MW01446014

"A book for such a time as this. From the op[...] throughout American and American church [...] lives in ways we may not even see'—Karen John[...] the stories of twentieth-century Christians who[...] Here at Koinonia Farm, we are grateful that Kare[...] the spirit of our community and Clarence Jord[...] her ordinary heroes, writing, 'He insisted that [...] that White Christians share spiritual, social, an[...] all Christians—including Black ones.' Karen echo[...] call must come through all humility. Read this b[...]
Bren Dubay, director of Koinonia Farm

"In this bewildering moment for church and soci[...] timely but a breath of fresh air. With all the c[...] wisdom of a committed believer, she recounts t[...] who nevertheless did the small faithful thing [...] markable effect. Readers will find here not only a[...] but also sparks of inspiration toward a more faith[...]
Heath W. Carter, associate professor of American Chri[...] Theological Seminary

"*Ordinary Heroes of Racial Justice* is an extraordinar[...] This thought provoking, self-revealing, challengin[...] painful time in history that is well worth your tim[...] investigating whether you may be on the right side [...] can potentially lead you to a deeper understanding [...] and our living a disciple's life."
Scottye Holloway, president of The Mendenhall Ministri[...]

ORDINARY HEROES OF RACIAL JUSTICE

A HISTORY OF CHRISTIANS IN ACTION

KAREN J. JOHNSON

ivp
Academic

An imprint of InterVarsity Press
Downers Grove, Illinois

InterVarsity Press
P.O. Box 1400 | Downers Grove, IL 60515-1426
ivpress.com | email@ivpress.com

©2025 by Karen J. Johnson

All rights reserved. No part of this book may be reproduced in any form without written permission from InterVarsity Press.

InterVarsity Press® is the publishing division of InterVarsity Christian Fellowship/USA®. For more information, visit intervarsity.org.

All Scripture quotations, unless otherwise indicated, are taken from The Holy Bible, New International Version®, NIV®. Copyright © 1973, 1978, 1984, 2011 by Biblica, Inc.™ Used by permission of Zondervan. All rights reserved worldwide. www.zondervan.com. The "NIV" and "New International Version" are trademarks registered in the United States Patent and Trademark Office by Biblica, Inc.™

While any stories in this book are true, some names and identifying information may have been changed to protect the privacy of individuals.

The publisher cannot verify the accuracy or functionality of website URLs used in this book beyond the date of publication.

Cover design: Faceout Studio
Interior design: Jeanna Wiggins
Images: © mikroman6 / Moment via Getty Images
   © belterz / E+ via Getty Images
   © ilbusca / DigitalVision Vectors via Getty Images

ISBN 978-1-5140-0998-7 (print) | ISBN 978-1-5140-1000-6 (digital)

Printed in the United States of America ∞

Library of Congress Cataloging-in-Publication Data
A catalog record for this book is available from the Library of Congress.

32 31 30 29 28 27 26 25 | 13 12 11 10 9 8 7 6 5 4 3 2 1

For Eric, Jack, Evelyn, Kate, and Sophia

CONTENTS

Acknowledgments ... ix

Introduction ... 1

PART I: TELLING TRUE STORIES
CATHERINE DE HUECK AND FRIENDSHIP HOUSE

1 A Different Take on History ... 17
2 The Significance of Money ... 25
3 Segregated Cities ... 39
4 The Mystical Body in Black America ... 54

PART II: CONTEXT MATTERS
JOHN PERKINS AND THE GOOD NEWS IN MISSISSIPPI

5 The Gospel and Civil Rights ... 71
6 Mississippi: Is This America? ... 85
7 How Place Influences Faith ... 94
8 The Tasks of the Church ... 117
9 The Church's Role in Seeking Justice ... 127

PART III: HUMILITY
CLARENCE JORDAN AND THE COTTON PATCH GOSPEL

10 Faith Is Betting Your Life on Unseen Realities ... 143
11 A Demonstration Plot for the Kingdom ... 155
12 Exclusion, Not Embrace ... 172
13 It's Not So Simple ... 196
14 Cotton Patch Gospel ... 206
15 The Soil Never Loses Its Claim on Us ... 223

PART IV: SEEK FIRST TO UNDERSTAND
ROCK OF OUR SALVATION EVANGELICAL FREE CHURCH AND CIRCLE URBAN MINISTRIES

16	An Unlikely Pair	235
17	Going Back to the Fundamentals	245
18	The Funky Gospel	259
19	Life in the Austin Neighborhood	269
20	The Challenges of "Colorblindness"	283
21	Prophetic Hope	299

Conclusion	313
Timeline	319
Suggested Reading	331
Index	333

ACKNOWLEDGMENTS

The research and writing of this book was collaborative in so many senses, and I am grateful for all who supported me. It felt like God was opening doors at every step of the journey.

This project took me to Mississippi and Georgia for substantial visits. The John Stott Endowment of the Human Needs and Global Resources program at Wheaton College provided the funding for those trips and for an additional semester of sabbatical, which enabled me to inhabit the places I was writing about. Laura Yoder of Wheaton's Human Needs and Global Resources program encouraged me to apply for funding, and what a difference it made. Wheaton College granted me sabbatical, and my colleagues in the history department, especially our then-chair Melissa Harkrider, cheerfully supported my research leave. The Calvin Institute of Christian Worship awarded me the Teacher-Scholar Vital Worship Grant, which enabled me to write not only about Christians but, in a sense, with them, and create spaces to wonder about race and Christianity. The grant provided a course release and helped me to workshop my chapters with current and former members of the Mendenhall Bible Church in Mississippi, Rock of Our Salvation Evangelical Free Church in Chicago, and Church of the Resurrection in Wheaton.

In Mississippi, friends from the Mendenhall Ministries welcomed me and then my family with open arms. They provided space to research, read my work and offered feedback, and shared their stories informally and formally through oral history interviews. I am grateful to Scottye Holloway, Josie Holloway, Dolphus Weary, Rosie Weary, Artis Fletcher, Carolyn Fletcher, Rosemary Bethune, and Suzanne Keye. Others in Mississippi helped me to see how race has worked there as I traversed the state, and I am grateful to Otis Pickett, Robby Luckett, Susan Glisson, Chuck Westmoreland, Elbert McGowan, and Patrick Weams for sharing their wisdom and hard-earned knowledge. Deborah, Elizabeth, Priscilla, John, and Vera Mae Perkins were open to collaborating despite the constraints of Covid and more generous than I could imagine.

ACKNOWLEDGMENTS

In Georgia, Koinonia Farm members provided my family and me hospitality, meals, conversation, and their feedback on my writing. Bren Dubay opened "the closet" for research and continues to be a faithful presence in her leadership at Koinonia. Elizabeth Dede and Sue Morrison helped us navigate the logistics of bringing a large family to stay at the farm. Ainsley Quiros connected me to Evan Kutzler, who helped me understand Americus as a place more deeply. The staff at the Hargrett Library was welcoming, and Mary Linneman was so efficient when I asked for images.

Members of Rock Church, past and present, shared their insights through oral history interviews. I am grateful to Sheila Anderson, Louise Bonner, Charles Butler, Doug Hansen, Reggie Harris, Sareta Harris, Andre Hinton, Shunelle Hollis, Arthur Jackson, Sandra Jackson, Lonni Kehrein, Merdise Lee, Trina McIlrath, Steve McIlrath, Lynwood Morris, DuRhonda Grant Palmore, Murray Sitte, Amy Soudan, Carole Stannard, Bob Stannard, Bethany Stannard, Paulette Washington, and Raleigh Washington. Rock's current pastor, Rob Stevenson, has been a champion for this project, my husband and me, and our family over the decades. Others at Rock have blessed me with their love and presence in my life, since this project has been incubating since I started attending the church in my twenties. Many of these, including Bridgette Stevenson, Pastor Cliff Kyle, Maggie West, Cynthia Banks, and Tommy Williams responded to the book's ideas and let me join their conversations about Rock's callings then and now.

Those who research and write about Catherine de Hueck have been so helpful. I found Catherine during my dissertation research years ago, and this book builds on that earlier work I did on Catherine and Friendship House at the Chicago History Museum, the Notre Dame Archives, the Schomburg Center for Research in Black Culture, and the Madonna House Archives. Archivists at each place were so helpful, and Jean Doucet and Mary Catherine Rowland welcomed me to live at Madonna House for several weeks while I pored through their archives. More recently, Kathy McVady provided me with scans of pictures of Catherine.

The book was also strengthened by my community—scholarly and not—in Wheaton. I am grateful to Church of the Resurrection congregants Ema Chester, Meaghan Falkanger, Bill MacKillop, and Marta Cedeno for reading portions of the manuscript and offering feedback. FIA friends Laura Black and Whitney Woerner also gave feedback on the manuscript, and others asked persistently how it was going. Also thanks to Rusty Hawkins and Cliff Williams for reading portions of the manuscript. Wheaton College's Evangelism and Mission's Archives enabled me to read sources from some of John Perkins's later work, Katherine Graber provided scans for some photos, and Paul Erickson's oral history interviews were invaluable. Paul modeled the sort of care and thoroughness I aspired to when I conducted additional interviews, which I plan to donate to Wheaton's archives.

My students at Wheaton have inspired me and pushed me further in my understanding of what it is to do history, who it makes us, and how to understand those I have written about for this book. Students in my Race, Justice, and Reconciliation classes over the past years have helped me determine who might work in a book like this and have puzzled over connections with me. My teaching assistants Hannah Smedley and Isabella Anderson, both now graduated, helped find secondary sources and read numerous drafts. Rachel Shaughnessy helped me with the timeline.

My departmental colleagues have pushed me to be a better teacher, and much of my thinking about what it means to do history and how that discipline shapes us as Christians has been sharpened by conversations with them. Thank you to Melissa Harkrider, Hanmee Kim, Matt Lundin, Tracy McKenzie, Jonathan Riddle, Amber Thomas Reynolds, and Joey Cochran. You have helped me see our discipline in new ways.

Those who work at IVP Academic have been professional and beyond helpful. My editor and fellow historian, Jon Boyd, has been a source of clarity and encouragement from our first coffee meeting, when I pitched my book. Rebecca Carhart helped see it through to completion.

My deepest thanks to my family. Members of my family have been with me—literally, at Koinonia Farm, in Mississippi, at Rock Church, and at Madonna House—every step of the way. My mom and dad, Marianne and Lynn Fricke, have been helpful in ways I am sure I do not even know, but my mom has traveled with me to Mississippi and Georgia, to support me when I was pregnant and to watch my children while I worked. My aunt, Linda Willard, came to Koinonia Farm with great cheer and sent me off early in the morning to the Hargrett with strong coffee. Other members of my extended family have asked about my work and cheered me on in so many ways. I am so grateful to Marlene Johnson; Todd Johnson; Phil Willard; Cheryl, Jeong, and Everett Hyun; Wayne and Rindy Fricke; and Sara, Andrew, Luke, Brooke, Blake, and Lilly Meyer.

Last, my children and husband. Our four kids, Jack, Evelyn, Kate, and Sophia, make each day worthwhile, and I aspire to love them well and to help them to grow in wisdom and courage. I am grateful for their joy and encouragement on this journey of research and writing. Eric, my husband, has been a rock. Thank you.

INTRODUCTION

A SHORT STORY

Race has mattered throughout American and American church history, and it continues to shape our lives in ways we may not even see. Some Christians in America have carried racial burdens more heavily than others. But today no Christian in America, no matter their racial background, can ignore race. This is a gift from God, a moment when we, the church in all its diversity, can seek justice and righteousness in all their fullness. We must not let this moment pass.

At least for some White Christians, including me, it has not always been this way. Based on factors such as where and when we have lived, we have been able to be blind to race in America. When I grew up in the suburbs of Chicago, the place where I lived and the circles in which I traveled limited my ability to see that race mattered. Had you asked me, a White person living in a mostly White, middle- and upper-class suburb, whether I thought race still affected people's experiences in America, I would have been puzzled by the question. Perhaps race affected people somewhere else, but not in my town. Things were peaceful there, and the racial minorities for the most part seemed very successful. And yet, my context was profoundly shaped by race. By context, I mean the place where I lived, the economic systems that enabled it to be as it was, the social norms, and even the evangelical Christian church where we worshiped. But because it was so homogenous and because the day-to-day patterns of my life were focused on other things, I assumed race did not matter.

Often we need to be with people we can trust to feel free enough to reconsider our core beliefs. For me, the secular liberal arts college I attended was not that safe space. My church, like most White evangelical churches in the 1980s and 1990s, implicitly taught me to mistrust those Christians who worked for what they called social justice because I understood that they held to a false gospel, the social gospel. While I could not have defined what the social gospel was precisely, I thought it was concerned more with people's bodies than with their souls, and I thought true Christians cared about people's spiritual relationships with God, which was somehow separated from questions of physical suffering. What I did not know was that my vague fear had a history, that my tendency toward concern only for a person's soul at the expense of their body was the result of complicated historical dynamics from nearly one hundred years prior. Nor did I know that generations of Christians—for thousands of years—had cared for people's eternal *and* temporal needs. As a Christian without knowledge of the history of those faithful followers who had lived before me, I was stranded in the present, unable to see that God's people should care about salvation *and* shalom, by which I mean the restoration of all things to the way God meant them to be. Therefore, I doubled down into my own personal righteousness.

My time at this secular college gave me many gifts, however, and one of the most important was a hard-won conviction that Christians need not fear ideas. When I read biblical higher criticism for a class on the New Testament, which did not assume Scripture's inerrancy and explained away Jesus' divinity, I was plagued with fear. Perhaps my faith was founded on lies and I could not trust that Scripture was God's Word. But God used a fellow Christian who lived about sixteen hundred years ago to help restore my faith when I took a philosophy class the next term. We read Augustine, that great father of the faith, who proclaimed that all truth is God's truth. As I prayed that term, my fear dissipated. If all truth is God's truth, then I do not need to fear what I might learn. God can handle it, and he will lead me into truth.

This freedom to explore and confidence in God's superiority and sovereignty was a gift I carried to the evangelical seminary where I worked on my master's degree. There, finally in a place where I could trust my teachers more fully, God taught me something new, something that now seems so obvious but then was fresh and amazing: because race matters in American life, the church, Jesus' body on earth, needs to address it. Even more, Satan has used race to cripple the church's witness to the world, fostering injustice and disunity. In seminary, God gave me eyes to see what had been there in plain sight. He gave me ears that heard and a mind that began to understand. And he gave me a call to speak to the body of Christ about what I was learning, to call my brothers and sisters of all hues into a messy, uncomfortable journey to help each other live out the unity Jesus already won for us on the cross.

THREE BITS OF WISDOM

I want to highlight three bits of wisdom derived from the journey I just described that can help us repent, which in the biblical Greek derives from a term meaning "to turn." They are (1) to ask how our context shapes us, (2) to recognize that we are historical beings, and (3) to practice courage in the process.

First, we all live in contexts that affect our ability to see the world. My context growing up blinded me to race's power in America. Like many people, I was so immersed in my context that I could not see how it was blinding me to what was actually happening. A joke about fish can illustrate this dynamic. It goes like this: "There are these two young fish swimming along, and they happen to meet an older fish swimming the other way, who nods at them and says, 'Morning, boys. How's the water?' And the two young fish swim on for a bit, and then eventually one of them looks over at the other and goes, 'What the hell is water?'"[1]

Part of growing in wisdom is realizing that we live in water and then understanding the character of that water. Christian life and worship are meant to be lived in our contexts, lived in the water where we swim. But our lives and worship as Christians, which extend well beyond church walls, also contain the power to transform our contexts because they should be transcultural and intercultural, reflecting the nature of the body of Christ. This book is meant to help us see our contexts better.

How can we begin to see more clearly? The answer to this question is the second nugget of truth from my story: history can help us see our contexts more clearly so we can better serve God faithfully in our generation. Studying history can give us what historians call a historical consciousness, the gift of seeing how things came to be as they are. Essentially, we can see that our present assumptions and ways of living have a history, and although they

---

[1]David Foster Wallace, "This Is Water: Some Thoughts, Delivered on a Significant Occasion, About Living a Compassionate Life" (speech, April 14, 2009, Kenyon College, Gambier, Ohio), http://bulletin-archive.kenyon.edu/x4280.html.

seem normal and perhaps inevitable, they are not. Rather, as cocreators with Christ, people God has put on this earth to be his hands and feet, we can make changes in the present so that our generation and our children's children can live differently. In this book, I will use history to help us see the water in which we swim. As we read about those from different eras and see our contexts more clearly, we also avoid what the British author and apologist C. S. Lewis calls "chronological snobbery," the belief that those of us living are better than and know more than those who are dead.[2] I believe we have much to learn from Christians who have lived before us, and this book offers a handful of men and women whose faith transformed their contexts.

This process of beginning to see requires courage. But, and here is the third key point, we have a faith that calls us to courage, not to fear. God is bigger than all we know, and he can handle our questions and our fumbling. Therefore, Christians need not fear the insights secular disciplines can offer. Nor should we fear the insights of those who are not believers. God's common grace falls on all people. We want to have our eyes open wide and to probe how our faith addresses the joys and sorrows of our time. As we do this, we should expect that God will teach us new things, that some of the assumptions—shaped by our historical contexts and our sin—that have undergirded our lives will be uprooted as he conforms us to the image of Christ. Trying to understand race in America as we seek to love God and love others takes courage. But, as Paul reminded Timothy, God has not given us a spirit of fear, but of power, love, and self-discipline (2 Timothy 1:7).

I write as an evangelical Christian who is a professional historian. I am a born-again Christian who believes in Jesus' divinity and that his death on the cross atoned for my sins. I believe that people must be converted and that Scripture is God's inerrant word. I believe that our faith must be lived out, not just held as a set of beliefs. My journey of following Jesus into the tangle of race in America brought me into a mostly Black neighborhood on Chicago's west side, where fellow members of an interracial church patiently taught me about racial reconciliation and God's love. That journey also brought me to graduate school to study race and urban history, and then back to the suburbs to teach at an evangelical Christian college, where I learned from the best

---

[2]C. S. Lewis and Owen Barfield, *Surprised by Joy: The Shape of My Early Life* (New York: Harcourt Brace Jovanovich, 1956).

INTRODUCTION 5

about how to weave together my faith with the discipline of history. I have come to believe that understanding the past with love can help us love our neighbors better in the present and bless our children's children, to a thousand generations. As a Christian and a historian, I wonder a lot. I do not know everything, but I can ask good questions. This book is the fruit of those questions, of wondering about race, God, and the church in US history.

WHY READ THIS BOOK?

You should read this book for three reasons.

First, we will learn what happened in America's recent racial past.

Centered on the twentieth-century exodus of many African Americans from the rural South to the urban North and the civil rights movement, the book will show how racial dynamics developed and worked on a broad scale, or, to use a word that has many meanings, a systemic level. People often think of *systemic* as relating to laws, but we will think about it more expansively. By systemic, I mean the bigger systems and patterns that shape our everyday lives: where we live, the quality of the schools we attend, who joins our churches and how our churches function, and our nation's economic dynamics. Again, we are trying to understand contexts, which are often invisible. We'll see how racial logics, assumptions, and hierarchies became embedded, sometimes intentionally, often unintentionally, in these systems. We'll also see how Christianity, Christians, and churches were actors in creating many of these painful dynamics.

Understanding what happened in the past is essential if we are to move forward in the present. As Christians, we must not stifle the truth but must rather courageously seek the truth to break the chains of the past.

We will also study a handful of examples of women and men who pushed against the racial dynamics of their times and places, including those sometimes unjust racial contexts created by brothers and sisters in Christ. History is by nature selective, and it is different from the past. The past is everything that has happened up until now, including the breath you just took and, before that, your decision to pick up this book. History, by contrast, is what people know, discuss, and remember about everything that has happened until now. The distinction is significant. No one can write a history that includes everything that ever happened in the past. Anyone who claims they have written *the* comprehensive book on a subject is exaggerating and doing history poorly.

I have chosen people for our study who allow us to glimpse racial dynamics in the North and the South, and the East and West Coasts, and whose lives allow us to think through much of the twentieth century. The people will lead us to focus on Black-White racial dynamics. Race in America is so much broader, and there are wonderful studies that also address Native American, Asian, and Latino racial histories. But the Black-White dynamics are also foundational to race in America and, therefore, essential to understand. The variety of racial, ethnic, and denominational backgrounds represented also offers us the benefits of diverse perspectives and experiences. Equally important, reflecting on the lives of our subjects can offer substantial wisdom for our time. These are people I have learned *from* as I have tried to understand their lives.

Prepare yourself to learn the stories of people who had a mighty impact in the kingdom. And remember too that God's economy is not the same as ours. While each person has had national and even international prominence, often their impact was felt most deeply by those with whom they broke bread in one another's homes. They are ordinary heroes. No person I discuss was perfect. But they offer glimpses of the "already but not yet" of heaven, moments where the world was the way it should be and will be when all things are made new.

We will start in the 1930s and 1940s with Catherine de Hueck, a Catholic Russian refugee from the 1917 Bolshevik Revolution. Catherine founded Friendship House to help her fellow Catholics fully embrace Jesus' teachings to care for the least of these in New York City's Harlem, a thriving center of Black Americans' relocation from the South. For Catherine, who became an American citizen, seeing African Americans' second-class citizenship in the nation and in the Catholic Church made her passionate about their lives. Next, we will wonder about John Perkins, an African American who fled Mississippi for California in the 1940s after his brother was murdered. In California, he became a Christian, worked closely with Black Christians, and was mentored by White Christians. But when John returned to rural Mississippi in 1960, his faith led him to join the civil rights movement, going against many White Christians who saw the movement as irrelevant or even anti-Christian. Staying in the South, we will meet Clarence Jordan, a White, southern New Testament scholar who insisted Christians should make no racial distinctions. His interracial Koinonia Farm and famed Cotton Patch translation of the New Testament into contemporary vernacular subverted racial norms in the 1950s and 1960s in Georgia. Last, we will ponder the story of the work and relationship between Raleigh and Paulette Washington and Glen and Lonni Kehrein, one Black and one White couple, who founded Rock of Our Salvation Evangelical Free Church and Circle Urban Ministries in Chicago. The Kehreins began applying their faith to their urban context in the 1970s, and in the 1980s and 1990s both couples sought to live out a form of racial reconciliation that would draw people to God and to one another.

The second reason you should read this book is that we will *do* history, which can help us become more faithful disciples. This book is an uncommon history book. Most books on history are written so they hide the tangled web of evidence and the complex decisions historians make to determine what happened and what it means. Most books share the final product. But I will not just describe the history of race in America. I want something more. I want us to think together about how we have come to know what we think we know.

I am inviting you into the process of determining what happened, the effort to weave together stories based on tangled and often scant threads of evidence, and figuring out what it means because this process is vital to repentance and reconciliation. I am convinced, furthermore, that many of the habits and practices historians use as they approach the past can help each of us become more faithful followers of Jesus. Together we will see how the act of studying history can strengthen our faith.

My commitment to welcome you into *doing* history, usually reserved for upper-level history classes, comes from my reading about and experience of how we grow as Christians. Christians across time and in different places have told us that being a Christian is not just about *thinking* rightly, but it requires cultivating our *loves*. We must pay attention to who and what we love. How we act reveals what we love. To change our loves, we must change our practices.[3]

---

[3] An accessible contemporary book on the subject is James K. A. Smith, *You Are What You Love: The Spiritual Power of Habit* (Grand Rapids, MI: Brazos, 2016).

Therefore, we will not just do history, as important as that may be. We will do it as Christians, embodying the traits that should characterize followers of Jesus at their best: love, humility, and awe. As I welcome you into the formative process of doing history, this book will go back and forth between what happened in the past, my efforts to understand the past and craft a compelling narrative, and what the stories and process has meant to me as I have sought to learn not just *about* the actors but *from* them as well. The process of doing history—of piecing together incomplete evidence to find a pattern, of puzzling over causality, of tracking change over time, of getting caught in a web of complexity, of trying to contextualize a source to understand what it means, of marveling at the contingency of events, all while seeking to love those we study—teaches us to *craft true narratives, to value context, to practice humility, and to exercise empathy*. Each section will highlight one of these habits of mind, habits that also help bring unity to the body of Christ. These habits of mind can help us develop rightly ordered affections; they can shape our hearts and minds.

You will notice that I often refer to the main historical actors in this book using their first names or a title and a first name, resisting the traditional way academic historians discuss their subjects. The reason comes from my process, which has made the actors feel just as alive as you or me. I have either lived in or visited for an extended time communities each of the main actors inhabited, from Madonna House in Canada (where Catherine de Hueck lived out her days), to Mendenhall, Mississippi (where John Perkins began his Mississippi ministry), to Koinonia Farm in Americus, Georgia (which Clarence Jordan founded), to the Austin neighborhood of Chicago (where I lived for over six years and where the Washingtons and the Kehreins lived). Additionally, the archival sources often refer to them by their first names, and when you spend months of successive days in the sources, you begin to feel like you know the people. There is risk beyond bucking academic conventions in my choice to use first names, however. It is a dangerous thing to close the gap between us in the present and those we study in the past, even in such a small way as to presume familiarity by using a first name. They are not just faded tin-type versions of us; they were different, and seeing the strangeness of the past is one of the most powerful parts of doing history. Nonetheless, I have chosen to call them by the names their friends used because it feels like I am their friend.

INTRODUCTION

You'll also notice that there are footnotes at the bottom of pages rather than endnotes buried at the back. I did this to emphasize that this narrative is based in primary sources and in conversation with secondary sources, others who have puzzled over these actors. Doing history is something we do with others.

The third reason you should read this book is that we will seek wisdom, which the book of Proverbs tells us is worth more than anything and will bring great blessings (Proverbs 3:13-28; 4:7-9).

Doing history while emphasizing Christian virtues is a way to seek out wisdom, that precious gift worth more than gold or silver. Because wisdom is not simply knowledge, we must not simply learn *about* the past. Wisdom is knowledge, rightly applied. We must learn, therefore, *and* apply what we know in our day-to-day lives. Together we will learn *from* the past, and I will provide opportunities to reflect on how you could apply the principles we observe to your particular context. You and I probably don't live in the same town or even the same state. Our contexts are different. But there is work of discipleship, racial healing, and justice to be done in each of our places. That is part of God's call on his church in this time and in each of our places.

That work can transform our worship in church along with our worship in our everyday lives. Because we live in particular times and places, our gathered worship will reflect our contexts. That can be good, unless we are unknowingly living out sinful aspects of our culture. Worship should be contextual, but it should also be countercultural (resisting a culture's idolatries), transcultural (not bound by a particular time and place), and crosscultural (breaking through contemporary cultural barriers). Wondering about these historical actors can help us see our own worship with fresh eyes.

We also worship throughout our day-to-day lives in mundane things such as working in a factory, meeting with clients, folding laundry, or reading a book. The apostle Paul tells believers to offer their *bodies* as living sacrifices, holy and pleasing to God, as their true and proper worship. He then says to not conform to the pattern of this world, but to let God transform us by renewing our *minds* (Romans 12:1-2). God will change how we think as we worship him. I invite you into this reading as an act of worship, praying that God would renew our minds as we worship him in our reading. We also offer our bodies as living sacrifices, and our emotions are part of our bodies. We must make room for emotions, because this work that we're doing is difficult, especially when we apply what we've learned closer to home, looking at our own family histories and our own communities.

HOW TO REMEMBER

Before we turn to the past, we must consider *how* we remember—and this is a process that involves all of who we are, bodies and minds included.

First, humans are sinful, and everything we touch is tainted by sin. Sin happens on an individual level, which is the way most American Christians understand sin. We remember that Jesus washed away *my* sins, that *I* am covered by the blood of Jesus. But Scripture also talks about sin as corporate, which means that sin can reside in all the systems—economic, political, geographical, and even religious—that make up the contexts of our lives. Evangelical theologian Millard Erickson observes,

> The particular social situation in which we involuntarily find ourselves—including the political and economic system, our intellectual and family background, even the geographical location in which we were born—inevitably contributes to evil conditions and in some instances makes sin unavoidable. Sin is an element of the present social structure from which individuals cannot escape.[4]

Without knowing it, we can participate in sinful systems. While there are several examples of unity and beauty to celebrate in American church history regarding race, much of what happened reveals how Christians have been complicit in and subject to individual and corporate sin.

But because of God's great love, we do not need to only celebrate or only condemn those in the past. It is easy today to fall into a habit of either extreme. We might want to celebrate our ancestors to honor and respect them. But we must remember that they were sinners like us, and they were products of their time. Or we may just want to condemn our ancestors—or even better, someone else's ancestors—wondering why they messed up so badly. But neither approach is appropriate.

---

[4]Quoted in Bruce Fields, *Introducing Black Theology: Three Crucial Questions for the Evangelical Church* (Grand Rapids, MI: Baker Academic, 2001), 69. I am grateful to the late Dr. Fields for all he taught me about theology and for his faithfulness in serving in a predominantly White institution.

INTRODUCTION 11

How Scripture treats heroes of the faith offers a model as we study our past. Scripture is thorough, telling the good and the bad. Abraham trusted God, yes, but not enough to protect his wife from being taken into Pharoah's house as a concubine, and not enough to reject Sarah's suggestion to have sex with Hagar to produce a child when God was slow in providing a son through her. Moses faithfully led the Israelites out of Egypt and then led them for forty years in the desert. But he initially would not do God's will until God gave him Aaron as his mouthpiece. Moses also got so angry at the Israelites that God would not let him enter the Promised Land. David, author of many psalms and a man after God's own heart, acted on his lust for Bathsheba when he should have been leading his army into battle. When he could not cover his lie, David essentially had her husband Uriah killed. Jesus' closest friends, the disciples, failed again and again. Peter denied he knew Jesus, none of the disciples understood what Jesus was saying about his kingdom until after his resurrection, and they constantly fought with one another. Paul, who wrote a significant portion of the New Testament, killed Christians before Jesus blinded him on the road to Damascus. Even after Paul surrendered his life to Christ, he could not live in harmony with his coworkers, splitting with Barnabas because Paul did not want to take John Mark, who had deserted them earlier, with them on a missionary journey.

These few examples show us that heroes need not be perfect. God uses imperfect people. He also transforms imperfect people as we offer up whatever we do as acts of worship.

....

Now let us puzzle over fragments of the past and try to piece together a story about race in the North in the 1930s. We will start with Catherine de Hueck, who founded a ministry called Friendship House to use love of God and love of neighbor to address economic, spiritual, and social effects of segregation in the North.[5] We start with Catherine because she brought a unique, outsider perspective to American race relations. Fleeing Russia by way of Canada, she had to learn about race in America. As someone who looked White and who could

---

[5]Note that Catherine de Hueck married Eddie Doherty and changed her name to Catherine Doherty. In the time period we are discussing, she was Catherine de Hueck.

see how being perceived as White gave her opportunities in the United States, Catherine observed how the meanings of race were historical creations.

Catherine was helpful to me early in my study of race in America because she was a Christian who came from a tradition with persistent strands that applied Christianity to the massive issues of poverty, poor working conditions, and the relationship between owners and workers. As a Catholic, she drew from the deep wells of Catholic social teaching. That tradition, while in no way perfect or perfectly applied, is thick and rich. Catholic social teaching is rooted in Scripture and was illuminated throughout church history, but it began in its modern form during the major conflicts between capital and laborers in the late nineteenth century. Pope Leo XIII's encyclical, or major teaching, *Rerum Novarum* crafted a middle way between excessive capitalism and communism, calling Catholics to create a world in which owners and workers provided for one another, emphasizing the dignity of each person made in God's image. While most Black Protestants in America resonated with this frame, contemporary White evangelical leaders were condemning worker strikes even as American workers were fleeing evangelical churches, believing that Jesus loved them but churches did not.[6] Regarding race, White evangelicals were turning from their fleeting support of Black southern Christians and were, as one historian puts it, reforging the White republic in the wake of the Civil War by reversing the fruits of Reconstruction and recreating a segregated society.[7] Catholic social teaching's dealings with money, materialism, and people's tendency to objectify others offered a prophetic witness in the late nineteenth century, in Catherine's time, and our own.

Catherine also lived in the North in Harlem and later Chicago. Why start in the North? Contemporary racial dynamics have reminded us that race is still an issue in the North today. But the dominant historical racial narrative is that racial conflicts, segregation, and oppression were a southern phenomenon. When writing about race in American history early in my classes, most of my excellent students say it was significant during slavery and the civil rights movement, which they understand as located in the South, despite

---

[6]See Heath W. Carter, *Union Made: Working People and the Rise of Social Christianity in Chicago* (New York: Oxford University Press, 2015).
[7]Edward J. Blum, *Reforging the White Republic: Race, Religion, and American Nationalism, 1865–1898* (Baton Rouge: Louisiana State University Press, 2005).

INTRODUCTION

evidence to the contrary.[8] While slavery was certainly more extensive in the South, it was also present in the North from the United States's founding. The civil rights movement as we commonly remember it, starting in the mid- to late 1950s and resolving with the Voting Rights Act of 1965, happened in the South. But Catherine and those who joined Friendship House understood themselves as among a cadre of northern civil rights pioneers.

Race in the North at midcentury can be characterized by geographic segregation. This segregation did lead to cultural flourishing for African Americans, but it also harmed Black and White people alike. While there is some weight to the argument that people will live by those with whom they are most comfortable, or that like attracts like, the geographic segregation was not simply due to personal choice. White homeowners, religious practices, and governmental programs that did not always intend to create racial hierarchies limited where African Americans could live.

But few people—and maybe no one—in the 1930s and 1940s could tease out the complicated intersections of these systemic dynamics. Catherine wondered about segregation as she searched for a location for a second interracial Friendship House branch in Chicago. She said,

> Slowly we walk the streets looking for suitable stores to rent. Friendship House always starts with a store front or two. People walk right into store fronts off the streets. This looks like the continuation of Harlem. Perhaps it is. New York, Chicago, Boston, Detroit . . . each has its Harlem, its Negro town within a town. Why? How many times have we asked ourselves that question?[9]

It is to de Hueck's question—and to what she did in light of that segregation—that we now turn.[10]

---

[8]There are many good works, but see, for instance, Joann Pope Melish, *Disowning Slavery: Gradual Emancipation and "Race" in New England, 1780–1860* (Ithaca, NY: Cornell University Press, 1998); Patrick Jones, *The Selma of the North: Civil Rights Insurgency in Milwaukee* (Cambridge: Harvard University Press, 2010); Thomas Sugrue, *Sweet Land of Liberty: The Forgotten Struggle for Civil Rights in the North* (New York: Random House, 2008).
[9]Catherine de Hueck Doherty, *Friendship House* (New York: Sheed & Ward, 1947), 84.
[10]For more on Catherine's work on race alongside many others, see Karen J. Johnson, *One in Christ: Chicago Catholics and the Quest for Interracial Justice* (New York: Oxford University Press, 2018).

PART I

TELLING TRUE STORIES

Catherine de Hueck and Friendship House

The walk past all the honky-tonks and slum smells to the store front with the sign Blessed Martin de Porres Library and Friendship House and the statue of Blessed Martin in the window, the exterior set in cavernous rows of sleezey stores, below the line of unbroken drab 6 story tenements. It was a slum alright. But once inside! The ambience was unforgettable: walls lined with books, a place of not many lights, muted by smoke. (The "B" [Catherine] as we called her smoked like a chimney then.) White faces, Black faces, talking, laughing, friendly, sipping coffee. How simple the solution all seemed then: the sooner we of different races learned to work together, to pray together, to eat, to study, to laugh together, the sooner we'd be on the way to interracial justice. Little did we know the complexities of the sin of segregation then.

ANN HARRIGAN, A WHITE IRISH CATHOLIC FROM BROOKLYN AND DIRECTOR OF FRIENDSHIP HOUSE IN CHICAGO, RECALLING HER FIRST VISIT TO CATHERINE DE HUECK'S FRIENDSHIP HOUSE IN HARLEM

1

A DIFFERENT TAKE ON HISTORY

How Catherine founded Friendship House and why questioning that story can make us better disciples.

FRIENDSHIP HOUSE LORE

Catherine de Hueck was captivating. Those who encountered her met a woman in love with God, who in her Russian accent pontificated about how to love God and love others. From the 1930s in urban Toronto, to Black Harlem in 1938, to Chicago's Black belt in 1942, until her death in rural Canada in 1985, Catherine called wealthy and middle-class White Catholics to not just say they loved Jesus but to love him by meeting the physical needs of people who had less. Like the prophets in the Hebrew Scriptures who called the people of God back to righteousness and justice, Catherine called people in her own time to cease worshiping their idols of wealth and comfort and instead practice righteousness and justice, two ideas that are inseparable in the biblical narrative. She modeled a different way of living through her countercultural, if profoundly imperfect, life.

Catherine's story was unexpected in midcentury America, and she knew it. In her 1946 book *Friendship House*, Catherine uses the strangeness of her story to attract her readers' attention and then, like Nathan speaking to David, turns the tables to point out their sin. In the book, Catherine asks how she, a White woman from Russia, ended up in Harlem, a center of African American life in New York. The immediate answer to her question became Friendship House lore. In 1938, she exited the subway in Harlem with a handbag, three dollars, and a typewriter, which she would use to write thousands of words, filling letters, newspaper articles, and eventually books. The man showing her the flat she intended to rent told Catherine she must be confused. Why would a White woman want to rent an apartment in Black Harlem? Catherine was not "slumming" like many White people who went to Harlem because she was not going to a club. Catherine responded that she was Russian, which seemed to satisfy the man. Catherine related that he assumed she was like the only other White people who stayed in Harlem (besides the White priests assigned to local parishes): she must be a communist. He showed her the flat.

The strangeness of Catherine's arrival and subsequent residence in Harlem cannot be overstated. Like most northern cities that had received the hundreds of thousands of Black migrants who moved away from farms where as sharecroppers they eked out a subsistence-level living and navigated a racial hierarchy that was characterized by lynching, New York was segregated. Catherine rented the flat and prayed that the Holy Ghost and the saints would provide furniture. They did, and the New York Friendship House was born.

Friendship House became an oasis of interracial Christian community in segregated New York. Friendship House functioned as a Catholic settlement house: it would grow to provide programming for young people, host a mother's club for local women, provide used clothing to those in need, offer African American history classes, and help people find jobs. Like other settlement houses, it also became a meeting place for people from different social, economic, and religious backgrounds, a place where new ideas were born. People who visited and stayed there worked to bring Black and White people together for two reasons: to grow in their relationships with Jesus Christ and to bring about interracial justice. For them, interracial justice meant stopping the suffering African Americans endured because of White Americans' intentional and unintentional actions.

LIGHT IN THE DARKNESS

Catherine was a lifeline to me when I first encountered her, a light in the darkness. I had begun my doctoral coursework wanting to understand how race had worked in American history. My first class on race in early America had been deeply frightening and nearly paralyzing. My professor was amazing, smart, kind, and wise—and wanted the class to be useful to his students. I regularly sat in the rocking chair in his office during office hours and asked questions, turning ideas around in my mind. But as intellectually stimulating as that was, the subject was awful. We had probed how race had been experienced and intellectually constructed, and I felt a portion of its crushing weight.

For my research project the next semester, I was looking for hope. I wanted to study some Christians who had resisted the darkness and the division that characterized so much of race in US history. I took the train from our inner-city west side neighborhood to the Chicago History Museum on the north side with a list of potential organizations to research in more recent US history that had been doing interracial work. After a few days exploring other collections, I happened upon the Friendship House papers and was hooked. Catherine and her comrades wrote with passion, drawing living water, it seemed, from a deep well of thought and practice that talked as much about people loving one another as it did individual righteousness and people loving God. Their ideas resonated with the Black church tradition that was nurturing me in the interracial—but mostly Black—church I was attending.

Friendship House became the middle of my first book.[1] I had found a historically significant organization and researched what happened before and after the group's founding in Chicago. I spent months in archives in Chicago, Milwaukee, South Bend, and Catherine's intentional community, Madonna House, in rural Canada researching Friendship House. While I soon saw the group's imperfections, its thinking on race and interracialism formed me personally. My questions then revolved primarily around Catherine's approaches to race and theology; I thought economics mattered, but I subsumed them under the category of race.

ANOTHER STORY

Despite my spending years studying Catherine and Friendship House, she continued to captivate me, as she had so many when she was alive. Some of my old questions lingered, like how she ended up in Harlem and what it meant. But when I turned to Catherine for this current book, my rereading of the sources prompted two new questions. Last time, I had glossed over her life in the early 1930s, thinking her arrival in Harlem was of primary concern

---

[1]Karen J. Johnson, *One in Christ: Chicago Catholics and the Quest for Interracial Justice* (New York: Oxford University Press, 2018).

to me because it was then she started talking about race. This time I began wondering more about her years in Canada and her anticommunism. How did her views of economics shape her? I wondered. I also had some ten years of teaching undergraduate students how to do history under my belt and had puzzled with them over how to use sources and how to craft narratives. As I returned to Catherine's life and writings, I asked more about how she portrayed herself to outsiders. I was curious about the notion of histories as stories and wanted to see how Catherine had used them.

While I suspect the Friendship House lore about Catherine, her three dollars, and her typewriter is true, I cannot say for certain that it is. In my initial research, I found Catherine to be sometimes inaccurate and inconsistent in her descriptions of facts and events. Some of Catherine's closest American friends grew frustrated, too, with her at times because she seemed to hold the truth about events in the past loosely. Catherine was fiercely consistent in her passion for God and commitment to moral truths, but her stories were not always accurate in the factual sense. As one colleague observed, "That woman never told a story the same way twice."[2] Catherine would sometimes dismiss particular facts if they did not serve the moral truths on which she was expounding. But Catherine was not concerned with factual accuracy in the same sense I am; she was concerned with how stories would illuminate larger, deeper truths. All these points have pushed me to treat her work with care and to value contextualizing her so as to tell a true story.

That Catherine and I approach the past differently can make clear a key point necessary for doing history—and being in relationship with others, including God—well: history and the past are not the same. Historians can never fully know the past; only God, who knows the number of hairs on my head, who knit you together in your mother's womb, and who knows when a sparrow falls, knows all the past. Humans write history, which is the remembered past, parts of the past we piece together to tell a story that answers a question we have about the past. As we puzzle through Catherine's story and try to make sense of it, I want us to resist the notion that some histories are simply true and others are revisionist. Crafting histories always requires interpretive decisions; history is not simply an objective list of names and

---

[2]Quoted in Ellen Tarry, Oral History, interview by Lorene Hanley Duquin, 1991, 1998.052-072, Madonna House Archive.

dates. Our narrative, therefore, about how Catherine came to Harlem will, by necessity, be incomplete and will highlight certain aspects of her story.

But unlike humans, not all histories are created equal. Good histories must be *true stories*. Let me be clear: I am not embracing relativism. I am asking us to read the past using wisdom, weighing competing narratives, grounding arguments in evidence, and recognizing the limits of what we can know. But good histories are *stories* in that the storyteller makes choices, often depending on the historian's questions and purposes, and the scope of their research. They are also *true*. That is, they are based in careful analysis of sources created in the time period, sources historians call primary sources. True stories must have evidence that supports the stories, and that evidence must be used carefully. As we study Catherine, we will think deeply about the stories we tell, the narratives we have about different issues. I will take Catherine's story that she often told about her founding Friendship House and expand on it, problematize it, and reframe it.

As Christians, we must pay attention to the stories we tell not only about other people but about God and God's work in the world. When we think about God, do we emphasize that he is a God of justice, or do we downplay that aspect of the story? When we think about our roles in God's work, do we think that God's work relies on us or that we can join God in God's work, with ultimate responsibility lying on God's shoulders? Do we think God can handle our sin? Do we think—and act—as though God is on the move? Do we tell stories of people struggling or of people struggling and overcoming? Do we look around our world and see the pain and suffering as an end, or do we know that God will redeem it all? Do we think that this world is good, or do we tell a story that says that God is better, even if God seems more fleeting? Do we believe that what is here will pass away, or do we think of what is in front of us as somehow eternal? Our answers to these questions, and the stories our answers constitute, will shape our imaginations and actions. The discipline of telling of true stories about the past can help us see that we also need to tell—and live into—true stories about God.

The stories we tell are shaped by when we begin and end them. I choose to start in Russia, because of the economic dynamics Catherine experienced there. There, Catherine de Hueck was born Ekaterina Fyodorovna Kolyschkine in 1896 to a noble family. Her parents baptized her into the Russian

Orthodox Church (a fact she downplayed later in life) and raised her largely abroad in cosmopolitan settings. When they were home in Russia, her mother went to the peasants to serve them and taught Catherine to do manual labor, insisting she must know how to do the work she would later expect her servants to do.[3] At fifteen, she married Boris de Hueck, who gave her a diary as a wedding present and in his inscription to his young bride wrote that she should write all her ideas and feelings in there for him to read. He would be unfaithful to Catherine.

When World War I began, Boris served in the First Russian Army, and Catherine followed him to the front to serve with the Red Cross. There she saw great horrors. She remembered carrying amputated limbs, covered in blood; retreating among refugees on the roads. "I have seen children slowly dying of hunger, while their mothers lost their reason over tragedy," she said. "I have seen a field green with grass one day and literally stripped of every blade the next by people who had nothing else to eat. I have seen towns without a single roof on the houses because the straw of the thatching was taken to be boiled and eaten."[4] There on the front, she wondered where God was. The answer that came to her was that "it is we who have brought about the wounding of our solders, the widows, the orphans, by entering into another war. We always enter into another war. It is our will that does it, not God's."[5]

When the Bolsheviks took over Russia in 1917, Catherine's life became endangered at the hands of her own people. In 1919, communists trapped her and Boris in their family estate in Finland, intending that they starve to death. Catherine remembered,

> I was dragged into my own house. All foodstuffs were taken away, but water and fuel were left me—that I might myself prolong my agony. . . . Long, interminable days began—and the cold cruel face of death by hunger came closer, closer, ever closer. The temptation of Satan came with it. It would be easy to close the flue in the fireplace. The merciful fumes of carbon dioxide would fill the room, and cheat starvation. Long interminable nights went by.[6]

---

[3]Lorene Hanley Duquinn, *They Called Her the Baroness: The Life of Catherine De Hueck Doherty* (Staten Island, NY: Alba House, 2000), chaps. 2–5.
[4]Quoted in Duquinn, *They Called Her the Baroness*, 34-35.
[5]Quoted in Duquinn, *They Called Her the Baroness*, 35.
[6]Catherine de Hueck Doherty, *Friendship House* (New York: Sheed & Ward, 1947), 4. Carbon monoxide, not carbon dioxide, is lethal. Catherine did use the word *dioxide* in her text.

For three months, they suffered. Lying by the fire, nearly unconscious, Catherine told God, "If you save me from this, in some sort of way I will offer my life to you." Then she became unconscious and awoke to the shouts of the Finnish White Guards, who had defeated the Bolsheviks.[7]

After a brief reunification with their families, the couple went to Murmansk, Russia, where Boris served in the White Army against the Bolsheviks. Catherine again worked as a nurse and saw the violence and atrocities the Bolsheviks committed, following Lenin's words that "revolution is in itself an act of terrorism. . . . It is likewise evident that when the revolution is most in danger the dictatorship must be most pitiless."[8] That explained the castrated solders, the ones tied to trees with their intestines sliced open, the ones with the missing arms and legs. Catherine saw the depths of evil that humans could commit.

When the British evacuated northern Russia and Boris was injured, the couple left for England under the guidance of the British military. Within five months, the Bolshevik army defeated the White Army. In England, Catherine fulfilled a childhood dream to join the Catholic Church. Soon they emigrated to Canada, where Catherine gave birth to her only child, George, in 1921.

They needed money, and so Catherine worked first in manual labor and then, starting in 1924, quite lucratively as a public speaker telling exotic tales about her experiences in Russia for the Community Chautauqua of Canada, an outdoor university of sorts that brought cultural events, entertainment, and lecturers to small towns across Canada. Catherine's greatest trial was being away from George, her son, whom the unemployed Boris kept even as he saw a mistress. Catherine sent money to them to support George, but it funded Boris's lifestyle. She went to New York to work, but the work was unstable as she lectured and helped book lectures for a lecture bureau. She helped Boris secure a visa, hoping their lives could be rebuilt together, and she faded in her faith. Boris again took up with his mistress, and Catherine lost hope for reconciliation. But she could not shake the nagging thought that God had saved her for something more than this. But what? The answer brought her back to her roots, to persecution by those who were poor when she was rich. Her answer was in forgiveness and repentance.

---
[7]Duquinn, *They Called Her the Baroness*, 51.
[8]Quoted in Duquinn, *They Called Her the Baroness*, 56.

QUESTIONS AND IMPLICATIONS

How historians think about history is different from definitions of history in popular media. There you may have encountered debates over what the "real" history actually is. I offered a definition of history as "true stories." They are true in that they must be grounded in evidence. They are stories in that they are shaped by the questions we ask, and we make decisions about what to include or not to include while remaining committed to being as honest as possible. Catherine's lore about Friendship House's founding is incomplete, and when we ask additional questions, which I focused around her relationship to the least of these, I was able to write a more complex, fuller story about the origins.

- How would you define *history*?
- How is the definition I offer similar to or different from that?

Although historians are committed to telling true stories, they often disagree with one another about questions related to causality, significance, change over time, and other matters. These debates are, in a sense, similar to disagreements people can have with friends, colleagues, and family members. As a historian and a teacher (and in my best moments as a parent, spouse, daughter, and friend), I am committed to being able to articulate someone's position on a subject in a way they would say is accurate, even if I do not agree with them. Psychologists call this reflective listening.

- How might this definition of history as interpretive (and often debated) be helpful in strengthening your relationships with others?

Narratives about history are contested because they are not only about the past but also about who "we" are. For instance, are Americans a people characterized by freedom, or are we fundamentally oppressive? You may have heard debates between proponents of revisionist history and traditional narratives, with each side claiming that theirs is *the* right way to interpret the past.

- How could a more complex understanding of what constitutes history offer a different lens into these debates?

2

THE SIGNIFICANCE OF MONEY

> How Catholic social teaching gave Catherine
> a way to respond to urban poverty and why
> her repentance is a good model.

CONFESSING SIN

In 1932, Catherine began an undercover assignment for Archbishop McNeil of Toronto, Canada. Her job was to infiltrate communist reading rooms to learn why so many poor workers found communism appealing. Her fluency in Russian no doubt helped her work. She would refer to this assignment obliquely in later writings, describing the awful working conditions people faced and the precarious moral situations that resulted, especially for young women. I suspect some of her descriptions of working-class folks come from this time in her 1947 book *Friendship House*, which she wrote to share with others her vision of God's love for poor people and his concern about racial injustice.

Catherine's approach to communism in word and in deed was striking. She thought communism held false promises and may have even been evil, but she never condemned communists. This distinction is important, and in this chapter I want us to ask what we can learn *from* Catherine's approach to a worldview and people with whom she vehemently disagreed. Catherine exemplified humility in her approach, a posture essential to doing history and Christian discipleship (which we will return to in later chapters). People tell a story—although unverified with evidence—about Catherine's contemporary G. K. Chesterton, who, when answering the question "What is wrong with the world today?" responded simply, "I am." I suspect Catherine would have answered similarly. Together, we will puzzle over Catherine's approach using, among other things, her 1947 memoir, *Friendship House*.

Although she could have written disparagingly about her Russian neighbors and other poor Russians who tried to kill her during the Bolshevik Revolution, Catherine described herself as complicit in the oppressive context that led to their sin in her book, *Friendship House*. When she wrote about being trapped in her manor, Catherine said she realized then that she, like "most Christians, Catholics included," had given to "God only 'intellectual allegiance'" and had worshiped the idols of "wealth, power and fame." While nearly starving to death, she realized, "I too had been guilty, rendering to Christ lip-service only. I had failed to show my fellow-men the Face of Christ shining through my soul, and I had been found out. Having failed to integrate my belief into my daily life, I had no right to complain. My sin had found its punishment in this world instead of in the next."[1]

We must treat this passage with care. We cannot argue, based on a published book in 1947 and no other evidence, that in 1919 Catherine realized that her sin led to her destruction. I have not read sources closer to the 1919 event that substantiate this narrative. The claim I *can* make as a historian, however, is that in 1947 Catherine told a story of her life that made her complicit in the evils resulting from the Communist Revolution. She came to believe, or at least publicly proclaimed, that she and other Christians like her who had not aligned their lives with the gospel, thinking they could worship God and not work to end poverty, were at least partly to blame for others' turn to revolution. This position is powerful because she did not set herself apart from idol worshipers but rather made herself as one who had worshiped idols but now sought to love God instead.

LEARNING WHAT IT WAS LIKE TO BE POOR

Catherine's prophetic witness was first about the physical suffering of people, and she came to this position because changing her context changed her perspective. Even if Catherine had realized in 1919 that she had worshiped mammon, when she began lecturing on the Chautauqua circuit in 1920s Canada, she earned a steady income and lived comfortably. She claimed,

---

[1] Catherine de Hueck Doherty, *Friendship House* (New York: Sheed & Ward, 1947), 4-5.

though, that she could not escape the nagging feeling that God had saved her life for more than her personal comfort.

McNeil's request that she investigate why so many workers were becoming communist provided an opening to a new life. Catherine undertook a yearlong, secret study of the working class, living among them and gathering the data that she would turn into a ninety-five-page report for McNeil, to whom she would later dedicate her book *Friendship House*. The archbishop's question of why workers were attracted to the Communist Party is an important one and reflects both the inheritance of deep Catholic thinking in Catholic social teaching about the relationship between workers and those who employed them, and McNeil's sensitivity to the dynamics of working-class life.

But his request also seems odd given *when* Catherine began her research. She did the investigative research starting in 1932, when she was thirty-six years old. Less than three years later, in the summer of 1935, the Communist Party in Russia instituted a new strategy that effectively increased its influence among workers around the world. Fascism was a rising political threat, and party leaders thought defeating it mattered more in the short term than promoting world revolution. The Communist International or Comintern, an international communist organization led by Russia, instructed Communist Party branches around the world to change tactics, becoming less sectarian and instead coming out into the open. Many Canadians in the throes of the Depression blamed the state's failure for their economic hardship rather than their own failures. They were willing to listen to an organization that promised to revive Canada. Communists opened club rooms, where they fostered vigorous political debate, hosted parties for high school students, ran summer camps for adults and children, engaged in electoral politics (a shift from their earlier eschewal of elections), emphasized their own respectability, and pointed to the compatibility of Christianity and communism. In August 1937, the year after Catherine would leave Toronto, one of the Communist Party clubs provided games, community singing, swimming, bands, sports, and a popularity contest at their second annual picnic in Toronto. Efforts like these made the Canadian Communist Party's membership explode, jumping from five thousand members in 1934 to about fifteen thousand members in 1937.[2]

---

[2] John Manley, "'Communists Love Canada!': The Communist Party of Canada, the 'People' and the Popular Front, 1933–1938," *Journal of Canadian Studies* 36, no. 4 (2002): 59-86.

But Catherine moved to the slums and lived among working-class immigrants *before* the Popular Front period, when the Communist Party was still relatively small, which made me wonder how Archbishop McNeil understood the urgency of the question. A historian's work on anticommunism and Catholicism in Toronto helped me answer the question. Part of McNeil's concern was ideological. In the 1920s, McNeil knew that the party denounced religion as the opiate of the masses and promoted atheism. McNeil's work with Toronto's Red Squad shaped his perspective. The Red Squad was a police force that tried to stop the spread of communism by jailing party members for passing out propaganda, stopping meetings held in foreign languages, and preventing communists from campaigning. It used violence and force. While McNeil may not have known about the violence, he supported the surveillance. Confidential files from the Red Squad starting in 1923 are in the Archdiocese of Toronto's archives, suggesting how involved with the Red Squad McNeil was.[3] It is possible, then, that McNeil thought violence against people who were communists was permissible if it stopped what he saw as the greater evil of communism's spread.

If concerns about communism's ideological and spiritual danger formed part of McNeil's motivation for sending Catherine undercover, another part may have been a belief that the communists were more effective in converting working-class immigrants than they actually were. The Red Squad's Inspector Douglas Marshall estimated there were forty thousand communists active in Toronto. Thus, even though historical data suggests that in 1932 communists were not successful in recruiting workers to the party, McNeil saw them as a numerical threat.

Given this context, how should we tell the story of Catherine's study of the social problems facing immigrants in working-class Toronto? This same historian portrayed Catherine as a spy who collaborated with an unjust, inhumane system. After all, she was working for an archbishop who colluded with the Red Squad, a form of state-sponsored oppression, and she did not reveal her intentions to the communists she met while on this mission. This scholar, concerned with the dangers of state and private surveillance, wrote that Catherine's "Russian heritage and ability to speak several Slavic

---

[3] Paula Maurutto, "Private Policing and Surveillance of Catholics: Anti-communism in the Roman Catholic Archdiocese of Toronto, 1920–1960," *Labour / Le Travail* 40 (1997): 119.

languages allowed her easy entry into communist organizations. Living among the immigrant poor, in October 1931, Catherine began infiltrating communist organizations and compiling a survey of their activities."[4]

Catherine, however, wrote about her study of communism's spread among workers not as infiltration, which suggests evil, but as an act of love. She understood poor workers' problems as exacerbated by the Depression but fundamentally rooted in the problems of industrial capitalism. These problems, she said, were inadequately addressed by the Catholic Church, which drove people away from the church and into the arms of communists. Catherine's intent does matter.

McNeil likely would have understood his actions similarly. McNeil was the first bishop in Canada to formally introduce Catholic social thought, the intentional questioning of what Catholicism has to say to economics and the problems of poor people, into his archdiocese. In an era of great inequality between the wealthy and the poor, Catholic social teaching offered a way forward that honored the image of God in each person.

WHY CATHERINE RETURNED TO THE SLUMS

After her investigative work ended, Catherine wanted to return to live among the poor to show them Jesus. Her work of learning and studying the problem had changed her, and she wanted to act. She believed that sharing life with those suffering would offer hope to them. As she would write years later about her Friendship House in Harlem,

> We had to be poor as they were poor. We had to experience the way of life they experienced. We had to experience the crowded apartments with their poor ventilation; unbearably hot in the summer and unbearably cold in the winter. We had to experience the poor plumbing which, at times, could threaten our very lives. . . . Because we identified in these ways, those who received things from us did not hate us. They began to love us. The law of love, the law of Christ, began to work in Harlem in a tangible way.[5]

McNeil gave Catherine permission to return to the slums and to open Friendship House, intended to bring working-class people to the church by

---

[4]Maurutto, "Private Policing and Surveillance," 41.
[5]Doherty, *Fragments of My Life*, 160.

caring for them materially and providing Catholic answers to their economic concerns. Shortly after opening, the St. Francis Friendship House relocated to 122 Portland Street, which was populated by Czechoslovakians, Poles, Russians, and Ukrainians. Catherine strategically located the house across from the Protestant Church of All Nations and a communist hall.[6] Catherine modeled Friendship House on communist reading rooms, providing books to read, clubs for children, and fellowship for adults, except that she fed those who came a strong diet of Catholic social thought.

Catherine's Friendship House operated in an alternative economy, one of trust in God's provision. She earned no income and had no insurance. Catherine reported that God did provide: "'We just trust in the Holy Ghost.' The Holy Ghost not only sent us the Brothers Christopher who must be fed, and the poor boys and girls of the neighborhood who must be fed and clothed and taught and kept off the streets as much as possible, and all the others who come to us with their needs . . . but He also sent us the things we must have to minister to them."[7] She believed God equipped her for the work he called her to.

From this context of living among the poor, Catherine critiqued the church and her fellow Christians for their pursuit of individual advancement. "These are tragic days," Catherine reflected.

> Humanity has forgotten God. Because of that, some of us who still remember Him, have left homes and friends. We have come to live among the needy and the poor, to help them atone for the rich who have forgotten their brothers, the poor. We feel we are privileged and rich beyond the dreams of men, for we are doing it for Christ whom we see in all the poor and downtrodden.[8]

A SPIRITUALITY THAT INCLUDES CARING FOR THE POOR

If Archbishop McNeil and Catherine were seeking to apply Catholic social teaching in Toronto, why were so many Catholics in the category of those who had forgotten God, as Catherine said? The pair was on the cutting edge of Catholic social teaching but represented a smaller stream of theology within Catholicism. Most Catholics' spiritual formation did not adequately

---

[6] Maurutto, "Private Policing and Surveillance of Catholics," 129.
[7] Doherty, *Friendship House*, 39.
[8] Doherty, *Friendship House*, 35.

address deep suffering of the era—both as experienced by workers and as perpetuated in part by employers. Catholic spiritual formation, broadly, was concerned mostly with the individual, and confession manuals and the like helped individual Catholics avoid specific, personal sins. While Catholics viewed sin as serious, a matter of heaven and hell, they saw it as relating mostly to their own personal piety, not the social order. For most Catholics, this conception of sin as an individual problem continued through the 1960s. As one version of the Baltimore Catechism puts it, "[Actual sin] is a sin which we actually commit *ourselves*. Actual sin is any *willful* thought, desire, word, action or omission which God forbids us to do."[9] But McNeil, Catherine, and others argued that while a person should be concerned with their individual righteousness, they also must see themselves as part of a whole with which they were concerned.[10]

They rooted their understanding of sin and God's call on God's people in Catholic social thought, whose foundational document was Pope Leo XIII's 1891 encyclical *Rerum Novarum*. Also known as *Rights and Duties of Capital and Labor*, the encyclical calls for a middle way between communism and unfettered capitalism. It argues that owners and workers have mutual responsibilities to each other. The encyclical affirms the right of private property but recognizes that, in a society where those who own the means of production can leverage more power, workers need special protection. It also observes, contrary to a prosperity gospel, that God cares for the economically and spiritually poor: "God Himself seems to incline rather to those who suffer misfortune; for Jesus Christ calls the poor 'blessed'; (Matt.5:3) He lovingly invites those in labor and grief to come to Him for solace; (Matt. 11:28) and He displays the tenderest charity toward the lowly and the oppressed."[11] While the encyclical is conservative in that it promotes change through changing people's attitudes rather than structural change in society, in its context people saw it as radical because it calls for help for the poor and lays out the

---

[9] Quoted in Maria C. Morrow, "The Change in the Conception of Sin Among Catholics in the United States, 1955–1975," *American Catholic Studies* 122, no. 1 (Spring 2011): 59.

[10] Peter Ernest Baltutis, "To Enlarge Our Hearts and to Widen Our Horizon: Archbishop Neil McNeil and Social Catholicism in the Roman Catholic Archdiocese of Toronto, 1912–1934" (MA thesis, University of St. Michael's College, 2006), 41.

[11] Leo XIII, *Rerum Novarum*, 1891, www.vatican.va/holy_father/leo_xiii/encyclicals/documents/hf_l-xiii_enc_15051891_rerum-novarum_en.html.

responsibilities of capital. In 1931, Pope Pius XI published *Quadragesimo Anno*, updating Catholic social teaching in light of the Depression, and argued to restructure society along more corporatist lines.

McNeil brought Catholic social teaching to his archdiocese, believing that social Catholicism "comprehends not only the care of those in actual want and distress, but the prevention of causes of want and destress, and the promotion of rehabilitations, physically, morally, and vocationally."[12] McNeil, along with Catherine and other Catholics who tried to find this third way in their day-to-day lives between capitalism and communism, wanted to both change individuals *and* address systemic problems.

When we think about how to narrate Catherine's move into the slums, we must account for her commitment to Catholic social thought in the context of her efforts to fight communism. Historians know that accounts will vary, depending on the questions people are concerned with and the sources they use. But they cannot just dismiss critiques, accounts, or evidence that does not mesh nicely with what they want to say. Catherine did go undercover. She likely lied about her identity, and she participated in a system of relationships that did oppress citizens and immigrants—all made in the image of God—who promoted communism. Even if she did not know about the details of the Red Squad, she was implicated in their work because of the connections. But we cannot dismiss her as simply duplicitous because the situation was more complicated. She did this work out of a conviction that was like the communists'. She wanted to make the world better for workers, to end their suffering, and in so doing to bring them back to the faith.

WE HAVE FALLEN SHORT

Catherine insisted that her fellow Catholics not blame workers for finding communism appealing and said Catholics must consider how they were to blame. She wrote, "We rave and rant about 'foreigners' being Communists in our cities yet never stop to think of our responsibility for their being there and being such."[13] Catherine's argument is significant. Her immersion in a poor context made her acutely aware of her neighbors' suffering. Her faith led her to believe that God did not like their suffering.

---

[12] Quoted in Baltutis, "To Enlarge Our Hearts," 55-56.
[13] Doherty, *Friendship House*, 23-24.

Like the Hebrew prophets of old, few Catholics wanted to listen to her. Priests and laypeople alike called her communist for her insistence that the church work on behalf of the poor. After McNeil died, a panel of five priests investigated Catherine and Friendship House and determined that Friendship House would be better run by priests. Catherine wrote to her friend Dorothy Day of the Catholic Worker movement, "FH Toronto is closed down. The reasons? To you I can tell the truth: too radical Catholic Action stepping on ecclesiastical and rich people's toes. Priestly jealousy. That is all."[14] Catherine's letter suggests the raw emotion of her "deportation," as she called it, and is an effective description of the immediate context.

But Catherine's narrative does not account fully for the priests. It is possible, as she suggested, that they were too concerned with wealth and their own authority. But their context may also not have equipped them to receive prophetic calls from a single laywoman saying something profoundly different from what they had known. When McNeil came to Toronto as archbishop, few people had heard of Catholic social thought. In the whole of Canada, he was the first person to try to systematically introduce it into his archdiocese, which he did through seminary education, periodicals, and speakers. At least the older priests' seminary training and everyone's Catholic culture did not equip them to prioritize social justice and hear and respond with humility to a layperson speaking prophetically to them.

COMMUNISM'S APPEAL TO BLACK NEW YORKERS

Immediately after fleeing Toronto, Catherine landed in New York, staying with Dorothy Day.[15] Then she went to Europe for a year to study Catholic action, a way of spiritual formation that taught practitioners to study a situation, judge what a Christian response would be, and then act to bring the situation in line with Christ's kingdom. Always the future for Catherine seemed uncertain.

After two years, in 1938, Catherine sensed a call to New York, where, like in Toronto, she would resist communism's advance among poor workers.

---

[14]Robert Wild, ed., "Catherine de Hueck to Dorothy Day, November 25, 1936," in *Comrades Stumbling Along: The Friendship of Catherine De Hueck Doherty and Dorothy Day as Revealed Through Their Letters* (New York: Alba House, 2009), 52-53.

[15]For their friendship, see Wild, *Comrades Stumbling Along*; Karen J. Johnson, *One in Christ: Chicago Catholics and the Quest for Interracial Justice* (New York: Oxford University Press, 2018).

Catherine would later report that Father John LaFarge, a Jesuit priest who was a leader in the Catholic interracial movement, wanted her to come to New York and found a Friendship House in Harlem to combat communism among Black New Yorkers. It is likely that Catherine had known the priest at least since 1927. Catherine's Black colleague, Ellen Tarry, reported in an oral history that Catherine's husband, Boris, had tutored LaFarge in Russian.[16] LaFarge asked Father Michael Mulvoy of Harlem's St. Mark's parish to invite Catherine to Harlem. Mulvoy did, and Catherine moved into Harlem.

The neighborhood she entered was home to the Harlem Renaissance, a flourishing of Black literature and arts. Yet for all its rich literary, musical, and artistic culture, it was poor. As Black poet Langston Hughes observed, "The ordinary Negroes [in Harlem] hadn't heard of the Harlem Renaissance. If they had, it hadn't raised wages any."[17] When the Great Depression wracked the world, some Black Americans would argue that not much changed. As one worker remembered, "The Negro was born in depression. It didn't mean too much to him, The Great American Depression, as you call it. There was no such thing. The best he could be is a janitor or a porter or a shoeshine boy."[18] Nonetheless, the Depression hit Harlem hard, an extensive impact caused in part by White racism. Unemployment was about 60 percent in Harlem throughout the Depression, and half of families were on relief as White workers replaced Black workers in jobs such as house cleaning. Overall, the number of skilled workers declined by 50 percent.[19]

Figure 2.1. Catherine de Hueck in Harlem, late 1930s or early 1940s. Courtesy of Madonna House Archives, Combermere, Canada

In this context, communism was appealing to many African Americans, although this appeal was by no means

---

[16] Ellen Tarry, oral history, interview by Lorene Hanley Duquin, 1991, Box 1998.052-072, Madonna House Archives, Combermere, Canada.
[17] Quoted in Lauri Johnson, "A Generation of Women Activists: African American Female Educators in Harlem, 1930–1950," *Journal of African American History* 89, no. 3 (Summer 2004): 224.
[18] Clifford Burke interview with Studs Terkel, quoted in David E. Shi and Holly A. Mayer, eds., *For the Record: A Documentary History*, 5th ed. (New York: Norton, 2013), 2:197.
[19] Johnson, "Generation of Women Activists," 224-25.

THE SIGNIFICANCE OF MONEY

natural or inevitable. In the 1920s the Communist Party had little appeal for most Black Americans. During that decade, the Communist Party in the United States largely avoided addressing what came to be called "the Negro question," which meant the particular and pervasive discrimination Black Americans faced. Instead, most communists adopted a colorblind approach, saying the real issue was not social equality but economic freedom. Even after the White-on-Black riots across America in 1919, the party held that the issue was not race but class. A handful of Black American communists, including Jamaican immigrant and author Claude McKay, who would later convert to Catholicism through Friendship House, argued that African Americans' situation demanded special attention from the Communist Party because they suffered not primarily because they were working class but because they were Black.[20] The Comintern, however, deferred to the mostly White Communist Party USA leadership on racial matters, and those leaders adopted a perspective that prioritized economic matters as separate from and over and above racial matters. This position made the Communist Party irrelevant to most African Americans.

The situation changed, however, when the Communist Party's legal arm, International Labor Defense, joined the defense of the Scottsboro boys. In 1931, two poor White women who had been riding the rails claimed that nine Black teenagers had raped them when the train was stopped in Alabama by a posse of White men looking for a group of White youth. Following the South's racial logic and despite what most people thought were false accusations, the young men were charged with murder and sentenced to death. The boys' mothers, however, worked to defend their sons and welcomed the help of the Communist Party alongside the National Association for the Advancement of Colored People (NAACP) in court, along with organizing mass demonstrations, writing editorials, and going on national and international speaking tours. As Janie Patterson, one of the mothers, said, "I haven't got no schooling, but I have five senses and I know Negroes can't win by themselves. . . . I have faith that they will free him [her son, Haywood Patterson], if we all is united behind them. . . . I don't care whether they are Reds, Greens,

---

[20]J. A. Zumoff, "The American Communist Party and the 'Negro Question' from the Founding of the Party to the Fourth Congress of the Communist International," *Journal for the Study of Radicalism* 6, no. 2 (2012): 53-89.

or Blues. They are the only ones who put up a fight to save the boys and I am with them to the end."[21] Their combined efforts made the case widely known and made many African Americans appreciate that there were some White people, communists, who were willing to help them in what they knew was a trumped-up case.

If the communists' defense of the Scottsboro case made Black Americans realize that White communists were the only White people in America who seemed to care about their situation, the Communist Party demonstrated that concern in sustained ways throughout the Depression. Because of their higher rates of unemployment, Black Americans were hungrier and evicted from their homes at higher rates than White Americans. But communists helped them in Harlem and Black communities throughout the nation. Mothers, desperate to shelter their families, upon an eviction notice would turn to communists to help. Contemporary Black sociologists Horace Cayton and St. Clair Drake observed that when an eviction notice came, "It was not unusual for a mother to shout to the children, 'Run quick and find the Reds!'"[22]

But White communists did more than help African Americans. They treated them as equals. As Arthur Falls, a Black Catholic medical doctor who would later welcome Catherine's Friendship House to Chicago, observed in 1931 about the Communist Party, "One sees white and colored sharing in the positions of responsibility in the organization, as well as in the rank and file. One sees white and colored marching side by side in their parades, funerals, and other public demonstrations. To a large number of Negroes, this is the first contact with a group of white people who say 'Comrade' and seem to mean it." Those who joined the party, Falls noted, did believe "that the Communist Party offers the only chance of true 'equality of opportunity' for which the group has been fighting so long."[23]

Friendship House leader Ellen Tarry reflected the mixed views many Catholics working for interracial justice held toward communism. On the one hand, they admired that communists were actually living what they preached: that

---

[21] Quoted in Lashawn Harris, "Running with the Reds: African American Women and the Communist Party During the Great Depression," *The Journal of African American History* 94, no. 1 (Winter 2009): 21-43.
[22] Quoted in Harris, "Running with the Reds," 23.
[23] Arthur Falls, "The Spread of Communism Among Chicago's Negroes," *St. Elizabeth's Chronicle* 4, no. 9 (September 1931): 577-78.

Black and White workers could unite together and work for justice. Communists' actions profoundly contrasted White Catholics (and White Protestants), who preached a universal church, open to people from all racial backgrounds, but in practice actively excluded Black Catholics from their parishes and turned a blind eye to their calls for justice (as we will discuss more in the next chapter). Tarry was disgusted with White Catholics' responses to Black Americans' turn toward communism. She gained a national audience in 1940 when reviewing Richard Wright's book *Native Son*, which won wide acclaim. Tarry wrote in the White Jesuit magazine *Commonweal* that she was concerned that "in Catholic circles many have lamented the fact that the Negro writer who has arisen as the spokesman for his race should be a communist." Tarry noted that Wright, whom she called a God-fearing communist, "was not born a communist. Existing social, economic and political conditions have made him so." She noted that Catholics were "among those who are responsible for some of the conditions that have led Richard Wright and scores of others into the ranks of the reds," and that it was time for "Christian America to shed its coat of hypocrisy and admit its sin."[24]

While no more than one thousand Black Harlemites joined the Communist Party, many found its universal call and advocacy for their well-being appealing and appreciated their activism. When Catherine moved to Harlem, communists were some of, if not the only, White people who actively worked for Black people's benefit. There was the rare exception, of course, such as Father Michael Mulvoy, who was known as the blackest White man in Harlem. But that he and then Catherine were exceptions to the overarching pattern in Catholicism—and even liberalism—in the North cannot be overstated. As Catherine noted, "Here [in Harlem] poverty, misery, race discrimination bring much hardship and sorrow. Here Communists find fertile ground for their claims that they the godless, have the only solution of the Race problem."[25]

QUESTIONS AND IMPLICATIONS

Catherine argued at the end of her life that it would have been impossible for her to fully understand the experiences of African Americans had she not

---

[24]Ellen Tarry, "Native Daughter: An Indictment of White America by a Colored Woman," *Commonweal*, April 12, 1940.
[25]Doherty, *Friendship House*, 42.

lived with them, sharing the difficult living conditions they faced. She and other leaders in Friendship House would regularly note that they gained credibility among their neighbors by living in their communities, rather than coming in to work and leaving at the end of the day for a safer neighborhood. Because they were neighbors, their help was received with love, rather than disdain. As we will see, all of the people in this book moved close to those suffering within economic and racial systems.

- How can you learn what your neighbor's experience is like?
- Are you close to those who are suffering because of economic issues? What would stop you from moving closer?

Catherine did not condemn communists and those who joined their ranks, and neither did the African Americans who appreciated White communists' help when their backs were against the wall. To Catherine and to many African Americans, White communists seemed to be the only White people who were acting in a "Christian" manner by treating people equally and helping poor Black people.

- In what ways may others who are not Christians be acting in a more Christian manner than you or your church? Than our contemporary Christian culture?
- What role do you play in contributing to a culture in which Christians do not live as Christians are called to live? How can you repent as Catherine did?

Catherine confessed her sin of not loving God as she ought and not loving her neighbor as herself as she reflected on the rise of communism. She placed the blame for the problem not "out there" but in her own life.

- Do you have a tendency to blame others?
- What do you need to confess?

In contemporary society, we often hear debates about what matters more in fostering inequality in American society: race or class. Catherine's experiences and critiques, written in a different context from our own, break down that race-versus-class binary and show how complicated and intersected they are.

- To what extent do you think the debate matters? How does it function in your own context?

3

SEGREGATED CITIES

> Why Catherine's home in Harlem was so segregated and how Christian beliefs and practices contributed to racial inequalities.

CATHERINE'S CONTEXT: A SEGREGATED LAND

When Catherine moved to Harlem in New York City in 1938, she moved to one of the most significant receiving cities for Black migrants from the South, into a city with an inherited racial geography that had shaped her neighbors and would shape her and her ministry. She was an immigrant to the United States and early on was in a crash course of sorts about race in America. Because she sought to understand why Harlem was as segregated as it was, so must we.

The story we will tell accounts for two of the key themes implicit in the quote from Catherine's dear friend and White coworker Ann Harrigan in the epigraph for part one. The epigraph comes from an unpublished manuscript Ann wrote about her experiences at Friendship House during the 1940s. Ann typed the draft at the end of her life, between 1982 and 1983, working either from her home in Canada, where she had married Catherine's cousin, or at Notre Dame, which had given her a grant to work on the project and which now houses Ann's papers (and where I spent weeks researching Friendship House one summer). Ann talked about Friendship House's neighborhood, the "slum smells" that characterized the walk up to Friendship House's storefront "in cavernous rows of sleezey [sic] stores, below the line of unbroken drab 6 story tenements."[1] She also talked about complexity, pointing to the difficulty of understanding and dismantling racial hierarchies. Ann contrasted the simplicity of people from different racial backgrounds "talking, laughing, friendly, sipping coffee" in the haven of Friendship House with "the complexities of the sin of segregation."

As Catherine and Boris faced starvation at the hands of Bolsheviks, the faces of New York City and other northern American cities were changing. Black American southerners began moving north from the southern plantations where they sharecropped. Historians call this movement the Great Migration, and it was the largest population movement in US history, with some six million African Americans going north between 1916 and 1970. Sometimes an entire church congregation would move north, reestablishing itself in a northern city with members living close to one another.

Historians have found that migrants' reasons for leaving varied. Echoing the exodus narrative so prominent in African American Christian thought, many were pulled by the hope of a "promised land" where they could experience racial and economic freedom. They saw the North as a land where women did not need to fear for their safety, where all eligible voters could vote, and where a man could advance economically and not fear being labeled an "uppity Negro." Northern companies advertised in Black newspapers that made their way South, carried by the all-Black Pullman porter staff that worked in the Pullman luxury overnight cars (hired because the Pullman company thought Black servants would make White people comfortable psychologically), calling for workers to fill the booming economy. Many were pushed by declining farming opportunities, with increased mechanization and decreased cotton crops plagued by the boll weevil.[2]

As the American economy expanded in the roaring twenties, these southern sharecroppers took trains north, so their migration patterns followed the rails. They did not ride in the Model T cars that Henry Ford, in a brilliant financial decision, priced at costs accessible to his northern workers.

---

[1] Ann Harrigan Makletzoff, "Finished Works and Drafts" (n.d.), Ann Harrigan Makletzoff Papers, Box 3, Folder 5a, University of Notre Dame Archives.

[2] There are many excellent books on the Great Migration, including Isabel Wilkerson, *The Warmth of Other Suns: The Epic Story of America's Great Migration* (New York: Random House, 2010); James R. Grossman, *Land of Hope: Chicago, Black Southerners and the Great Migration* (Chicago: University of Chicago Press, 1991).

Those from Florida, Georgia, South Carolina, North Carolina, and Virginia stayed along the East Coast, usually ending up in Harlem. Folks living in Mississippi, Alabama, Tennessee, and Kentucky usually went to the Midwest, stepping off the train in cities such as Chicago, Milwaukee, Detroit, Cleveland, and Pittsburgh, although some got off earlier in Louisville, on the border between North and South. Those from Arkansas, Louisiana, and Texas often went west to Los Angeles and the Bay Area.

Industrial plants in these cities needed workers. In 1924 Congress passed the Johnson-Reed Immigration Act, limiting the number of immigrant workers who could migrate to the United States and making Black southerners an appealing group of laborers for northern industrialists. Senators and representatives, concerned that immigrants from southeastern Europe were unable to assimilate to American culture and were spoiling America's bloodlines, wanted to reshape what they called the nation's racial stock. The act excluded immigrants from Asia and aligned other immigration with the 1890 US Census, which reflected the population before immigrants from the "less desirable" southeastern European countries came to the United States.[3]

At first, sociologists who studied the Great Migration as it happened thought that African Americans would assimilate into the cities' labor force and neighborhoods as many immigrants in previous decades had. However, Black Americans experiences were different, and great violence initially characterized race relations in northern cities.

As soldiers fought in World War I's last days in the summer of 1919 and Catherine and Boris recovered in England, riots rocked the United States as Whites attacked Blacks in the context of labor competition and housing conflict. Unlike in previous racial conflicts, African Americans fought back. Black poet and author Claude McKay, whom Friendship House later befriended, captured this ethos in his 1919 poem "If We Must Die." He wrote of "New Negroes," men and women who had fought abroad for freedom in the Great War and were unwilling to cower when attacked at home.

> If we must die, let it not be like hogs
> hunted and penned in an inglorious spot,

---

[3]For more on immigration and race, see A. R. Zolberg, *A Nation by Design: Immigration Policy in the Fashioning of America* (Cambridge, MA: Harvard University Press, 2006).

while round about us bark the mad and hungry dogs,
making their mocking at our accursed lot.
If we must die, O let us nobly die
. . . Like men we'll face the murderous, cowardly pack, pressed to the wall
but fighting back![4]

As Black Americans grieved their losses in the months following that summer, Catherine and Boris were evacuated to England, where Catherine converted to Roman Catholicism. Soon after the couple would immigrate to Canada.

By the 1930s, as African Americans' migration to northern cities slowed because of the Depression, there was some successful integration in industry. In 1935, labor organizers formed the Congress of Industrial Organizations (CIO), which organized all workers, not just skilled and White workers. While historians' more recent assessments of the CIO on racial matters have been mixed, contemporary Black leaders appreciated the CIO's leadership. W. E. B. Du Bois, the Black intellectual, cofounder of the NAACP, and civil rights activist, observed that the congress had "thrown together, Black and white, as fellow workers striving for the same objects. There has been on this account an astonishing spread of interracial tolerance and understanding. Probably no movement in the last 30 years has been so successful in softening race prejudice among the masses."[5] As the congress was fostering a measure of interracialism in the United States, Catherine's response to economic suffering was to move into a Toronto slum and found the first Friendship House.

Back in the United States, the pockets of integration among workers in the workplace did not lead to many White people having a desire to live by African Americans. These housing dynamics led to Harlem's segregation. Some of the segregation, of course, was by choice. People rented flats by those they knew from down South.

But despite some personal preferences, Black urban dwellers found their housing options limited by White residents' actions and systemic factors they—and Catherine in the 1930s—knew little about. Part of the complexity

---

[4]Claude McKay, "If We Must Die," *The Liberator* 2, no. 7 (July 1919): 21.
[5]W. E. B. Du Bois, "Race Relations in the United States, 1917–1947," *Phylon* 9 (1948): 234-47, quoted in Michael Goldfield, "Race and the CIO: The Possibilities for Racial Egalitarianism During the 1930s and 1940s," *International Labor and Working-Class History*, no. 44 (1993): 1-32.

of these dynamics lies in the complicated ways economic and racial logics intersected, and the often unintended racial consequences of economic choices. These housing dynamics had profound negative social, economic, and spiritual effects on Black families and individuals. But because these dynamics were created by people, they were never "natural."

Some mechanisms of segregation were more obvious. Frequently, when Black families moved into "White" neighborhoods, they would encounter angry mobs that attacked the properties they had rented or purchased. White newspapers did not cover the violence, hoping to prevent more White people from joining the mobs, but Black newspapers did.[6]

Even White residents who thought of themselves as racially liberal worked to keep Black folks out of what they saw as their neighborhoods. They hosted so-called neighborhood improvement associations to encourage neighbors to keep their properties well-cared for, hoping that respectability would keep property values high and keep potential Black homeowners out. Women and men in local neighborhoods covenanted together to not sell their homes to a particular racial group—often "Negroes" and Jews (until about the 1930s, most White Protestants thought of Jews as a different race)—and would add restrictive covenants to their home titles. Residents could not enforce these covenants, however, and although restrictive covenants were widespread by the late 1920s, they were ineffective in keeping Black neighbors out. Attorneys from the NAACP, working for racial progress through the courts, argued successfully against restrictive covenants in the 1948 Supreme Court case *Shelly v. Kramer*. The court decided that while an individual could place a restrictive covenant on their house, the state could not enforce it. While some White people who supported restrictive covenants thought that Black people were inherently biologically inferior, many thought that Black folks could make good neighbors, but they were more concerned with the potential that a neighborhood would be "overrun" by Black residents and lead to dropping property values.

Perhaps surprisingly, these White folks' racialized economic concerns were legitimate, although not entirely for the reasons they believed. Neither they nor their potential Black neighbors knew the details of the hidden

---

[6]Arnold R. Hirsch, *Making the Second Ghetto: Race and Housing in Chicago, 1940–1960* (Chicago: University of Chicago Press, 1998).

mechanisms promoting segregation. During the Great Depression of the 1930s, President Franklin Roosevelt created the Federal Housing Authority and the Home Owners Loan Corporation to help the housing industry and prevent people from defaulting on their mortgages. The Federal Housing Authority, which insured mortgages, created a series of neighborhood-based maps that assessed how likely residents were to pay back their loans. They used a racialized logic (which sociologists in the 1940s debunked) that assumed that Black homeowners were less likely to pay back their loans. They colored Black and interracial neighborhoods red on these maps to indicate they were "dangerous" places to make loans.[7]

Because the maps expressed faulty racial assumptions, the Federal Housing Authority would not insure Black homeowners, thus ensuring segregation and forcing potential Black buyers into a secondary, more expensive mortgage market. Private banks began using these maps, extending segregation across cities. Because the maps focused on particular places, even the occasional White buyer—including the White Catholics who followed Catherine de Hueck—who wanted to live in an integrated neighborhood would have difficulty finding mortgage money. When a Black family, usually a middle- or upper-class, moved into the neighborhood, they often paid a premium for their new home, sometimes two to three times what a White family might pay because so few people were willing to sell to them.[8] Realtors who made money by what was called "blockbusting," moved in quickly, knocking on doors and telling homeowners they should sell quickly because the neighborhood was turning over. Initially, then, housing costs went up but then fell because of the lack of mortgage money and then a vast supply of houses, created by the fear blockbusting realtors flamed. This meant that, as White people feared, Black neighbors meant their property values would fall eventually. But it was not because Black homeowners defaulted more on their mortgages; it was because the government assumed they would and so did not want to insure their loans.

---

[7]Kenneth T. Jackson, *Crabgrass Frontier: The Suburbanization of the United States* (Oxford: Oxford University Press, 1987).

[8]For a gripping narrative, see Beryl Satter, *Family Properties: Race, Real Estate, and the Exploitation of Black America* (New York: Metropolitan Books, 2009).

HOW FAITH FOSTERED SEGREGATION

There is another complicated factor that helped segregate northern cities: religion. When Catherine wrote about White Catholics and housing segregation, she pointed to individual instances of White Catholics' discrimination against Black Americans, Catholic or otherwise. She did not discuss another important aspect of Catholicism's contribution to segregation in northern cities. I want to expand the true story she told with more context.

Catherine was steeped in a faith whose geographic sensibilities meant that White Catholics stayed in their neighborhoods longer than their Protestant and Jewish counterparts when Black neighbors moved in.[9] Although this faith was characterized by a theology that in theory crossed color lines, Catholics in the mid-twentieth century practiced it in an insular way. Historians of the urban North have shown how Catholicism's very rhythms and religious frameworks intersected with the Great Migration's dynamics to foster segregation, revealing how careful historical work can bring into focus dynamics that were not always obvious on the ground.[10]

In the late nineteenth and early twentieth century, as immigrants entered the United States, they worshiped in national parishes, which intended to reach specific national or racial groups. These immigrants' identities were fluid. When Sicilians and Tuscans, who identified themselves by their region, came to the United States, they became "Italian." In America, to be "Italian" was to be one of the many "White races." This identity was changing, however, and by the 1930s, as Catherine was moving into Harlem, the many White

---

[9]For Jewish responses to Black neighbors with housing, see G. H. Gamm, *Urban Exodus: Why the Jews Left Boston and the Catholics Stayed* (Cambridge, MA: Harvard University Press, 1999). For the complicated Protestant responses, which usually resulted in leaving a neighborhood, see Darren Dochuk, "'Praying for a Wicked City': Congregation, Community and the Suburbanization of Fundamentalism," *Religion and American Culture* 13, no. 2 (2003): 167-203; Mark Mulder, "Evangelical Church Polity and the Nuances of White Flight," *Journal of Urban History* 38, no. 16 (2012): 16-38; Mulder, *Shades of White Flight: Evangelical Congregations and Urban Departure* (New Brunswick, NJ: Rutgers University Press, 2015).

[10]John T. McGreevy, *Parish Boundaries: The Catholic Encounter with Race in the Twentieth Century Urban North* (Chicago: University of Chicago Press, 1996). This is the foundational book for understanding these dynamics. Other books that deal with racial geographies and Catholicism include Timothy Neary, *Crossing Parish Boundaries: Race, Sports, and Catholic Youth in Chicago, 1914-1954* (Chicago: University of Chicago Press, 2016); Matthew J. Cressler, *Authentically Black and Truly Catholic: The Rise of Black Catholicism in the Great Migration* (New York: New York University Press, 2017); Karen J. Johnson, *One in Christ: Chicago Catholics and the Quest for Interracial Justice* (New York: Oxford University Press, 2018).

races had largely become "the White race."[11] When the Great Migration began in the 1910s, though, Italians worshiped at Italian-speaking parish, Poles in a Polish-speaking parish, Irish in an English-speaking parish.

Right as the Great War broke out across Europe and as Anglo-Protestant Americans' anxiety about the purity of the bloodlines was rising, American Catholic bishops increased their efforts to "Americanize" the Catholic faithful. In Chicago, for instance, Archbishop Mundelein stopped creating national parishes to accommodate immigrants and instead designated parishes as geographic. In a geographic parish, the parish priest was responsible for those living in a particular neighborhood. Because people often lived by others who were like them, those living in their parish boundaries were usually from the same national background. Although nationality mapped onto geography, the logic had changed from a national/racial one to a geographic one.

Black parishes, however, were the one consistent exception to this rule. Bishops set aside national parishes for Black parishioners and staffed them not with regular clergy, trained in diocesan seminaries, but with missionary priests who had callings to "the Negro race" at home and abroad. Even in the categories of leadership, Black Catholics were segregated.

As Black Protestants moved to northern cities, many did convert to Catholicism, drawn by what they saw as its colorblind theology, reserved style of worship, and good schools. Few migrants wanted to send their children to the crowded public schools, and many who could afford it sent their children to Catholic schools, staffed by nuns who wanted to serve African Americans. Schools required parents to learn the tenets of the faith, and many converted.

But they soon learned that White Catholics did not want Black Catholics to practice their faith—or live—outside the increasingly crowded Black belts. Many bishops essentially mandated segregation for Black parishioners who wanted to attend White churches and schools. While Black parishioners were technically free to attend any parish they wished, priests in non-Black parishes would often deny them the sacraments, segregate them in the pews, and not admit their children to the parish Catholic school, saying that Black Catholics had their own parishes. Making Black Catholics the exception to

---

[11]See, for instance, Matthew Frye Jacobson, *Whiteness of a Different Color* (Cambridge, MA: Harvard University Press, 1998).

the geographic parish logic therefore furthered White Catholics' implicit bias against Black neighbors, even if those neighbors were Catholic.

Black Catholic responses were complicated. Some were grateful and praised their bishops for trusting them with their own parishes. Others were concerned, seeing how the other races were merging while "the Negro race" was being set apart.

This geographic parish mentality among White Catholics shaped northern cities, where Catholics made up large proportions of the population. Priests encouraged their working-class parishioners to buy their homes, and the parishioners invested their savings in bricks and mortar. Parishioners built Catholic worlds within walking distance of their homes, participating in Catholic clubs, sending their children to the local parish elementary schools, and sacrificing for church building funds. While this place-based mentality fostered a vibrant sense of belonging and meaning for local residents, their insularity meant that they were often resistant to outsiders, particularly those who were not Catholic. Therefore, White Catholics thought Black Protestant neighbors threatened the parish both because they were Black and because they were Protestant.

While reports of physical violence on church grounds were rare, White Catholics' resistance to Black neighbors was often violent in the neighborhood, which reflected a spiritual formation that allowed for attacking Black neighbors or at least turning a blind eye. They attacked the apartments and houses Black neighbors moved into, and their priests usually either failed to condemn the actions or actively supported them. Until 1951, much of this violence went unreported in White newspapers. That year, however, the violence received international attention when a suburban police force could not contain it. Harvey Clarke, a Black Catholic, attempted to move his family into the all-White and mostly Catholic suburb of Cicero. Residents of Cicero and nearby Berwyn attacked the apartment building, burning it and destroying the Clarkes' belongings, including their piano, which the mob threw out the window. After the mob settled down, many priests denied that their parishioners had participated, but other witnesses argued that Cicero's shame "belongs partly to the Catholic schools and churches of Cicero."[12]

While the violence in Cicero was obviously wrong—and by the 1950s more Catholics, often influenced in some measure by Catherine's and Friendship

---

[12] William Gremley, "The Scandal of Cicero," *America*, August 25, 1951.

House's ministry, were beginning to call race prejudice sinful—this resistance cannot be dismissed as simply prejudiced, although most likely held prejudiced views. Once again, it was complex. There were many layers, not easily solvable simply by individuals changing their racial views. These White Catholics were part of a larger economic system, with the redlining and the blockbusting, whose logic perpetuated racial inequality and prevented integrated neighborhoods. Because their priests had encouraged them to buy a house in the parish and because they were working-class folks, they would lose a lot if property values in their neighborhoods plummeted. Many White families felt the sting several times, moving out of the parish when Black families moved in. While Catholicism held within it a vision, and even an ontological reality, that Catholics were indeed one in Christ, the logic of this place-based faith meant that religious outsiders were a threat to a thriving parish because they would literally take up physical space in a community but not contribute financially or socially to the parish life. Thus, when the place-based practice of parish life merged with racial prejudice, economic systems promoting segregation, and a faith that assumed segregation between "Whites" and "Negroes," the results were detrimental.

COSTS OF RACIAL SEGREGATION

Why did pioneering Black families want to move into "White" neighborhoods? Why face angry mobs at worst and cold shoulders at best? Most also paid more money for their housing in these new neighborhoods because they were forced to the secondary mortgage market or because there were so few homes available to them. Why go to the trouble? They were willing to endure these hardships to move to nicer neighborhoods because they were tired of the overcrowding in Black neighborhoods and, reflecting their class status, wanted to live with others of a similar class level.[13]

They were leaving behind neighborhoods plagued with difficulties caused in large part by systemic issues. Catherine wrote about the poor living conditions, including the incessant bedbugs in Harlem. She could have added more. When a neighborhood became Black, city government and landlords often stopped providing regular services and maintenance. Arthur Falls, a

---

[13]William Cooley, "Moving on Out: Black Pioneering in Chicago," *Journal of Urban History* 36, no. 4 (2010): 485-506.

Black Catholic medical doctor and acquaintance of Catherine's, recalled in his memoir that when he first rented an office for his practice,

> The building was kept in spotless condition with two janitors on call. As white tenants moved out and colored moved in, the owner, although he was charging us a higher rent than our predecessors had paid, took one of the janitors off so that we had only half the service we previously had had. Ultimately, when the only tenants in the building were colored, the service became abominable and the building rapidly deteriorated. This in spite of the fact that all of us were not only paying more rent than the white persons who preceded us, but our rent steadily was being increased.[14]

As Dr. Falls and so many other Black tenants experienced, White landlords could become rich at their expense. For those who owned property, Black ghettos were profitable.

Those trapped in them, however, experienced lower quality of life, beyond deteriorating buildings and fewer garbage pickups. Mothers feared that rats would bite their sleeping children at night. Landlords converted large apartments into several smaller kitchenettes, making their buildings more profitable. Fires racked these buildings, often because the conversions did not follow building codes. The overcrowding led to higher rates of communicable diseases such as tuberculosis among Black city dwellers. Black and White doctors knew, as Dr. Falls remembered, that "to correct the health situation the living conditions of the people had to be corrected . . . we emphasized the necessity of strict enforcement of the building code, better garbage collection, and beyond that, access to housing on an equal opportunity basis by colored people."[15] As Catherine summed it up, in Harlem, "poverty, misery, race discrimination bring much hardship and sorrow."[16] This segregation would have generational effects, most obviously in quality of life but also in the ability to pass on wealth from one generation to the next.

BLACK AGENCY

The situation, however, was even more complicated. While Catherine focused on very real hardships in her narratives about Harlem, she failed to write about

---

[14]Arthur Falls, "Memoir Manuscript" (1962), 247, Marquette University Archives, Milwaukee, WI.
[15]Falls, "Memoir Manuscript," 277.
[16]Catherine de Hueck Doherty, *Friendship House* (New York: Sheed & Ward, 1947), 42.

another side of the story that further complicates our understanding of segregation in the North. Similar to how we needed the work of historians to understand why cities were so segregated, we need other sources to get a more complete sense of day-to-day life in Harlem. We must resist simple binaries, resist the ease of writing about segregation as simply oppressive to its victims, although it *was* oppressive. But that is not the whole story. Within those segregated communities, African Americans created art, music, poetry, and beauty.

When she moved to Harlem, Catherine had moved to a center of Black intellectual and artistic life. There, Black culture had been flourishing in the Harlem Renaissance of the 1920s, and the effects bubbled over into the 1930s. For Black artists, authors, and musicians, Harlem was *the* place to be. Black immigrants from the Caribbean such as Claude McKay, a famous poet, author, and leader in the Harlem Renaissance, composed about twenty percent of New York's Black population by the 1920s.[17] Some remain famous today, such as McKay and Langston Hughes; others are less well known, such as Ellen Tarry, a Black author and Catholic who would support Friendship House in Harlem and help found the Chicago Friendship House branch. But there in Harlem, many artists, writers, and musicians played jazz, wrote novels, poetry, and plays, and painted.

The Black leader W. E. B. Du Bois's iconic 1903 book *The Souls of Black Folk* shaped their imaginations. In it Du Bois describes African Americans' lives as hidden behind a veil, impenetrable and held in place by the color line, which he argued was *the* central problem of the twentieth century.[18] Behind this veil and responding to the racial discrimination they could not avoid, Black culture-makers sought to "advance the race," making America more democratic and Black life more vibrant. Tarry's books for children reflect this sensibility, and she portrays strong Black characters who often cooperate interracially in solving everyday problems. Many artists and writers reflected on African Americans' place in American society, and some concluded, long before formally trained Black theologians thought about Jesus as Black, that had Jesus come to America, he would have been Black. In a nation whose

---

[17]J. A. Zumoff, "The American Communist Party and the 'Negro Question' from the Founding of the Party to the Fourth Congress of the Communist International," *Journal for the Study of Radicalism* 6, no. 2 (2012): 55.
[18]W. E. B. Du Bois, *The Souls of Black Folk*, centennial ed. (New York: Modern Library, 2003).

government refused to make lynching a federal crime, they imagined that he would have been lynched, and they painted him this way.[19]

Catherine not only read their work; she came to know many of the Black intelligentsia through her friend Ellen Tarry. Tarry, as her friends called her, like so many Harlem residents, was a transplant. She had moved north from Alabama, and her experiences of the Klan and police brutality in the South framed her understanding of race in America. She was willing to be a bridge for Catherine, bringing this strange Russian woman into her community because, as she reflected in her memoir, she had become convinced that "Negro and white Americans must first come to know one another before they can be expected to understand or respect each others' problems," and that "constant separation of the races is the greatest barrier to mutual understanding."[20] In other words, Tarry thought friendship was a starting point to ending racial discrimination, and Catherine was offering a place in segregated New York where friendships could be formed.

Harlem's vibrant life influenced Catherine, and she integrated its insights with her Catholic faith in her writing. In her book *Friendship House*, Catherine makes Du Bois's veil central to her depiction of Harlem and critique of White Catholics. She writes about Black Harlemites as trapped behind "the veil," which was "hard to get out from under.... A grasping Veil that suffocates and enfolds all those who want to lift it and pass beyond its light-killing darkness."[21] Catherine reflects that she and other White folks at Friendship House could "pass through the thick folds of the Veil. WE ARE WHITE.... We can stay and we can go.... THE NEGRO CAN'T."[22] Catherine prophesies against White Catholics who ignore the plight of Black Americans, saying, "Is it Lucifer himself, or the Veil? ... That laughs and shouts.... 'Even the Cross cannot tear me today, for the Children of Light are walking in darkness.... The salt of the earth is losing its flavor.'"[23]

---

[19] Paul Harvey and Edward Blum, *The Color of Christ: The Son of God and the Saga of Race in America* (Chapel Hill: University of North Carolina Press, 2012). The most prominent theologian reflecting on Jesus' theological Blackness is James H. Cone. See Cone, *God of the Oppressed* (New York: Seabury, 1975); *The Cross and the Lynching Tree* (New York: Orbis Books, 2000).
[20] Ellen Tarry, *The Third Door: The Autobiography of an American Negro Woman*, 2nd ed. (London: Staples, 1965), 150.
[21] Doherty, *Friendship House*, 59.
[22] Doherty, *Friendship House*, 60.
[23] Doherty, *Friendship House*, 62.

READING EVIDENCE

Although Harlem's Black intelligentsia clearly influenced Catherine, she failed to acknowledge their influence on her thinking or really even their presence. Instead, she painted a picture of Harlem as solely suffering in her 1947 book *Friendship House*, one of her main pieces of writing about Harlem, which echoes many of her news and personal letters. Why did Catherine hide these parts of Harlem's story in her book? I do not have a clear answer to this question based on the primary sources I have read. But we can tease out an answer by considering *Friendship House* in three ways: (1) as a text (which I recognize you probably have not read); equally important (2) in a context, puzzling over who it was written for and why; and (3) interrogating its subtext, or the assumptions undergirding the text.

Why did Catherine write *Friendship House*? She did not write it to describe the richness, joys, and sorrow of Black life in America, nor did she write it to convey a nuanced understanding of Harlem. Rather, she wrote the book to help White Catholics turn from what she saw as their worship of money and comfort. Conveying African Americans' suffering to her readers showed the cost of her readers' idolatry.

Catherine may have glossed over these Black non-Catholic influences because of her own context: she attended Mass daily and was immersed in a Catholic world that was largely separated from Protestant influences. Also, given her past experiences with priests and the controversial nature of her message, I wonder whether Catherine assumed she needed to show herself as a legitimate Catholic authority, which was no small task when she was a laywoman writing about Catholic social action. Trying to figure out how to contextualize *Friendship House*'s odd last chapter helped me reach this conclusion. The last chapter is different from the previous ones because Catherine does not ground her narrative in a place but rather describes her spiritual influences, all influential saints, naming St. Thomas Aquinas, St. Augustine, St. Ignatius, and John Bosco. She also mentions Blessed Martin de Porres, the son of a Spanish man and a freed Black slave from Panama, who had been beatified in 1837 and would be sainted in 1962. Perhaps Catherine thought it best to point to more vetted sources as theological influences rather than African Americans who were not Catholic. She also may have been concerned that her readers might fear that communists were influencing her work because by the

1930s the Communist Party was popular among the Black intelligentsia. Catherine's actions—if not her message—were fiercely anticommunistic.

Accounting for Catherine's purpose in writing does not mean we should dismiss her work as biased and throw it out as a source. Every source has bias. Or, said another way, there is no unbiased source. Every person has a perspective and a purpose. Using sources responsibly means recognizing that accounts will vary, and we need to use them with care.

QUESTIONS AND IMPLICATIONS

This chapter showed how the segregation in the North, where Catherine lived, was not natural or the result of simple personal preference. I aimed to help us develop a historical consciousness about housing segregation. We live in inherited geographies and cannot dismiss this history as irrelevant because it set the trajectory for contemporary racial and class segregation.

- How does knowing this history (if it's new to you) change your perspective on where people live today?

This story is one that includes unintended consequences from religious rhythms stacked with racial dynamics. White Catholics valued place-based community, and their spiritual logic meant they resisted Black neighbors.

- What spiritual logics are at work in your community that foster exclusion or inclusion of others who are different from you, particularly if they share the same faith?

Narratives that address oppression but also show agency are more true because they account for complexity and context.

- When you think about America's racial past or the histories of other racial groups, do you tend toward complexity or simplicity? What are the benefits of either position?

We thought about how we cannot simply read Catherine's *Friendship House*—or any other source—at face value. Would you trust an advertisement that promises certain benefits if you just buy the product, or would you do more research? We must always think about purpose and context: Who is the author, and why did they write?

- How might this habit of mind be helpful in other contexts?

4

THE MYSTICAL BODY IN BLACK AMERICA

> How Catherine responded to racial inequality and why her Black friends had to help her resist a White savior complex.

DISCOVERING RACE AND PRIORITIZING IT

Living in Harlem helped Catherine to see economic dynamics with fresh vision. While she left for speaking tours or to visit friends, she was embedded in a ghetto that many working-class Black Harlemites were unable to leave. There she began to see things differently and added a racial critique of White Catholicism to her economic critique as she discovered how race operated in America. This critique emerged from her immersion in Black culture, learning about the history of race in America, and discovering some of the continuing mechanisms that trapped Black Americans in economic ghettos. She wrote of weeping on the linoleum floor, asking God why he had allowed such oppression and why he had called her to this place. And she knew that, as her friend and White Chicago Friendship House leader Ann Harrigan had observed, friendship between White and Black people mattered. But "the sin of segregation" and its solutions were not solvable by friendship alone.

As in Canada, Catherine blamed wealthy—but now also White—Catholics for the suffering of Black Harlem. She described the pain she and other Friendship House members experienced when they read over the names and addresses of the children who came to their club, choosing which members of the children's club to send to camp, because they did not have enough money to pay for everyone's fees. Were these simply "Names, addresses, lists? . . . No. [They were] Humanity crying to heaven for vengeance—because the justice of God had been forgotten by His children—madly engaged in building temples to selfishness and greed."[1]

She critiqued White Americans not only for their selfishness and greed but for their ignorance of Black lives born in part because they did not know one another. Catherine recounted the story of a White visitor to Friendship House who commented, "I love this Harlem. . . . It's dirty and noisy and verminous, but it has a flavor. The Negroes don't mind anything. They laugh. And oh, the right warm laughter one hears! They are a happy-go-lucky people." The White man pointed to a group walking by as evidence, and Catherine, who knew the passersby as neighbors, observed that one woman had cancer and another a PhD but was unable to find work suitable to his station. She responded by addressing many White stereotypes of Black Americans:

> Their laughter is born of despair, Mister, and defiance, and a nobility of soul hard for anyone not a Negro to understand. The rich warm laughter of the Negroes! That kind of talk makes me sick. It's the way men talk who think all Negroes are lazy, that they won't work for a pittance because they have a pittance; that they are all thieves; that they want only watermelons and pork chops; that they lust for every white woman they see no matter how ugly or old she may be; and that they're all abysmally ignorant and always will be—all of which is just balderdash.[2]

MYSTICAL BODY AND CORPORATISM

Catherine called Catholics to change their ways of being in the world. She wanted them to both become more holy and to see themselves as part of a whole, as members of the mystical body of Christ. Although Pope Pius XII gave the doctrine official sanction with the encyclical *Mystici Corpus Christi* in 1943, Catherine was working out pieces of it on the ground as she lived among poor people in Toronto and Harlem. The doctrine of the mystical body of Christ, based in the apostle Paul's letters, states that all those who are "in Christ" are part of Christ's body here on earth.

---

[1]Catherine de Hueck Doherty, *Friendship House* (New York: Sheed & Ward, 1947), 49.
[2]Doherty, *Friendship House*, 58.

Because of her experiences living in Harlem, Catherine understood Jesus to be living among Black Americans, "the least of these," who faced racial discrimination and segregation. She reached this understanding through her reading of Catholic social teaching and Scripture, regularly referring to Jesus' parable of the sheep and the goats in Matthew 25. Matthew describes Jesus telling his disciples that some of his followers, the sheep, would enter into the his glory when he returned, "for I was hungry and you gave me something to eat, I was thirsty and you gave me something to drink, I was a stranger and you invited me in, I needed clothes and you clothed me, I was sick and you looked after me, I was in prison and you came to visit me" (Matthew 25:35-36). When the righteous ask when they cared for Jesus in these ways, he responds, "Truly I tell you, whatever you did for one of the least of these brothers and sisters of mine, you did for me" (Matthew 25:40). Jesus' other followers, the goats, would be sent into eternal fire because they did not care for the least of these.

Catherine translated this passage into her context. As she remembered years later,

> I ended all my lectures this way: "Sooner or later, all of us are going to die. We will appear before God for judgment. The Lord will look at us and say, 'I was naked and you didn't clothe me. I was hungry and you didn't give me anything to eat. I was thirsty and you didn't give me a drink. I was sick and you didn't nurse me. I was in prison and you didn't come to visit me.' And we shall say, 'Lord, when did I not do these things?'" I would stop here, pause, and in a very loud voice, say "*When I was a Negro and you were a white American Catholic.*" That was the end of the lecture. That's when the rotten eggs and tomatoes would start to fly![3]

For Catherine and others at Friendship House, being a sheep meant practicing what Catholics called the corporal and spiritual works of mercy. These acts, such as feeding the hungry, visiting the sick, and encouraging the downtrodden, took time away from personal advancement. But performing these practices regularly won Friendship House friends, such as Claude McKay. When he was sick, Ellen Tarry, who was back working full time as a writer, asked the Friendship House staff to care for him. McKay eventually converted to Catholicism through a network of Friendship House–related Catholics. As Catherine wrote, members of Friendship House wanted to be generous toward God,

---

[3] Catherine de Hueck Doherty, *Fragments of My Life* (Notre Dame, IN: Ave Maria, 1979), 152.

Figure 4.1. Official blessing of the Harlem Friendship House's library by Father Michael Mulvoy, October 1939. Mulvoy is the White priest labeled on the left. Catherine is seated by the window. It is clear how Friendship House, like a storefront church, was close to the street and accessible. The myriad books and crucifix reveal Catherine's commitments to learning and transformation. Courtesy of Madonna House Archives, Combermere, Canada

to perform the spiritual and corporal works of mercy. To suffer in this upside down world, where the unimportant things take up so much of our time, leaving so little for the important things. Friendship House is a movement which is trying to put order into social life by taking first things first. God, eternity, the soul, our neighbor—these are the first things, and should take up a large part of our time.[4]

Because Catholics were members of the mystical body, they could not seek their own good alone. Instead, they must remember that they belonged not to themselves but to the body, to one another. This connection meant that, as one Friendship House White resident learned, "One's spiritual growth made the 'Body' more radiant . . . more beautiful, and that every Christian shared in this growth. I was my Brother's Keeper . . . supernaturally as well as naturally."[5] Catherine warned that Catholics "were never to forget that their primary duty was personal sanctification, and that the heresy of good works should at all times be watched for."[6] That is, they must not believe that their works would make them worthy of God's love, but they must act in response

---
[4]Doherty, *Fragments of My Life*, 91.
[5]Mary Jerdo, quoted in Doherty, *Fragments of My Life*, 82.
[6]Doherty, *Fragments of My Life*, 6.

to God's love. The mystical body doctrine also meant that since all Catholics were ontologically united as one, if one part of the body suffered—such as Black Catholics trapped in Black ghettos—all of the body suffered.

CHRIST IN THE NEGRO VERSUS CHRIST AND THE NEGRO

When Catherine moved to Harlem, she translated this idea into her context and called for rich White Catholics (by which she meant all White Catholics) to serve "Christ in the Negro." The phrase "Christ in the Negro" became common parlance in Friendship House literature, and it functioned prophetically. If Christ was in "the Negro," then, returning to the logic of Matthew 25, if Catholics did not help Black Americans, they were literally leaving Jesus to suffer in Black ghettos.

But some of Catherine's Black friends and supporters resisted the language of "Christ in the Negro" because of how White people—usually unconsciously—used it. We must pay attention to these voices, looking at our subjects from as many perspectives as possible.

Ellen Tarry, the Black writer who joined Friendship House and would serve for almost a year helping to start the Chicago Friendship House branch, was a dissenting voice. Tarry loved Catherine deeply. But she was also well aware that Catherine was not perfect. After Catherine's death, when someone promoting Catherine's canonization cause asked Tarry to fill out a form to support the cause, Tarry declined, saying she did not know Catherine "like that," like a saint.[7] Tarry agreed to found Friendship House in Chicago with Ann Harrigan, but when she wanted to leave Friendship House in a formal capacity because of conflict with Ann and Catherine, Tarry submitted her resignation to Catherine in a letter. She knew that she would not be able to withstand Catherine's entreaties to stay in person. And after Catherine moved to rural Canada, Tarry refused to visit, although many Friendship House friends and affiliates went up. As Tarry remembered, she did not want to let Catherine "get within a mile of me because if she does, I'm hers. . . . She could convince you that you were supposed to do what she was telling you to do. . . . My resignation and everything was done in writing. I couldn't look her in the eye and say I'm leaving. I knew better than that."[8]

---

[7]Ellen Tarry, oral history, interview by Lorene Hanley Duquin, 1991, 1998.052-072, Madonna House Archives, Combermere, Canada.
[8]Tarry, oral history.

While Tarry did not contradict Catherine's phrase "Christ in the Negro" explicitly, Tarry did not use the language "Christ in the Negro." Instead, when she talked about Friendship House, she said that it was serving "Christ *and* the Negro." Why? While Tarry did not say, context can help us answer the question.

The phrase could too easily be used to promote Black subordination, even as White Catholics tried to help Black people. It could be used in a way that assumed that White people would somehow save Black people, and, in ways similar to how Catherine wrote about Harlem mostly as a poor ghetto in need of help, it could be implied to diminish African Americans' agency. This framework operated according to an implicit (although not intentionally malicious but harmful nonetheless) framework that put White people in positions of power and leadership, and Black people in positions of needing help. As Tarry remembered in her autobiography *The Third Door*, which she published in 1955, shortly before the start of the Montgomery bus boycott, she both wanted to help Catherine with Friendship House and realized, "I would have to get more Negroes to help me and we would have to explain to these well-intentioned white boys and girls that, instead of working *for* the Negro, they would have to work *with* us."[9]

A framework of White people and Black people operating as equals—and even Black people helping or leading White people—was challenging to most White Catholics (and White people generally in the 1930s and 1940s, and in some contexts even today). Because the Catholic hierarchy appointed Black priests only in Black parishes, few White Catholics had experienced Black priestly leadership. At factories and other industrial work, because Black workers were the last hired and first fired, it was rare for a Black person to be in authority over a White person. And in social settings, Black and White folks were usually segregated because, while White northerners may not have been concerned if *other* White people fraternized with African Americans, sociologists found that *they* did not want to interact socially. That is, White people in the North did not mind if other White people ate with Black friends or married into Black families, but they did not want their families doing that sort of thing.[10]

---

[9]Ellen Tarry, *The Third Door: The Autobiography of an American Negro Woman*, 2nd ed. (London: Staples, 1965), 144.

[10]See St Clair Drake and Horace R. Cayton, *Black Metropolis: A Study of Negro Life in a Northern City* (Chicago: University of Chicago Press, 1993).

Dr. Arthur Falls's experience leading the first Catholic Worker meeting in Chicago (connected to Dorothy Day's and Peter Maurin's Catholic Worker in New York) epitomized the experiences of Black folks when they tried to lead Whites.[11] After Peter Maurin, the White, French cofounder of the New York Catholic Worker, spoke, Falls led the discussion. Dr. Falls recalled in an oral history interview that "a middle-aged woman got up right in the middle of the church and said just because she was a Catholic didn't mean she had to associate with niggers."[12] While many of the White participants remained, they were shocked that a Black person would lead the discussion. John Cogley, who would later run *Commonweal* magazine and help John F. Kennedy navigate Protestants' fear of a potential Catholic president, recalled in his autobiography that a Black man's leadership was "unheard of . . . in a general Roman Catholic undertaking." Dr. Falls's confident manner surprised Cogley too, who was used to deference from Black people. Cogley described Falls as "remarkably sophisticated, almost patronizing to his inferiors," with an attitude "opposite of the subservience which the few Black people we had known affected for white people."[13]

Catherine, who saw herself as a White woman, had difficulty listening to Tarry's advice. The reasons were not entirely racial, but race and culture no doubt played a role. Tarry's papers at the Schomburg Center for Research in Black Culture contain letters from Catherine, scrawled in her barely legible handwriting and typed with a typewriter. While they do not contain Tarry's responses, reading between the lines can help unpack the conflicts between the two women, who both loved the church and wanted to end Black suffering. Catherine wrote to Tarry that she understood that her friend wanted Friendship House to listen to what Harlem wanted, not "to come to a Community and force things down people's throats."

Why would Tarry say such a thing? Context can help again. A few years before this letter exchange, Tarry had published an article in the Catholic

---

[11] For more on the Chicago Catholic Worker and Falls, see Johnson, *One in Christ*; Lincoln Rice, "Confronting the Heresy of the 'Mythical Body of Christ': The Life of Dr. Arthur Falls," *American Catholic Studies* 123, no. 2 (Summer 2012): 59-77; Rice, *Healing the Racial Divide: A Catholic Racial Justice Framework Inspired by Dr. Arthur G. Falls* (Eugene, OR: Pickwick Publications, 2013).
[12] Arthur Falls, oral history, interview by Rosalie Troester, 1990, 19, Marquette University Archive, Milwaukee, WI.
[13] John Cogley, *A Canterbury Tale* (New York: Seabury, 1976), 8. For Cogley on Kennedy's campaign, see John Cogley, interview by John F. Stewart, February 20, 1968, John F. Kennedy Library Oral History Program.

Interracial Review in which she encouraged African Americans to take pride in their culture and heritage, lest they become a "badly blurred carbon copy of the American white man."[14] The letter exchange expresses Tarry's unease, as Tarry appears to have been deeply concerned that Friendship House was promoting assimilation to White culture.

Catherine, however, criticized Tarry's choice to emphasize her Blackness and instead used a colorblind framework, but one that assumed Black people's assimilation to White cultural norms. She asked, "Aren't we all human being with the same FUNDAMENTAL COMMON DENOMINATORS. . . . The more we harp on differences, the more we so to speak underline them. . . . I have such a bruning [*sic*] desire to eliminate them that as you say I must be a walking mistake. . . . But to me the Negro IS NOT A NEGRO but a human being . . . like me." We do not have Tarry's answer but can pretty fairly assume that Tarry *did* want to be seen as a human being. But Catherine's next point suggests what may have been Tarry's concern with the colorblindness: that it was not actually colorblindness but assimilation to Whiteness. Perhaps Tarry thought that prioritizing seeing people simply as people, while denying their race, would mean that Black people would have to give up their culture.

Catherine seems to have assumed this too, saying that since African Americans were a minority in America, "[The Negro] he too has to consider the white man's ways. . . . And that whereas he MUST BE INTEGRATED IN JUSTICE AND CHRISTIANITY AS WELL AS DEMOCRACY INTO THE STREAM OF AMERICAN CHRISTIAN LIFE . . . it will have to be done the American way i.e. the white way."[15] Catherine did not think it was possible for White people to embrace elements of Black culture and religious life; she assumed Black people would assimilate. We should note that Catherine was not asking African Americans to do anything she had not; as an immigrant, Catherine had assimilated to American and Canadian culture in many ways.[16]

---

[14]Tarry, "Lest We Forget Our Heritage," *Interracial Review* (May, 1940).
[15]Catherine de Hueck to Ellen Tarry, January 8, 1943, in Ellen Tarry Papers, box 1, folder 20, "Doherty, Catherine de Hueck—Letters, 1942," Schomburg Center for Research in Black Culture.
[16]Once in Canada at Madonna House, Catherine did work to bring together her Eastern spirituality with Western spirituality in her Christian practice. She taught, for instance, the practice of Poustinia, or going into a bare cabin to fast and pray. See Catherine's discussion in Catherine Doherty, *Poustinia: Encountering God in Silence, Solitude, and Prayer*, 4th ed. (Combermere, Canada: Madonna House Publications, 2021).

Ultimately, though, "Christ in the Negro" was a complicated term that could both undercut and implicitly reinforce racial hierarchies.

Nonetheless, the idea of the mystical body of Christ empowered Black and White laypeople to act. Tarry was a cradle Catholic, born in Alabama and raised in a church that taught her, like every other American Catholic, to see priests as God's literal agents on earth, who were to be obeyed and honored. Tarry, Catherine, and other Catholics working for interracial justice were at odds with most priests in the American Catholic Church, who, as we have seen, supported racial hierarchies and segregation, if not in their thinking then in their actions. Nonetheless, the mystical body doctrine empowered these laypeople to persevere because they saw themselves as members of Jesus' body, people put on earth to love him and obey him, which meant bringing his kingdom to come on earth as it was in heaven. Thus, while Catherine and Tarry honored priests, they did not always obey and instead navigated the complicated political dynamics of going against what priests said. Imagining themselves as Christ's hands and feet enabled them to do this.

As Catherine applied the mystical body, she expected that individuals would be transformed as they radically depended on God and that they would leaven society. As she told Tarry, "Everything built on sacrifice—and giving up of a few individuals in love with God . . . that *IS* my vision . . . above all others. The rest are human means." Catherine insisted that they rely on God to work: "The H.G. [Holy Ghost] He will do most for it. . . . Yet we must work to—all lawful weapons—some always—some rarely—That is it!"[17] Remember, here, that Catherine assumed that those who already were in Christ had been sinning and needed to be awakened to the call of interracial justice. And these individuals would bring social transformation that would enable evangelization. As she wrote, "Catholics cannot forget that before the war-torn, hungry, naked, miserable world can listen to their voices, they must alleviate its material misery. Christ cannot be preached to empty stomachs."[18]

In the end, we return to our initial question: How did Catherine end up in Harlem? Her story about the three dollars and a typewriter may have been

---

[17]Catherine De Hueck to Ellen Tarry, December 31, 1942, in Ellen Tarry Papers, box 1, folder 20, "Doherty, Catherine de Hueck—Letters, 1942," Schomburg Center for Research in Black Culture.
[18]Doherty, *Friendship House*, 12.

true. But her journey also had many more layers, as I think she would agree. It was shaped by her experiences with the Bolsheviks, her life among working-class immigrants in Depression-era Toronto, the racial dynamics of Catholicism and housing as they intersected with the Great Migration, and her desire to live out the social teachings in Catholicism, especially as a member of the mystical body of Christ in her racialized context. Catherine's application of the mystical body was shaped by her context and her blinders. She preached from Friendship House, a place surrounded by "honky tonks" and six-story tenements, immersed in a Black, poor context. She sought to apply her faith to this context and found that the church, the body of Christ, was not living up to its calling. She called Catholics to turn from their sin of worshiping wealth and comfort, wanting them to live up to the faith they received, and she asked no less from herself. She stepped into something messy, and while at times it seemed like simple friendship would overcome the segregation and discrimination characterizing American life, she and others at Friendship House knew that the sin of segregation was much more complex. And they disagreed on the way forward. While Catherine did not always emphasize the agency of those with the empty stomachs, she also offered a powerful critique of the church, placing the blame for people turning away from Christianity not on those who refused the faith but on the church for not offering a winsome, holistic, and helping embodiment of what it really meant to live faithfully.

Catherine would go on to found several more Friendship House sites around the United States. In 1947, she moved to Combermere in rural Canada to serve among the poor there, founding Madonna House. While Madonna House today speaks little about race, Catherine's work in the 1930s and 1940s was truly radical, in the sense that she was getting at the root of why Christians do not embody Jesus as they could.[19] For her, the systemic issues facing African Americans in the United States were due to a failure of the church to live up to its calling—its ontological reality, really—as the body of Christ. She took full responsibility for her own failings and repented. Her journey to Harlem—through nobility in Russia and the subsequent suffering wrought

---

[19]For more on Catherine's move to Madonna and the heartache that developed within the Friendship House community, see Johnson, *One in Christ*; Lorene Hanley Duquinn, *They Called Her the Baroness: The Life of Catherine De Hueck Doherty* (Staten Island, NY: Alba House, 2000).

by the rise of communism there, into the slums of Toronto, where she sought to learn from communist solutions to poverty, to segregated New York—gave her eyes to see what most White people in the United States missed or ignored: that race in America was bound up in economics and an unwillingness to love one's neighbor as oneself. This was the story she told herself—and as we have learned from Catherine's narration of her arrival in Harlem, the stories we tell ourselves and the narratives we step into shape our lives in profound ways.

QUESTIONS AND IMPLICATIONS

Catherine loved the church, the body of Christ. As she learned about the church's complicated complicity first in the suffering of poor people and then, when she moved to Harlem, in the segregation of and discrimination against African Americans, she did not turn away from the history or the present reality. She looked clearly at the situation and tried to understand it. This seeing required her to listen. Although Catherine had a way of speaking loudly, she also had the humility to listen to the experiences of others through personal conversations, by observing their lives when living alongside them, and through reading their literature. In this, she was open to hearing a new story, rooted in new evidence she had not previously considered.

- What would it look like for us see the pain of those suffering because of economic and racial dynamics in our contexts? To listen to their stories? To ask how Christians historically and today contribute to their suffering?
- What stories do you know and tell about Christianity and racism? Are they stories that comfort or that convict?

As she saw things anew, Catherine judged the situation—which means not that she condemned it and turned away but that, entering the pain, she determined it was not right, not in accordance with God's call on the people of God. Catherine believed that loving Christ meant trying to stop people from turning to communism, which in her time usually meant turning away from God. But she never condemned those who looked for economic help among the communists or called them the enemy. Rather, she condemned the church, which was not living up to its holy calling to care for Jesus among those who suffered. In her judgment of the church's complicity in racism, Catherine did not excuse herself although she could have. After all, she was an immigrant, a newcomer to American society whose family had been separate from American racial dynamics. But instead she confessed her sin of worshiping mammon and comfort.

- When people turn away from Christianity to seek justice, how do you respond? Do you dismiss Christianity's complicity in the suffering of some people? Or do you name it and even work for justice even if it wins you criticism from fellow Christians?
- What would it look like for us to judge our own situations, holding up ours and others' experiences to our understanding of the gospel, considering whether those experiences bring God tears or joy?

Catherine acted in light of the true stories she had learned about the church's complicity in African Americans' suffering. Catherine put herself in proximity to those who could not leave the ghettos that trapped them and provided spiritual and social goods such as friendship, teaching on Catholic social thought, and clubs for local children. She also sought to provide physical care, visiting the sick, feeding the hungry, and clothing those who needed a winter coat or a new pair of shoes. Seeing this pain, she tried to convince the church to act, to convince her fellow Catholics to reshape their worlds, and to live according to their faith in a radical way, so as to change the social structure. She tried to live in such a way that honored the unity Jesus won for Christians on the cross, that recognized that when one part of Christ's body suffered, all parts suffered. For Catherine, this meant crossing economic, national, and class barriers.

Catherine's work was imperfect. While her thinking and actions directly resisted segregation and discrimination, she also implicitly perpetuated the idea that White people should lead and not follow, as Ellen Tarry's witness attests to. Research on contemporary interracial churches suggests that often White people assume that Black people will conform to White cultural norms and limit Black leadership influence.[20]

- What would it look like to act according to what you humbly know?

---

[20] Korie Edwards, *The Elusive Dream: The Power of Race in Interracial Churches* (New York: Oxford University Press, 2008).

- At your church and in your faith settings, does White culture prevail? Do people of color have equal leadership opportunities to White people? Does your church's racial and theological logic assume integration and reconciliation are good but expect people of color to give up more than White people to participate in the fellowship?

Catherine also tried to walk in the wisdom of Catholic social thought, not just learning about it but acting on it. Catholic social thought developed in response to the human suffering caused by the Industrial Revolution. As much as the economic growth benefited people, it also caused the gap between the rich and the poor to grow, separated people from one another, and led to lack of hope and poor living conditions for workers. While these patterns have changed in some ways, in others they endure. For Catherine, walking in a third way between communism and capitalism meant voluntary poverty. She chose to live without the security of an income and relied on the goodwill of people to provide for her. Voluntary poverty can be a freeing way to live, as St. Francis demonstrated, because those in it have the holy freedom and joy to depend on God. Not all Christians are called to voluntary poverty, however. But God does offer each of us the freedom of simplicity, which can enable us to trust in God's provision and be used by God to provide for our neighbors.[21]

- In what ways might you need to experience the freedom of simplicity, which would bless your neighbors?
- Do you put yourself in positions to see God provide, or do you try to manage things on your own?

We must tread this journey of seeing, judging, and acting with humility because our contexts, including our assumptions about the world, can blind us to what is happening.[22] Remember that Catherine did not begin her journey pleading for White Catholics to stop ignoring African Americans' plight, nor did she begin working to care for poor immigrants right after she escaped potential death at the hands of poor communists in Russia. Rather, she grew in her concern for economic suffering when she moved into a poor Toronto neighborhood and studied the suffering of working-class immigrants. But in Canada she knew little about African Americans' experiences.

---

[21]Richard J. Foster, *Freedom of Simplicity* (San Francisco: Harper & Row, 1981).
[22]See, judge, act is the model of Catholic Action, which was a part of Catholic social teaching.

Only in Harlem did she learn how racial discrimination trapped African Americans in special ways; only there did she see how race mapped onto class.

- Like Catherine, each of us is shaped by our contexts and our stories. How clearly can you see your context? What can you do to see it better? How has your context shaped you?

Catherine was an unexpected prophet who lived counterculturally to both the American church she adopted as her home and to American society.

- What do you take from Catherine's story?

PART II

CONTEXT MATTERS

John Perkins and the Good News in Mississippi

Faith by itself, if it is not accompanied by action, is dead. . . . As the body without the spirit is dead, so faith without deeds is dead.

JAMES 2:17, 26

5

THE GOSPEL AND CIVIL RIGHTS

> Why John and Vera Mae Perkins's commitment to the gospel led to John's beating by White police and how paying attention to context can help us discover our blind spots.

JAILED FOR HIS FAITH

Reverend John Perkins lay in his own blood on the floor of the Brandon jail in Rankin County. This was Mississippi justice in 1970, six years after Congress prohibited discrimination on the basis of race or color in the 1964 Civil Rights Act. White police officers had tortured John because he was leading "their Negroes" to upset the racial order. John and other Black people in the small town of Mendenhall had boycotted downtown Mendenhall's stores to convince White residents to stop discriminating racially.

Black boycotters wanted what the federal government deemed was theirs as US citizens. They demanded proportional employment in downtown Mendenhall and city services, an end to segregation in the public recreational facilities, the prohibition of "backdoor cafes" that demanded Black patrons go around back to be served, an end to police brutality targeting African Americans, that the Black community's streets be paved, and, among other things, a biracial Human Relations Committee to review complaints concerning jailers, sheriffs, and police.[1] For White folks, the problem was not only what Black citizens wanted but that they demanded it.

---

[1] John Perkins, "Demands of the Black Community," in *A Quiet Revolution: The Christian Response to Human Need . . . a Strategy for Today* (Waco, TX: Word, 1976), 225-26.

We cannot underestimate what John was up against. He was resisting a culture that had trained him to not look a White person in the eye and that threatened to kill him if he did. That culture was undergirded by a significant swath of White Christianity, which insisted that the concerns John raised were "political" and not relevant to the faith. Mississippi was different from Harlem, but it exemplified the American South and was, more fundamentally, part of America.

John had chosen this path, though he could have taken an easier one. He had fled Mississippi justice after a White police officer had killed his brother, joining the Great Migration. John had landed in California, where his hard work paid off as he advanced economically. He had married his wife, Vera Mae, and converted to Christianity. Though he attended a Black church, White fundamentalist Christians had nurtured him in the faith. But like Catherine, John felt like God was calling him to give up comfort. And so in 1960, the couple moved their family back to Mississippi to evangelize among Black rural folk. They also had to face the wrath—and sometimes indifference—of White Christians.

The boycott emerged almost by accident in the immediate context but reflected the larger patterns of race in Mississippi. Two days before Christmas in 1969, John Perkins and Doug Huemmer had driven Perkins's Volkswagen Bug to the local grocery store in uptown Mendenhall to purchase country cane syrup for Huemmer's parents. Huemmer was going home to California for Christmas and wanted to bring his parents a taste of Mississippi. The pair had noticed signs on the highway saying, "White people unite, defeat Jew/Communist race mixers."[2] White people in Mississippi had a different approach to communism from Catherine de Hueck. Huemmer was in his twenties, a White man living in the Black quarters who served with Perkins at his church and ministry, the Voice of Calvary. At the store, they saw Garland Wilks, a local Black man who had been drinking, get into a conflict with the clerk. Concerned for the man's safety, they ushered him into the car to take him home. But the shopkeeper had already called the police, who stopped the three and arrested the man.

John and Doug drove back down to the Voice of Calvary, which was next door to the Perkins family home. A group of young people, children through

---

[2]John Perkins, *Let Justice Roll Down: John Perkins Tells His Own Story* (Ventura, CA: G/L, 1976), 132.

college students, were practicing at the church for the Christmas program. Carolyn Albritton, a freshman home from Los Angeles Baptist College, told John that her cousin, Roy Berry, had just been arrested and beaten badly at the jail. Many White people were resisting the increasing national and local Black pressure to reform their beloved southern way of life.

The "southern way of life" was both a way of being and a concept. As a way of being, it meant how southerners did things. It referred to the beauty and the hospitality that characterized southern life and was rooted in an agrarian attachment to the land. But it also included racial hierarchy and gave Black children poor educations, cheated Black workers out of equal pay for equal work, and made it all legal by preventing Black people from voting to change the laws. As a phrase, it became more common when it was contested during the civil rights movement.[3]

Perkins had seen the number of police beatings and arrests increase since he had moved back to Mississippi in 1960, responses to the pressure to change. Concerned that police would beat Wilks, John, Doug, and Mrs. Wilks (Wilks's mother) went back uptown to the jail, bringing seventeen young people with them. John thought there was safety in numbers and that "17 people of all ages, including junior high kids, surely would not be jailed. In fact, four of my own kids were in that nervous, noisy group of folk."[4]

But when the jailer saw the group and heard their demand to see Wilks and Berry, he became nervous and arrested them all. The jailer knew he had made a mistake in arresting everyone without cause, and so with the support of the highway patrol, the jailer tried to convince the children to leave the jail quietly. They refused to budge. John's wife, Vera Mae Perkins, and others came up to the jail after calling as many supporters as they could find. The Perkins children yelled to their mom that the police had beaten their daddy.

The police had made another mistake. They had put John in a cell with a window, facing the street. Sensing the crowd was becoming agitated, John

---

[3] Like most ideas, the term has been debated. Was it based in racial hierarchy or agrarianism? Did White southerners universally accept it, or was it contested? See Wilma Dykeman, "What Is the Southern Way of Life?," *Southwest Review* 44, no. 2 (Spring 1959): 163-66; Charles Reagan Wilson, *The Southern Way of Life: Meanings of Culture and Civilization in the American South* (Chapel Hill: University of North Carolina Press, 2023).

[4] Perkins, *Let Justice Roll Down*, 135.

first encouraged them to remain peaceful. "I warned them," he recalled, "that if we gave in now to anger and violence and hate, we would be just like the whites. And we would be doing the very same things to them that they were doing to us. But they would be the winners and we would be the losers."[5] Then John was inspired with an idea that could lead to substantial change in Mendenhall: a selective buying campaign.

The boycott was an effective civil rights strategy of confronting power with power that Blacks had used across the South. Martin Luther King Jr., Rosa Parks, and the Black citizens of Montgomery, Alabama, had shown the effectiveness of the strategy in 1955 and 1956, when they boycotted buses because of mandatory segregation. Finally, in 1956, the city of Montgomery had to bow to a Supreme Court decision that affirmed a local court's decision to outlaw segregation. From the window of his jail cell, Perkins asked the people to institute a boycott.

The boycott would be costly to Black residents and White businesses alike. Vera Mae and the others stayed up, making signs and organizing their plan. She was the backbone of their ministry. As much as John was the visionary and entrepreneur, Vera Mae executed the vision. Both were hard workers who had for ten years welcomed volunteers, local young people, traveling evangelists, and, since 1964, civil rights workers in their home, teaching their eight children to practice hospitality as they made room in their two-story white house. Starting Christmas Eve, they would ask local Black citizens to neither make the final payments nor pick up the Christmas gifts they had bought on layaway. In coming weeks, they wanted to keep Black money out of Mendenhall's White business district. They organized carpools to take people south to Magee or north to Jackson to shop. John was released from jail and continued to lead the boycott.

Reflecting both segregation and the illusion that race relations were fine, the local newspaper, the *Simpson County News*, did not cover the boycott. News coverage during the boycott instead included updates on the development of the segregation academy, which would be available to White parents when the federally mandated integration took effect the following school year. The only evidence of the boycott could be found in the

---

[5]Perkins, *Let Justice Roll Down*, 141.

advertisements, reminding people, "Your community is what you make it. Shop in Mendenhall first."[6]

Each Saturday, students from the mostly Black Tougaloo College in Jackson, about forty miles away, came to Mendenhall to support the boycott. The police monitored them, and Voice of Calvary volunteers who shuttled the students back and forth had to pass checkpoints on Highway 13, the road going in and out of the Black part of town. These activists may have suspected that the FBI and the Mississippi State Sovereignty Commission, the state-funded watchdog segregationist agency that used backdoor tactics to maintain segregation, were keeping tabs on them too. Evidence from the Mississippi State Sovereignty Commission archives shows that the commission and the FBI collaborated to monitor John and his colleagues.

It was the events on a drive back to Jackson one Saturday in February 1970, after John had been released from prison, that led to John's second arrest and beating in the Brandon jail. Doug Huemmer was driving a Dodge van carrying of nineteen students back to Tougaloo, followed by a Volkswagen with the remaining students. Officer Douglas Baldwin pulled the van over immediately when it crossed the border from Simpson County to Rankin County. Rankin County had a reputation for Klan activity and violence. Its sheriff, Sheriff Edwards, had been sued previously for beating a Black person attempting to register to vote, although the court's majority opinion had understood Edwards's behavior as an isolated event and not as part of a larger pattern.[7] As Doug later testified, the policeman asked whether they were demonstrators from Mendenhall. When Doug replied yes, Baldwin said, "Well, we're not going to take any more of this . . . anymore, and we're not going to take any more of this civil rights stuff." Then he called other units, saying, "I've got a couple of niggers and whites, they are armed, come on down and help me clean them all out tonight." Six squad cars arrived, and they took the students and Doug to the Brandon jail. Doug was placed in a separate car, and Officer Frank Thames of the Highway Patrol, who had previously threatened his life, beat him on the way to the jail.[8]

---

[6]*Simpson County News*, January 8, 1970.
[7]Perkins, *Let Justice Roll Down*, n17.
[8]John Brown, Reverend John M. Perkins et al., *Petitioners-Appellants v. State of Mississippi*, Respondent-appellee, No. 470 F.2d 1371 (US Court of Appeals for the 5th Circuit, 1972).

The occupants of the Volkswagen returned to Mendenhall to report what had happened. John, Joe Paul Buckley, and Rev. Currie Brown, the head of Simpson County's NAACP, drove to Brandon to check on Doug and the students and hopefully bail them out. They were armed with two rifles, a shotgun, and a pistol, all of which were in plain sight in the back seat and all legally in John's possession.[9] Reports from the Mississippi State Sovereignty Commission noted too that they were armed.[10]

The decision to carry firearms was common among civil rights activists, although noting the presence of firearms complicates civil rights movement narratives. It shows the diversity of approaches to the movement along with the extreme violence activists faced. John's life had already been threatened several times, and he knew that to some White people his life mattered little. Civil rights activists faced regular threats on their lives, sleeping with their phones off the hook. Several had been murdered. Some, such as Vernon Dahmer and Medgar Evers, were killed in their own homes with their children nearby. Others, such as James Chaney, Andrew Goodwin, and Michael Schwerner, had been ambushed and murdered while following up on civil rights violations on country roads not unlike Route 49, which John, Brown, and Buckley took north.

When thinking about the civil rights movement, most people want to emphasize its nonviolence. Rightly so, as nonviolence as a radical act of love for one's enemies is to be admired. Its practitioners committed themselves to sacrificing their bodies, being beaten and spit on without fighting back, because they believed their attackers and those who stood by silently would humbly repent and admit their sin. It might be tempting to think of those who carried arms, those who were prepared to fight back, as somehow wrong. But we need to understand all African Americans were up against in a society that did not acknowledge all people's humanity.

When John, Brown, and Buckley exited their vehicle at the jailhouse in Brandon, their weapons did not help them. John quickly realized they had been set up, ambushed. The police had not wanted the Tougaloo students;

---

[9]Brown et al., *Petitioners-Appellants v. State of Mississippi*.
[10]"Report," February 9, 1970, SCR #2-90-0-45-1-1-1, Mississippi State Sovereignty Commission, Mississippi Department of Archives & History, https://da.mdah.ms.gov/sovcom/result.php?image=images/png/cd05/033784.png&otherstuff=2|90|0|45|1|1|1|33227|.

they wanted the boycott leaders. They were arrested too, and the jailhouse became John's Golgotha, the place where he was crucified.

Sheriff Edwards said that the violence began when John swung at him for no apparent reason. I find that claim unlikely because the state never charged John with assaulting an officer. John and others who were arrested offered another story, saying that he was beaten without provocation as the sheriff referenced their civil rights activity. Not only did the officers beat the men, but they also shamed them, pouring moonshine whiskey on their heads and shaving their facial hair and heads. John did not remember a lot of the details because he was passed out on the floor, although he did remember the blood, how officers bent a fork and shoved it up his nose, and how they looked like animals, distorted by hate.

When she heard John was in jail, Vera Mae notified as many people as possible. She refused to let the deeds of darkness remain in the dark. She called Artis Fletcher, a young man they had mentored who was now studying at Washington Bible College in Washington, DC, who worked as a capitol police officer to help pay his tuition. Artis had grown up in church but became a born-again Christian when he was seventeen. John and Vera Mae met Artis when they preached at Prentiss Academy, a local private junior college for African Americans, and taught him about the faith. When Artis went away to school, John reminded him he must return home to help his community. Upon hearing of his mentor's arrest, Artis went to the FBI headquarters to report what had happened. Back home in Mississippi, rumors spread at the jail that the FBI was coming. The police demanded John clean up his own blood, and when the FBI did not arrive, they became even more brutal.

Vera Mae also called Dolphus Weary, Jimmie Walker, Rosie Marie Camper, and Carolyn Albritton, all Black students from Mississippi whom the couple had discipled and who were attending Los Angeles Baptist College. The Perkinses had connected these young folks to the college through friends from California. John had become a Christian as an adult in California, and White Christians there had mentored him in the faith. Los Angeles Baptist College was a White fundamentalist Bible College, and these young Black Mississippians, who had integrated the school, were often the first African Americans their White friends had met.[11] The students called together friends to pray. These White Christians, knowing little of Mississippi justice, were confused as to why the Black students were so scared for John.

Carolyn and the others explained to their White Christian friends that John might be killed, pointing to their own experiences with the police. She had been arrested with John at Christmas in the incident that began the boycott. Although Carolyn had been scared, she had consistently joined any march she could, thinking, "This was part of my duty as a Christian. Whenever there was a march I participated, although I was always afraid with all the police, guns, and dogs."[12]

Like many other northern White Christians, their White college friends saw no connection between their faith and civil rights activism. Carolyn and her peers had told their friends about John's civil rights leadership, but their friends had responded, "Why doesn't he as a Christian just stick to preaching the Word and get out of civil rights?" Carolyn remembered, "We tried to explain that preaching the gospel involves our total life, that we can't separate our bodies from our souls while we live here on this earth."[13]

WHY WE HAVE TO PAY ATTENTION TO CONTEXT

Carolyn's testimony about why John was imprisoned raised an important question for me. Were these two different gospels? Did Carolyn, her Mississippi friends, and John and Vera Mae follow one truth, while the White Christians in California followed another? We will explore this fundamental question as we piece together a history of John and Vera Mae's work in Mississippi in the 1960s in the years leading up to John's Golgotha experience. I am convinced that understanding context is key to answering the question. We began accounting for context when analyzing Catherine's book *Friendship House*, piecing together why she was so concerned about economics and why Harlem was so segregated. John and Vera Mae's story can help us see how the characteristics of a place influence how a person understands the implications of their faith, and why we need Christians from other contexts to more fully understand the implications of the Gospel.

---

[11]This school is now the Master's University.
[12]Carolyn Albritton Fletcher, quoted in Perkins, *Quiet Revolution*, 172.
[13]Carolyn Albritton Fletcher, quoted in Perkins, *Quiet Revolution*, 172.

THE GOSPEL AND CIVIL RIGHTS

In Mississippi during the 1960s, John asked what the gospel had to say to the dehumanizing systems of poverty and oppression African Americans endured. The gospel John had observed as a child and young man in Mississippi seemed irrelevant to Black people's physical oppression. When he was young, John thought African American churches were more like a social group that pointed people beyond their troubles to heaven. White churches were worse; someone could beat up a Black man on Saturday night and worship the Lord on Sunday morning. In California, John converted to Christianity and developed relationships with White Christians. The gospel John was discipled into by his White Christian mentors there emphasized right knowledge of the Word of God and evangelism—they very things Carolyn's White friends thought were the extent of Christianity.

But in Mississippi, John discovered that though God's truth—orthodoxy—does not change, Christians may not always understand its fullness. Further, the application of God's truth—orthopraxy—must look different in different contexts, and even Christians can miss the mark. He realized that the ways of Christian living he had observed as a child in Mississippi and learned as a young convert in California were not a full application of Christianity. Our study of John will show us how he came to this conclusion, how he lived out the Gospel faithfully, and how that commitment ultimately led to his beating in the Brandon jail. John's story will lead us to ask how context can shape what we can and cannot see, and to ponder our own blind spots, which every generation has.

Understanding how our context can blind us can help us walk more faithfully, like the saints described in the book of Hebrews. In Hebrews 11, we read of Abel offering his acceptable sacrifice; of Noah, who believed God concerning events unseen; of Abraham, who went out to a new place and later offered up the child of the promise; of Sarah, who received power to conceive because she believed God was faithful; of Moses' parents, who refused to obey the king's edict to kill Hebrew baby boys; of Moses, who scorned the fleeting pleasures of Egypt to lead God's people from Egypt because he was looking for a greater reward; and so on. All these, the author tells us, could see beyond their immediate contexts, whose logics demanded one set of responses. Instead of identifying with those earthly contexts, they lived as citizens of heaven; they lived according to a different set of rules.

Developing eyes of faith like those saints demands that we see the illusions of our own current moments, the cultural assumptions that we—even Christians—take for granted as true, good, or at least normal. For John, eyes to see the blind spots in his Christian practice came from a change of place, going from an affluent society in California back to a poor one in Mississippi. The author of Hebrews models another way to discern our blind spots: by considering those saints, such as John Perkins, who lived before us. One of my favorite authors, C. S. Lewis, knew well how our own contexts blind us. In addition to writing beloved children's books, Lewis was a scholar of medieval and Renaissance literature. The people from the past he studied helped him gain heavenly eyes, because they helped him see a different way of life, that the ways of his own time and place were not universal or normative. Lewis argued that people needed to read old books to help them see the illusions of their own time more clearly, saying, "None of us can fully escape this blindness, but we shall certainly increase it and weaken our guard against it, if we read only modern books. . . . The only palliative is to keep the clean sea breeze of the centuries blowing through our minds and this can only be done by reading old books."[14] Old books—and stories like John's pieced together from old sources—can fuel our prophetic imaginations, helping us imagine a different way forward when we realize how we can inadvertently place limits on the gospel because parts of it do not mesh well with what we think life should be.

Being wary of how our context influences us teaches us to distrust what we think is *obviously* true because that thing that seems so, well, obvious may actually be contextual. Accounting for context means that we will realize our great need for the perspectives of Christians from other centuries and other places. It also means asking God what the gospel, which does not change, means in our time and place.

In Mississippi, John realized that the gospel had the power not only to change individuals but to change a society. His solution to societal change, however, was not the individual heart change that most White evangelicals thought would leaven the world. John believed in individual conversion, but he also knew, like Catherine, that Christianity had a social component. He

---

[14]C. S. Lewis, "Preface," in *On the Incarnation*, by Athanasius (Yonkers, NY: St. Vladimir's Seminary Press, 2011).

suffered in jail because he had refused to conform to the pattern of his world, a pattern that demanded subservience. Instead, he had spoken truth, calling Black people to live out their human dignity. He had tried to change the system White people created that insisted African Americans were not equal in worth. As he suffered in the Brandon jail, John, like Jesus, experienced the wrath of a people who did not want to be confronted with truth. But his battle had not really been against people; it had been powers and principalities that had used the chains of the past to imprison White and Black southern Christians. They were a people shaped by the weight of their history, people who had inherited a tradition and were unable or unwilling to separate the wheat from the chaff. And it seemed that John, like Jesus and so many of the prophets before him, would die because of his testimony.

MEETING DR. PERKINS

Spoiler alert: John did not die in the Brandon jail. And I am deeply grateful because he changed my life too. I first read some of John Perkins's work in seminary, when he was a national leader in evangelical Christian circles. His call for Christian community development, which crystalized in the Christian Community Development Association, which he founded in 1989, seemed like the answer to how race and class stacked in American society. Dr. Perkins came to campus and called Christians with more resources to the three R's: relocation, reconciliation, and redistribution.[15] Like he had when he returned to Mississippi, we could move into impoverished communities and live with the people. Dr. Perkins's vision of this shared life was summed up in a Chinese proverb he often quotes: "Go to the people, live among them, learn from them, love them. Start with what they know. Build on what they have, but of the best leaders, when their task is done, the people will remark, 'We have done it ourselves.'" United together through Jesus in local churches, people would then be reconciled to God and to one another across racial and class lines. The move into communities would also redistribute resources, bringing social capital and ideas into communities

---

[15]When I speak of my own interactions with Dr. Perkins, I refer to him as Dr. Perkins to show respect. I have learned in my years of research and from my church in a Black neighborhood the importance of respect and honor among African Americans, especially when they have rarely received it from White people. When I speak about Dr. Perkins in the 1960s, I will refer to him as John because most of the people in his context used that name at his request.

with deep need. I visited with Dr. Perkins, and he, in his typically encouraging and empowering way, encouraged me to follow what I heard as God's call in my life. By the end of that year, I could not imagine living anywhere but a poor community.

When we got married soon after, my husband and I followed Dr. Perkins's call and moved into Chicago's Austin neighborhood, joining a church there whose founders were friends with Dr. Perkins (see part four for more on that story). When I started working as a professor, we moved to the Chicago suburb of Wheaton, where my school is located, so I could save hours a week commuting, reducing the time away from our infant son. Dr. Perkins's call stuck with me, and I wrestled with the implications of where we live in front of my students as I taught.

When I teach, I learn and ask questions right alongside my students. I began to wonder about Mississippi, a place where many of my Black friends in Chicago had roots. Was it an anomaly, or was it America? During the civil rights movement, Mississippi was known as the belly of the beast. As one historian puts it, Mississippi was not the tip of the iceberg; it was the middle of the iceberg.[16] It was there that Fannie Lou Hamer lived. Hamer was a Black sharecropper who loved Jesus, but did not know she could legally vote until Student Nonviolent Coordinating Committee leader Bob Moses told her so. For her efforts to register and to help others, she, like John, wound up beaten in jail in 1963. But Hamer refused to back down from God's call on her life. In the summer of 1964, even as civil rights activists were being murdered and terrorized, Hamer helped organize the Mississippi Freedom Democratic Party (MFDP), to counteract the Democratic Party in Mississippi, which had an all-White primary. The MFDP was open to any voter. At the 1964 Democratic National Convention, delegates, including Hamer, from the MFDP demanded the seats representing Mississippi. When Lyndon Johnson tried to compromise and offer them at-large seats, Hamer and the other delegates refused. Hamer gave a speech at the convention, wondering, "Is this America, the land of the free and the home of the brave where we have to sleep with our telephones off the hooks because our lives be threatened daily because

---

[16]Charles Payne, "The View from the Trenches," in *Debating the Civil Rights Movement, 1945-1968*, by Steven Lawson, Charles Payne, and James T. Patterson, 2nd ed. (Lanham, MD: Rowman & Littlefield, 2006).

we want to live as decent human beings, in America?"[17] It was a place where Black people had better know their place or they'd risk their lives. It was a place many people, including John Perkins, left, unwilling to stay in his place. It was the place Perkins returned to in 1960 after finding faith in Christ among White fundamentalists and Black Christians in California. There he and Vera Mae founded the Voice of Calvary. And it was a place I wanted to try to understand.

Although I had read about how race had worked in Mississippi's history, spending six weeks immersed in its history, living in Mendenhall—the small town where John had moved in 1960—gave me a thicker perspective. In the Mississippi heat, I read John's work and learned about Mississippi during the civil rights movement, when John was there. I talked with other historians and visited museums. I stayed in the Black quarters of Mendenhall and took walks, committed to seeing a place on foot. I conducted oral history interviews with those who had been involved with John's ministry, Voice of Calvary, and who had worked for civil rights. In Jackson, John and his family generously shared their time, speaking with me about the ministry casually and granting me oral history interviews. The Mendenhall Ministries, which still does gospel-centered community development, hosted me as I hammered out and revised early drafts of my chapters on John. Those leading the Mendenhall Ministries and Mendenhall Bible Church (which John's Voice of Calvary became) welcomed me into the community, sharing their stories and offering feedback on chapter drafts. My family came too, and the kids thought of Mississippi not as a place to leave—as many people do—but a place where they were welcomed by southern hospitality, Black and White.

The world looked different to me from a poor town in Mississippi compared to the town of Wheaton, the wealthy suburb where I was living. The median household income was a third of Wheaton's, and the median house value less than one-fourth. And as I reckoned with John's history and Mississippi's past, I continued to ponder the question civil rights leader Fannie Lou Hamer asked at the Democratic National Convention in 1964: Is this America?

---

[17]Fannie Lou Hamer, speech at the 1964 Democratic National Convention, August 22, 1964. Available online via Mississippi Department of Archives and History (https://www.mdah.ms.gov/new/wp-content/uploads/2014/08/Lesson-Five-Mississippi-in-1964-A-Turning-Point.pdf). For a gripping narrative of the summer of 1964, see Charles Marsh, *God's Long Summer: Stories of Faith and Civil Rights* (Princeton: Princeton University Press, 1997).

QUESTIONS AND IMPLICATIONS

Learning the history of Christianity's different theological perspectives concerning race and human dignity can be difficult. It would be easy to fall into relativism, assuming each person can have their own truth. Another option would be to ignore the different theologies Christians have believed and practiced, assuming that we in the present are right. Neither of these positions accounts fairly and honestly for what has happened, for how context shapes people's understanding of their faith, for people's inability to understand truth. The second option suggests a chronological snobbery that assumes we in the present are somehow more enlightened than those in the past.

- What do we do with the historic, regional, and racial diversity of Christian beliefs regarding race?
- Do your assumptions about Christianity fit more with Carolyn's and John's, or Carolyn's White friends from college? What can you learn from these different perspectives? Is one more right?

A helpful way forward is to approach our present beliefs with humility, knowing they are shaped by our context and knowing that sin limits our ability to understand God's truth. I have found the Wesleyan quadrilateral helpful as a way to navigate the limitations of my knowledge. It suggests that we can know truth through four intersecting fields: Scripture, reason, experience, and tradition (or what the church has known throughout history). Also, accounting for the voices of Christians from different backgrounds (including and perhaps especially those different from our own) can give us more confidence that we are approaching truth.

- What beliefs does your church hold that are reflective of your context?
- What different voices might you need to listen to, to enable you to change your contexts as an expression of your faith and bring others to Jesus?

6

MISSISSIPPI: IS THIS AMERICA?

How John's growing up and flight to California reveal racial dynamics in Mississippi and why those of us not from the state are still implicated.

AFRICAN AMERICANS' PLACE IN THE CLOSED SOCIETY

John's mother, Maggie, died from starvation when he was seven months old. The technical term for the cause of her death is pellagra, a disease caused by a nutrient deficiency of niacin, which is found in fish, meat, and nuts. The disease is common in less developed countries. John was still nursing, and he later wondered whether he had sucked the life out of his mother. Milk would have helped Maggie, but the man whose land her family sharecropped said he could not spare land for families to raise cows, and the family was too poor to buy milk.

Maggie's death was not an accident of circumstances. Nor was it due simply to the landowner's selfishness or to her baby's need for milk. John lost the gift of his mother, Maggie, because of how race and class worked in Mississippi. And race and class worked in such deadly ways because people—Christians and non-Christians alike—in the state and across the country allowed it to do so.

My first and very human response to Maggie's death is both grief and distance. It's not my fault, I want to respond. And on one level, that's true. I did not live there and my family is not from the South. But Maggie's death is the result of human sin, embedded in society. And so, following Catherine's example, I want to let the loss of John's mother drive me to reflect on my own sin and the sins of my time and place. My response, then, can be a prayer of confession: "Most merciful God, we confess that we have sinned against you in thought, word, and deed, by what we have done and what we have left undone. For the sake of your Son Jesus Christ, have mercy on us and forgive us; that we may delight in your will, and walk in your ways, to the glory of your Name."

Rightly oriented and seeking to understand, we can now ask: What was this place where John grew up like? And what did John overcome to become a leader who worked to change Mississippi so other poor people would not suffer like his mother?

The road was not easy. Jap Perkins, John's father, left John and his four siblings around the time of Maggie's death. John grew up in his Grandma Babe's house on Fred Bush's plantation until he was seven. Then Babe made the strategic decision to move the family to smaller farms to sharecrop. On smaller farms she could more discreetly run her bootlegging business, which catered to White and Black customers.

Although technically a dry state, Mississippi was known as the "wettest dry state." It had been the first state to ratify the Eighteenth Amendment, which instituted Prohibition. But the amendment only made illegal to sell or transport liquor, not to consume it. Mississippi knew a good thing and passed a black-market tax, recovering millions of dollars.

Perhaps ironically, bootlegging benefited John by giving him a sense of his dignity as a human being. The business gave his family a source of income independent from White folks. They were known to be tough, "one of the toughest families around," Vera Mae would later recall. "Everybody was afraid of the Perkins, even some of the white folks."[1] When Perkins saw his grandmother stand up to a White sheriff, he knew that he was not inferior to White people just because they said so.

Mississippi's segregation tried to stamp out African Americans' human dignity, and for John and his fellow activists to later convince their Black neighbors to march for their civil rights was close to a miracle. If bootlegging helped John, owning land also helped the small number of Black people who could afford it to stand up.

---

[1] Quoted in John Perkins, *A Quiet Revolution: The Christian Response to Human Need . . . a Strategy for Today* (Waco, TX: Word, Incorporated, 1976), 24-25.

In both cases, a key difference was a means of sustaining a family apart from White people. Landowners such as Artis Fletcher's family, who owned a 540-acre farm, could live and work apart from White folks.[2] While Artis (who later became one of John's mentees) knew what White people could do to him, he remembered feeling safe as a child because he rarely interacted with White folks. Unlike most Black parents, his father did not have to send his children to work for White employers.

Even those with a little independence learned early, as John did, that White people wanted African Americans to stay "in their place." Staying in one's place meant saying yes sir and yes ma'am to White folks and never looking them in the eye. It also meant earning less money and complying when cheated out of fair pay for a crop or charged exorbitant interest. When living in town, it meant living in the worst part of town, often closest to the river, where the muddy waters regularly flooded houses and shacks. It meant going to school for fewer days of the year because Black children had to work in the fields, driving to school in run-down school buses that let in the cold winter air, and, when they were in school, using secondhand books that White schools had passed along.

Beyond quality of life, staying in one's place was also a matter of life and death. It meant that parents must teach their children—and especially their sons—to interact in specific ways with White women. Parents told their children stories of lynchings, like Emmett Till's murder in 1954, when Artis Fletcher was ten. He learned well the lesson that if a White person killed a Black person, no one would be punished.

Most of the time, White folks, and especially genteel ones who could afford distance from Black people, frowned on racial violence that ended in death. But they would protect their own—White men who had killed Black people—when push came to shove. If Till's murder taught Artis and many other young African Americans the danger of getting out of their place and the paucity of Mississippi justice, it also revealed White people's unity in moments of crisis, such as J. W. Milam's and Roy Bryant's trial for murdering Till in 1954 in Mississippi's delta region, with its rich soil, plantation economy, and extremes of wealth and poverty.

---

[2]Artis Fletcher, interview by Paul Ericksen, 1987, in Collection 374, Oral History Interviews with Artis Fletcher, Evangelism & Missions Archives, Wheaton College, https://archives.wheaton.edu/repositories/4/resources/24.

Till, like so many Chicagoans with family in Mississippi, had come down for a few weeks in the summer when he was fourteen. While the details are debated—did he whistle, did he ask her on a date?—Till had interacted with a White woman working at her family's grocery store in a way that all southerners knew demonstrated he did not know "his place." The woman's name was Carolyn Bryant. Her husband and brother-in-law went to "whip [Till] and scare some sense into him," teaching him a lesson about staying in his place and to protecting the family's reputation. But the men reportedly decided to kill him when he boasted about dating White girls back in Chicago. As Milam, who sold his story to a reporter for *Look* magazine after being acquitted in the trial, said of their decision to murder Till, "Well what else could we do? He was hopeless. I'm no bully; I never hurt a nigger in my life. I like niggers—in their place—I know how to work 'em. But I just decided it was time a few people got put on notice. As long as I live and can do anything about it, niggers are going to stay in their place."[3]

But Till's mother, who lived in the relative safety of a Chicago suburb, refused to stay in her place. Ignoring the state of Mississippi's demand that she not open the box Emmett's body was shipped in back to Chicago, Mamie Till Bradley held an open-casket funeral, displaying her boy's body so "all the world can see what they did to my boy." The Black press, also based outside Mississippi, made Till's murder a national story, inspiring a generation of civil rights activists to act.

While the Delta's wealthier Whites funded Milam's and Bryant's successful defense, after the trial they distanced themselves from the men. They wanted to have little to do with these poor White men who had brought such negative attention on their state and way of life. As Milam complained a year after his acquittal, "I had lots of friends a year ago. . . . Since then some of those friends have been making excuses. I got letters from all over the country congratulating me on my 'fine Americanism'; but I don't get that kind of letters anymore. Everything's gone against me. . . . I'm living in a share-crop

---

[3]Quoted in William Bradford Huie, "The Shocking Story of Approved Killing in Mississippi," *Look*, January 24, 1956. As a source, Huie's *Look* articles must be used carefully. They narrate a murder tale that involves only two killers when the Black press and others wrote about several others who were involved. See Dave Tell, *Remembering Emmett Till* (Chicago: University of Chicago Press, 2019).

with no water in it. My wife and kids are having it hard."[4] While Milam's and Bryant's families struggled, they could at least hold onto the message the South taught them: their White skin made them better than Black folks.

Although many poor Whites sharecropped, Black sharecroppers lived in a labor system that intended to keep them bound to the land. After Reconstruction ended in 1877, Mississippi's constitution, which became the model for other southern states, created laws that limited Black residents' work options, intending to hold captive a Black labor force as much as possible. Black landownership was an exception, and this rural state replaced slavery with sharecropping. In return for farming on a (usually White) landowner's land, sharecroppers gave a portion of the crop to the landowner. But they also borrowed against their crop to purchase supplies for farming from the landowner or a White store. Usually, at the end of the year the Black family would discover they were in debt or had broken even, no matter how abundant a crop they had produced.

Dolphus Weary, another man who John mentored, remembered his family's season of sharecropping as an education in exploitation. As a school-age child, Dolphus became interested in the family's income. The first year sharecropping on a new place, the White landowner told the family they had broken even. The second year, Dolphus thought that the improved crop yield would give his family a profit, but the landowner had the same response: they had broken even. By their third year sharecropping, Dolphus had learned enough math in school that he and his sister decided to keep their own record of their purchases. They wanted evidence in writing at the end of the season for what they owed. When they presented their log that demonstrated the family had made a profit, the landowner agreed but refused to let them continue to work his land. He must have wanted someone he could control more easily.[5]

Few Black people resisted this culture that told them they were inferior in such an upfront way as Dolphus. Oral history interviews I and others have

---

[4]William Bradford Huie, "What's Happened to the Emmett Till Killers?," *Look*, January 22, 1957. For a powerful narrative about Till's murder and its significance for all of us, see Wright Thompson, *The Barn: The Secret History of a Murder in Mississippi* (New York: Penguin Random House, 2024).

[5]Dolphus Weary, interview by Paul Ericksen, 1987, in Collection 373, Evangelism & Missions Archives, Wheaton College.

conducted with Black Mississippians repeatedly describe that the system was designed to teach them that they were inferior. Few had the energy or willpower to resist such an all-encompassing system because they struggled with the poverty of day-to-day life. As John observed, "When you've spent your whole lifetime with limited opportunities, spent your whole lifetime being told your place is at the bottom—that entire mixture helps create a low image of yourself. After awhile, assertiveness or anger or whatever it's called just sort of dries up, like a muscle that never gets used."[6]

RESISTING THE CLOSED SOCIETY

But there are turning points in history, moments where something changes for a people. If World War I had been a turning point for Black Americans living in the North, for Black Mississippians, World War II was a turning point. That generation of Black men returned from fighting in Europe and the Pacific transformed. Of Mississippians, 237,000 served, and about 85,000 of those soldiers were African Americans.[7] When talking about Mississippi, historians often point to this generation—members of the so-called Greatest Generation—as the one that began the civil rights movement. Many of them began doing the unthinkable—registering to vote, refusing to sit in the segregated part of movie theaters, defending themselves when attacked by White folks.

Mississippi native Medgar Evers, who was later murdered because of his civil rights activism, returned home after fighting in the Battle of Normandy and attempted to vote. White people turned him away at gunpoint. He began selling insurance and organizing NAACP chapters, hoping to change Mississippi from the bottom up. The NAACP asked him to be the first field organizer in Mississippi, and he agreed. He went on to drive forty thousand miles a year on Mississippi's narrow roads, organizing people to resist segregation.[8]

Many other returning Black soldiers did not become civil rights organizers but were nonetheless changed by their experiences. Clyde Perkins,

---

[6]John Perkins, *Let Justice Roll Down: John Perkins Tells His Own Story* (Ventura, CA: G/L, 1976), 23.
[7]Yasuhiro Katagiri, *The Mississippi State Sovereignty Commission: Civil Rights and States' Rights* (Jackson: University Press of Mississippi, 2001), xxi.
[8]Jerry Mitchell, *Race Against Time: A Reporter Reopens the Unsolved Murder Cases of the Civil Rights Era* (New York: Simon & Schuster, 2021).

John Perkins's older brother, was one of those changed men. As John recalled, Clyde returned home with combat ribbons, a Purple Heart, an honorable discharge, "and a new attitude about the white man in Mississippi. Clyde was determined not to be pushed around anymore. He was a hero to all us kids."[9] But this attitude was threatening to Whites, many of whom were poor and, like Milan and Bryant, had their Whiteness as a consolation. As Perkins observed, "Though they were a heap better off than the Blacks, the way of life of local whites was modest enough that any change in the way things were was a personal threat to them. And in those days, keeping things the way they were meant keeping Blacks in line."[10] One Saturday in 1946, Clyde and John were in downtown New Hebron, the closest town to where they lived. Clyde was waiting outside the Carolyn Theater with his girlfriend, Elma. As John recalled, "Nobody's real sure just what started it all. But some folks say Clyde was talking loud, maybe even arguing with Elma about something. Anyway, a deputy marshal standing on the sidewalk yelled at them, 'You niggers quiet down.'"

When Clyde turned to ask the marshal a question, the marshal clubbed him. Clyde grabbed the club in self-defense, and the marshal shot him twice in the stomach. Blacks watching carried Clyde to the doctor in town, who said Clyde needed to go to the hospital. John, a cousin, and his uncle drove the hour and a half to Jackson, the nearest hospital. John held Clyde's head in his hand. Shortly after they arrived at the hospital, Clyde died. John remembered that, like most situations when White folks killed Black folks, there was no "official inquiry. If any white stopped to think at all about my brother's death, they quite naturally took it for granted that whites in authority were always justified no matter what they did. No questions need ever be asked."[11]

This was Mississippi. This was America. This is our history.

Professor of history James Silver, a White son of the South, dubbed Mississippi "the closed society." Dr. Silver was teaching at Ole Miss, the state's beloved flagship White institution. His students were Rebels, their mascot harking back to the Civil War, or what they called the "War of Northern

---

[9] Perkins, *Let Justice Roll Down*, 17.
[10] Perkins, *Let Justice Roll Down*, 16.
[11] Perkins, *Let Justice Roll Down*, 23.

Aggression" or the "War Between the States." In 1962, African American student James Meredith integrated Ole Miss. Meredith had served in the integrated air force and returned from his post in Japan impressed by Japan's racial tolerance. Ole Miss students were not so tolerant. Students and other White people rioted for three days when he enrolled, leaving two people dead. Dr. Silver wondered aloud why White Mississippians resisted integration.

He concluded that Mississippi was the closed society. It was a place where White citizens accepted the orthodoxy of White people's superiority, a place from which those who voiced disagreement were either "hushed, silenced with a vengeance, or in crisis situations driven from the community. Violence and the threat of violence have reinforced the presumption of unanimity."[12]

White Mississippians' false sense of their history closed Mississippi to change. Dr. Silver observed, "The search for historical truth has become a casualty in embattled Mississippi."[13] Dr. Silver lost his job at Ole Miss because of his analysis. White people hardened their hearts to the truth. They dug in their heels, closing their ears so they could not hear because the truth was offensive to them, and they found no pleasure in it.

Many Black people fled. As we know from our study of Catherine, they went to the Harlems of the nation—places rich in life and also segregated. John was one of them. After Clyde's death, John moved north because his family thought White people would kill him if he stayed. John's experience in the North would bring new life, allowing him to shine a light in Mississippi's darkness.

QUESTIONS AND IMPLICATIONS

For those living outside Mississippi or the Deep South, it is tempting to dismiss these places as racial exceptions historically (and perhaps presently). The outright violence seems to contradict what America stands for. People I talked to in Mississippi insisted that the state is fundamentally American, that it reveals the best and worst of America. I think the evidence also keeps northerners like me on the hook: historically, the violence and inequality in Mississippi would not have been enabled had not the nation allowed it. For instance, Black activists worked for a national antilynching law, but until

---

[12] James W. Silver, "Mississippi: The Closed Society," *Southern Historical Association* 30, no. 1 (1964): 3-4.
[13] Silver, "Mississippi: The Closed Society," 3.

recently, the nation never had the will to overcome southern resistance and pass one. Further, when the federal government administered the New Deal's social security benefits, it benefited most Americans except farm workers and domestic servants, two professions that Black southerners filled.

While acknowledging differences is important, and racial change may best be accomplished at a local level, where individuals of all economic backgrounds can effect significant change, not distancing oneself from the violence and inequality in Mississippi if one is an outsider requires humility. As Jesus described, when a tax collector and a Pharisee went to the temple to pray, the tax collector beat his breast and prayed, "God, have mercy on me, a sinner" (Luke 18:13). The Pharisee looked at the tax collector and thanked God he was not like that sinner. But when they left, only the tax collector was justified (Luke 18:9-14).

- How can Mississippi's racial history act as a mirror for you to see your own context more clearly?
- What would it mean to identity with Mississippi's racial past, to lament it, and to repent?

Research on why people become involved in racial justice suggests that they often have a personal connection to someone who has suffered because of injustice. As an adult, John used his sorrow and anger at his mother's unjust death to fuel his energy to make things right for other poor people who failed to flourish.

- Whose stories grip you and motivate you to action? They could be people you know in person or people whose stories you've heard.

7

HOW PLACE INFLUENCES FAITH

> How John's understanding of the gospel's implications expanded when he moved from California to Mississippi, why White southerners' understanding of the gospel was so different, and why our response to painful histories must be one of embrace rather than exclusion.

THE FREEDOM CALIFORNIA OFFERED

John went to California. California meant freedom. Economic freedom, racial freedom, and, only then, spiritual freedom. While Los Angeles, where John landed, was not the Promised Land, it was a whole lot better than Mississippi. John found work at the Union Pacific Foundry, where he earned ninety-eight cents per hour. Back home, John could earn twenty dollars a week. For a forty-hour work week, John was earning nearly twice as much. Aware of the power of collective action, he voted for the workers to join the United Steel Workers, which was part of the interracial CIO union. John helped organize a strike that brought greater benefits for the workers and taught him the benefit of united action. His income, which at times neared one hundred dollars a week, allowed him to live comfortably.

John also found the freedom of not being defined by his Blackness. "In Mississippi," he recalled, "every move I made was defined in terms of my race. I worked on farms and fields, I behaved in certain ways toward my employers, and I received certain wages—all of this defined in terms of my Blackness.

And in every one of these areas there were different standards for whites."[1] In California, he worked alongside Whites and earned equal pay, and he did not face overt racism (although he later learned that "socio-economic structures in northern urban areas maintain the ghettos and white supremacy in a mechanical way, so northern whites have never had to be open, active racists as was true in the South").[2]

In this context, John began searching for religious truth, reading a variety of religious texts. Christianity was not high on his list. Despite living in the Bible Belt, he had grown up on the outskirts of Christianity because of his family's bootlegging. He had not admired the hardscrabble faith of the poor White and Black folks in the rural South, looking down on a faith that focused on the by and by, helping people endure the poverty that characterized their daily life until they could reach their heavenly reward.[3] Though uneducated, he had longed for good arguments and had despised Black pastors, few with seminary training, who preached sermons that gave parishioners emotional release. Perhaps the worst thing he remembered about Black Christianity was that it seemed to make the people submit to a dehumanizing system. John remembered that he "had always looked at Black Christians as sort of inferior people whose religion had made them gullible and submissive. Religion had made so many of my people humbled down to the white-dominated system with all its injustices. Religion had made them cowards and Uncle Toms."[4]

---

[1] John Perkins, *Let Justice Roll Down: John Perkins Tells His Own Story* (Ventura, CA: G/L, 1976), 52.
[2] Perkins, *Let Justice Roll Down*, 52. While there were clear racial differences between California and Mississippi, it would be wrong to assume that California (like "the North" generally) was a racial haven. Like other parts of the country, California faced racial and economic inequality. John and Vera Mae were sending their children to schools that drew more than half their funding from local property taxes. As happens today in many communities, because of the funding structure, children in poorer communities, populated mostly by Black and Latino families, attended schools that were not equal in quality to the schools of children who lived in wealthier neighborhoods. In the early 1970s, the California Supreme Court argued in a series of rulings from the *Serrano v. Priest* case that the state's system of funding was unfair to children from poorer communities. In 1978, voters passed Proposition 13, which reduced property taxes statewide and hindered the state's ability to fund public education. Wealthy areas found creative ways to supplement their schools' budgets or let the public schools languish and sent children to private schools. Poorer areas continued to struggle.
[3] Paul Harvey, *Christianity and Race in the American South: A History* (Chicago: University of Chicago Press, 2018).
[4] Perkins, *Let Justice Roll Down*, 57.

White Christians also drove him away from the faith. As John recalled, "I did not see white Christianity as meaningful either. To me it was part of that whole system that helped dehumanize and destroy Black people; that system which identified me as a nigger. So how could the white church really be concerned about me?"[5] Other African Americans, Christian or not, testified similarly. Dolphus Weary remembered, "We'd concluded that there were no white Christians in Mississippi, since in our limited world we rarely encountered whites who treated Black people with anything but contempt."[6]

Despite his disdain for Black Christianity, the Black church structured social life in Mississippi, and John participated when he went home to visit. Like everyone else, he had grown up going to the regular church association meetings, which gathered people from multiple churches together, and the weeklong revivals. Church was such a part of southern life that people who had moved away came home for revivals. In 1949, John attended one such revival at Pleasant Hill Baptist Church in Mississippi to see friends and family. The visit changed his life. He spotted a young woman sitting in a car with her friend and went up to talk with her. Her name was Vera Mae Bradley. Vera Mae had also been born in New Hebron, and she and John had sometimes played together while their daddies gambled.[7] Vera Mae's grandmother had largely raised her. Like many Black children, Vera Mae and her siblings had gone north to Mississippi's Delta region to pick cotton every year in the fall instead of going to school those first few months of the school year. But Vera Mae liked school and was good at it. At a school chapel program, she had become a Christian (not just joined the church). Unlike John, Vera Mae was on track to graduate from high school.[8] John knew that day, as he talked to Vera Mae in the church yard, that he wanted to marry her. He told her, "Vera Mae, you're going to be my wife some day."[9] When I asked Vera Mae what she

---

[5]Perkins, *Let Justice Roll Down*, 57.
[6]Dolphus Weary, *I Ain't Comin' Back* (Wheaton, IL: Tyndale House, 1990), 59. Black intellectuals throughout US history have had a fractured relationship to Christianity, as they have learned how the faith has supported their subjugation. When they interact with Christian institutions that fail to value their perspectives if they are not culturally White, it can be easy to dismiss Christianity.
[7]John Perkins, *A Quiet Revolution: The Christian Response to Human Need . . . a Strategy for Today* (Waco, TX: Word, 1976), 24-25.
[8]Vera Mae Perkins, interview by Joe White, 2003, Simpson County Historical and Genealogical Oral History Project, The Center for Oral and Cultural Heritage at the University of Southern Mississippi.
[9]Perkins, *Let Justice Roll Down*, 56.

thought about Perkins's proposal so soon after meeting her, she responded with joy, "He chose me."[10]

Soon after, Perkins returned to California. He courted Vera Mae, writing letters. They planned to marry, but their plans were disrupted in 1951 when he was drafted for the Korean War. Perkins was drafted into a military that, for the first time in US history, had been integrated. This fact is striking—prior to the Korean War, every military branch had been segregated. Black soldiers such as Clyde Perkins fought, and many died in World War II, fighting for freedom abroad in segregated units when there was oppression at home. After basic training, John and Vera Mae married, but then he was shipped overseas to Okinawa.

John's service ended in January 1954, but he and Vera Mae had become estranged. When Vera Mae gave birth to their first child, Spencer, in New Orleans in 1954, John was in California. Spencer was eight months old when John held him for the first time, only after Vera Mae decided to give their marriage another try by moving out to California.[11] Spencer would be the person whose testimony turned John to faith in Jesus.

John and Vera Mae continued to work hard and raise their family. Vera Mae attended church periodically while John continued exploring other religious. Spencer, their son, began attending children's church at a local holiness church. John could see "something was developing in [Spencer] that was beautiful, something I knew nothing about. I'd had no real experience before of seeing Christianity at work like that in a person's life. At work in a way that was beautiful—and good."[12] Spencer kept inviting his father to church, and John finally went.

John also finally gave in to invitations to attend church from Calvin Bourne, a friend from work. There John met people whom he remembered as "zealous Christians. These were folks who you could feel loved and cared for you."[13] At twenty-seven years old, John began to study his Bible and desire the contentment the apostle Paul promises comes from submitting to Christ.

---

[10]Vera Mae Perkins, interview by author, May 7, 2021.
[11]Spencer Perkins, interview by Paul Ericksen, 1987, Collection 364, Evangelism & Missions Archives, Wheaton College.
[12]John Perkins, *Let Justice Roll Down: John Perkins Tells His Own Story* (Ventura, CA: G/L Publications, 1976), 68.
[13]Perkins, *Let Justice Roll Down*, 68.

One Sunday, when the pastor preached on Romans 6:23, "For the wages of sin is death, but the gift of God is eternal life in Christ Jesus our Lord," John heard the gospel in language he could understand: economics. He submitted his life to Jesus.

John would later conclude that despite the high levels of church participation among Black Mississippians, many missed the central call of the gospel. They joined churches but did not understand that, as John later put it, "Jesus Christ could set me free and live His life in me." John said he never heard this message in his years of revival and occasional church attendance.[14] He would become convinced that others too needed to know this simple truth.

John's decision transformed their family. With his new faith and Vera Mae's renewed faith, the couple devoted themselves to the Christian life and began teaching children using the Child Evangelism Fellowship model. Child Evangelism Fellowship was a fundamentalist organization founded in California in 1937 by J. Irvin Overholtzer, who believed that children as young as five could hear and respond to the gospel. John appreciated the model because it was based in Scripture, offering solid teaching rather than emotional release.

He also met White Christians, "not just white church members," as he noted, "but white *Christians*—people who said that God had actually changed their lives."[15] Through Wayne Leitch, who discipled him and taught him the Bible, Perkins learned a truth shocking for a Black man from Mississippi: the gospel could change White folks too. For two years, the pair met regularly, "man to man," a habit that was a far cry from Whites' insistence in Mississippi that Black folks remain in their place.

The White Christians John knew in California were often a generation removed from their southern roots too, as many had moved west to work in the budding military industrial complex that built cities such as Los Angeles.

---

[14]Others who would come into John's ministry had similar experiences. Dolphus Weary had joined his family's church when he was eight, waiting a year on his mother's insistence that he was too young. But when Dolphus was a teen, he was convicted at a revival to raise his hand because he knew he was not a Christian. When the preacher asked those with their hands raised to join the church, Dolphus did not know what to do. He was already a church member, but he had only just then responded to Jesus' gift of salvation.

[15]Perkins, *Let Justice Roll Down*, 75.

These Whites were New Deal Democrats who, in a mostly White setting, were questioning some of their racial assumptions and beginning to imagine themselves as beyond the racial divide. As the economy expanded, they were optimistic and highly individualistic, convinced that if a man worked hard, he could pull himself up by his bootstraps and succeed. They were also convinced that economic differences no longer mattered, and the church family could include a farmer and a wealthy oil man who could interact equally.[16]

Those habits of mind of optimism, economic growth, and equality were shaped by systemic factors, and they became the water Christians in California swam in. They were implicit theologies—assumptions about how God works in the world and what God values that are often shaped by particular contexts—that came along with the explicit theology of the gospel of salvation through Jesus' atoning death on the cross, which John accepted.

Through his evangelistic work, John formed deep bonds with both White and Black Christians. One day, as he preached in a prison full of mostly African American inmates who, like him, had migrated from the South, Perkins realized that the problems facing Black folks in Mississippi were not resolved by moving out of the South. He could have easily been one of those imprisoned men rather than married with a large house, good-paying job, and beautiful family.

John felt like God was calling him back to Mississippi, to preach the gospel and teach the Bible to African Americans there. There was only one problem. Vera Mae had no desire to go. She did not want to raise her children in Mississippi, in a place where Black folks had to know their place and in the small towns that were so full of poverty.

John soon became ill. As Vera Mae remembered, "The Lord showed me that unless I would give in to his calling, what the Lord was calling him and us to do, that I wouldn't have no husband, that he would take him away from me. And the thought of having to raise five children alone . . . now, that was a frightful thing!"[17] She came to believe that although she did not feel God's call to return to Mississippi, since her husband felt called, their family was called. She relented and agreed, and almost immediately John became well.

---

[16]Darren Dochuk, *From Bible Belt to Sun Belt: Folk Religion, Grassroots Politics, and the Rise of Evangelical Conservatism* (New York: Norton, 2010).
[17]Quoted in John Perkins, *Quiet Revolution*, 22.

Their decision would cost them great comfort. They had just purchased a five-bedroom home with two indoor bathrooms, plenty of space for their growing family. They had a steady income with John's work in industry and Vera Mae's work as a beautician. Among their White and Black friends, they were valued as human beings. In Mississippi, they would move in with Vera Mae's mother and stay in a two-bedroom house with an outhouse, along with her brother's family.[18] There Vera Mae and John would have to teach their children to both maintain their dignity and navigate the White hierarchy. They would also raise their children in a poor community, a far cry from the middle-class Black community where they had lived. Vera Mae would remember later that she had raised her children in the "ghetto" of Mendenhall and note the honky-tonks and how predominant children born out of wedlock were.[19] But despite the costs, they responded to what they believed to be God's call affirmatively. When they looked back, they would not have done otherwise.

THE MISSISSIPPI TO WHICH THE PERKINS FAMILY RETURNED

They were stepping into a perilous context, a place that had grown even more dangerous for such a strong man as John.

Mississippi had changed, both for the better and for the worse. As had Catherine, they were moving to a place profoundly shaped by its history, a history we must understand. In the decade and a half since John had left, African Americans had increasingly resisted Jim Crow. In response to Black people's increasing militancy and the federal government's subsequent reluctant support, White Mississippians were developing new organizations and strategies to keep Black citizens in their place. While some White southern liberals increasingly supported racial change, most White southerners resisted it, albeit to varying degrees. White people in Mississippi seemed to believe that "their Negroes" were happy with the racial order—or at least they told themselves this. When African Americans protested, White

---

[18]Spencer Perkins, interview.
[19]Vera Mae Perkins, "My Life as a Mother" (n.d.), folder 4, Rough Drafts, Voice of Calvary Ministries, Evangelism & Missions Archives, Wheaton College.

people responded that they were being led by outside agitators or prompted by an interventionist, overreaching federal government.

I want to be clear here: the federal government did make changes. But, and I want to be even more clear now, African Americans and their handful of White supporters prompted those changes. Civil rights changes did not just sort of inevitably happen, nor were they led by White people. They were the result of activists—whom John and Vera Mae would soon join—literally placing their lives on the line and many times sacrificing their lives to reveal the contours of the violence and prompt enough dissatisfaction from the rest of the country to support change. National political leaders—nearly all White in this era—rarely had the moral or political will to make things more racially just on their own, and their White constituencies were not asking them for racial justice.

If White Mississippians were wrong about the source of the changes, their perception that the federal government was attacking their way of life was accurate by default.[20] In 1954, after the NAACP worked for decades in litigation against lawful segregation, the US Supreme Court ruled in *Brown v. Board of Education* that separate education was unequal and therefore unconstitutional, overturning the precedent set by the 1896 *Plessy v. Ferguson* case that gave federal support for the segregation White southerners were implementing during the rise of Jim Crow.

White Mississippians, like most White southerners, argued that the federal government was interfering with states' rights. John Bell Williams, a World War II veteran and one of Mississippi's representatives in the House, deemed the Monday of the Supreme Court's ruling "Black Monday." Two years later, Williams declared that the Supreme Court had violated the Constitution. Williams framed the issue as a constitutional one, not a racial one, saying, "For the purposes of discussion, let us set aside the emotional and political aspects of the subject matter involved as well as the merits or demerits of racial segregation, per se."[21] However, while Williams and other White

---

[20]Steven F. Lawson, Charles Payne, and James T. Patterson, *Debating the Civil Rights Movement, 1945–1968*, 2nd ed. (Lanham, MD: Rowman & Littlefield, 2006).

[21]John Bell Williams, "Interposition, The Barrier Against Tyranny" (1956), box 3, folder 17, in M393 McCain (William D.) Pamphlet Collection, McCain Library and Archives, University of Southern Mississippi, https://usm.access.preservica.com/uncategorized/IO_a5429ebf-9a9a-45a0-a03f-c63160684a89.

southerners were concerned about constitutional issues, we cannot disentangle their constitutional concerns with their desire to protect a way of life that subjugated Black citizens.

White Mississippians responded to *Brown* by creating the Citizens' Council, composed of grassroots organizations of respectable men and women—doctors, lawyers, accountants, teachers—that intended to resist school integration. Citizens' Councils wanted to silence White racial moderates who might support gradual integration and instead prioritize a unified White resistance to integration. Knowing well the effects of class divisions among White people, they also intended "to retain control of resistance to desegregation in the hands of the 'better people.'"[22] Locally, members of the Citizens' Council would resist civil rights activism, whether it was firing a Black worker who tried to register to vote or promoting White supremacy more generally. When Ross Barnett, a faithful member of First Baptist Church in Jackson, was elected governor in 1959, he granted the Citizens' Council state funding for its weekly television and radio programs. These programs—and the Citizens' Council more generally—aimed not to reach only Mississippi but to spread the message of segregation across the nation and the world.[23]

In 1956, the state government created the Mississippi State Sovereignty Commission, emerging from the fears both of a constitutional crisis and of the decline of their beloved way of life. The commission's founding documents emphasized protecting Mississippi's sovereignty, saying the commission could "do and perform any and all acts and things deemed necessary and proper to protect the sovereignty of the State of Mississippi, and her sister states, from encroachment thereon by the Federal Government."[24] While the founding documents did not mention segregation, in practice the commission was known as the "segregation watchdog agency," and "any and all acts" included working against civil rights activists such as John Perkins by spying on and harassing them. They would keep a file on John, watching him and colluding with local law enforcement, which documented his activities (and was a useful source for my research). The Sovereignty

---

[22]Quoted in Yasuhiro Katagiri, *The Mississippi State Sovereignty Commission: Civil Rights and States' Rights* (Jackson: University Press of Mississippi, 2001), xxx.
[23]Stephanie Rolph, *Resisting Equality: The Citizens' Council, 1954–1989* (Baton Rouge: Louisiana State University Press, 2018).
[24]Quoted in Katagiri, *Mississippi State Sovereignty Commission*, 6.

Commission also worked against justice in the courts. When Klan member Byron de la Beckwith murdered NAACP leader Medgar Evers, the Sovereignty Commission aided Beckwith's defense, leading to two successive hung juries in 1964.[25]

But we must allow for complexity. Studying the commission's history, much like the history of the Citizens' Council, reveals that White people were not all united in resisting racial integration. They disagreed about tactics and even ends. In 1973, the Sovereignty Commission was decommissioned, and after an extensive court battle, its records were made available to the public, enabling scholars and other interested parties to piece together the Sovereignty Commission's work in more detail. That history of the Sovereignty Commission—which included White people working to open them to the public—can remind us of the complexity of the past.

Into the heart of Mississippi, this state fraught with racial pain, moved the Perkinses, and because they wanted to reach Black Mississippians with the gospel, they moved into Mendenhall's Black quarters. Mendenhall was (and is) the county seat of Simpson County in the piney woods southeast of Jackson, the state capital. The Black quarters, where all the Black folks lived, were south of the railroad tracks in a low section of town next to Sellers Creek. The creek flooded often, adding a burden to the already difficult life of its residents. Many of Mendenhall's Black citizens lived in shacks, which was often the case for those in the country too. The White part of town was literally higher than the Black part of town, and Black folks walked uphill to cross the railroad tracks to the Main Street business district, where most services and businesses were located. The Simpson County Courthouse, a beautiful yellow brick building with graceful pillars, overlooked the business district. First Baptist Church sat a block away from the courthouse. Black people could go "uptown" for shopping or to go to the doctor (although they would have to wait in a separate, segregated waiting room). In the Black quarters, the Perkinses built a two-story white house, a bit of a luxurious concession to Vera Mae for the move back to Mississippi. But soon enough the house would be overflowing with visitors and guests.

---

[25]Jerry Mitchell, *Race Against Time: A Reporter Reopens the Unsolved Murder Cases of the Civil Rights Era* (New York: Simon & Schuster, 2021).

Figure 7.1. Fisherman's Mission, May 4, 2021. The original storefront John and Vera Mae Perkins used for their ministry is marked with a sign. It is located in what was the downtown part of the Black district, which is down a hill, close to the river, and across the tracks. While there is gravel up to the building, the road to it today is paved. Courtesy of Karen J. Johnson

Figure 7.2. Mendenhall Court House, May 6, 2021. The beautiful yellow brick courthouse was built in 1907 for $59,000; it was restored in 1987 for $1,750,000—both funded by Black and White taxpayers. It sits at the pinnacle of a hill, and the most direct route from the Black quarters to the courthouse is up the hill via the Main Street shopping district, which in the 1960s was all White. Today, a sign in front of the courthouse praises Mendenhall Ministries (which Perkins's group became) as a "model for faith-based community development," and notes that President George W. Bush granted it a Daily Point of Light Award. Courtesy of Karen J. Johnson

THE HOLISTIC GOSPEL: THE TYPE OF CHRISTIANITY RACISM AND POVERTY IN MISSISSIPPI REQUIRED

The faith John's White Christian friends had mentored him into in California was not adequate to meet the needs of Black people in Mississippi. This statement might seem odd at first because Christians seek to follow a God who is outside our time, outside our world. But just as the Son came to earth as a Jewish man living under Roman rule and spoke to people in those particular contexts, each person inhabits a context as they seek to live out the faith. When people today read Scripture, they must understand the context of Scripture's stories and statements before applying them to their own context. The challenge, of course, is that people live in contexts that are shaped by individual and corporate sin, and when they try to follow Jesus, they are limited in their understanding and action. All theology—the stuff humans put together to try to understand God, which must be distinguished from God's revelation, which we cannot fully understand—is lived out in a context. The assumptions implicitly accompanying Christianity in California could not account for Mississippi's racial and economic challenges.

When John and Vera Mae went back, John still knew the simple message that Jesus loves people and that they must repent and receive his forgiveness was foundational. But was that message, which in California had easily blended with individualism and economic advancement, enough? Did the gospel say more? Dolphus Weary, one of the young men Perkins discipled, helped me understand the question when we talked in Mississippi when I was there doing research. Dolphus put it this way: Is the gospel big enough to handle racism? Is the gospel big enough to handle poverty?[26]

John came to believe that the gospel *was* big enough to handle racism and poverty in the crucible of Mississippi. His context in Mississippi—the economic inequality, the pressure of having Black people "stay in their place," White folks' fears of change—required him to leave behind the implicit and false assumptions that characterized faith in California and adopt a truer set of assumptions about the world. John would develop a theology of the church, an ecclesiology, that insisted that to fully respond to God's call, local churches must fulfill four main responsibilities: (1) evangelism and discipleship,

---

[26]Dolphus Weary and Rosie Weary, interview by author, May 21, 2021.

(2) social action, (3) community and economic development, and (4) working for justice.[27] For John, Christianity had to be a gospel that addressed all aspects of a person's life (more on this in the next chapter). The gospel was holistic, as he put it, addressing the whole person. John developed a robust enough understanding of the gospel that his faith, and the faith of his family and brothers and sisters in Christ, could shape his context. There were many obstacles to living out his faith in such a robust way.

One of the most daunting was the Christianity White people practiced.

HOW WHITE CHRISTIANITY IN MISSISSIPPI SUPPORTED POVERTY AND RACISM

What? Weren't the White Christians on John's side? Didn't they care about poverty, at least? Answering these questions requires puzzling about the White Christians' implicit theologies—the assumptions that surrounded the core of their faith and were embodied in practice, which may or may not have been aligned with their explicit theologies, what they said they believed. From a historical perspective, it can be difficult to understand what people actually believed. For instance, on the one hand, we may have a statement people in the past signed condemning violence against civil rights workers or affirming that all people are made in the image of God, statements that cannot be taken lightly, particularly if they were public. But on the other hand, we also must account for what people did to help contextualize what they said and determine the extent to which their actions supported their stated beliefs. To try to understand White Christians' beliefs and practices, we will consider John's relationship with a local White pastor.

When John returned to Mississippi, he reached out to fellow pastors who were White. Through the ministry of friendship, White California Christians had changed John's perspective about White people, and he was open to relationships with them back home in Mississippi. Despite the ways White Christianity snatched the seed of God's Word away from the soil of John's heart, White Christians had helped John cultivate good soil for the good news. Few in Mississippi, however, responded with friendship. Robert Odenwald was one of them. But Rev. Odenwald learned, as did other White pastors who viewed Black Christians as equals, that preaching against the southern way of life was costly.

---

[27]Perkins lays these out in Perkins, *Quiet Revolution*.

Rev. Odenwald was pastor of Mendenhall's First Baptist Church, a short walk across the tracks and up the Main Street hill from Voice of Calvary. The two men were in similar life stages, both recently returning to Mississippi and both with young children (Rev. Odenwald had three daughters and a son). John visited Rev. Odenwald to inform him about Voice of Calvary's community projects. Their conversation drifted to theological issues, and John realized that Rev. Odenwald "was interested in whether or not I was a real, Bible-believing Christian. . . . As we talked, he became radiant—like it was a fire inside him to know we were preaching the same gospel."[28] The men developed a friendship.

White folks noticed. In part, at least, because of his relationship with John, Rev. Odenwald began speaking about Black people's human dignity. John remembered, "Cautiously, but surely, he [Odenwald] had tried to take the major step of trying to preach the real meaning of Christian love as it applied to the sin of racism."[29] Odenwald was bringing his explicit theologies in line with his changing implicit theologies. Rev. Odenwald's congregation did not appreciate this new turn. As John recalled, "I could tell this man was under great emotional stress, really strained. But I never understood at the time all that he was going through." While the details are unclear, in January 1966, Rev. Odenwald was checked into the Baptist Hospital in Jackson. He jumped from his fourth-floor window. The coroner ruled it a suicide. He was thirty-nine years old.[30]

What would cause Rev. Odenwald to kill himself? John suggested in his writing that Rev. Odenwald's death was tied to his preaching about racism as sin.

Taking John's answer as my starting point, my own conclusion comes from pondering Rev. Odenwald's context: the White Christians he pastored. His message that racism was a sin countered a pillar in the southern way of life. But just how racism and Christianity intersected in the South in the mid-twentieth century is debated.

Some say that White Christians ignored the truth of their faith. Lillian Smith, a White liberal who critiqued her beloved South, is an example of this

---

[28]Perkins, *Let Justice Roll Down*, 99.
[29]Perkins, *Let Justice Roll Down*, 100.
[30]"Robert Odenwald Obituary," *Simpson County News*, February 3, 1966; "Baptist Pastor Commits Suicide," *The Town Talk*, February 1, 1966.

perspective. In her 1949 book *Killers of the Dream*, published the year John and Vera Mae reconnected, Smith wrote about Christianity as containing a message similar to what John would later come to believe: that all humans held dignity and equal worth. She understood Christianity as a secondary force to the southern tradition of segregation. Smith lamented that, in their tortured way and aware of their sin, White southerners ignored Christianity's implications for segregation.[31] For a few generations, scholars followed Smith's suit. Books about the civil rights movement increasingly explored Black Christianity as a force animating the movement, but few considered how White Christianity fostered resistance.[32]

But was White southern Christianity subjugated to the southern way of life? Or is it impossible to disentangle White southern Christianity from the southern way of life? Put another way, when Rev. Odenwald suggested segregation was sinful, did White church members think he was attacking segregation or preaching heresy? Because of more recent historical work on White southern Christianity, I think it's possible that Rev. Odenwald's congregation thought he had strayed from the faith.

As historians have reconsidered Smith's framework, they have asked whether and how White southerners used their faith to support their resistance to integration. This different set of questions and fresh eyes on the evidence has offered new insights. As one historian—an evangelical Christian—puts it, "White Christians did not undertake their resistance to Black equality *in spite* of their religious convictions, but their faith *drove* their support of Jim Crow segregation."[33] White Christians believed segregation to be scriptural, a moral imperative supported in the Old and New Testaments, and interpreted passages in the Bible to support Black subordination.

Their faith had deep roots. White Christians' arguments for African Americans' inferiority emerged in the early days of slavery as the United States was transforming from a society with slaves to a slave society. White Christians in

---

[31] Lillian Smith, *Killers of the Dream*, 2nd ed. (New York: Norton, 1961).

[32] One of the most prominent books in this vein is David Chappell's *A Stone of Hope: Prophetic Religion and the Death of Jim Crow* (Chapel Hill: University of North Carolina Press, 2004).

[33] J. Russell Hawkins, *Because the Bible Told Them So: How Southern Evangelicals Fought to Preserve White Supremacy* (New York: Oxford University Press, 2021), 4. See also Carolyn Renee Dupont, *Mississippi Praying: Southern White Evangelicals and the Civil Rights Movement* (New York: New York University Press, 2013).

the 1600s and 1700s were troubled by slavery, concerned that if a person was a Christian, they would be disobeying Scripture if they held that person in slavery. By the 1700s, as more people of African descent became Christians, White Christians began reading Scripture to say that if an enslaved person became a Christian, their owner was not bound to free them. By the time of America's founding, many founders believed slavery was evil but assumed that it would become unnecessary and would eventually fade away. But as the invention of the cotton gin made cotton farming more profitable, and as Black and White abolitionists began to preach against slavery, White slaveholders, preachers, and trained theologians began to argue that slavery was an institution profitable to White and Black people alike.[34] After slavery ended, White Christians still believed Scripture supported the hierarchy slavery had embodied. For instance, when reading the story of Noah cursing his son Ham's descendants, saying they would serve their brothers, they understood "Negroes" as the descendants of Ham.

Like everyone, their experiences influenced how they read Scripture. Many White southerners also believed God commanded the separation of races. They read Israel's punishment for intermarrying with other nations as translating neatly into their own context, demanding racial purity. Acts 17:26 in their King James Bibles states, "And [He] hath made of one blood all nations of men for to dwell on all the face of the earth, and hath determined the times before appointed, and the bounds of their habitation." They interpreted this passage to mean that God had established divisions between the races that ought to be honored. (White southerners' interpretation stands in stark contrast civil rights supporters', which emphasized the first part of the verse, "and He hath made of one blood all nations of men."[35]) For many White southern Christians, integrating would lead to God's curse. Their resistance, then, was motivated at least in part by a belief that they were following Jesus. Certainly there was diversity among White Christians' approaches to Black civil rights, but those supporting Black equality, like Odenwald, did not fare well in Mississippi's White Christianity.

---

[34]Paul Harvey and Edward Blum, *The Color of Christ: The Son of God and the Saga of Race in America* (Chapel Hill: University of North Carolina Press, 2012), chaps. 2-4.
[35]Paul Harvey, *Bounds of Their Habitation: Race and Religion in American History* (New York: Rowman & Littlefield, 2016).

We must pay attention to complexity. White southern Christians were not monolithic in their response to the developing civil rights movement, which pushed for integration. Denominational affiliation was one marker of diversity. About 90 percent of Mississippi's Protestants were Baptists or Methodists, and the denominational governance structures affected White churches' responses. National denominational bodies were usually more progressive than local churches, but White Methodist churches struggled more mightily with their denomination than their Baptist counterparts. Among the Methodists, the struggle between local congregations and the national denomination was public and fractious in part because Black Methodists were part of the same denominational structure as White Methodists. Many White Mississippi Methodists remained staunchly loyal to their national denomination, unwilling to disassociate from it when they disagreed with its racial positions.

Even within a denomination, White people had different approaches to integration. In Mississippi, White Methodists resisting segregation faced opposition from their fellow White Methodists. For instance, in 1963, twenty-eight young Methodist ministers published "Born of Conviction," a statement reinforcing the national denominational body's support of integration. They wrote, "Our Lord Jesus Christ teaches that all men are brothers. He permits no discrimination because of race, color, or creed." The statement said right Christian practice would be to oppose efforts to close public schools rather than integrate, and it encouraged ministers to speak their conscience. But within a year, most of the ministers who had signed the public statement were no longer serving in Mississippi.[36] Some White Methodist ministers who came to believe segregation was sinful refused to leave the state but could no longer minister to White congregations. Such was the case of civil rights leader Ed King, who had to reframe his conception of what church was. When King could not find a placement in a White congregation, he became chaplain of the historically Black Tougaloo College in Jackson.[37] These leaders, including Odenwald, spoke up and faced serious consequences for their actions.

---

[36]Dupont, *Mississippi Praying*, 127.
[37]Charles Marsh, *God's Long Summer: Stories of Faith and Civil Rights* (Princeton, NJ: Princeton University Press, 1997).

But many others White ministers, who at the very least opposed racial violence, remained silent. Not speaking about race in a racially charged context was also a racial message. Why would they remain silent? Again, context can help. The assumptions guiding White ministers' preaching supported the racial status quo. White southern evangelicals preached a message that prioritized individual salvation and the purity of the individual's soul. Their morality was individualistic and ignored the structures of inequality, contrasting the emphasis John would develop on changing current social conditions *and* individual conversion. White pastors argued that addressing those structures was "political" and therefore something that Christians ought not concern themselves with. But even as they claimed they were focusing on Christianity and not politics, many of these pastors preached a political message that supported the status quo in the South, arguing that the federal government's overreach led to moral weakness.[38]

Presence also shapes power. Staunch segregationists' presence in prominent churches—undergirded by segregationist theology—led few White preachers to preach against segregation, or even to condemn the violence White southerners committed against civil rights activists. For instance, Mississippi's governor from 1960–1964, Ross Barnett, who campaigned on a segregationist platform, taught Sunday school and attended Jackson's First Baptist Church alongside the Hederman family, who promoted segregation through the state's two largest newspapers, the *Jackson Clarion-Ledger* and the *Jackson Daily News*. Less prominent segregationists were Christians too, everyday folk who were trying to be faithful as they saw fit. The murder of two white civil rights activists in the summer of 1964 alongside one Black activist drew national attention to the state's violence, although many in the movement thought if those killed had all been Black there would not have been such a national outcry. After that summer, White Christian leaders in Mississippi at least began speaking out occasionally against violent resistance. But as John's beating shows, the violence did not stop.

White Christianity and the policing of African Americans reinforced each other as well. Beyond Rev. Odenwald, local White people were troubled when

---

[38]Historians have used the most prominent southern pastor, Douglas Hudgins of First Baptist Church in Jackson, Mississippi, to illustrate these trends. See Marsh, *God's Long Summer*; Dupont, *Mississippi Praying*.

John brought White pastors into the Black quarters. In October 1964, a Sovereignty Commission representative reached out to Simpson County's sheriff to check the "race situation" (by which he meant voter registration, KKK violence, and any Black demonstrations). Sheriff Howard Varnar responded that he had seen no trouble but was concerned that John might begin doing some voter registration activity. Varnar reported that three White pastors and one woman, who he said was supposedly one of their wives, had come to Voice of Calvary. He had kept them under surveillance and reported their names, addresses, and license plate tags.[39] John's son Spencer observed how the police watched his family. He remembered looking out his second-story window and watching the police coming down the road to their house.[40] The police were letting the family know that they were being watched, and not in a friendly way.

In this context, pastors did not need to preach sermons or publish pamphlets supporting segregation (although some did). Their congregations knew the lessons so well already: the Bible told them that integration was evil. And when there was violence against civil rights activists, often committed with the knowledge of police by Ku Klux Klan members who assumed that they too were acting under Christian conviction, the pastors' silence or meager opposition enabled the culture of death. Regrettably, the violence and White Christianity's collusion would drive many Black activists away from Christianity and toward a secular and separatist version of Black Power.[41] And it may have contributed greatly to Rev. Odenwald's death.

WHY OUR RESPONSE TO TRUE STORIES MATTERS

Are people like this worth listening to—who wanted Black people like John to stay in their place? People who allowed a system that killed John's mother,

---

[39]Virgil Downing, "Investigation of Racial Attitudes in Copiah, Jefferson, Franklin, Claiborne, Simpson, Covington, Jasper, Clarke, Kemper and Newton Counties," October 23, 1964, Sovereignty Commission Files, Mississippi Department of Archives & History.
[40]Spencer Perkins, interview.
[41]Several members of the Student Non-violent Coordinating Committee turned away from interracial unity and beloved community toward separatist Black Power because of the violence they experienced in the South (see Marsh, *God's Long Summer*). Black Power has also been practiced and supported by Christians. See Kerry Pimblott, *Faith in Black Power: Religion, Race, and Resistance in Cairo, Illinois* (Lexington: University of Kentucky Press, 2017); Matthew J. Cressler, *Authentically Black and Truly Catholic: The Rise of Black Catholicism in the Great Migration* (New York: New York University Press, 2017).

Maggie, and his brother, Clyde? People who caused great stress for Robert Odenwald when he spoke about Black people's equality? Despite the complexity, White people's overwhelming resistance to change can seem so strange to most twenty-first-century people, who tend to assume, at least publicly, that all people are equal. But for White Mississippians, these changes bubbling up from Black activism and eventually supported by the federal government seemed like an attack on all they knew to be right and good. Acknowledging their perspective is an act of love, and while one may not agree with it, asking why can help build a bridge rather than sever a connection.

Building bridges allows us to lean into the interconnectedness of the body of Christ rather than imagining ourselves as individual islands. To build this bridge further, I want to ask again why and how White people could believe what they had to know were lies about how content African Americans were. Curiosity and a willingness to listen can help us understand others, although we do not have to agree with them.

One significant answer is the content of the history people chose to remember and their close identification with that history. Lillian Smith helped me understand the historical depth of White people's tortured perspective on race in the South. As we know, she was a White southerner who loved the South yet still critiqued its racial hierarchy in her 1949 book *Killers of the Dream*. She observed,

> We identified with the South's trouble as if we, individually, were responsible for all of it. We defended the sins and the sorrows of three hundred years as if each sin had been committed by us alone and each sorrow had cut across our heart. We were as hurt at criticism of our region as if our own name had been called aloud by the critic. We knew guilt without understanding it, and there is no tie that binds men closer to the past and each other than that.[42]

Smith reflected in 1961, the year after the Perkinses returned to the South, that civil rights activists "are not fighting people, they are fighting a past that bars them from freedom and responsibility."[43] Smith knew well it was not just the civil rights activists' contemporaries but all the ideas they had inherited that shackled them to a hierarchy that placed White people at the top.

---

[42]Smith, *Killers of the Dream*, 26.
[43]Smith, *Killers of the Dream*, 19. This quotation comes from her 1961 preface to the book.

Confessing their guilt rather than defending their actions could have led to freedom. Despite their denial—like you and I with our own sin—they still bore responsibility for their actions.

The past is heavy, and it is hard to change. This generation of White southerners' resistance to efforts to dismantle their racial hierarchy makes that clear. However, like them, we are not off the hook for our current racial dynamics. Like them, we live in an inherited world, with patterns of how to interact with authority, sensibilities of what we consider the good life, norms about where people should live. Yet it is difficult for people to see their own contexts—including their assumptions about how the world works and how it should work—for what they are. We need to press into the past, to seek to understand it—which is why opening previously closed records like the Sovereignty Commission's is usually a good thing. When people encounter different ideas, different practices, different people, they can either close their eyes, shut their ears, and resist change, or they can sincerely listen, humbly considering what they have heard.

QUESTIONS AND IMPLICATIONS

Considering the cost of what John and Vera Mae Perkins decided to do when they moved back to Mississippi can bear fruit. Like so many of the other people in this book, they were moving in a countercultural direction. The Perkins family's move back to Mississippi was an example of downward mobility, of giving up the American dream of having a better—by which we usually mean richer—life for each successive generation. This decision to resist the American dream and live in a poorer community would become a bedrock of John's philosophy in later years, and he would write about it as "relocation"—the message I heard while in seminary. One of the contexts for American Christianity today, by contrast, is the assumption of comfort and upward mobility as goals.

- In what ways can you and your church push against the culture for the gospel? In what ways does a desire for comfort limit how fully you live out the gospel?

I offered two ways to understand the relationship between southern White Christianity and race: one in which White Christians subjugated their faith to racial preferences and another in which their faith contributed to racial hierarchies. Both were likely true in some ways. John and Vera Mae Perkins had to adapt their faith, which they inherited in middle-class California, to Mississippi's soil. There they developed a theology of the church, an ecclesiology, that expanded the church's call from simply "saving souls" to engaging with all of who people were and all of what they were experiencing. Their evangelism drew them into social action, community and economic development, and justice work. They were able to see these needs because they placed themselves in a difficult situation among the poor. Once there, they sacrificed profoundly—from giving up middle-class comforts to the point of death—for the good of their neighbors. Both the Perkinses and White southern Christians resisting integration had a conception of Christian faith that was shaped by their context. As humans, we see through the glass darkly and our actions are bound by sin; we cannot understand truth fully nor can we live it out. Our limitations do not diminish the truth of the gospel, but they do require us to be on guard.

- How does your context shape your theology and your actions? What holes might there be in your understanding of what your faith requires?
- I often have to guard against prioritizing my own comfort and satisfaction above other goods, which is the very frame the Perkinses resisted. In what ways do you have a theology that prioritizes comfort—individually and corporately? In what ways could you sacrifice more? What fruit might that bear?

Lillian Smith argues that White southerners' resistance to racial change stemmed in part from how they related to the past. They identified closely with it and did not want to confess guilt in the present. Many people go in the opposite direction, wanting to ignore the past or claim no responsibility in the present for the results of our history.

- How do you relate to the past? We may not be responsible for what happened then, but we are called to love others in our own times and places. To what extent are you willing to ask for forgiveness and work for the good today?

Dolphus's questions of whether the gospel is big enough to handle poverty and race had deep resonance for me when I was researching in Mississippi, walking by shacks in the Black part of town on my morning walks. Living in the Chicago suburb of Wheaton, like (especially) White Californians in the 1950s, Dolphus's question might never occur to me unless I am intentional about asking it. The question is essential because if the gospel is not big enough to handle poverty and racism, then is the gospel just for those who are comfortable?

- Is the gospel you follow big enough to handle racism and poverty? In what ways are you living out that gospel?

8

THE TASKS OF THE CHURCH

How John and Vera Mae defined the callings of Christians as more than simply evangelism and discipleship and why we should listen to them.

THE CHURCH'S FIRST TASK: EVANGELISM AND DISCIPLESHIP

Despite the failure of discipleship among White Mississippi Christians, John's and Vera Mae's initial goal was not teaching White Christians the gospel. They wanted to teach the Bible to Black folks. They saw most rural churches as social clubs and were concerned about the emotionalism and lack of scriptural teaching. Vera Mae remembered that they were up against "a religion without a consistent grasp on the truths of the Bible." They were Bible teachers and would use their Child Evangelism Fellowship training in the hamlets around Mendenhall and in schools across the county. They were active, speaking to ten thousand young people a month in the early 1960s.[1]

The Perkinses also threw their lot in with the people. Few Black pastors of rural congregations lived with the people at the same economic level. Many pastors lived far away and preached once a month. The church folks could be proud of their pastor's fancy car and nice suit and would honor him out of their poverty. A sharecropping family might feed their pastor a meal with two meats as the children—who rarely ate meat—waited for him to finish before

---

[1] John Perkins, *A Quiet Revolution: The Christian Response to Human Need . . . a Strategy for Today* (Waco, TX: Word, 1976), 30.

they ate the leftovers. Pride would fill them as they watched their pastor drive away from their small shack because he looked prosperous.

John was different. He never took up an offering after preaching or teaching. He and Vera Mae relied on their manual labor—hauling railroad ties, farm work—and the goodwill of local people who shared their garden produce. John also had what most Black pastors lacked: supporters outside Mississippi who contributed financially to their ministry. People from the White Calvary Bible Church in Burbank, California, supported his ministry in Mississippi, and he named the ministry after the church: the Voice of Calvary. The church sent their young people to help John on short-term trips.

People noticed the difference between John and most Black pastors. Eugene Walker, a farmer from Vera Mae's home church, Oak Ridge Missionary Baptist Church, invited John to teach Sunday school. He observed,

> Rev. Perkins wasn't like most preachers who had about four churches. And a lot of times at Oak Ridge folks would say something like, "But I can't understand that he isn't going to take up an offering." Most preachers take up offerings, but he didn't and that had the people spellbound. They said, "Well, how is he gonna live?" . . . I would have to say he made it by the help of God, that's all I know.[2]

John's actions also amazed Dolphus Weary, whom John would later mentor. Dolphus met John in 1963 under the big green-and-white tent John purchased for revivals. When the White preacher, Rev. Wallace, invited people to be saved, Dolphus responded. He remembered, "What I knew of Rev. Perkins didn't seem to fit my image of Black preachers. Everyone called him 'John' instead of 'Rev. Perkins.' He lived simply, just like the rest of us. And he walked around town in jeans and a shirt, just like the rest of us. I thought, *If this guy's a preacher, where's his Cadillac?*"[3]

But despite his connection with the people, John failed to build strong relationships with other Black pastors. He critiqued their absenteeism, lack of scriptural teaching, and practice of taking money from their flocks. He blamed out-of-wedlock births and honky-tonks—both prominent in Black

---

[2]Eugene Walker, quoted in Perkins, *Quiet Revolution*, 53.
[3]Dolphus Weary, *I Ain't Comin' Back* (Wheaton, IL: Tyndale House, 1990), 42.

Mendenhall—on them. Churches, John argued, should make their communities better by teaching conservative morals that would stabilize families and provide wholesome activities. John's critiques were public, and Black pastors resisted his presence in their churches. Robert Archie Buckley, an older man who mentored John and offered him work on his farm, observed, "He was so heavy that he scared some of the pastors out in the churches. I was in charge of the youth church in our church, so I asked Rev. Perkins to come and be the guest speaker. The pastor didn't like it and he challenged my choice by taking it to the folks. The folks backed him up—they didn't want to cross the pastor."[4]

THE CHURCH'S SECOND TASK: SOCIAL ACTION

Living in the community, working side by side with people hauling wood, picking cucumbers and greens, and speaking in schools, brought John and Vera Mae face to face with people's felt needs. To address only physical needs would be paternalistic, John thought. So he told people that God could change their lives, starting in the present and "sharing with them the understanding that they can have a new quality of life with God that lasts forever."[5]

The kingdom was coming and had come. John and Vera Mae could not divide body from soul. If they were going to preach Jesus' salvation, they had to meet physical needs too. As John reflected, when they went out into the community and worked with the people, "we could not escape seeing firsthand the desperate physical needs of many of our people."[6] People would come to them, asking for help and advice about specific needs they had. They realized that "filling those needs had to be a basic part of our strategy and that it might be key to reaching the community." As they tried to address the needs people raised, they "stumbled on a key biblical principle: that a response to the needs which people feel most deeply fleshes out the meaning of the gospel which we proclaim. We now call this the 'felt-need concept,'" which means "the best way to communicate to a person's most

---

[4]Robert Archie Buckley, quoted in Perkins, *Quiet Revolution*, 50. Many Black pastors' suspicion of John would take a change in leadership to overcome, and Perkins's successors, Artis Fletcher and Dolphus Weary, worked to build bridges to other pastors through the Pastors Development Program.
[5]Perkins, *Quiet Revolution*, 66.
[6]Perkins, *Quiet Revolution*, 62.

basic, spiritual needs is through his physical needs, or the needs he can best identify for himself."[7]

Pause and note: John did not want to provide physically what *he* thought people needed but rather what *they* thought they needed. This would become a pillar in his philosophy of Christian community development that he taught me in seminary. John and Vera Mae tried to help folks out in small ways early on, giving money or food. They then moved to more institution building to provide for needs, founding a daycare and, by the early 1970s, founding a health center to provide quality care to Black and White people who were willing to be treated by a Black doctor.

Many Christians are good at social action. White folks in Mississippi would even cross racial lines to provide some forms of social care for Black folks when they faced great trouble—such as a part of town being leveled by a tornado or an excessive flood. But John quickly realized social action's limits. It might help someone in the moment, but it would not address the underlying problems leading to their poverty. For that, John and Vera Mae knew they needed to develop people and strengthen the community economically. Social action was like seeing people who did not know how to swim drowning in a river and tossing them life-saving devices. John and Vera Mae began to teach them to swim through economic and community development.

THE CHURCH'S THIRD TASK: ECONOMIC AND COMMUNITY DEVELOPMENT

In 1966, the Perkinses used the Johnson administration's War on Poverty funding to morph their daycare into Head Start. Many of President Johnson's programs were designed to address the economic inequality that motivated the political action of the civil rights movement.[8] Head Start was a comprehensive, culturally responsive program designed to involve not just the children in preschool themselves but entire families. It addressed children's

---

[7]Perkins, *Quiet Revolution*, 64.
[8]In later years Perkins critiqued big-government funding of poverty programs. He argued that too often they passed money *through* poor communities and sent it back into the hands of the rich rather than actually developing those communities. The cost of infrastructure also concerned him. See Lauren F. Winner, "The Church as Family and the Politics of Food Distribution," in *Mobilizing for the Common Good: The Lived Theology of John M. Perkins* (Jackson: University Press of Mississippi, 2013), 16-31.

education and their health, nutrition, and social and emotional needs, and had great buy-in from the poverty-stricken communities it served. With Head Start, the Perkinses were able to gain access to resources to further a like-minded vision that would develop people and communities.

Pregnant with their eighth child, Elizabeth, Vera Mae went to Tuskegee Institute in Alabama to train in the early development program so she could direct the Head Start program.[9] Vera Mae was a strong leader in the position, and John admired her ability to draw people together. People across Simpson County knew her from their Child Evangelism Fellowship and school discipleship, and they trusted her. Voice of Calvary's facility could host the children—more than one hundred a day—who came. They provided education and good food, essential in a poor community. On one level, the program was a form of social action.

But it was also more. It became a center for community and economic development. Head Start's evolving employment situation revealed the need for economic and community development. Most Black folks in Simpson County worked, but they did not get paid enough to escape poverty. Head Start offered a fair wage. About 150 people applied for the approximately twenty teacher, cook, and secretary positions available. John and Vera Mae were troubled. They wanted to hire only Christians, but Christians and non-Christians alike volunteered, hoping to make it to the top-of-the list when a position opened. Many might have appreciated the Christian perspective, but they cared mostly about the money.[10]

The demand for good-paying jobs helped the Perkinses see that their community needed a stronger economic base. To build the base, people needed to be developed. For John, community development could not just mean providing economic opportunities; it had to grow people. Their philosophy encompassed both personal and systemic solutions: prioritize individuals growing into opportunities and working hard, *and* deal with the structures that kept Black people "in their place."

Worship was at the core of their philosophy. John understood why Black churches valued emotional release, reflecting, "It was a strain to live in a

---

[9]Vera Mae Perkins, interview by Joe White, 2003, Simpson County Historical and Genealogical Oral History Project, The Center for Oral and Cultural Heritage at the University of Southern Mississippi.
[10]Perkins, *Quiet Revolution*, 71-72.

world where you were 'free,' but still not having any real control over important parts of your life, over matters that affected you and your community. The Black minister who had some skill in drawing out or transferring that strain and emotion helped maintain the sanity and mental health of a people suffering and oppressed."[11] But John believed worship must also engage "the mind or the understanding." Without knowing biblical truths, Black people cowered when the Bible would call them to stand up and resist injustice. As Vera Mae observed, "All my folks were religious back in those days. And I saw again and again how their religion made them humble down to the white structure, with all its injustice."[12] The church's first task, evangelism and discipleship, was essential to community development, because strong biblical teaching not only raised people up; it kept in the fold those craving a faith that addressed their intellect.

In 1966, John found another way to develop his community. He discovered cooperatives through Father A. J. McKnight, a Black Catholic priest who was using Ford Foundation money to develop the Federation of Southern Coops.[13] Cooperatives could address both the personal-growth and systemic-change aspects of community development. Systemically, they enabled poor people to gain ownership in the economic system rather than being just consumers or producers. Personally, they required that individuals learn about economics. John was elated for the opportunity "to raise more people who knew about economics."[14]

John had learned his lesson on the importance of ownership early. He would often tell the story of when, as a child, he worked for a White man hauling hay all day. After the day's work, he expected to be paid a fair wage, a dollar and a half or two dollars. At the end of the day, however, the man gave him fifteen cents, a buffalo dime and one nickel. John was disgusted; to accept such a paltry sum would hurt his dignity, but to refuse it would be getting "out of his place." John took the money. But he also learned a lesson:

---

[11] John Perkins, *Let Justice Roll Down: John Perkins Tells His Own Story* (Ventura, CA: G/L, 1976), 124.
[12] Vera Mae Perkins, quoted in Perkins, *Quiet Revolution*, 25.
[13] Perkins, *Let Justice Roll Down*, 122-25. For McKnight, see A. J. McKnight, *Whistling in the Wind: The Autobiography of The Rev. A. J. McKnight, C.S.Sp.* (Opelousas, LA: Southern Development Foundation, Inc., 1994).
[14] John Perkins, interview by author, May 15, 2020.

That man had the capital: the land and the hay. And he had the means of production: the wagon and the horses. All I had were my wants and needs—and my labor. So I was exploited. . . . And if you're going to make it in this society, you've got to somehow or other get your hands on the means of production. Once you get the means of production, you can do good or evil with it. And this man done evil with it.[15]

John wanted to help his people do good.

Cooperatives had a slow start in Mississippi. They were subversive, after all, especially when Black people were involved. In 1946, when John fled the state, the *Monthly Labor Review* reported, "Cooperatives are few in Mississippi." The state had the lowest number of credit unions in the United States, which was the most common type of cooperative in the South.[16] African Americans involved with cooperatives not only grew as people and profited economically; they also upset the racial hierarchy. Cooperatives could create a separate economic system independent from White people, which could subvert the labor and consumer patterns that kept Black people in their place. When Black organizers developed some of the first Black cooperatives in the South through the National Federation of Colored Farmers, they intended "to make life on the farm more attractive and more profitable, and to build up in this nation a Negro group of organized, influential, and satisfied producers."[17]

The first local unit, organized in the town of Howard in Mississippi's Delta region, found they could buy supplies at slightly less than wholesale prices and sell them to members at *half* the cost sharecroppers had to pay when they bought supplies from White merchants. The White planters and merchants banded together and told the Black co-op it must leave the county. It refused, pointing to the legality of their organization, and amazingly, the state's attorney general supported the co-op, telling the planters that they too could purchase supplies cooperatively.[18]

By the 1960s, cooperatives were becoming more common in rural areas.[19] In 1966, there were sixteen cooperatives in ten counties, and three years

---

[15]Perkins, *Let Justice Roll Down*, 48-49.
[16]"Cooperatives in the South," *Monthly Labor Review* 63, no. 4 (1946): 585. See also Charles M. Smith, "Observations on Regional Differentials in Cooperative Organization," *Social Forces* 22, no. 4 (1944): 437-42.
[17]John Hope II, "Rochdale Cooperation," *Clark Atlanta University* 1, no. 1 (1940): 39-52.
[18]Hope, "Rochdale Cooperation."
[19]Monica M. White, *Freedom Farmers: Agricultural Resistance and the Black Freedom Movement* (Chapel Hill: University of North Carolina Press, 2019).

later, famed civil rights leader Fannie Lou Hamer would found her freedom farm.[20] But there was still work to be done. At home, John helped form the Simpson County Development Corporation and used federal money to help build five duplex houses. He helped organize a farmers' cooperative to purchase supplies, and Voice of Calvary opened a cooperative thrift store. In 1969, as schools in Mississippi prepared to integrate, John had fewer opportunities to evangelize in schools, so he agreed to serve as a state organizer for the Southern Cooperative Development Corporation, helping local people organize cooperatives. The Sovereignty Commission and the FBI took note.[21]

As Voice of Calvary worked to grow African Americans' economic base in Simpson County and across the state, John and Vera Mae remained committed to a particular type of people development. They wanted to teach people to grow themselves so they could help others grow. John reflected, "In a poor community the motivation for helping ourselves must come out of more than just self-interest. There must be a deep and strong commitment to each other, to unity."[22]

They sought to develop local leaders who would have as much of a commitment to the community as they did. The couple mentored young people, sharing their homes with Dolphus Weary, Artis Fletcher, Carolyn Albritton, and Rosie Marie Camper. They also knew they needed to expose these young people to a world beyond rural Mississippi. As Vera Mae reflected, their living in California "gave us exposure to a world much bigger than the one we grew up in. We later found this essential in our development of strong, Black, Christian leaders in Mississippi and we began to send our young converts outside the South for education and experience so that they could come back as more fully developed and mature believers."[23] Out of Mississippi, these young men and women could experience life, as Vera Mae and John had, away from the daily hatred and oppression they had to endure at home.

---

[20]Mississippi Museum of Civil Rights History.
[21]Mississippi State Sovereignty Commission, "Report on Perkins and Huemmer" (n.d.), SCR ID # 2-90-0-38-1-1-1, Mississippi Department of Archives & History.
[22]Perkins, *Quiet Revolution*, 117.
[23]Quoted in John Perkins, *Quiet Revolution*, 29.

THE CHURCH'S FOURTH TASK: JUSTICE

As they evangelized, met social needs, and developed people and communities, the Perkinses prayed for the civil rights movement to come to Mendenhall "as earnestly as we prayed for the kids and adults we shared with to become Christians."[24] This might seem strange. Isn't eternal salvation more important than temporary situations? But remember: the Perkinses' theology demanded they answer the foundational question, Is God big enough to handle poverty and racism? John and Vera Mae were concerned both with eternal damnation and salvation, *and* with how the gospel could change a person's life today. Their faith demanded they work in the civil rights movement. If social action was passing out lifesavers to people drowning in a river and community development was about teaching people to swim, then seeking justice was stopping those people, laws, and systems who were throwing people into the river in the first place. And, as we will see, John and Vera Mae were willing to lay down their lives for justice.

QUESTIONS AND IMPLICATIONS

Part of John's freedom to serve came from financial partnerships outside Mississippi. We see this pattern in the New Testament when churches that had more sacrificially shared with Christians in need.

- Whom could you partner with?

Financial partnership can come with unintentional strings attached. When I spoke with later leaders of the ministry, they commented how they had to resist (and sometimes failed at) structuring the ministry around what donors wanted rather than what the people needed, which contrasted with John's vision to empower people and help them provide for what they perceived they needed. Those relationships could be difficult, as seen in the different perspectives between the White Christian supporters and the Black Christians in Mendenhall about how their faith ought to be lived out (for example: Should Christians work for civil rights?).

- If you are financially supporting a ministry, to what extent do you trust the leadership? How can you submit to their leadership while also offering your own gifts?

---

[24]Perkins, *Quiet Revolution*, 106.

When Perkins wrote about the church's tasks of evangelism and discipleship, social action, economic and community development, and justice, he wrote about them from a corporate perspective. It was not the individual who was to accomplish these tasks but the church.

- John was pushing against the individualism that creeps into Christianity in America with a biblical perspective. To what extent do you think about yourself as part of the church doing these things?
- Which of the following—evangelism, social action, community and economic development, and justice—does your church prioritize? Which might you need to focus on more?

THE CHURCH'S ROLE IN SEEKING JUSTICE

How John and Vera Mae lived their faith
in the civil rights movement and were able to
forgive White people for John's suffering.

VOTING

In 1965, White civil rights organizer John Longstreet was looking for Black partners in Simpson County to help him register African Americans to vote. No one would host him. His plight was not uncommon. While many Black churches became hubs of civil rights organizing, they paid dearly for it. Those opposed to the movement bombed those churches, and insurance companies refused to insure them. It was dangerous and costly to organize for the movement. But John and Vera Mae said yes. They invited Longstreet into their home and opened Voice of Calvary's facilities.[1]

Longstreet and the Perkinses were building on the previous summer's activism in Mississippi led by the Student Nonviolent Coordinating Committee, a grassroots civil rights group that focused on developing indigenous leadership. While Mississippi Blacks could technically vote in national elections, the state had several barriers to their registration. Furthermore, the Democratic primary was all White. The Student Nonviolent Coordinating Committee had wanted to send delegates to the Democratic National Convention

---

[1] John Perkins, *Quiet Revolution*, chap. 12.

from the Mississippi Freedom Democratic Party, which was open to Black and White voters. The committee invited White college students to join them in Mississippi. The committee's move was strategic; they knew violence against the White, mostly northern students would garner national attention. A Black citizen's murder would be unnoticed by the nation.

Mississippi's White residents had violently resisted what they saw as an attack. Early in the summer of 1964, civil rights workers James Chaney, Andrew Goodman, and Michael Schwerner, two White and one Black, went to investigate a church burning in Philadelphia, Mississippi. Police arrested the men and released them to the Ku Klux Klan, whose imperial wizard, Sam Bowers, had ordered their executions. KKK members killed the men and buried their bodies in an earthen dam. The Student Nonviolent Coordinating Committee was right. That two of the men were White drew national news coverage. The FBI recovered the bodies. Although there was clear evidence pointing to Bowers and others involved in the murder, the all-White jury would not convict them.[2]

Voting mattered. The jury hearing Bowers's case was selected from those registered to vote. Voters elected officials who decided whether to employ Black workers in government service and who set policy. Voting could make systemic change and be personally empowering.

John worked with other African Americans such as Voice of Calvary supporter Jesse Newsome and a handful of Whites to register Black voters. They canvassed Black residents, never alone, because of threats to their lives. John reported that Newsome registered over one thousand people, a huge feat in a county with a population of under twenty thousand.[3] In 1966, they organized the Simpson County Civic League and elected Nathaniel Rubin chair. Federal marshals set up a voter registration site at the only federally owned site in town: the post office. They built an outpost off the back of the post office, and Black organizers brought people there to register. As more Black folk registered, they began to feel their power. One election, John asked John D. Smith, the long-term incumbent candidate for highway commissioner, whether he

---

[2] For the Freedom Summer and the murder, see Anne Moody, *Coming of Age in Mississippi* (New York: Doubleday, 1968); Charles Marsh, *God's Long Summer: Stories of Faith and Civil Rights* (Princeton, NJ: Princeton University Press, 1997).

[3] John Perkins, *A Quiet Revolution: The Christian Response to Human Need . . . a Strategy for Today* (Waco, TX: Word, 1976), 107.

would hire Black workers. If Smith did not agree to hire Black workers, Perkins told him Black voters would vote for opposing candidate, Shag Pyron.

Questions like that put the Perkins family in danger, but their Black friends rallied around them and refused to cow to pressure. The Sovereignty Commission took note of John's voter registration activity. The commission—directly opposed to civil rights—had canvassed Mississippi sheriffs to see whether they were "having trouble" with the NAACP and the Council of Federated Organizations (Mississippi's umbrella civil rights organization). Simpson County's sheriff reported that he suspected John and some outside White ministers may be beginning some voter registration work.[4] White people also began making threatening phone calls. After one particularly sinister one, which said he needed to flee the county by 8:30 p.m. or they would kill him, John flagged down NAACP leader Mitchell Hayes, who was on his way home from church. Hayes recalled, "He told me what happened and said he wasn't leaving. We began organizing a guard for his house that night." They recruited around thirty-five to forty men to protect Voice of Calvary and the Perkins house, and the following day scattered around town, protecting John so he could go about his business as usual. Black citizens ended up voting Smith out of office, which Hayes remembered as one of "the high points for us."[5]

TYPES OF NONVIOLENCE

Arming themselves, as they did to defend the Perkins house, was not uncommon for Black civil rights activists especially in rural areas. When Perkins began receiving threats, he took the advice of his friend Charles Evers, Medgar's older brother, and armed himself. Medgar's 1963 murder in his driveway by White Klansman Byron de la Beckwith was still fresh. Like Medgar, Charles Evers carried guns to protect himself. When he visited Mendenhall, Charles would announce his presence—and that he was armed—on the police scanner.[6]

Although he carried weapons, John understood his activism as nonviolent.[7] He was not going to attack others, but—in a very American sense—he

---

[4]Mississippi State Sovereignty Commission, "Report on Perkins and Huemmer" (n.d.), SCR ID # 2-90-0-38-1-1-1, Mississippi Department of Archives & History.
[5]Mitchell Hayes, quoted in Perkins, *Quiet Revolution*, 118.
[6]Jerry Mitchell, *The Preacher and the Klansman* (Jackson, MS: Clarion-Ledger, 1999), 24.
[7]Carolyn Fletcher, interview by author, May 14, 2021.

was going to defend himself, his family, and members of his community if they were attacked. John's perspective was common among African Americans, including the somewhat misinterpreted Malcolm X and some members of the Black Panther Party, who promoted self-defense. While John was not as in-your-face as the Black Panthers who marched around cities wearing guns and ammunition, he did take physical precautions.

John's and his fellow Black activists' approach was practical. Clyde's death so many years before had only solidified what John knew: there was no protection from the law. John's nonviolence was different from Martin Luther King Jr.'s. King refused to let his bodyguards carry guns, convinced that he must model nonviolence. King and other nonviolent activists such as the Student Nonviolent Coordinating Committee in the early 1960s adhered to nonviolence as a philosophy, a way of life. King's organization, the Southern Christian Leadership Conference, required those marching with them to sign statements declaring their commitment to the philosophy of nonviolence, which meant absorbing the violence of those who attacked them without striking back. John loved his enemies, but on a backcountry road he wanted guns to deter them.

EDUCATION

In addition to voting, African Americans were concerned about their children's education. For years, the NAACP had litigated cases to show that separate education was inherently unequal. But Black families valued the opportunities and resources available to White students and did not prioritize integration intrinsically.

White southerners also cared about their children's education and saw the Supreme Court's *Brown v. Board of Education* ruling in 1954 as forced integration that would lead to the destruction of their families. For White folks, school integration was dangerous. Black and White children would be interacting socially, which could lead to romantic interests and eventually marriage—or at least sexual encounters. Interracial sex, they believed, would lead to the "mongrelization" of the races. Of course, that had already happened—for years during slavery, White men had had unwelcome sexual liaisons with Black women. White men, knowing their past, sought to protect "their women" and feared Black men would do to White women what they had done to Black women. Often, when White men lynched a Black man, they cited rape as the reason (although the reason was often the economic advancement of a Black man).

White people were to blame for African Americans' poor education. Public education in Mississippi was underfunded compared to other states, and Black students had a decreasing piece of the pie. In 1890, during Jim Crow's early days, the state spent two times more money educating White students than Black students. By 1935, the state funded White students' education at three times the rate of Black students'. By World War II, as Perkins was leaving the state, only 13 percent of state monies went to Black students, although they were about half the state's population.[8]

Despite the Supreme Court ruling, southern states moved at a snail's pace to end school segregation. Mississippi finally began a "freedom of choice" plan in 1965. It meant Black students could voluntarily go to White schools, and White students could voluntarily go to Black schools. Legislators knew no Whites and, because of the danger, few Blacks would take up the offer. But some Black children and their families did. I have gotten to know a few of the brave people who integrated Simpson County schools.

Scottye Holloway was one. Scottye is now president of the Mendenhall Ministries, which John's Voice of Calvary became fifty years ago. He holds a master of divinity and a doctorate of ministry, and pastored multiracial churches for many years. A few years ago, he moved back to Mississippi to lead the ministry. Scottye welcomed me during my sojourn in Mississippi.

When he was in first grade, Scottye's father, a pastor, asked Scottye whether he wanted to go to Black school or White school. Scottye responded that he wanted to attend White school. Scottye knew, even as a six-year-old who had never attended school, that he would receive a better education in the White school. They had the better books, the better buses, the better school buildings, and the longer school year. Scottye's parents agreed that he could attend the White school.[9]

John saw voluntary integration as an opportunity to push forward civil rights. Unlike Scottye, John's children were not eager to go to White school.

---

[8] Jerry Mitchell, "Separate and Unequal: Mississippi Has Left Its Public Schools in the Hole," *Biloxi Sun Herald*, February 21, 2019, www.sunherald.com/news/local/education/article226512855.html.

[9] Scottye Holloway, interview by author, May 5, 2021.

Spencer Perkins, John and Vera Mae's oldest child, was in eighth grade when he and his other siblings began attending White school.

White neighbors in Mendenhall felt threatened by Black children and teens and were determined to not integrate. Scottye remembered that his teacher placed him in the back of the classroom and refused to read his work. She just wrote "F" on each paper. Scottye boarded the bus from his aunt's house along with some other children voluntarily integrating. One night, White people, likely Klan members, shot up the house, barely missing his aunt. The next day, they had no trouble. Scottye did not know it then, but a group of armed Black men hid for several weeks in the woods, protecting the children and the house so they could continue attending school. Today Scottye suspects John was among the group. Other children experienced similar harassment. Scottye's friend Deborah Payne, whose mother helped register Black voters, had also voluntarily integrated the school. Payne was nearly kidnapped when the school bus dropped her off at the end of her road. Like Scottye, she did not know who had tried to steal her, but after that someone always escorted her from the bus.[10]

John's and Vera Mae's son Spencer started at the White high school with about a dozen other Black children, but by the end of the year, only he and one other student remained at the school. White peers called him "nigger" throughout the day, even in front of teachers, who did not intervene. One teacher called him a "Negra," a derogatory way to say "Negro." Vera Mae drove Spencer to school every day, and every day the police stopped her, harassing her and asking for her driver's license.[11] When asked about the two years he was voluntarily integrating the high school, Spencer responded that they were "probably the worst two years of my life, eighth and ninth grade."[12]

In the short run, segregationists mostly had their way. At the end of the school year, when Scottye received his final report card, he learned he had failed the first grade. His friend Deborah Payne had also failed. That day as he rode the bus home, Scottye wondered how he would tell his parents. He also noticed a blue Chevrolet Impala tailing the car but did not give much

---

[10]Deborah Payne, interview by author, May 13, 2021.
[11]Vera Mae Perkins, interview by author, May 7, 2021.
[12]Spencer Perkins, interview by Paul Ericksen, 1987, Collection 364, Evangelism & Missions Archives, Wheaton College. See also Spencer Perkins and Chris Rice, *More Than Equals: Racial Healing for the Sake of the Gospel* (Downers Grove, IL: InterVarsity Press, 1995).

thought to it. Impalas were top-of-the line cars, so the person driving it had money. When Scottye exited the bus, the Impala's driver stopped and started shooting at the first grader. Scottye sprinted to his house, somehow safe. The next year, Payne stayed at the White school, but Scottye returned to Black school. After two years, the Perkinses pulled their kids out of the White school, tired of the constant harassment. It looked like the White folks in Mendenhall had avoided integration.

But in 1970, the federal government declared Mississippi's voluntary integration plan was not sufficient. Mississippi had to integrate. Few White residents in Simpson County agreed. The *Magee Courier*, a newspaper from a nearby town, seethed that the Department of Housing, Education and Welfare would no longer give funds to schools that did not comply with mandatory desegregation. In a common refrain, paper's editor argued that the federal government was destroying public schools by removing White parents' choice to send their children to segregated schools. There was no freedom of choice, one editor claimed. He either ignored or missed the fact that the current segregated system destroyed freedom of choice for Black parents.[13]

While White Mississippians blamed the federal government for destroying public schools, they were the ones to blame for the ensuing decline of public education. Necessarily speaking in race-neutral terms, they created segregation academies, arguing that as Christian parents they were protecting their children.[14] Over the next few months, the *Simpson County News* consistently ran front-page stories detailing the rise of Simpson Academy. The paper reported on January 15 that over four hundred people attended a meeting at Robert Odenwald's former church, First Baptist Church in Mendenhall, to discuss setting up a private school. The newspaper seemed to support the move, noting that 260 families had registered their children and cautioning readers to not judge their neighbors who did not join the private school. Private schools, after all, cost money, and not all Whites could afford to maintain their God-demanded racial purity that way. Following editions laid out the fee structure, the football calendar, and a note from Senator M. M. McGowan, who would

---

[13] Thomas Sensing, "Destroying the Public Schools," *The Magee Courier*, January 1, 1970, Simpson County Chancery Office.
[14] J. Russell Hawkins, *Because the Bible Told Them So: How Southern Evangelicals Fought to Preserve White Supremacy* (New York: Oxford University Press, 2021), chap. 5.

later speak at Simpson Academy's groundbreaking ceremony and who praised their efforts, saying, "In my humble opinion this is the only way we are going to rescue America from socialist and communist ruin. It is going to take sacrifice, labor and toil to do this. But the salvation of America is at stake."[15]

FINDING THE FREEDOM TO FORGIVE

Let us now return to the beginning of our story about John. In 1970, as White readers read about the new private, segregated school while sipping their morning coffee, John languished in jail, beaten for teaching and living out the gospel in all aspects of his life. He had joined others to register folks to vote, he had worked to develop people and resist an economic system that subordinated Black people through cooperatives, he had supported an economic boycott demanding police reform and equal employment in Mendenhall, and he had advocated for school integration. All this had been in the five years *after* the Voting Rights Act prohibited racially targeted voting restrictions and six years *after* the Civil Rights Act banned segregation in public places.

When we step back and consider the timing of these events, the goals and means of the civil rights movement become more complex and expansive. Black folks' concerns—and perhaps the good of all Americans—were not resolved just by legislation and court cases. They had to be enacted on the ground, by people who exercised great courage and a commitment to their community.

The night after John was ambushed and arrested for his refusal to back down on the boycott, Vera Mae found someone to drive her and some others up to the Brandon jail. Sherriff Edwards would let only the women into the jail. As Vera Mae met John, he whispered, "Get me out of here. Get me out of here because they gonna kill me first."[16] Nathaniel Rubin, president of the Simpson County Civil League, which Black citizens had founded a few years prior, traversed the county asking Black property owners to post their property for bond for those in prison. Alfoncia Hill had enough property to cover John's bond and signed the note.

---

[15]"Charter Received by Directors of Private Academy," *Simpson County News*, January 29, 1970, Simpson County Chancery Office.

[16]John Perkins, *Let Justice Roll Down: John Perkins Tells His Own Story* (Ventura, CA: G/L, 1976), 167.

Once out of jail, John eventually settled in court with the state of Mississippi. He and the Black community saw the settlement as a victory because he had refused to roll over and submit completely to Mississippi justice. As John noted, "The local court lost the power to intimidate Blacks. And local Blacks won a great moral victory."[17] The *Simpson County News* reported on the front page that Perkins's case was being heard but gave little detail. White people in Simpson County seemed only to be hardening their positions toward Black equality.

John paid a profound cost in his body and soul for the beating. That summer, John was planning to officiate the wedding ceremony of Dolphus Weary and Rosie Marie Camper. Like all the White folks, Rosie ran an ad in the *Simpson County News* announcing her wedding. She wanted Black folks to know they could do the same. Crippled by his wounds, John could not officiate.[18] He was soon hospitalized in Mississippi's Delta region, where he had been organizing cooperatives. Through the summer and fall of 1970, John was in and out of the hospital in Mound Bayou. There a White Catholic doctor and a Black doctor treated him.

As an all-Black community, Mound Bayou provided a sanctuary for John away from the evil he had experienced at White people's hands. He remembered, "That kind of separate existence among Blacks was the only thing I could take during those months of pain." He knew so many Black people who had come to a point where they gave up hope that White people could change and turned toward separatist Black Power—Stokely Carmichael, Rap Brown, George Jackson, Eldred Cleaver. He knew of others who had turned away from Christianity, building their lives apart from what they saw as a White God. John was in a moment of crisis: "My whole humanity, my whole self was telling me to reject everything I had once worked for. Not to give up. Oh no! But to work for something different. To give up on whites and white Christians and to work only for me and mine."[19] While he had seen growth and leadership development among fellow Blacks, he had seen so few White Christians change. He wrote, "I believed that the gospel was powerful enough

---

[17] John Perkins, *Let Justice Roll Down*, 187.
[18] "Engagement for Miss Rosie Marie Camper to Dolphus Weary Is Being Announced," *Simpson County News*, July 30, 1970, Simpson County Chancery Office. See also Dolphus Weary and Rosie Weary, interview by author, May 21, 2021.
[19] Perkins, *Let Justice Roll Down*, 201.

to shatter even the hatred of Mendenhall. But I had not seen it. Especially in the churches."[20]

Somehow, John did not give up hope. The White doctor's presence helped him, meeting him "on the level of my humanity" and not just on a theological level. He pondered the few other White people who had helped him, "who believed in justice. Who lived love. Who shared themselves. Who joined our community." He remembered how he had seen people, young and old, in Mendenhall transformed. And he remembered that Jesus too suffered deeply, facing an unjust trial, a lynch mob, and finally murder. He wanted to be like Jesus, to forgive. Finally, "The spirit of God kept working on me and in me until I could say with Jesus, 'I forgive them, too.'"[21]

As John walked through this valley of the shadow of death, hovering between hatred and forgiveness, Vera Mae tended to the family. She drove up to see him, carrying her youngest child, Elizabeth, with her in the car. John's doctor told Vera Mae that they needed to move out of Mendenhall or the stress would kill her husband. Vera Mae purchased a house in Jackson, the state capital.[22]

TRANSFERRING LEADERSHIP

Moving to Jackson changed the Perkinses' relationship to Mendenhall and marked a turning point in their calling. Initially, the Perkinses lived in Jackson and commuted to Mendenhall to work in the ministry on the weekends and full time during the summer months, when they ran Christian enrichment camps for children. The camps, which remain a mainstay of the Mendenhall Ministries, worked to help children to be successful in the newly integrated schools.[23] John began to see Jackson as an opportunity to expand his reach, to mentor more people from all racial backgrounds in how to live the gospel holistically. By the 1980s in Jackson, he would develop his three *R*'s of Christian community development, which called people to *relocate* among the poor, to *reconcile* people to God and to one another, and to *redistribute* resources to restructure their local contexts so all could flourish.[24]

---

[20] Perkins, *Let Justice Roll Down*, 203.
[21] Perkins, *Let Justice Roll Down*, 204-5.
[22] Vera Mae Perkins, interview.
[23] Priscilla Perkins, interview by author, May 10, 2021.
[24] For the vision, see Wayne Gordon and John M. Perkins, *Making Neighborhoods Whole: A Handbook for Christian Community Development* (Downers Grove, IL: InterVarsity Press, 2010).

In Mendenhall, ministry leadership passed to Artis and Carolyn (Albritton) Fletcher and Dolphus and Rosie Weary. Artis served as pastor of the church, and Dolphus led the ministry arm. The pair understood themselves as the second generation of leadership, carrying the torch that John and Vera Mae had lit. To distinguish the work in Mendenhall from that in Jackson, they named the Mendenhall work the Mendenhall Ministries.[25] John's work in Jackson remained the Voice of Calvary.

In the coming years, the Mendenhall Ministries' actions would upset Mendenhall's racial geographies, establishing organizations in places that would seem out of place according to White folks' standards. The Wearys and the Fletchers oversaw the establishment of a medical clinic with a Black doctor, Dennis Adams, in uptown Mendenhall (the White section) that would treat Black and White patients equally. Even then, Whites resisted. The ministry was able to purchase the building only because the widow of the White doctor who had owned the building sold it to another White person, who covertly sold it to the ministry. They helped bring a law services office to the Black quarter. The movement of places chipped away at the hierarchies and distance between Black and White residents. Yet hierarchies and destructive racial norms remained. They established a Christian school, which was open to all people, but only a handful of White people ever attended.

The church and its ministry arm also worked at the legal level to establish justice. The law office's lawyer, a White woman named Suzanne Keys (now Griggins), who converted to Christianity through Pastor Fletcher's ministry, provided services for poor people and led action-impact legislation to change Mississippi's systems.[26] They sued the Simpson County Board of Education for paying Black educators unequally and hiring them on a discriminatory basis. For their efforts, members of the ministry faced persecution. Sometimes it was subtle, like when Rosie Weary tried to join a Bible study run by White women and was told she was not welcome. Other times it was more violent, like when the Fletchers and the Wearys were threatened by the Klan. But they persisted, trying to live out an answer to that old question: Can the gospel address poverty and racial injustice in substantial ways?

---

[25]See Dolphus Weary, *I Ain't Comin' Back* (Wheaton, IL: Tyndale House, 1990).
[26]Suzanne Griggins, interview by Paul Ericksen, 1987, Collection 375, Evangelism & Missions Archives, Wheaton College.

People associated with the Mendenhall Ministries continue to evangelize and disciple, do social action, develop the Black community, and work for justice. Scottye Holloway, who had voluntarily integrated a school in Mississippi, now leads the Mendenhall Ministries alongside Artis Fletcher, who still pastors the Mendenhall Bible Church. Scottye, whom Weary and Fletcher mentored, moved home to Mendenhall after decades of ministering in the Midwest. Dolphus and Rosie Weary moved north toward Jackson to work with Mission Mississippi, which explicitly fosters relationships between Black and White Christians, and founded the Rural Education and Leadership Development Fund to continue the work of people development.[27]

Artis, Carolyn, Rosie, Dolphus, and Scottye were among the many people who shared their stories with me when I stayed in Mississippi to immerse myself in the state's racial history so I could better understand John's and Vera Mae's work in the 1960s. Questions of what changed and what remained the same loomed over me, intellectually and personally. I was not at a distance, in my comfortable Midwestern house. I was walking Mendenhall's streets that hot, sticky summer, with stories of the Klan persecuting the people I had met racing through my mind, somewhat anxious for my family who joined me. Would someone target us because one daughter carried around a Black baby doll?

Many patterns from the past persisted, both good and bad. The town remains profoundly different on either side of the railroad tracks, the dividing line between the Black and White parts of town. I stayed in the Black part of town, across from the Perkinses' old house in a house that had recently been rebuilt by volunteers after a tornado partially destroyed it. But run-down shacks bore witness to the poverty that persisted. I was pregnant with our fourth child, and I searched for a pool, longing for the relief water's buoyancy would offer my aching body, in vain because the town had filled their pool in rather than integrate. Truly, we live in a world shaped by the past. And yet, people at the Mendenhall Bible Church are growing in their relationship with God and have a powerful faith in his goodness and provision. The Mendenhall Ministries continues to live out the fullness of the gospel. Continuities continue to exist.

---

[27]Peter Slade, *Open Friendship in a Closed Society: Mission Mississippi and a Theology of Friendship* (New York: Oxford, 2009).

Yet some things had clearly changed. Now the streets in Mendenhall's Black quarter are paved, and the town is not entirely segregated. The medical clinic Voice of Calvary started treats Black and White patients. Those working for racial changes no longer face constant harassment and fear. Houses Voice of Calvary built with a cooperative provide decent housing. Some Black-owned businesses thrive, patronized by White and Black customers alike, such as Café 320, where I purchased donuts for my kids.

John's and Vera Mae's efforts to put their faith to work alongside that of many others have changed Mendenhall and Mississippi in some ways. But the questions this context demands still remain: How does the gospel speak to racism and poverty? In Mississippi, those questions cannot be ignored as easily as they can from my perch in the Chicago suburb of Wheaton.

Those questions cannot be answered without dealing with the weight of Mississippi's racial history—both the (sometimes false) stories people tell themselves and the truth of what happened. Over sixty years ago the Perkinses moved home. But Mississippi has over two hundred years of racial dynamics—starting with the forced removal of the Chocktaw and Chicasaw people west of the Mississippi so a race-based plantation economic system could take root. I ought not expect two hundred years to be undone in just sixty years. The inheritance of the past is too strong.

But our faith can change our context. As Dolphus wrote in 1979, "We need to constantly be aware that we can look back in history and see the way things were and then look at our present situation to determine how God would have us move."[28]

QUESTIONS AND IMPLICATIONS

John understood the problems of Black Americans—and poor people generally—to be both individual and systemic. Because of his perspective, he cannot be categorized neatly as a contemporary liberal, radical, or conservative.

- Do you approach problems in society more from a systemic or an individual level?

---

[28]Dolphus Weary, "From the Desk of the Director," *The Mendenhall Ministries*, November–December 1979.

- What have you learned about seeing systemic contexts? What have you learned about individual action?
- How would incorporating both systemic and individual understandings of sin and change affect how you approach race and poverty?

Perkins came to reconciliation, to preaching to White and Black people only after working sacrificially for justice. His focus on reconciliation, for which he is more well known, was not a main point in this chapter because the chapter did not extend chronologically to his developing commitment to racial reconciliation. During his beating in the Brandon jail—which took a massive toll on his body—and in his recovery, he came to a point where he believed he needed to preach to White *and* Black folks. He has spent his life since then preaching to people with love from all racial backgrounds—offending and encouraging them equally. The order of his experience is significant, though, preventing his efforts for reconciliation from being cheap. He worked for Black empowerment before working for reconciliation. Often White Christians today want to prioritize reconciliation without accounting for the suffering and inequality we are inheriting.

- Do you prioritize reconciliation over justice or vice versa?
- How would accounting for both change your actions and perspectives?

PART III

HUMILITY

Clarence Jordan and the Cotton Patch Gospel

*The crowning evidence that [Jesus] lives is not
a vacant grave, but a spirit-filled fellowship.
Not a rolled-away stone, but a carried-away church.*

Clarence Jordan, *Incarnational Evangelism*

10

FAITH IS BETTING YOUR LIFE ON UNSEEN REALITIES

Why White farmer and pastor Clarence Jordan did not follow the norms of White southern Christianity and why humility is necessary to faithfully piece together his story.

A WORKER IN THE FIELD

"I think there's a universal attraction to working toward . . . dreams, like the idea of being a fool for Christ," reflected Dorothy Day the year after Clarence died.[1] Being a fool for Christ got her into the mess in the first place. Shots rang out in the dark, and those in the car who fired yelled out in the night. Dorothy's heart sank down to her boots. She was committed to nonviolence, but she did not want to die. She marveled at how Clarence took the violence in stride. "He was a southerner, he knew the hatred. . . . It's something diabolical."[2] Then it was over. She was alive. She and her fellow watchperson just stayed on watch and reported what happened when they were relieved. It was Lent, and the men were planting, so the women insisted on taking turns sitting up all night to deter attacks. There had already been so much violence.

This was not Korea, where John Perkins served in an official war. This was southwest Georgia, the heart of the Bible Belt in the mid-1950s. There

---

[1] Dorothy Day, interview by Dallas Lee, January 27, 1970, Koinonia as Others See Us, Koinonia Farm Archive.
[2] Day, interview.

White Christians waged an unofficial war against Koinonia Farm and Clarence Jordan.

Dorothy first heard Clarence at a church in New York, sharing about the persecution the community that lived at Koinonia Farm was enduring. Dorothy was a friend of Catherine de Hueck and ran a ministry called the Catholic Worker, which had close ties with Friendship House.[3] Clarence preached a message Dorothy tried to live. He insisted that faithful Christian witness demanded that White Christians share spiritual, social, and economic fellowship as equals with all Christians—including Black ones.

Clarence and his bride, Florence, tried to live that out in everyday life as farmers outside the town of Americus, Georgia. In 1942, as World War II raged, they founded the farm with fellow missionaries Martin and Mabel England. Clarence had a draft exemption because he was a minister, though he would have been preferred the conscientious objector status. The Jordans were missionaries of a sort to White and Black American southerners. They wanted to preach the gospel as they taught their poor neighbors the latest in scientific farming (Clarence had a bachelor's degree in agriculture). They also believed that the gospel called them to share possessions freely, even holding them in common, as had the early church. They joined their local Baptist church, and Clarence, who also held a master of divinity and PhD in Greek New Testament from the Southern Baptist Theological Seminary, preached regularly there and around the country.

At first most of their White neighbors liked them well enough, although many were troubled by their pacifism. But after the Supreme Court's decision in *Brown v. Board of Education* in 1954 made the White neighbors feel pressured to change the southern way of life, Koinonia Farm's White neighbors had begun an economic boycott and violently attacked the farm and its residents. The persecution had thrust Clarence and Koinonia Farm into the national spotlight, with press coverage in White and Black, Christian and secular circles. That's how Dorothy had ended up sharing the passion—the suffering—of Koinonia Farm that Lent.

Clarence and his son had Lenny picked Dorothy up at the train station. Clarence was "tall, handsome with a shock of auburn hair, sparkling eyes,

---

[3]For their correspondence, see Robert Wild, ed., *Comrades Stumbling Along: The Friendship of Catherine De Hueck Doherty and Dorothy Day as Revealed Through Their Letters* (New York: Alba House, 2009).

expressive face, muscularly powerful with almost unlimited energy."[4] He was quick to tell a joke and often smiled. He loved children and spoke to them as much at the dinner table as he did to adults. Clarence was creative; he had invented the first mobile peanut harvester. And Clarence shared abundantly; he never patented the machine but let others use the design. Clarence spoke in a measured way—probably too slow for a northerner like Dorothy. When he sat under a shade tree talking with a friend, he was gentle and listened to understand their point of view. Clarence turned ideas over in his mind thoroughly, measuring the problems, his son Jim remembered, "with the gospel of Jesus as his square and ruler."[5] When he knew what course of action to take, he moved.

Clarence acted because he wanted to live rightly, to align himself with his understanding of Scripture. Like John, he wanted consistency between his beliefs and actions. For Clarence, faith was not an intellectual assent, nor was it "belief in spite of the evidence but a life in scorn of the consequences"—faith was doing what you knew was right, even if it cost you everything.[6] He also wanted others to act—especially the White southern Christians whom he saw as enslaved to the god of mammon. They supported the boycott against the farm and were mostly silent when people shot into the families' houses on the farm, blew up their roadside stand, or cut down fruit trees they had planted years before. Blue jeans were his uniform, except for when he donned a plain suit for preaching. From the pulpit he sometimes thundered but more often explained thoughtfully how he understood Scripture speaking on war, brotherhood, and materialism. Clarence thought that people's right understanding of Scripture would cause them to change.

As we study Clarence, we will practice humility, which doing history (and walking faithfully as a Christian) requires. Humility, for Thomas Aquinas, was the beginning of Christian virtue. But our focus will not be on the extent to which Clarence was a humble person. Instead, we will first pay attention to our own limits as people—in this case, our limited ability to understand what happened. Humility—and good historical thinking—does not lead to

---

[4]Conrad Browne in Kay Weiner, ed., *Koinonia Remembered* (Americus, GA: Koinonia, 1992), 94.
[5]Jim Jordan, in Weiner, *Koinonia Remembered*, 96.
[6]Clarence Jordan, "The Substance of Faith," in *Clarence Jordan: Essential Writings*, ed. Joyce Hollyday (New York: Orbis Books, 2003), 43. Clarence's definition of faith is used regularly when talking about him. See, for instance, Frederick L. Downing, *Clarence Jordan: A Radical Pilgrimage in Scorn of the Consequences* (Macon, GA: Mercer University Press, 2017).

proud assertion of what we know. Nor does it lead to a sense of superiority over those in the past because of what they did not know or do, compared to us in the present. Humility leads us to specify our ignorance, stating clearly what we do *not* know. Humility requires us to ask wondering questions. It necessitates sitting in those questions, not fully resolving them, and then only with messy answers. Humility actually requires a great deal of courage and being uncomfortable. But God has not called us to comfort.

THE RED SOIL: SEGREGATION IN GEORGIA

The word *humility* comes from the root word *humus*, or "soil." The soil in Georgia is striking. Clarence grew up in Talbotton, Georgia, about sixty miles north of where he later founded Koinonia Farm, playing in Georgia's red soil made famous by the film *Gone with the Wind*. The first time I touched that soil at Koinonia Farm, I was in awe. It was so bright red, it seemed almost unreal. It stained my running shoes and got into the cracks in my son's rain boots. And it had captured my mind as a child when I encountered the book and the movie *Gone with the Wind*. With Scarlett O'Hara, I wept at the destruction of her plantation, Tara—which meant the dirt, that red soil. I believed that she, and by extension other kindly slave owners deeply hurt in the War of Northern Aggression, would rebuild her life because, after all, tomorrow is another day. The movie *Gone with the Wind* came out in 1939, the year Hitler invaded Poland, and became the highest-grossing film in America, surpassing even *The Birth of a Nation* (1915). These films' success reveals that the vision of the old South and comfort with segregation was not just a southern thing but a vision that captured the hearts and minds of many White Americans across the nation.

The two films had similar themes that resonated with White Americans across the country. They lamented the loss of the old South during the Civil War and portrayed enslaved African Americans as contentedly serving loving masters. But they denied the inhuman commodification of Black people's bodies; ignored the destruction of Black families as children were sold away from their mothers; passed over the curiously light-skinned babies of Black mothers, impregnated by their White masters; overlooked the suffering of White women as they turned a blind eye to their husbands' abuse of Black women and then beat the hell out of Black women to make them pay for the

White mistress's pain; disregarded the unjust labor conditions Black and White sharecroppers faced separately, prevented by race from uniting and working for just labor conditions; discounted the distortion of White Christians' souls as they devalued their Black brothers and sisters, ignoring the *imago Dei*. As I read many books about slavery in the United States, the Civil War, and Reconstruction, I realized that these truths were undoing the powerful *Gone with the Wine* narrative that had shaped my own imagination. Today, these truths seem self-evident to me, but they were not acknowledged in Clarence's world.

Clarence was a son of the South, born into a locally prominent family that did not question segregation. Enslaved Africans and their descendants had farmed the soil for about three hundred years alongside and for White owners. By the early twentieth century, Whites had established segregation in southwest Georgia. Like in John's experiences in Mississippi, White people thought that "Negroes" should stay "in their place" in society. As Ossie Little, an African American Koinonia resident, remembered, "Blacks had to walk to school while the whites took the bus. Whites had Black children sweep yards. We only interacted with the whites when we worked for them. We had to go in the back door of restaurants. We had to sit on the Black side and we were served there. At the movies we had to go in the back door."[7]

In the 1930s and 1940s, Americus, the largest town close to Koinonia, saw the establishment of several separate "colored" institutions, which could make it appear progressive. Newspapers report the establishment of a separate playground for "Negro" children in 1930, a separate hospital in 1940— which demonstrated how well the White citizens cared for "colored" folks (no matter that Black citizens endured the 1919 flu pandemic without a hospital), a separate theater in 1948, and a "Negro" library in 1955.[8] But as in Mississippi, segregation fundamentally kept Black people in their place, even as White and Black people lived closely together. Jimmy Carter, a White man who became US president in 1976 and grew up close to Americus, remembered:

> All my playmates were Black. We never went to the same church or school. Our social life and our church life were strictly separate. We did not sit together on the two-car diesel passenger train that could be flagged down in Archery

---

[7]Ossie Little, n.d., "Segregation," Koinonia Farm Archive.
[8]Historian Evan Kutzler made this observation to me when he gave me a historical tour of Americus.

[where his home was]. There was a scrupulous compliance with these unwritten and unspoken rules. I never heard them questioned. Not then.[9]

LOVE LIFTED ME

If no White people questioned segregation, as Jimmy Carter said, how did Clarence come to do so? It would be easy to think of Clarence Jordan as a singularly unique southern White man, a lone ranger who came to his convictions on his own. But our work on John and Vera Mae Perkins's theology and experiences shows that a person's context matters. Historians have probed exceptions to the norm Jimmy Carter described—not only the few White southern pastors who joined the civil rights movement in the 1950s but social gospel White and Black southerners who partnered (often on unequal terms) to advance African American education, the interracialism of the 1920s and 1930s that worked within the segregated system to address racial problems, and the radical Christian labor organizing of the 1930s that drew together sharecroppers across racial lines.[10]

Yet the question still remains: How did *Clarence* come to believe in—and then live out in sometimes limited ways, but ways askance to his culture—the equality of African American and White people? Clarence's own telling of his story in later years contains several key moments, moments that have resonated with others who have written about Clarence. As we use his memories, we will remember—as we saw with Catherine de Hueck—to treat these sources carefully as we seek to tell a true story. With memory, we do not always know the significance of a moment as it happens, but when we look back, we can see that it was a turning point. For Clarence, there were key moments when he saw the world clearly and knew how he wanted to live in light of foundational church lessons about loving God and loving others.

TALBOTTON

Born in 1912, Clarence grew up as a middle child in a prosperous family with seven children. He lived in town by the courthouse and jail, a location that

---

[9]Jimmy Carter, quoted at Jimmy Carter Boyhood Farm, Archery, Georgia, visited March 2023.
[10]See, for instance, Elaine Allen Lechtreck, *Southern White Ministers and the Civil Rights Movement* (Jackson: University Press of Mississippi, 2018); Tracy Elaine K'Meyer, *Interracialism and Christian Community in the Postwar South: The Story of Koinonia Farm* (Charlottesville: University of Virginia Press, 2000), chap. 1.

would have a profound impact on him. His family attended First Baptist, and Clarence loved the song about Jesus loving all the little children, "red and yellow, Black and White." But it seemed like God might love some children more, no matter what he was taught in church. After all, Clarence noticed, "At Christmas, the white children were given the good oranges while the Negro children got rotten oranges from the merchant's garbage pail."[11]

Clarence also remembered cognitive dissonance arising from the prison system. A 1911 survey of chain gangs in Georgia counted 2,000 African American and 180 White prisoners.[12] Clarence would talk to the Black inmates who lived close by and observe their conditions. He recalled,

> I saw men with short chains locked between their feet to keep them from running, men bolted into the agonizing shame of primitive pillories, men beaten with whips or their bodies torn under the stress of the "stretcher"—a small frame structure in which a man could be placed with his feet fastened at the floor and his hand tied to ropes above him that extended to a block and tackle on the outside. I saw that almost all these men were Black. This made a tremendous, traumatic impression on me.[13]

Two hot summer nights stuck out in Clarence's mind. He had been at an evening revival at church and had seen the White jail warden praising God, singing "Love Lifted Me." Revivals, times of frequent gatherings and intense spiritual focus, were common in the South. The next night, Clarence heard one of the inmates' cries of agony as that same warden put him on the stretcher and tortured him. "I was torn to pieces," Clarence said. "I identified totally with that man in the stretcher. His agony was my agony. I really got mad with God. If the warden was an example of God's love, I didn't want anything to do with Him."[14]

COLLEGE

Though his family was well-to-do, Clarence lived in a poor place where people eked out a living from the soil. He observed that "preachers were always thundering about Hell and brimstone when it seemed to me they should have spent

---

[11] Quoted in Ansley Lillian Quiros, *God with Us: Lived Theology and the Freedom Struggle in Americus, Georgia, 1942–1976* (Chapel Hill: University of North Carolina Press, 2018), 17.
[12] Mills Lane, *People of Georgia: An Illustrated History* (New York: Beehive, 1975).
[13] Quoted in Hamilton Jordan, *No Such Thing as a Bad Day* (New York: Pocket Books, 2000), 126.
[14] Quoted in Jordan, *No Such Thing*, 127.

a little time telling about phosphate and limestone," which would have fertilized the crops.[15] Clarence determined to use agriculture to deal a blow to the sharecropping system that kept Black farmers on the lower rungs of society. He went to study agriculture at the University of Georgia in Athens, meaning "to come back to my people to help unite them in Christian love and brotherhood."[16]

Clarence joined the ROTC in college but became a pacifist during a summer training camp. As he wrote,

> The class that day was a mounted drill on the edge of the woods. I was on horseback and galloping through the woods with my pistol and saber drawn. We were to shoot the cardboard dummies and stick the straw dummies with our sabers. Every time I would shoot one of those dummies, that verse, "But I say unto you, love your enemies," would flash through my mind.[17]

For Clarence, "it was crystal clear that Jesus was going one way and I was going another." He resigned his commission.

By his senior year, 1932–1933, Clarence began to think that success in farming might not solve African Americans' problems. He wrote to his mother, "Whites seemed to have the very things I wanted Blacks to have . . . and the whites were living in such a hell. Why should I feel that Blacks would be in any less of a hell if they had these things?"[18] Adequate food and standard of living mattered, but Clarence was meditating more on things of the spirit. He concluded "that men do not live by bread alone but by words that proceed from the mouth of God. So I went to the Southern Baptist Seminary to learn what those words of God might be."[19] Clarence would soon develop a sensibility about the gospel that differed dramatically from the mangled White southern Christianity that had nurtured him. Love was lifting him to a new way of living.

LOUISVILLE

Southern Baptist Seminary was in Louisville, Kentucky, the end point for some Black migrants in the Great Migration. Clarence's years in Louisville were significant for three reasons.

---

[15]Clarence Jordan, "Ordeal by Bullets," *Liberation*, May 1957.
[16]Jordan, *No Such Thing*, 137.
[17]Quoted in Jordan, *No Such Thing*, 127.
[18]Letter quoted in Quiros, *God with Us*, 19.
[19]Jordan, "Ordeal by Bullets."

First, Clarence fell in love with the Scriptures. Second, he fell in love with Florence Kroeger. Florence worked at the library and, as the daughter of German immigrants, was an outsider.[20] Clarence shared his dream of returning home to "do something for the poor" with her, and she agreed.[21] The couple married in 1936, the year Clarence finished his master's in theology. Clarence continued his studies of New Testament Greek because he wanted to get as close to the New Testament church as possible, with only limited interventions because of translation, denomination, and tradition.[22] Clarence and Florence also created a fellowship of students—a Koinonia—who pooled their financial resources and shared a common life.

Scholars usually emphasize that Clarence came to his theological positions—especially on race—through reading the Scriptures. And Clarence fueled this perspective by observing how helpful it was to have a PhD in New Testament Greek in such a Bible-steeped culture, especially when he was speaking prophetically to that culture. His biblical expertise gave him credibility in a culture that emphasized reading the Bible, and he could—and did—say he was just following what it said.

But I wonder how much African Americans influenced his perspective on the Scriptures. The contexts in which we read Scripture shape the questions we ask of it. An intense scholarly focus *was* significant for Clarence. But he also received the gift of learning from mature Black Christians about the implications of the gospel while in Louisville. I wonder whether Clarence underemphasized his tutelage under Black Christians when talking to White Christians about how he reached his positions because most fellow White Christians *could* abide by the standard of the Bible but would not abide by the testimony of Black brothers and sisters.

As we will see in later chapters, there were limits to his relationships with African Americans. But this is the third significant point—in Louisville, Clarence worked with Black Christians in contexts that bordered on and maybe achieved equality. Let us consider the significance of Clarence's interactions with Black Christians and wonder how it shaped his perspectives on

---

[20]Obituary of Florence Jordan, in 2A. Iii)b) Florence Jordan, Koinonia Farm Papers, Americus, GA.
[21]Quoted in Joyce Hollyday, "The Dream That Has Endured: Clarence Jordan and Koinonia—Koinonia Farm," *Sojourners*, December 1, 1979, www.koinoniafarm.org/history-center/articles/the-dream-that-has-endured-clarence-jordan-and-koinonia/.
[22]Quiros, *God with Us*, 20.

Scripture and life, while still accounting for Scripture's influence on his decisions. Let us practice humility.

As Clarence finished his PhD in 1939, he began working at the Sunshine Center in Louisville's West End. It was a Baptist outreach arm that evangelized Black migrants, funded by White Christians. Clarence received a great deal as he worked on more equal footing with African Americans. He petitioned to change the name to the Fellowship Center, reflecting his growing sense of partnership. He wrote, "The only way . . . constructive work, agreeable to both groups can be done [is if White workers] 'understand that they are *helpers* rather than bosses and put on equal footing with the other workers.'"[23] Clarence sounds here like he had learned the lesson Catherine's friend and coworker Ellen Tarry taught: that White people must work *with*, not for, African Americans. But a sense of paternalism would be hard for a White man to shake, especially living in a culture that idealized him as the benefactor.[24] I wonder, then, the extent to which Clarence lived out this ideal.

Clarence also worshiped under the leadership of Black Christians. From 1936–1941, he taught at Simmons University, which served African American preachers.[25] Since he was working in a Black community, Clarence joined a "Negro" church, to the chagrin of his White denominational employers. Clarence responded that the early church's fellowship among Jews and Gentiles ended the distinctions between racial groups.[26] Clarence later described his experience working in the Black ghetto as a "spiritual awakening." Alongside Black Christians, with fellow White seminarians, and with Florence, he observed that the church was failing in three areas: race, war, and materialism. That he was in fellowship with Black Christians during his time in Louisville is essential, I think, to understanding how Clarence broke out of the mold cast for southern White preachers.

---

[23]Quoted in Quiros, *God with Us*, 20.

[24]For a powerful discussion of how theological education socializes people toward independent mastery of material rather than connection, holding this up as the ideal that White men especially must live into, see Willie Jennings, *After Whiteness: An Education in Belonging* (Grand Rapids, MI: Eerdmans, 2020).

[25]William S. Lee, "FBI Report on Koinonia Farm," Atlanta, May 11, 1951, Federal Bureau of Investigation, Koinonia Farm Archive. In 1940, Clarence became director of the Baptist Fellowship Center, and the following year he was the superintendent of missions for the Long Run Association of Baptists.

[26]Quiros, *God with Us*, 20.

Clarence's experience in urban Louisville convinced him he would be more useful back in a rural setting. At Fellowship Center, Clarence met people who had relocated from Georgia and Alabama, looking for work and a better life. But unlike John Perkins, who would leave Mississippi for California within the decade, these folks had not found success. As Clarence later reflected, "The city was grinding them up. It drove me to get back to the areas that were vomiting these people up and see if we couldn't reverse the trend from the farms to the city."[27] Clarence wanted to solve the problems of urban ghettos by going to what he saw as the root—the poor economic conditions for Black sharecroppers—and he wanted to do this while living the gospel in fellowship with other Christians.

QUESTIONS AND IMPLICATIONS

Clarence thought each generation needed to learn and live out anew the good news of God. For him, the church, as Jesus' body, was the continuation of the Word—Jesus—becoming flesh and dwelling among us. As he wrote in a 1949 Sunday school book for high school students, the kingdom of God grows from seeds, not from roots. Referring to the parable of the soils, Clarence observed that the seeds must be planted into the soil—the hearts—of each new generation, which then must embody Jesus. He said of the first disciples:

> They were demonstrations (witnesses, they called themselves) of the things which the Lord Jesus had done in and through them. And *your* witness to this generation is as vital as theirs was to their generation. The rest of the world will understand only so much of the kingdom as they see in *you*. . . . Why can't a world torn asunder by racial prejudice look upon men and women who have learned from Jesus the lesson of love so well that they dwell together as brethren? . . . Why can't a world rotten with economic greed and exploitation be shown little groups of spiritual families who share with one another everything their good Father has given them? Can it be that *you* have anything to do with the answers to these questions?[28]

- How would you answer Clarence's questions as an individual Christian and as a part of your church?

---

[27]Quoted in Quiros, *God with Us*, 21.
[28]Clarence Jordan, *Lord and Master: Part I*, Judson Keystone Graded Course XI, Part 1-Pupil (Philadelphia: Judson, 1949), 71.

- Clarence almost lost his faith because of what he saw as the hypocrisy of White Christians. The cost of hypocrisy, coupled with a lack of repentance and humility, is high. For what do you all need to repent? How would repentance prepare the next generation's soil?
- Sometimes turning points happen to us and we do not plan them. But other times, we can plan turning points—or peak moments—for ourselves and for others. If the seeds have to be planted in each generation, how are you putting yourself and the next generation in contexts where they can be witnesses of what God has done to this generation?[29]

Studying and writing history requires humility, a word rooted in the Latin *humus*, which means "grounded or from the earth." It requires observing what you do not know, making clear to yourself and others where you are making educated guesses. When we do make claims about what happened in the past, we do so carefully because we know how limited we are in our ability to know what happened. Studying history can also open our eyes to the vastness of the human experience, and done well, it pushes us out from the center to the margins. This posture—a willingness to look for gaps in our knowledge—is contrary to contemporary society.

- How would leading with humility change your relations with others?
- What would a church characterized by humility look like?

---

[29] Chip Heath and Dan Heath, *The Power of Moments: Why Certain Experiences Have Extraordinary Impact* (New York: Simon & Schuster, 2017).

11

A DEMONSTRATION PLOT FOR THE KINGDOM

How those at Koinonia Farm sought life as though Jesus were actually among as they farmed and educated others, and why we should listen to them.

DEMONSTRATION PLOT

The soil on a four-hundred-acre plot of land sixty miles south of Talbotton that Clarence and Martin England visited was "about average" for that part of Georgia—erosion swept away the red dirt in the heavy summer rains, and it was poor in nutrients.[1] That soil was kind of like people, in need of redemption and restoration before it could produce abundant harvests. "The soil seems to be kin to humanity," Clarence commented. "It seems to know that we, too, are just soil. It reacts very slowly."[2] The plot would be perfect as a demonstration plot for the kingdom, to bring about the restoration of all things. It would be a place Clarence loved.

The term *demonstration plot* came from Clarence's undergraduate training in agriculture. It describes a portion of land set aside to experiment with new farming techniques and to teach others. Demonstration plots brought scientific approaches to agriculture into farming. Clarence wanted to use Koinonia Farm to teach others to restore the soil and to help

---

[1] Clarence Jordan and Martin England to friend, December 1942, Koinonia Farm.
[2] William S. Lee, "FBI Report on Koinonia Farm," Atlanta, May 11, 1951, Federal Bureau of Investigation, Koinonia Farm Archive, 18.

sharecroppers improve their profit. The farm was a demonstration plot for spiritual ideas too. As they stated in an early pamphlet, they intended to "experiment with the application of the teachings of Jesus to a typical Southern rural community."

The Jordans, Englands, and others who joined them wanted to show their neighbors what it meant when people lived as though God were actually among them. They saw themselves as continuing the incarnation—God's dwelling among people—by embodying the good news. Florence said the incarnation was the "fleshing out of Jesus' teachings: through changed attitudes and lifestyle and through action."[3] As they wrote in their first newsletter, they were convicted about "the brotherhood of *all* men, about the way of love as an alternative to hatred and violence, about man being more valuable than mammon, about Christian communal living."[4]

They called their community Koinonia Farm. *Koinonia* is the Greek word for "fellowship," which Clarence took from the description of the early church in Acts 2:42. As Clarence translated it, "They were all bound together by the officers' instruction and by the sense of community, by the common meal and the prayers."

VALUE ONE: CARE FOR THE LAND

A demonstration plot for the kingdom required loving the land, nurturing it, and honoring it because it provided for them. Clarence loved the land. He later remembered,

> We bought that old, run-down, eroded piece of land. It was sick. There were gashes in it. It was sore and bleeding. I don't know whether you've ever walked over a piece of ground that could almost cry out to you and say, "Heal me, heal me!" I don't know whether you feel the closeness to the soil that I do. But when you fill in those old gullies and terrace the fields and you begin to feel the springiness of the sod beneath your feet and you see that old land come to life, and when you walk through that little old pine forest that you set out in little seedlings and now you see them reaching for the sky and hear the wind through them. . . . Men say to you, "Why don't you sell it and move away?" They might as well ask you, "Why don't you sell your mother?"

---

[3]Florence Jordan, spring 1982, in 2A. iii)b) Florence Jordan, Koinonia Farm Archive.
[4]Koinonia Farm, "Newsletter," December 1942, Koinonia Farm Archive.

Somehow God made us out of this old soil and we go back to it and we never lose its claim on us.[5]

The work was hard. In 1942, Clarence and Martin went to the farm before their wives and children to prepare it. They planted a garden, clearing the knee-deep Bermuda grass and hitching each other to the plow because they had no mule. Although Clarence had agricultural training, he knew little about the practical aspects of farming in that specific region and would joke that they decided when to plant their crops by copying their neighbors. But they also invested for the long term, planting trees and perennials—"apple, pecan, peach, walnut, pear, plum, fig, apricot, nectarine, Chinese chestnut, Japanese persimmon—and other fruit and berries, grapes, scuppernongs, muscadines" (which Clarence would use to make his favorite wine), "strawberries, raspberries, improved Blackberries, Youngberries, and Boysenberries." In the first four years, they terraced forty-six thousand feet, added about two hundred tons of lime, phosphate, and slag to the soil, and increased the fertility by 20 percent.[6]

For both families, the farm was an act of faith. Clarence observed that Florence always said God would supply their needs but that she was one of the few people who would "give Him a chance to do so."[7] When Mabel and Florence brought their children to the farm, they felt like it was an adventure. Florence remembered that there was no running water; they made their meals on a wood stove and cleaned their clothes in an iron pot outside.[8] But they also quickly found more economic success than most of their neighbors. One key reason was that they worked together, farming in community.

VALUE TWO: SHARING LIFE IN COMMON

Clarence believed Christians should share life in common, with everyone having what they needed materially. He read the Luke's description of the early church in the book of Acts as normative.

What did life in common look like?

---

[5]Quoted in Bren Dubay, "Setting the Table at Koinonia Farm," *Plough Quarterly* (Winter 2015): 9.
[6]Lee, "FBI Report on Koinonia Farm," 18.
[7]Clarence Jordan to Florence Jordan, November 18, 1942, in 2A iii) b) [i] Florence's Writings, Koinonia Farm Archive.
[8]Florence Jordan, spring 1982.

First, families remained intact. As Florence observed, "Though we consider the whole group as one spiritual family, we recognize the place of the biological family and live in separate houses or apartments, grouped in a little village."[9]

Second, they shared the planning, work, and play of the farm. They met daily for prayer and worship and frequently convened to discuss the farm and governance. They worked together on the farm, ran a Bible school for local children, played softball, held parties for themselves and their neighbors, picnicked at old Picnic Hill, went swimming in the river, and welcomed visitors—the town drunk, members of other intentional communities such as the Hutterites, the curious, and FBI men. The women usually watched the children, canned, and prepared the food, while the men worked in the fields. As more individuals and families joined the community, they were folded into the daily patterns. By the early 1950s, the promise of community life, not the desire to teach others to farm (or even necessarily to farm themselves), drew people to Koinonia, and the community included about sixty people—both full members and those who participated deeply in the life of the community but had not signed the covenant.[10]

Life together was challenging. While Clarence was clearly the spiritual leader, he avoided asserting himself during group deliberations (although when he did choose a course of action and pushed for his perspective, some of the other children mocked the four Jordan kids, saying their daddy was a dictator). Community members regularly had to forgive one another, and few who joined stayed long term. As member Claud Nelson commented, "Our group feels keenly its own failures to make its ideal of love and unity fully real, particularly in its relationships with some who have left Koinonia."[11] Nelson observed, "Several people have left the group, usually because of a spouse who could not adjust to group living. It seems hard to find *two*, man and wife, who are interested together. To join such a group is really just as much of a decision as getting married."[12]

---

[9] Florence Jordan, "Koinonia Community, Americus, Ga." (circa 1960), in 2A iii) b) [i] Florence's Writings, Koinonia Farm Archive.

[10] Andrew S. Chancey, "Koinonia Farm," in *New Georgia Encyclopedia*, 2005, www.georgiaencyclopedia.org/articles/arts-culture/koinonia-farm/.

[11] Claud Nelson to Marcia and Dick Cowles, April 6, 1954, Claud Nelson correspondence, Koinonia Farm Archive.

[12] Claud Nelson to Don Wetzels, August 18, 1952, Claud Nelson correspondence, Koinonia Farm Archive.

Third, and most contrary to typical American sensibilities, life in common extended to their money, and they resisted accumulating wealth. "Man is more valuable than mammon," Clarence observed repeatedly. While wealth and possessions influenced a person's social position in churches and more generally, the Koinonia held their financial assets in common to prevent the group from kowtowing to those who had the most money.

Is Christian love real when ownership is private?

That question reverberated at Koinonia Farm. The vast differences in standards of living between brothers and sisters in Christ that characterized Sumter County troubled the Koinonia. Poor people lived in run-down shacks with no running water but plenty of roaches, and wealthy people lived in nice houses with plenty of plumbing and no cold nights due to a lack of fuel. But at Koinonia, everyone lived at a similar standard of living. Common ownership meant, as Clarence said, that "we join our lives with others. We are brothers. . . . When you proceed on this basis then people become more important than property. How long could Christian love last with private ownership?"[13]

Members of Koinonia sought to live simply and take what they needed. Clarence reflected that Christians should distribute goods according to need, not greed.[14] Each member or family shared with the community what their needs were, and they received money from the common purse to meet those needs. One person's needs were different from another's. Clarence noted that for him, books were a need, perhaps even more than food. He had to have books to live, but others did not share his love of reading. If he came to the community and said, "I need money to buy some books," they would provide it for him.[15] When asked how one knew how much one needed, Clarence responded, "The emptier a man is on the inside, the more he feels he has to have on the outside."[16]

Living like this demanded that members reorder their loves. When Clarence translated 1 John from the Greek, he read, "Don't love the old order or the thing which keep it going. If anyone loves the old order it is not the Father's love that's in him. For everything that's in the old order—the hankering for physical comforts, the hankering for material things, the emphasis

---

[13] Clarence Jordan, "AT 100-4223" (n.d.), Federal Bureau of Investigation, Koinonia Farm Archive.
[14] "Legacy of Clarence Jordan: His Final Interview," *Faith at Work*, April 1970.
[15] "Legacy of Clarence Jordan."
[16] "Legacy of Clarence Jordan."

on status—is not from the Father but from the old order itself."[17] Like the apostle Paul, Clarence said, "A person who is deeply satisfied at the spiritual level and has learned the deeper secrets of life can be happy with relatively few things" and won't seek after baubles. Clarence was learning "the secret of both feasting and fasting, of being loaded and being broke. With the help of him who empowers me, I feel up to *anything*."[18]

For Clarence, living simply did not mean embracing poverty, contrary to Catherine de Hueck. Clarence believed in living modestly but celebrating with abundance. "Jesus loved the feast and feast means abundance," Clarence argued. "But at the same time he rebuked those people who set their lives on possessions."[19]

Clarence thought many American Christians worshiped the false god of mammon. Americans were, he said, "so success oriented, so status-conscious, so materialistic," and imagined success was based on possessions. Materialism both hurt the one who worshiped material things and exploited others. But if you lived simply, you had enough to share.

Because the Koinonia held all things in common, many called them communists. As local pharmacist Dr. Wallace Frick observed, "They don't live according to Southern traditions. It seems like a communistic way of life, whether they have any Communist affiliations or not."[20] In the 1950s, during Koinonia's most intense persecution, a grand jury investigated the situation. The grand jury asserted in its findings that the farm appeared to be a communist front but wanted to let people draw their own conclusions.[21] In other words, they really did not have any evidence, but they were suspicious and so suggested the label. This label of *communist* has a history, and White southerners—and White Americans more generally—often used it to dismiss people.

The context for the accusation of communism also was significant. As we have seen in the North, White communists in the 1930s were some of the only

---

[17]Clarence Jordan, *The Cotton Patch Gospel* (Macon, GA: Smyth & Helwys, 2004), 1 John.
[18]Clarence Jordan, "Smithville, Alabama (Philippians)," in *The Cotton Patch Version of Paul's Epistles* (Piscataway, NJ: New Century, 1968), Philippians 4:10-13.
[19]Michael Ginsberg, "Koinonia Embraces All Beliefs," *Greenville Piedmont*, December 29, 1977, in Primary Resources 1970s, Outside Articles 1970s, Koinonia Farm Archive.
[20]John Pennington, "Koinonia Story—No. 6: What Citizens of Americus Really Think of Biracial Farm," n.d., in 2F—Primary Resources 1950s, Outside Articles 1950s, Koinonia Farm Archive.
[21]"Bi-racial Farm Appears to Be a Red Front, Americus Jury Says," n.d., in 2F Primary Resources 1950s, Koinonia Farm Archive.

White people concerned with African Americans' civil rights, and the Communist Party had some appeal for many Black people. Hardly any White Christians were concerned about the injustice African Americans faced in the North or the South—but White communists (who were rarely Christian) did care because they led with economic questions. By the late 1950s and into the 1960s, White southerners hurled the epithet *communist* at many of the activists—particularly those from the North—who came south for civil rights. In the context of the Cold War, which set the "Judeo-Christian" United States against the "godless" communists, this label meant someone was a dangerous outsider not only economically but also religiously and socially.

Not only was Koinonia accused of being communist, but the community had connections to others who were accused similarly, including Highlander Folk School in Tennessee.[22] Highlander Folk School had initially worked to organize labor, and after World War II it focused on training people in forms of nonviolent protest to desegregate the South. Like Koinonia, it was one of the few places in the South where people could hold interracial meetings. Both were outposts in a sea of segregation. When a court injunction forbid Koinonia Farm from hosting an interracial summer camp, they took the camp to Highlander. Highlander trained Rosa Parks before she refused to give up her bus seat in Montgomery. Koinonia resident Conrad Browne left Koinonia and worked at Highlander in 1963, when the farm was not making enough money to support his family, and civil rights activist Fannie Lou Hamer was one of the students at the first workshop Browne led.

Koinonia Farm improved life for Sumter County's White and Black residents materially and spiritually, and this concern for their neighbors was an extension of their communal living. They planted more than they could eat so they could share their produce. They developed a cow library, "where," Clarence said, "a family could come and take out a milk cow and keep her until she went dry and then take out another one."[23] They offered scientific farming classes and shared plans for Clarence's mobile peanut harvester. They introduced poultry farming, which Clarence had studied in college, to the region. Previously, Georgia imported about nineteen million dozen eggs from other states. In 1957, Clarence reported that Georgia "comes pretty close

---

[22]Conrad Browne, "Walking with a Saint," n.d., Con Browne, Koinonia Farm Archive.
[23]Clarence Jordan, "Ordeal by Bullets," *Liberation*, May 1957.

to supplying its needs."²⁴ They ran Vacation Bible Schools during the summers. They drove Black children, who had no bus, to school.

Figure 11.1. Clarence Jordan in the chicken house. Clarence was deeply committed to improving the lives of others through economic development and spiritual growth and brought chicken farming to the region, though Koinonia Farm later had to liquidate their stock because of the boycott against them. Courtesy of Hargrett Rare Book and Manuscript Library / University of Georgia Libraries

Their actions benefited everyone—White and Black. But their communal focus subverted the racial order. Martin observed that helping Black children get an education "was slapping all the good white Southern traditions in the face. For a farmer to mess up his truck" hauling around Black children "was just too much."²⁵ Even worse, those kids' education might lead them to resist their place in life. While there were comments, and the occasional threat from the Klan, early on Koinonia Farm's views on race and economic sharing were more of a theoretical problem to White neighbors but not one that led to tremendous resistance. "The South thought it had another century to change," Clarence later quipped.²⁶

---

²⁴Jordan, "Ordeal by Bullets."
²⁵Quoted in Ansley Lillian Quiros, *God with Us: Lived Theology and the Freedom Struggle in Americus, Georgia, 1942–1976* (Chapel Hill: University of North Carolina Press, 2018), 29.
²⁶Nicholas Von Hoffman, "A Rights Hero in Faded Blue Denims," n.d.

VALUE THREE: BROTHERHOOD OF ALL MEN

But the kingdom demanded change now. Applying Scripture's principles to his own context, Clarence knew what the apostle Paul called the "secret . . . that the Negros are fellow partners and equal members, co-sharers in the privileges of the gospel of Jesus Christ." It was Jesus, Clarence translated from the letter to the Ephesians, who

> is our peace. It was he who integrated us and abolished the segregation patterns which caused so much hostility. He allowed no silly traditions and customs in his fellowship, so that in it he might integrate the two into one new body. In this way he healed the hurt, and by his sacrifice on the cross he joined together both sides into one body for God. In it the hostility no longer exists.[27]

Koinonia Farm's commitment to the "brotherhood of all men" (and women) disrupted the foundational economic and racial systems that undergirded a significant part of White southern Christianity. Christianity, race, and economics were intricately intertwined. As Florence Jordan remembered years later, "What we were doing . . . was preaching the end of the world—their world. . . . The end of the big plantation owners, the end of the man who'd sit on his porch and let somebody else do his work for nothing."[28]

Flesh is put on the gospel in the mundane.

At Koinonia Farm, brotherhood manifested in the ordinary stuff of food and pay, which in the 1940s and 1950s was radical. Clarence and Martin ate with the Black workers they hired at mealtime. Annie Bell Jackson, a Black employee, recalled the day she met Clarence as "one of the happiest days, because he allowed us the chance to work, and sit to the table with white people. He treated us like we were white, just human people."[29] Brotherhood, based in a belief that all people were made in God's image, was not only a matter of where one ate, but what one ate. Lorene Floyd, who played at Koinonia as a child, remembered that at Koinonia, she was able to eat hog ham, not just the chitlins.[30]

---

[27]Clarence Jordan, "The Letter to the Christians in Birmingham [Ephesians]," in *Cotton Patch Version*, Ephesians 3:6; 2:14-16.
[28]"Florence Jordan."
[29]Kay Weiner, ed., *Koinonia Remembered* (Americus, GA: Koinonia, 1992), 52.
[30]Lorene Floyd, "Interview," n.d., XYZ Misc–Seniors Interviews, Koinonia Farm Archive.

The farm paid Black workers the same wage as White workers and paid them the best wages they could afford. Jackson remembered that when she started working at the small pecan-processing facility that Koinonia Farm would later develop, she earned a dollar an hour, compared to the standard $0.75 an hour that was minimum wage. She was delighted one Christmas when Clarence gave each employee a twenty-dollar bonus: "That's what I call a friend," she said.[31]

But shared meals and fair wages defied the mores of southern life.

Slowly—because of the danger, because it was strange, and perhaps because Koinonia does not appear to have formed strong connections with Black churches—Black neighbors began to participate in life at Koinonia. They attended the farming classes, sent their children to Vacation Bible School. In the meantime, the farm work continued.

Some African American families joined the community. In 1944, as Clarence and others terraced the land, planted seventy-eight acres of soil-building crops, and built a new house for one of the families, two Black families moved to the farm—the Joe Johnson family and the Jasper "Candy" Johnson family. In the mid-1950s, Rufus and Sue Angry, who sharecropped about five miles away, moved to the farm with their six children. Sue was thirty and knew the decision was dangerous. But she and Rufus wanted to be part of the community. "It was like a big family," she remembered. "You gave what you had and took what you needed. The idea was to help each other."[32] Other Black neighbors such as Collins McGee and Alma Jackson participated in the community more informally.

The community was transformative. As Sue remembered, "You begin to see the other person as you do yourself."[33] That's mundane and profound.

THE RACIAL LIMITS OF KOINONIA

Yet, very few African Americans joined Koinonia. People admired it from a distance, and later during the civil rights movement leaders would say Koinonia's witness bolstered their own courage. Why the disconnect? I can see at least three answers.

---

[31] Weiner, *Koinonia Remembered*, 52.
[32] Quoted in Art Carey, "A Witness to History at Civil-Rights Frontier," *Philadelphia Inquirer*, February 7, 2008, in 2Aiii) l) Sue Angry, Koinonia Farm Archive.
[33] Quoted in Quiros, *God with Us*, 29.

First, Koinonia's common purse required African Americans to give up the possibility of economic advancement in a society that wanted to keep them in their place. That's a lot to ask.

Second, Clarence does not seem to have built strong relationships with Black ministers and churches. Here I am making an argument from relative silence. I saw evidence of individuals who praised Koinonia but little reporting on Clarence speaking in Black churches or submitting himself to Black leadership, as he had in Louisville. Why? Perhaps because of the danger even of simple friendship. I have not read any sources that indicate whether Clarence thought about joining a Black church rather than a White one. But he would have known that in a rural area, and particularly in southeast Georgia where the Klan's presence was strong, it would be more dangerous to do so than in the relative anonymity of a city like Louisville. Or perhaps it was because (as we shall see in the next chapter) pressure from White Christians led Koinonia to turn inward and interact less with their neighbors.

Last, and perhaps most important, Koinonia's racially equal fellowship was dangerous. Being at Koinonia could get a person killed. In April 1958, as Dr. Martin Luther King Jr. was gaining national prominence, Clarence gave a lecture series at King's church in Montgomery, Alabama. King recalled,

> When I first invited him to speak at Dexter Street Baptist Church . . . , Clarence told us about his interracial commune in rural South Georgia. It was shocking and inspiring . . . and sounded too good to be true. Here was a son of the old South, a White Baptist preacher doing what we were just talking about doing. I went to Koinonia later to see it for myself and couldn't wait to leave because I was sure the Klan would show up.[34]

King's colleague Andy Young said that when he and King first heard about Clarence,

> We considered it too radical, too dangerous. Martin and I were trying to get folks the right to ride the bus and to shop where they wanted . . . huge challenges back then. But here Clarence was—smack dab in the middle of Ku Klux Klan country—going for the whole loaf. Clarence did not spend all his time telling others what to do or making a fuss about it . . . he just kept living

---

[34]Quoted in Hamilton Jordan, *No Such Thing as a Bad Day* (New York: Pocket Books, 2000), 122.

his faith. And Clarence put the rest of us to shame until we did something about it.[35]

Clarence understood African Americans' position. He commented often during the boycott that it was harder on the Black members of the community than the White members because Black members faced additional danger. I expect that Clarence took comfort in Paul's letter to the Galatians, where Paul, as Clarence translated it, says, "Now if, in our struggle to be true to Christ, we ourselves wind up segregated, does this make Christ a party to segregation! Heavens no! But if I try to rebuild a wicked system which I've already knocked down, then I may consider myself a violator. For as far as the Southern way is concerned I died, so I could be alive toward God. I was strung up with Christ."[36] In their community they had broken down the walls of segregation, and they would not rebuild them.

VALUE FOUR: THE WAY OF LOVE VERSUS WAR AND VIOLENCE

Clarence knew he was in a battle, but he insisted on using spiritual weapons, not physical ones. He translated Ephesians 6: "Put on God's uniform so as to be able to withstand all the Devil's tricks. For we're not fighting against ordinary human beings, but against the leaders, politicians and heads of state of this dark world, against spiritual wickedness in high places."[37] For this battle, they used "the pants of truth, the shirt of righteousness, and the shoes of the good news of peace. Above all, take the bulletproof vest of faith, with which you'll be able to stop the tracer bullets of the evil one. Also, wear the helmet of salvation, and the pistol of the Spirit, which is God's word."[38]

Clarence and Martin England preached this message when they founded Koinonia Farm in 1942—as the United States was engaged in World War II. Clarence observed that their neighbors—who sent their sons to war—were more troubled by the community's pacifism than anything else initially. Clarence faced his pacifism head-on. Clarence's draft classification was 4D,

---

[35] Quoted in Jordan, *No Such Thing as a Bad Day*, 122-23.
[36] Clarence Jordan, "The Letter to the Churches of the Georgia Convention [Galatians]," in *Cotton Patch Version*, Galatians 2:17-20. See also Clarence Jordan, "Jew and Gentile," n.d., Koinonia Farm, 1958–1965 (white binder), Koinonia Farm Archive.
[37] Jordan, "Letter to the Christians in Birmingham," Ephesians 6:11-12.
[38] Jordan, "Letter to the Christians in Birmingham," Ephesians 6:14-17.

for "the feeble-minded and preachers," but he "objected, because I don't think a preacher should be exempt any more than a deacon or layman."[39] The draft board disagreed. Pacifism remained a commitment for the farm. Several who came, such as Will Wittkamper, who arrived in 1953 with his family, had been conscientious objectors (Will was one in World War I). And the community remained committed to "the way of love" even when persecuted by their neighbors by seeking their neighbors' good. Clarence observed, "We believe that Jesus taught *more* than non-violence: he taught active good-will, the overcoming of evil with good."[40]

QUESTIONS AND IMPLICATIONS

"We have tried to keep [Koinonia Farm] from being merely a Negro project," Clarence told a White audience. "The Negro is a natural, normal part of it."[41] Clarence thought putting flesh on the gospel included unity between Black and White Christians, but it was bigger. Sometimes I wonder whether Clarence did not go far enough.

- Can you start a fellowship and just try to embody equality without dealing with the hurt of the past? Can you try to have a small fellowship of brothers and sisters in Christ, and even pay people equally, without addressing the economic and racial systems subjugating one group?

Koinonia Farm's commitments conflicted with key aspects of the culture of Christianity at their time and in their place. Clarence believed that following Jesus meant forsaking all others. He saw in the life of Judas, who betrayed Jesus, an example of what happens when a person tries to follow Jesus *and* be accepted by a religious culture that is contrary to the way of Jesus. Clarence's interpretation of what Judas's experience would be like in the twentieth-century South is striking, and I want to relay it here so it might be a mirror to see ourselves more clearly today. The narrative below—and Koinonia Farm's central commitments—make me wonder: What aspects of how Christianity today is practiced are not in line with Jesus' teachings, and in what ways are you like Judas? Keep these in mind as you read about Clarence's rendering of Judas.

---

[39] Lee, "FBI Report on Koinonia Farm."
[40] Jordan, "Ordeal by Bullets."
[41] Quoted in Jordan, "AT 100-4223."

In Clarence's mind, Judas had been profoundly shaped by religious (translated "Christian" rather than "Jewish" in the Cotton Patch version) culture. Clarence observed that Judas was from Judea, "the Bible belt of the nation," which in the South ("Palestine, that is") could not have escaped its influence. Judea was full of Christian churches and home of the Holy City, the denominational headquarters, seminaries, and publishing boards. Judas would have "inhaled its religious atmosphere," his "daddy" a deacon and his "momma" president of the Ladies Missionary Society. Judas "loved the church and was faithful to it," and no one was surprised "when he announced he was entering the ministry."[42]

But Judas soon found another master. When Jesus arrived and "called on men to reshape their lives and join the movement," Judas was "deeply attracted" to Jesus, although he did not think he needed to make any changes because he was a good church member. Judas "followed Jesus around like a puppy dog," going against his parents' wishes. Jesus made Judas feel "loved and wanted." Judas thought how great it would be for Jesus to hold a youth crusade at his church but knew Jesus couldn't because the elders had heard that Jesus had been run out of Nazareth for preaching integration. Clarence emphasized that Jesus loved Judas, and after a night of prayer chose him to become one of the twelve.[43]

Judas continued to crave the power and acceptance the church culture offered him, though he knew it was corrupt. He thought he could have both the religious structure's acceptance and Jesus, and so planned to follow Jesus in the immediate future and then later attend seminary. Clarence imagined Judas as chair of the disciples' social action committee and knew he got "burned up" when people wasted money. But Judas was alarmed by the high priest Caiaphas's response to Jesus. Judas had great respect for Caiaphas, even though he knew the whole church structure was "shot through with hypocrisy, greed and corruption." Judas did not want Jesus and Caiaphas to be enemies because they served the same God and read the same Bible. Clarence wondered whether perhaps Judas dreamed of himself as the go-between, the one who would unite the "old structures and the new order." And if he was successful, "he would be hailed as the leader of the greatest church merger of

---

[42]Clarence Jordan, *Judas: The Man from Gadara*, n.d., Koinonia Farm Archive.
[43]Clarence Jordan, *Judas: The Man from Gadara*, n.d., Koinonia Farm Archive.

all time." When Judas "casually mentioned" his idea to Jesus, Jesus nearly shouted that nobody puts new wine in old wine skins.[44]

When Jesus entered Jerusalem on a "jackass" (Clarence was known for his earthy language) on Palm Sunday, the tension between Caiaphas and Jesus was as great as the warring in Judas's own soul. Caiaphas sent Judas a note, inviting Judas to meet him in his study. Caiaphas received Judas "warmly," Clarence imagined, saying he had been thinking of Judas and praying for him since he heard Judas was not going to seminary. Caiaphas flattered Judas with fond remembrances of pastoring Judas's parents when he was in seminary but observed that Judas had fallen in with a "dangerous gang," whose teacher had been investigated by the House Un-Roman Activities Committee. Their report (similarly to one the grand jury gave about Koinonia Farm) definitely proved Jesus was a communist, and the Romans were about to convict them all, Caiaphas said. Then he reminded Judas that those who engage in subversive activities against the Romans ended up on crosses. Saying he thought Judas was a good boy and that he didn't want to see him executed, Caiaphas shared that the situation in the city was becoming dangerous. Jesus, that "cotton picking rabbi," was upsetting people, turning them away from "old time religion," and they wouldn't pay for the $75,000 pipe organ, the $25,000 fountain, or the new educational building. The ministerial organization was convinced that if Jesus was in town for the feast, there would be a riot. "For the good of all concerned," Caiaphas said, they should put him in prison until the feast ended.[45]

Caiaphas then asked for Judas's help identifying Jesus in the night so they could lock him up quietly. Caiaphas pressed relentlessly—asking Judas to do it for the sake of himself, his parents, his church, even his rabbi. Judas finally agreed, saying Jesus would be the one he "kissed." The word for "kiss" Judas used, Clarence observed, was unemotional, kind of like "shaking hands." Caiaphas gave Judas a small "love offering," and Judas, "half-crazed, stumbled away." Later that night, he led the "carefully selected group" from the high priest to Jesus. When Judas kissed Jesus, it was not the unemotional "handshake" kiss but a kiss that revealed how much Judas loved his rabbi.[46]

---

[44]Clarence Jordan, *Judas: The Man from Gadara*, n.d., Koinonia Farm Archive.
[45]Clarence Jordan, *Judas: The Man from Gadara*, n.d., Koinonia Farm Archive.
[46]Clarence Jordan, *Judas: The Man from Gadara*, n.d., Koinonia Farm Archive.

Clarence understood Judas's kiss to reveal Judas's deep love for Jesus, even as he was pulled toward the acceptance of his Christian church structure. The word Luke used was one that described repeated kissing, with much feeling, even to the point of tears. Judas, Clarence imagined, "flung himself" around Jesus' neck, tears streaming down his face. Jesus hugged him tightly, asking him, "Friend"—using an intimate word, like our "buddy"—what have you decided to do? Jesus knew the answer when Caiaphas's men took him away.[47]

What was Judas's response? Clarence wondered whether Judas collapsed on the ground and sobbed till morning, then the next day learned Jesus had been condemned to death. Perhaps he dashed into Caiaphas's office and slammed the money on the table. The unsympathetic Caiaphas told Judas he was on his own, and Judas then tied a rope to the end of a tree and the other around his neck. The tension of gravity pulling down and the rope pulling up toward the tree pulled Judas apart and killed him. "We are told," Clarence said, "that he busted in the middle and his guts poured out." Judas's body and soul were torn apart.[48]

Judas, in Clarence's mind, did not die of too little religion; he died of too much. "It wasn't that he had no master, but two, and he hated neither. He loved them both," Clarence said. Judas had double vision, trying to "follow a road that forked and was broken in the middle."[49]

Equally important as the question of Judas's double vision was Jesus' continuing love for his lost sheep, his dear friend Judas. Clarence believed that in eternity, Jesus and Judas would meet again and Jesus would clasp Judas in his arms, take him back to the Father, and say, "Rejoice with me, I've found my lost buddy."[50]

- What two masters might you—and your church—be trying to serve?
- In what ways are you like Judas? Do you hope that Jesus will come for you, his "buddy," his "lost lamb"?
- Do you resist Clarence's hope that Jesus will come for Judas? Would you condemn him? Why or why not?

---

[47]Clarence Jordan, *Judas: The Man from Gadara*, n.d., Koinonia Farm Archive.
[48]Clarence Jordan, *Judas: The Man from Gadara*, n.d., Koinonia Farm Archive.
[49]Clarence Jordan, *Judas: The Man from Gadara*, n.d., Koinonia Farm Archive.
[50]Clarence Jordan, *Judas: The Man from Gadara*, n.d., Koinonia Farm Archive.

A picture I see often in archival research is of Martin Luther King Jr. sitting at the Highlander Folk School in Monteagle, Tennessee, in 1957. Koinonia and Highlander had a relationship, as described above. The Georgia Commission on Education sent an undercover photographer to the event and then sent the photo across the South to discredit King, claiming it showed him attending a communist training school.[51] It might be easy to do the same with Koinonia Farm—although it was not communist, its economic practices were certainly not capitalist. Many, as we have seen, asserted Koinonia was communistic. As the Cold War began after World War II, there was little room in American life for nuance. American Cold War propaganda portrayed the battle as the Judeo-Christian, capitalistic, democratic United States against the atheistic, "godless" communists. That binary breaks down, however, and if we dismiss the economic questions Koinonia Farm raised, we miss an opportunity to learn.

- Do accusations of communism mean we should dismiss Koinonia Farm?
- What labels do you use to dismiss people?
- Koinonia's emphasis on shared life and spending on yourself only what you need is contrary to an implicit (and often explicit) ethos in American life that emphasizes consumption. Jordan may have overreached when he said that the more you consume, the emptier your soul. But rather than dismissing his sensibility, let that be a mirror for you personally and corporately. How much do you consume? Do you take more than you need? How much does your church spend on itself versus giving money to those who might need it?

---

[51]"Highlander Folk School," The Martin Luther King, Jr., Research and Education Institute, April 26, 2017, https://kinginstitute.stanford.edu/encyclopedia/highlander-folk-school.

12

EXCLUSION, NOT EMBRACE

How most White neighbors treated members of Koinonia Farm and how it is difficult to know just what their most famous neighbor, future president Jimmy Carter, did during their persecution.

REHEBOTH BAPTIST CHURCH

Initially, Koinonia Farm's White members participated in their county's White social life through their church, Reheboth Baptist Church. Clarence joined soon after arriving and did not speak forcefully about his views on race, materialism, and pacifism, hoping to win church members over to his perspective through friendship. This small church community would be the first to exclude members of Koinonia.

At least by the 1940s, Clarence fully expected that Christians would experience persecution because, like their king, Jesus, they could not help but conflict with their culture. Clarence was most concerned about the culture the White churches created (contrary to a perspective today that can emphasize "the church" versus "the world"). Clarence longed to see White church culture change because he believed it was enslaved to false gods. Clarence understood Jesus as persecuted not by the "gangsters and murderers and thieves and racketeers, but the 'good people'—property owners, religious leaders, successful businessmen, society folk, the upper crust—people trusted with the maintenance of the status quo." These folks, Clarence said, "sincerely didn't want to do him any harm, and wouldn't have if only he had left them alone. They didn't mind his preaching of dangerous doctrines, and they thought some of his thinking was stimulating. But he was going too far and too fast when he started *practicing* some of those things."[1]

Relations between White Koinonia members and other Reheboth members could be tense. An undated internal Koinonia document describes how under Pastor Jesse Bell's leadership, the deacons asked Koinonia members to withdraw their membership. When they refused, the church "took the position that no one at Koinonia should hold any office or place of responsibility in the church. The pastor, Jesse Bell, resigned."[2] Under Pastor Ira Faglier, relations soured more as Koinonia members refused to respect southern White racial sensibilities. Harry Atkinson, a White Koinonia member, invited his Black friend to his Sunday school class, transgressing racial dynamics both in principle and personally because the Black friend chauffeured for one of the other White Rehoboth members. In 1949, Harry and Allene Atkinson asked for "their letters," resigning from the church.

In 1950, Reheboth Baptist Church expelled the other White Koinonia members. When the Koinonians brought a dark-skinned Hindi man visiting the farm from India to visit their church, church members accused them of trying to integrate. Within a week, they summoned Koinonia members to a churchwide meeting addressing their status as church members, presenting a resolution to expel Koinonia members from the fellowship because of their racial beliefs.[3] Florence represented everyone since the men were going to be out of town.

When faced with the church's accusations, she agreed that they did believe in equality between the races but would not renounce their position. If the church insisted on expelling them, there was nothing else to do but support that decision. Florence motioned to adopt the church's resolution to expel Koinonia members because they believed in racial integration. Other

---

[1] Clarence Jordan, *Lord and Master, Part 2*, Course XI, Part 2, in the New Judson (Keystone) Graded Course for High School Young People (Philadelphia: Judson, 1949), 74.
[2] "Memo on Reheboth Baptist Church," n.d., in 2EV Race Relations Civil Rights, Koinonia Farm Archive.
[3] Tracy Elaine K'Meyer, *Interracialism and Christian Community in the Postwar South: The Story of Koinonia Farm* (Charlottesville: University of Virginia Press, 2000), 59-60; Charles O'Connor, "A Rural Georgia Tragedy: Koinonia Farm in the 1950s" (PhD diss., University of Georgia, 2003), 31. See also Charles S. O'Connor, "The Politics of Industrialization and Interracialism in Sumter County, Georgia: Koinonia Farm in the 1950s," *The Georgia Historical Quarterly* 89, no. 4 (2005): 505-27.

congregants were surprised at Florence's actions. Clarence remembered, "Well, the people didn't want to vote with her, and they didn't want to vote against the motion." When the preacher called for a vote in favor, a few people struggled to their feet. When he called for those opposed to stand, no one stood, but everyone remained silent. Then, "someone started to sob; then another, and another, and for about 5 minutes the whole church just sat there weeping. Finally, very quietly, one by one they got up and tiptoed out and got in their cars and went home."[4]

Clarence was surprised the church had expelled their own—White southerners. I wonder whether he thought being White would protect him from that sort of exclusion. Koinonia members forgave and sought reconciliation, telling Reheboth members, "It is our fervent prayer that all of us shall heed the command of our Lord Jesus to forgive each other 'until seventy times seven;' to pray for one another, and to love those 'who despitefully use you.'" But Koinonians were not willing to compromise their convictions. They wanted to be in fellowship with the church, even though they disagreed vehemently. The Koinonians added, "May there be a ready willingness for a reconciliation which would involve no sacrifice of conscience or compromise of our Lord's truth."[5]

Others in the area observed what happened. Sheriff McArthur and W. T. Beauchamp of the Georgia Bureau of Investigation advised the FBI, which kept tabs on potential subversives, of the conflict. The sheriff noted, too, that he had been warned of potential violence against Koinonia because of their interracialism. Sheriff McArthur asked other White people to help prevent violence, talking with "level-headed residents" in the area "to enlist their aid in forestalling possible violence."[6]

Clarence told supporters that other churches in the area extended a welcome to the excluded Koinonians, but they had declined to switch their membership. He did not say whether those other churches were White or Black. Initially, Koinonia members wanted to see whether Reheboth would reopen the doors of the church.[7]

---

[4] Clarence Jordan, "Ordeal by Bullets," *Liberation*, May 1957.
[5] "Memo on Reheboth Baptist Church."
[6] William S. Lee, "FBI Report on Koinonia Farm," Atlanta, May 11, 1951, Federal Bureau of Investigation, Koinonia Farm Archive, 20.
[7] Clarence Jordan to Ben, December 6, 1950, in 2)A)iii)a) Clarence Jordan, Koinonia Farm Archive.

EXCLUSION, NOT EMBRACE 175

When Reheboth members did not change their position, the Koinonians ultimately decided against joining another institutional church. In January, they wrote in their newsletter that while they were saddened

> by the break of fellowship with those we love and feel that it is a tragedy for the whole church, we rejoice in the clarity that it brings to us regarding our witness on this element of the gospel. Our witness is no longer divided. We are now whole-heartedly committed to the complete brotherhood across all barriers with no other commitments to compromise our witness.[8]

The break with Reheboth and the social relationships that church membership offered marked a turn inward for the Koinonia community. They began to see themselves as their own church. They continued to welcome visitors, and in the late 1940s and early 1950s between eight and ten thousand visitors and volunteers came per year. Few joined, but many testified to a renewed commitment to live out the gospel in their own time and place. Community members rejoiced when people joined them and grieved deeply when people left the fellowship, even if it was just to form a new community close by.[9] By the mid-1950s, about sixty people, including children, lived at the farm. About a quarter of the residents were Black. They went about their interracial life quietly, not making a demonstration of it in town. For the most part, White people left them alone.

BOYCOTTS AND VIOLENCE

That all changed in 1954. The Supreme Court ruled in *Brown v. Board of Education* that separate schools were inherently unequal and then in 1955 subsequently ruled that segregated schools needed to integrate with all deliberate speed in *Brown II*. White southerners felt attacked by outsiders. People regarded as respectable formed White Citizens' Councils to keep their schools segregated, White Christians lamented the court's trampling on what they saw as God's truth ordaining segregation, and many politicians made segregation foundational to their campaigns.[10] Georgia's solicitor general, Charles

---

[8]The Koinonia to Friend of Koinonia, January 12, 1951, Koinonia Farm.
[9]Clarence to Dick, 1953, in 2Aiii)a)I Clarence's Manuscripts and Other Writings, Koinonia Farm.
[10]For citizens' councils, see Stephanie Rolph, *Resisting Equality: The Citizens' Council, 1954–1989* (Baton Rouge: Louisiana State University Press, 2018).

Burgamy of Americus, publicly stated that he wanted a revival of the Ku Klux Klan to protect White citizens' rights.[11]

Koinonia Farm became a lightning rod for local White people's frustrations. Clarence observed, "Koinonia became the integrated hole in the segregation dike. We were an obscure farm, too small to hurt anyone, but we were told if we were removed, Georgia would be white, whole and pure once again. The White Citizens' Council said we were a cancer that would have to be cut out."[12] Local Whites used a two-pronged attack to convince Koinonia Farm to move. First, they boycotted the farm—refusing to buy farm products, carry products in stores, or sell them any supplies. Second, they used violence. Clarence later observed that he was most disappointed in the "good White church people" who would not take a public stand against the boycott, even more than in those who committed the violence.

VIOLENCE: PERSECUTED BUT NOT DESTROYED

The violence began in 1956. It correlated with Clarence's efforts to help two Black students, Thelma Boone and Edward Clemons, register at the University of Georgia's business school.[13] A Black friend of Clarence's in Atlanta, Sam Williams, asked Clarence to help the students since one admission requirement for prospective University of Georgia students was that an alum support their admission—a process that kept Black students out on a de facto basis *if* the White alumni toed the segregation line. Clarence agreed to help because Williams assured him the students genuinely wanted to attend the school and were not applying primarily because they wanted to integrate it. Clarence wanted to support civil rights actions that arose in the course of everyday events. He made the one-hundred-mile trip north to Athens in May 1956. Clarence was unable to sponsor the students on a technicality: he was an alum of the agricultural school, and they wanted to go to the business school. But by the time Clarence returned to Americus, the governor had called Sumter County's sheriff to ask who Clarence was. The White *Americus Times-Recorder* newspaper ran a headline saying he had tried to integrate the

---

[11]"Solicitor Asks Revival of KKK at States Rights Meeting Here," *Albany Journal*, 1956, in Koinonia Farm 1949–1957, Koinonia Farm Archive.
[12]Nicholas Von Hoffman, "A Rights Hero in Faded Blue Denims," n.d.
[13]K'Meyer, *Interracialism and Christian Community*, 84-85.

University of Georgia. NAACP lawyers wanted to make the situation a test case, but Clarence declined because he did not want to force others to do what he saw as right.[14]

The next month, someone attacked the farm's produce stand. After that, the violence picked up and was coupled with the boycott of the farm. Few businesses would sell to the farm or carry their products. In November, someone shot into Koinonia homes from the highway. Residents responded with posting an unarmed guard (which guests such as Dorothy Day took turns participating in) and piling up firewood around the outsides of the houses to stop the bullets. The children learned to drop to the ground when they heard gunfire. Vandals chopped down their road signs, cut down three hundred fruit trees that Clarence and Martin had planted over a decade before, and shot into the mechanism of the new gas pump, destroying it. In January, someone bombed the produce stand and destroyed it. Farm residents left the detritus up as a silent call for people to change their ways. It often seemed to be only God's grace that saved them. Twice, bullets barely missed a sleeping child.

Koinonia members were courageous in the face of terror. Members knew they could disappear like Emmett Till and countless other African Americans had. Clarence noted, "I am always scared, particularly for my wife and children. But being scared is not the question. . . . The question we face every day is whether or not we will be obedient to a system and to a group of people who insist that we hate and mistreat our fellow men."[15] Courage is not being unafraid. It is doing the right thing despite fear.

African American members of Koinonia Farm dealt with more acute fear. For Sue Angry and her family, remembering the night people shot at them when they were out playing volleyball fifty-one years after it happened brought tears to her eyes.[16] The community sent her and her family north to New Jersey with other members, attempting to found a Koinonia branch there. The branch ultimately failed because northern White neighbors

---

[14]"Gunfire Is Irony in 'Fellowship,'" *The Daily Times*, May 9, 1957, Federal Bureau of Investigation, Koinonia Farm Archive.
[15]Quoted in Hamilton Jordan, *No Such Thing as a Bad Day* (New York: Pocket Books, 2000), 121.
[16]Quoted in Art Carey, "A Witness to History at Civil-Rights Frontier," *Philadelphia Inquirer*, February 7, 2008, in 2Aiii) l) Sue Angry, Koinonia Farm Archive.

resisted an interracial farm in *their* backyard. By 1958, fewer than ten people (including children) remained at the farm in Georgia.

The few Black families who allowed their children to attend activities at Koinonia or did business with the farm faced serious repercussions. Lorene Floyde remembered that a cross was burned on her parents' lawn, and they were told to keep the kids away from Koinonia. Black farmer Rowe Edwards's testimony in the White *Americus Times-Recorder* reflects the fear White attacks caused for African Americans. He said that while his children had visited Koinonia and he had sold them a load of hay, he did that before "any of the facts of the object of the farm were brought out" and had nothing to do with them since the violence.[17] Like at the Floyde home, Whites had burned a cross at Edwards's place. Cross burnings were meant both to intimidate the family affected and to be a warning to everyone else, and they were largely effective in keeping Black supporters away from the farm. The handful of Black friends who continued to supply the farm did so at great risk.

Clarence and the others at Koinonia reported the violence to the local police but received only superficial investigations. I was not surprised that local police appeared to do far less than due diligence to investigate the violence and support the farm. As I read Clarence's FBI file, it confirmed my response. Sheriff Fred Chappel was one of the FBI's reliable informants. If he was feeding information on Koinonia Farm to the FBI, then he probably felt like he was on the side of the southern way of life that Koinonia so blatantly violated. When Koinonia received no help from the sheriff or the FBI, Clarence appealed to President Eisenhower "as a last resort, with the hope and prayer that you might find some course of action before it is too late."[18]

Eisenhower passed the letter along to FBI head J. Edgar Hoover, who spoke with the Georgia attorney general. Under pressure, Americus began a grand jury investigation concerning the violence against Koinonia. Koinonia members thought the grand jury was unfair from the start. They observed that Solicitor General Charles Burgamy "was responsible for assembling the facts and presenting them to the Grand Jury," and they knew of Burgamy's

---

[17]"Negro Denies Farm Association," *Americus Times Recorder*, February 20, 1957, in 2F Primary Resources 1950s, Koinonia Farm Archive.

[18]Clarence Jordan to Dwight Eisenhower, January 22, 1957, in 2Aiii)a)I Clarence's Manuscripts and Other Writings, Koinonia Farm Archive.

address to a States' Rights Council meeting during the violence, when he said, "Maybe that's what we need now, is for the right kind of a Klan to start up again and use a buggy whip on some of these race mixers. I believe that would stop them." At the same meeting, Burgamy had suggested that the recent roadside bombing of Koinonia's market stand was a false flag destruction; that is, it could have been done by Koinonia members to gain sympathy and attention. When they saw the results, Koinonia members argued, "Mr. Burgamy has used the prestige of the Grand Jury to distort the facts to fit his preconceived theory."[19]

The widely read report implicitly legitimized the boycott and violence. Following Burgamy's claim, it suggested that Koinonia members had committed the violence against themselves to gain national attention. Second, the grand jury asserted, rather than argued, that while they could not say for sure, it sure looked like Koinonia was a communist front organization (assertions are unsupported by facts; arguments are based in evidence). The report said the jury was "pleased to leave to the good judgment and understanding of the people who read these Presentments the question whether there exists extremely close kinship between the Communist Party and Koinonia, Inc."

Finally, the grand jury concluded that Koinonia was not really Christian: "We find its claim to Christianity sheer window dressing and its practice of Christianity has no precedent in the religious annals of the United States." The grand jury was ignoring hundreds of years of Black Christian history that agreed with Koinonia's racial stance. Koinonia responded that the statement was "a dangerous abuse of authority by a secular agency of the state. Do the people of Americus and Sumter County wish to grant to the Grand Jury the power to pass on the Christian sincerity of other citizens?" While Koinonia members noted their own frailty, they said that like other Christians "we are earnestly striving to follow the teachings of Jesus as we understand them."[20]

While the jury did not issue an indictment, Clarence and others at the farm believed that it "gave official undergirding to the campaign against us."[21] Farm members took out newspaper ads defending themselves and wrote their

---

[19] "Grand Jury: 'Koinonia Its Own Enemy,'" *The Daily Times*, May 9, 1957, Federal Bureau of Investigation, Koinonia Farm Archive.
[20] "Grand Jury: 'Koinonia Its Own Enemy.'"
[21] Jordan, "Ordeal by Bullets."

version of the situation to their supporters. They stated, "We do not seek pity, we understand the deep differences that divide us from many of our neighbors, but we believe that love and understanding will surmount these differences. We cast ourselves now on the mercy of the community. We shall neither defend ourselves nor retaliate. We have faith in the goodness of God and the goodwill of our fellows."[22]

BOYCOTT: PRESSED ON ALL SIDES

The boycott that accompanied the violence may have been more devastating. People and businesses the farm had been working with for years refused to do business. State Farm Insurance canceled their policy. Feed and seed dealers refused to sell to them. Service stations and car dealers would not serve them. The airplane company refused to dust their cotton crops for boll weevil. The grocery store would not sell to them or buy from them. Citizens Bank of Americus, where they had borrowed and repaid $200,000 without being late, closed their line of credit. Without a market for eggs, which was their largest income-generating product, they had to liquidate their chickens. In a deep irony, the people who had brought poultry farming to the county could no longer participate. The children faced persecution at school. Clarence's son, Jimmy, was harassed by a local man who called him a "nigger-lover," and the White high school students at the segregated school followed suit, leading Clarence and Florence to send Jimmy to a Hutterite community in North Dakota for high school for his mental and physical safety.

White Bible-believing Christians—leaders in their community—refused to advocate for Koinonia or even resist the boycott. The White bank president was a leader at Americus's First Methodist Church.[23] When Koinonia members asked him and other businesspeople why they joined the boycott, they would respond, "Now understand, there's nothing personal with me. I think the world of you people, but it's either that or my business." When Koinonia members replied that the businesspeople faced "the same alternatives we are: to be true to their convictions or to sell out to their business," the businesspeople would not change.[24]

---

[22]Quoted in Jordan, "Ordeal by Bullets."
[23]Koinonia Farm, "Newsletter," November 23, 1956, Koinonia Farm Archive.
[24]Jordan, "Ordeal by Bullets."

Koinonia members hoped some White Christian leaders would stand with them. They sent a delegation to the Sumter County Ministerial Association asking for help. The association appointed three men to study the situation, who determined that at least twenty-five businesses were boycotting the farm. They publicly condemned the violence, but under pressure some members took out newspaper ads to reassure White residents that the ministers themselves, though they did not like the violence, did not support Koinonia's commitment to equality and race mixing. The White southerners who wrote editorials against the violence similarly observed that the violence was wrong because it impinged on others' ability to follow their convictions.[25]

The ministers' lukewarm rebuke did little to quell the violence seven miles away from downtown Americus, and the farm and its supporters endured at least eight more shootings, three cross burnings, and many fires.[26] After a large Ku Klux Klan rally in Americus at which two White ministers spoke, one using Scripture to support segregation, more than seventy cars came out to Koinonia asking them to sell their land.[27]

Koinonia members were deeply disappointed in the "good White Christians" who refused to stand up and buck the boycott. Clarence said, "I would rather face the frantic, childest [sic] mob, even with their shotguns and buggy whips, than the silent, insidious mob of good church people who give assent to the boycott and subtle psychological warfare. What can I say for those who know the word of God and will not speak it?"[28]

Even Clarence's brother Robert refused to help. Robert was a World War II veteran and a lawyer with political ambitions. In 1958 he would become the vice president of the Georgia Bar Association. Robert declined Clarence's pleas for help because he did not want to isolate himself from White citizens. Clarence reminded Robert that when they joined the church, the preacher asked them both:

---

[25]Typical is Thad Gibson, "Over the Coffee Cup," *The Albany Journal*, May 10, 1957, Federal Bureau of Investigation, Koinonia Farm Archive.
[26]"Gunfire Is Irony in 'Fellowship.'"
[27]"Klansmen Meet in City; Motorcade Goes to Koinonia," *Americus Times Recorder*, February 25, 1957, Federal Bureau of Investigation, Koinonia Farm Archive.
[28]Quoted in Bo Turner, "The World Turned Upside-Down," n.d., in Primary Materials 1970, Koinonia Farm Archive.

"Do you accept Jesus as Savior and Lord?" His brother responded, "Clarence, I follow Jesus up to a point." "Could that point," asked Clarence, "be the cross?" "That's right," said his brother. "I follow him to the cross but not on the cross. I am not going to get myself crucified." "Then I don't think you are a disciple," said Clarence. "You are an admirer of Jesus, not a disciple."[29]

Standing with Koinonia did mean climbing on the cross, as White businessman Herbert Birdsey learned. Birdsey lived in Macon, where several Koinonia supporters lived, and had known Clarence's parents.[30] When Birsdsey ordered the Americus branch of his feed store to break the boycott in May 1957, the store was bombed. Authorities believed someone in a passing car tossed several sticks of dynamite into the store. The blast damaged three buildings and "ripped a hole 10 inches long, 3 inches deep, and 5 inches wide in a concrete sidewalk." Birdsey Feed Store's glass fronts caved in, and "about 14 windows were shattered in a four-story bank building across the street and one window was broken in the county courthouse diagonally across the street."[31]

The Birdsey Feed Store bombing was the last of the outright violence. Americus Chamber of Commerce members had turned a blind eye to violent attacks out in the country, but such obvious cruelty in town was another matter. They did not want potential northern business investors to think poorly of their town.[32] They visited the farm, asking members to move. Again Clarence refused. So the business leaders put pressure elsewhere, finally using their influence to stop the violence when it might hurt them.[33]

Ironically, the boycott expanded Koinonia's influence nationally. The farm shifted to selling pecan products out of state—a costly endeavor when they had already invested capital into traditional farming. They developed a small

---

[29]Quoted in Henlee Barnette, "Clarence Jordan and His Incarnational Evangelism," *Baptists Today*, October 2002. Barnette also wrote *Clarence Jordan: Turning Dreams into Deeds* (Macon, GA: Smyth & Helwys, 1992). Barnette and Clarence Jordan were friends. Robert's gamble paid off in one sense; in 1972 Jimmy Carter, who was then governor, appointed Robert to Georgia's Supreme Court. Robert served as its chief justice from 1980 to 1982. According to Barnette, before he died, Robert said, "Clarence is the greatest Christian I have ever known."
[30]Michael Nelson, "Koinonia: This Christian Commune in the Heart of Carter Country Has Been Proving That Small Is Beautiful for Thirty-Five Years," *The Washington Post Magazine*, December 4, 1977, in Primary Resources 1970s, Outside Articles 1970s, Koinonia Farm Archive.
[31]"Racial Angle Seen in Georgia Bombing," n.d., Federal Bureau of Investigation, Koinonia Farm Archive.
[32]O'Connor, "Politics of Industrialization." For Birdsey living in Macon, see Nelson, "Koinonia: This Christian Commune."
[33]O'Connor, "Politics of Industrialization."

pecan-processing facility and a kitchen, where they made products with the pecans. They quipped that they were "shipping the nuts out of Georgia." People nationwide responded. One Minnesota church asked over one thousand other churches in their state to form Koinonia Nut Committees to encourage sales. Others suggested buying nuts from the farm for Lent.[34] When insurance companies and banks refused the farm's business, Koinonians asked people around the country to invest in the farm by making small insurance pledges and loaning small amounts of money. Many did.

MODELING HUMILITY TO UNDERSTAND JIMMY CARTER

Beginning to understand a subject demands considering multiple perspectives even as humility reminds us of the limits of our knowledge. As I read about Koinonia Farm's trials, I inadvertently developed a binary framework that pitted the people of Koinonia against the White citizens of Sumter County (despite Birdsey's choice to break the boycott, which complicated matters). I had come to Koinonia Farm with a hyperfocus on the farm, and I am somewhat embarrassed to say that it took me being in the place to realize the significance of Koinonia's proximity to Plains, Jimmy Carter's hometown (to be fair, my dad had mentioned it, but it did not initially seem relevant to the time period I was studying). When I stayed at Koinonia, I went cycling and often rode toward Plains. As I pedaled, I wondered about the former president's relationship to the farm during the 1950s and how he fit into the binary. I had not brought a stack of books on Carter with me, but partly as tourist and partly as historian, my family and I visited the National Park Service's historical sites at Jimmy's old high school and the Carter farm in next-door Archery. They gave me some insight about Jimmy as a person and politician. Time in the archives helped me answer my questions and I followed up with secondary sources when I got home.

It turns out that Jimmy's relationship with Koinonia Farm was (and is) complicated and can remind us about the limits of what we can state using evidence.

In my first pass through the evidence, it seemed like Jimmy must have supported the farm. I read Jimmy's introduction to a 2012 version of

---

[34] "A Letter from Clarence Jordan of Koinonia Farm," *The Minnesota Message*, n.d., in 2F Primary Resources 1950s, Koinonia Farm Archive.

Clarence's Cotton Patch translation of the New Testament and was a little surprised to learn that Jimmy regularly read it and kept a copy on his desk. Jimmy observed, "It is one thing to read and imagine the gospel story set in centuries past; it is altogether different to see our own stories, failings, and prejudices as part of Christ's story."[35] Jimmy spoke at a 2012 symposium at Koinonia Farm honoring Clarence and Florence and said he had been proud to shell Koinonia's peanuts, although Clarence refused to buy seed, feed, or fertilizer from him because Clarence could get them cheaper somewhere else.[36] When I was eating lunch one day at the farm, I met former Koinonia member Don Mosely, who was on his way to drop off blueberries and visit his friends Jimmy and Rosalynn. It took me a moment before I realized Don was referring to former president Jimmy Carter and first lady Rosalynn.

My sense of Carter's support for Koinonia was forming—after all, Koinonia (as we shall see below) birthed Habitat for Humanity, which Jimmy and Rosalynn were active in. But my understanding about the 1950s, while present in Jimmy's recollections, was still inferred. I could say more confidently that Jimmy seemed to have a positive relationship with the farm after his US presidency. But I still had a nagging sense that there was more to the story. Two questions kept echoing in my mind: If Jimmy was such a supporter during the trials of the 1950s, why was his support not featured more prominently in all the histories of Koinoina Farm I had read, given his prominent role as US president? And what would make him so different from most other White Christians in Sumter County?

In 1976, when Jimmy was running for president, presidential reporters worked hard to catch him in a lie. He seemed too honest, too good to be true. He puzzled national reporters with his description of his born-again evangelical faith, and he seemed like such an honest, humble man. By then, Clarence had been dead seven years, and much of the knowledge of Jimmy's interactions with him and Koinonia were buried at Picnic Hill. Reporters from the *Chicago Daily News* and *Playboy* magazine learned about Koinonia's

---

[35]Jimmy Carter, "Introduction," in *The Cotton Patch Gospel*, by Clarence Jordan (Macon, GA: Smyth & Helwys, 2012).

[36]Jimmy Carter, "Opening Remarks for the Clarence Jordan Symposium," in *Fruits of the Cotton Patch*, ed. Kirk Lyman-Barner and Cori Lyman-Barner, vol. 2 (Eugene, OR: Wipf & Stock, 2014), xiii-xvi.

1950s travails and asked Jimmy what his response had been.[37] Jimmy answered that he had helped Koinonia Farm during the boycott by shelling their peanuts and that he had visited a few times.

My interest was piqued: here was evidence from 1976, not 2012 or 2022. But, like all evidence, I needed to treat it carefully. Jimmy was running a presidential campaign in 1976, when the nation's tenor on race had shifted— would he speak honestly? And if he did support the farm, might it look different than I expected?

Then I came across archival material that floored me. I read a 1976 letter from the same Don Mosely, with whom I had eaten lunch, to Jimmy's mother, Lillian Carter. Don told Ms. Lillian that reporters had been asking Koinonia members what they thought of Jimmy Carter. He said that while their response was "quite positive overall," that was "seldom what they [the reporters] were really asking."[38] They wanted to know whether Jimmy had stood by Koinonia. Don wrote that none of the three people at the farm who were there during the boycott remembered any contact with the Carters. Furthermore, they had gone through all purchase orders from that time period and saw no evidence of the Carters doing business with the farm. While they wanted to believe Carter was supportive and wanted to "do more," they were unwilling to "fabricate a story."[39]

Florence Jordan's testimony was similar. She wrote in a letter that she had told reporters she could not confirm Jimmy's statement that he had supported the farm because she did not know Jimmy in the 1950s. Nor could she find any evidence that they had paid the Carters' business for processing their peanuts. Florence had told the reporters, "Although we live just seven miles from Plains, I am not acquainted with Mr. Carter. Most of our business has been done in Americus and Albany, much larger trading centers. When we have done business in Plains, it has been with Mr. Williams. So far as I know we have never done, much, if any with Carter."[40] She told another reporter that while she did not want to "throw a monkey wrench in his campaign," she had to be honest: "I'm sorry, but I don't even know him and we've been living

---

[37] Nelson, "Koinonia: This Christian Commune."
[38] Don Mosely to Lillian Carter, n.d., in Folder 2A iii) b) [i] Florence's Writings, Koinonia Farm.
[39] Mosely to Carter.
[40] Florence Jordan to Howard Willets, September 13, 1976, in 2A iii) b) [i] Florence's Writings, Koinonia Farm Archive.

here for thirty-four years. People come here from all over the world, but he hasn't come seven miles."[41]

What to do? Could I reconcile the evidence? Had Carter lied in 1976, saying he had broken the boycott because the nation's racial sensibilities had shifted? Was he misremembering years later, perhaps given his later appreciation of Clarence? Had he actually supported the boycott—or at least done nothing to stop it? That would not be surprising, given that he was a White Christian in southwest Georgia. A floodgate of other questions opened too. If Carter had broken the boycott, how did he survive in Georgia's politics? After all, White locals such as Jimmy's friend Warren Fortson, a lawyer who stood with civil rights workers just a few years later, were socially isolated.[42]

CARTER AND RACE IN THE 1950S-1970S

I decided to go back over what I knew about Carter and race and create a timeline. When Clarence founded Koinonia in 1942, Jimmy had just graduated high school and soon would leave Sumter County for his military career. Carter received a naval commission in 1946, and he and his young bride, Rosalynn, returned in 1953 to run the family business when Jimmy's father, Earl Carter, died. When the boycott began in 1956, Jimmy was living seven miles from Koinonia Farm.

Given the proximity between Plains and Koinonia, it is likely that Jimmy's father, Earl Carter, had known about Koinonia. It is also likely that Earl had disagreed with Koinonia's integrationist stance. Jimmy often stated that his father was a segregationist, while his mother pushed racial boundaries because of her work as a nurse.

An oral history talking about Earl Carter's relationship with Clarence offered some insight. A friend of Clarence remembered Clarence telling him,

---

[41]Quoted in Nelson, "Koinonia: This Christian Commune."
[42]For civil rights in Americus, see Ansley Lillian Quiros, *God with Us: Lived Theology and the Freedom Struggle in Americus, Georgia, 1942–1976* (Chapel Hill: University of North Carolina Press, 2018), chaps. 4–6. For Fortson, see Douglas E. Kneeland, "A 'Mean' Town in Georgia in the '60s Sinks into Euphoria While Awaiting Carter Election," 1976; Bill Banks, "Warren Fortson, 92, Paid a Price for Supporting Integration," *The Atlanta Journal-Constitution*, August 13, 2020; "Warren Candler Fortson," *Cremation Society of Georgia* (blog), accessed August 30, 2023, www.csog.com/obits/warren-candler-fortson/.

Jimmy Carter's father, like Clarence a deacon [in his local church], shut off all buying and selling by Koinonia in his elevator at Plains. So Clarence called on Deacon Carter to remonstrate as a Christian. Mr. Carter was most generous, kind and troubled. He knew that God was on Clarence's side of the problem. His ultimatum was: "Clarence, my customers will not allow me to break out of the boycott of Koinonia."[43]

We have to treat oral histories carefully. They are valuable for teasing out what matters from the past to a person in the present, but they can be inaccurate regarding what actually happened. In this case, I thought the statement conflated Earl Carter with other business owners because Earl Carter had died three years before the boycott began. Since the oral history was in 1991, after Jimmy Carter's presidency, the likely mix-up made sense. But the sensibility described—of White owners thinking it was wrong to boycott Koinonia but not taking a stand—matched other evidence.

But it is also possible Earl Carter held friendly feelings toward Koinonia. Jack Singletary, a former White member of Koinonia who started his own farm in nearby Plains, offered evidence that complicated matters. Singletary said in 1976 that Earl Carter cut and threshed his farm's clover when no one else would, suggesting that perhaps there was informal resistance to doing business with Koinonia friends prior to the boycott. Evidence also suggested that Singletary sat with Earl Carter as the older man lay dying.[44]

Could the context of Jimmy Carter's race-related actions in the 1950s and 1960s help answer my questions? Historians argue that while Carter did not publicly advocate for integration, he worked for Black advancement. Jimmy refused to join the local White Citizens' Council, formed in the wake of *Brown v. Board of Education*. When he was appointed to the school board in 1955, he brought other members on a tour of Black schools and determined to improve African American education, albeit within a segregationist framework.[45] Jimmy remembered that Clarence had influenced his work on the school board: "I didn't have very much to do with Clarence until I became a

---

[43]Jim Wyker in Kay Weiner, ed., *Koinonia Remembered* (Americus, GA: Koinonia, 1992), 74.
[44]Robert Scheer, "Jimmy We Hardly Know Y'all," *Playboy*, November, 1976, in Box: TBO Internal Array, Koinonia Farm Archive. The Singletary family left along with the Atkinsons and the Ballards. The Atkinsons later returned to Koinonia. See Elaine Allen Lechtreck, "Pastor with a Hoe," n.d., Koinonia Farm Archive.
[45]Quiros, *God with Us*, 177.

member of the Sumter County School Board. But I had been listening to what he said."[46] Jimmy supported school consolidation because he thought it would lead to improved education for all the children, even though in that fraught climate consolidation was often billed as a vote for integration. In 1965, when his church in Plains wanted to bar African Americans from worship, Jimmy dissented, even though he knew it was a losing fight.[47]

But still, in 1960 after the boycott ended and before Sumter County schools were integrated, Jimmy did not intervene for Koinoina in a school-related conflict. White Koinonia high school-age students Billy Wittkamper (fifteen), Laura Ruth Browne (thirteen), and Jan Jordan (thirteen) applied to Americus High School and were refused admission because of their religious belief in equal fellowship across racial lines. Jimmy did not intervene when the school board refused their request.[48] After discussion with school authorities, as a last resort Koinonia parents sued the school based on religious discrimination. They won the case and the children were able to attend, although the other students isolated and harassed them.[49]

ANSWERS?

Stepping back to assess what I thought I knew and specifying my ignorance about what I did not know made me see Jimmy as complex. This evidence may have supported one historian's claim that: "Whether the issue was school desegregation or consolidation, Carter's primary concern remained his own stature in the community, the economic success of his family's farm, and increasingly, his political ambitions."[50]

At the same time, I still wanted to believe Jimmy and reconcile the conflicting evidence somehow (I know that my bias is to think the best of people). Could Jimmy have understood himself as supporting Koinonia in some way? Returning to a *Playboy* magazine article by freelance writer Robert Scheer, I found in Koinonia Farm's archive shed light on the situation for me. Scheer puzzled over similar questions and pushed himself to uncover the complexity of the situation.

---

[46]Carter, "Opening Remarks."
[47]Quiros, *God with Us*, 183.
[48]Quiros, *God with Us*, 177.
[49]*The Macon News*, September 15, 1960, in Civil Rights, Koinonia Farm Archive.
[50]Quiros, *God with Us*, 177.

Scheer reported that he talked with Jack Singletary—a name I remembered reading in the archive—and found another thread of evidence. During the boycott, Singletary no longer lived at Koinonia Farm but on a farm in nearby Plains. I returned to the documents and looked through my notes for Singletary. I found that John Leonard (Jack) Singletary was a Georgia-born White man who had served in the Navy during World War II but who had apparently served jail time for refusing to register under the Selective Service Act of 1948.[51] While a student at Mercer University, not far from Koinonia, he joined an African American church, receiving wide attention for his actions. Clarence had written him a note, commending Singletary's "courageous action." FBI research indicated that Singletary was at the farm during the boycotts, but some years later he moved from Koinonia to Plains to start a similar community.[52] The timing of Singletary's move mattered, but I set that aside (was he at the farm or not during the boycott?).

Singletary told Scheer that when his child was dying of leukemia, the family would go to Mrs. Howell's store to call the doctors in New York to manage the treatment. The White citizens' boycott extended to friends of Koinonia, including White ones, and Mrs. Howell stopped letting the Singletary family use her phone. Jack took the situation to a merchants' group of which Jimmy Carter was a member, and the group agreed the Singletary family should not be hurt by the boycott in this situation. When the child died, Rosalynn Carter brought a ham to the family and insisted her pastor do a memorial service.[53] Scheer saw these actions as bringing complexity to Jimmy Carter, which I appreciated. While this was not shelling peanuts, Jimmy's group did use their influence to bend the boycott.

But I still wondered about the relationship between Jimmy and Clarence, specifically in the 1950s. One other piece of evidence made me wonder further. Clarence's nephew, Hamilton Jordan, reported in an autobiography that he had visited his Uncle Clarence in 1969, shortly before Clarence died. When Hamilton, who served as Jimmy's executive secretary and helped run

---

[51] Clarence Jordan, "AT 100-4223" (n.d.), Federal Bureau of Investigation, Koinonia Farm Archive, under "Willie Pugh."
[52] FBI, "Re: Koinonia Farms, Inc., Americus Georgia," May 6, 1957, Federal Bureau of Investigation, Koinonia Farm Archive.
[53] Scheer, "Jimmy We Hardly Know Y'all."

his presidential campaign, told Clarence about working with Jimmy, Clarence responded, "He's a nice fella, Hamilton, but he is just a politician."[54] I suspect that if Jimmy had stood up more substantially, Clarence would have remembered and conveyed that to Hamilton.

Perhaps the Carters' business had shelled Koinonia Farm's peanuts before the boycott, before Koinonia Farm stopped producing peanuts and shifted to their mail-order pecan business. And perhaps Jimmy admired Clarence then but was not willing to take the sort of stand Clarence did.

In 1966, when Jimmy was at a personal low after losing the race for governor, he had a conversion experience of sorts, recommitting himself to Christ and calling it his moment in which he was "born again." Privately, he began to read authors such as Clarence, Reinhold Niebuhr, Martin Luther King Jr., and Benjamin Mays, who pointed him toward "justice and mercy for all."[55] Jimmy later reflected that by 1980, he kept a copy of Clarence's Cotton Patch translations on his desk at the Carter Center, and as he put it,

> Now I began to equate the crucifixion with lynching. And I began to bring the Holy Land into Georgia. Those kinds of things were heartwarming, but also stretched our hearts and minds to look on the resurrection and incarnation of Christ not just as an invitation someday to go to heaven, but, as Clarence would say, it was to indicate God's presence permanently with us.[56]

But in the 1950s and in 1976, those at Koinonia Farm thought not taking a stand was compromising and not living as a true Christian, and saw Jimmy's inaction as inadequate.

Other White people may have interpreted Jimmy's—and their own—actions as upright if they were working for justice in some small way, given the magnitude of resistance to Black citizens' advancement. Warren Fortson, a friend of Jimmy's and an Americus lawyer, thought along these lines. During Jimmy's campaign, he observed that Jimmy, who had represented Americus as a state senator in the 1960s, "wasn't running around screaming his head off one way or the other, but he was no redneck. It wouldn't have done him any

---

[54] Quoted in Quiros, *God with Us*, 185; Jordan, *No Such Thing*, 138.
[55] Quiros, *God with Us*, 182.
[56] Carter, "Opening Remarks," xv.

good going around screaming for integration as a state senator."[57] People forget, Fortson argued, "how mean things were in those times."[58]

Florence Jordan certainly knew the meanness of people. Her take on Jimmy Carter in 1976 was stark. She observed that Carter did take a stand on racial issues in the 1950s, but not enough to alienate him from other White folks.[59]

Back home, access to a library allowed me to review additional secondary and published primary sources. But they failed to help me find clarity. Some secondary sources perpetuated the idea that the Carter warehouse had helped Koinonia Farm, and others said the Carters did nothing to stop the boycott against the farm. The story about the Singletary family and Rosalynn's intervention was repeated, and I suspect, therefore consistent.[60] In his 1992 book *Turning Point*, Jimmy mentions Koinonia Farm as the "one notable exception" to the Southern way of life, which had been rarely challenged in Georgia prior to the 1950s. He makes no mention of the Carters selling seed peanuts to Koinonia or processing their peanuts, and perhaps from silence suggests that he did not know Clarence in that period, when Jimmy notes that "the only local person I knew who ignored the strict social separation of the races was my mother."[61]

Though it was not simple, trying to understand Jimmy Carter's relationship to Koinonia Farm bore fruit. First, it reminded me of how difficult it can be to actually determine what happened, which is a gentle reminder about humility. The past is vast, and we can only know a little bit about it, and even then we must carefully determine if what we think we know is accurate. Second, I reevaluated the binary I had created. There was a sort of binary among White people related to race in the 1950s that Florence referred to— those whose actions led to persecution and those whose actions did not. But historians draw in shades of gray, and I want add a layer of nuance to Florence's interpretation. Jimmy's case reminds me that looking at a situation

---

[57]Kneeland, "'Mean' Town in Georgia."
[58]Kneeland, "'Mean' Town in Georgia."
[59]Jordan to Willets, September 13, 1976.
[60]For the former, see Randall Balmer, *Redeemer: The Life of Jimmy Carter* (New York: Basic Books, 2014), 16. For the latter, see Jonathan Alter, *His Very Best: Jimmy Carter, a Life* (New York: Simon and Schuster, 2020), 111-12. My teaching assistant looked through the indexes of all the books on Carter in the college's library and brought me the ones that mentioned Koinonia.
[61]Jimmy Carter, *Turning Point: A Candidate, a State, and a Nation Come of Age* (New York: Times Books, 1992), 16-17.

from another perspective reveals the complexity of people in the past. If we let our encounter with these complex people change us, they can provide insights into our own responses, revealing how we are culturally situated when it comes to issues of justice and righteousness.

QUESTIONS AND IMPLICATIONS

How should we today tell stories about the people who attacked Koinonia, who may seem so blatantly wrong from our perspective? Or what about those who were like the apostle Peter was with Jesus, afraid to stand with them in their time of trial? We should tell them in ways that recognize the limits to our own knowledge alongside their limited ability to transcend their contexts. But as Florence's analysis of Jimmy Carter indicates, all are responsible to God for their actions.

Clarence modeled humility by seeing those who persecuted Koinonia as human beings with limits. One day, a visiting friend commented to Clarence that White folks in Sumter County seemed "unusually mean spirited." Clarence responded that "they were the most generous people in the world on most issues." Shortly after, a farmer pulling a trailer full of cattle had a flat tire in front of the farm—Clarence proceeded to help the man change the tire.[62] Clarence was following Paul's admonition to, as Clarence translated it, "never act competitively or for self-praise, but with humbleness esteem others as above yourselves. Don't confine yourselves to your own interests, but seek the welfare of others. In this regard, you all think as Christ Jesus did."[63] Our stories of the past must be stories laced with love.

Good history—and humility—demands that we understand people in their context first, as I have tried to model with Carter. It does not demand that we accept as good, right, and true what people did, nor does it mean we adopt a relativistic model. Recognizing that people's standards of living, habits, etiquette, and so on are time bound teaches humility. This perspective can remind us that our own ways of living are time bound, place specific, and shaped by personal and systemic sin.

---

[62]Lynn and Ginny Coultas in Weiner, *Koinonia Remembered*, 84.
[63]Clarence Jordan, "Smithville, Alabama (Philippians)," in *The Cotton Patch Version of Paul's Epistles* (Piscataway, NJ: New Century, 1968), Philippians 2:3-4.

As British author C. S. Lewis notes, our own age has illusions, ways of being, that are false, but we often accept them because they seem so normal. He argues that we needed to study the past because we need an "intimate knowledge of it," since

> we cannot study the future, and yet need something to set against the present, to remind us that the basic assumptions have been quite different in different periods and that which seems certain to the uneducated is merely temporary fashion. A man who has lived in many places is not likely to be deceived by the local errors of his native village: the scholar has lived in many times and is therefore in some degree immune from the great cataract of nonsense that pours from the press and microphone of his own age.[64]

Humility requires us, then, to wonder how we too might be misshaped by our own time and place. As Clarence described Koinonia members' expulsion from Reheboth Baptist Church in the midst of the boycott and violence,

> I tell you this, not to reflect bad or evil on any one but to show you the tremendous struggle going on in the hearts of the Southern people. Like all of us, they are people with the good and the evil pulling inside them, with a struggle between an ideal and a tradition. They want to do what they know Christ teaches but they are not strong enough to break with the tradition in which they find themselves.[65]

- Humility requires having a right view of yourself. What traditions do you have that seem normal but might require breaking from?

Humility also demands that we become clear with ourselves where we are making educated guesses and where we can be more confident in what we think we know.

- What does jumping to conclusions do to relationships? To understanding the past well?
- How could you resist jumping to conclusions?

During the boycott and violence, the Koinonia community read encouraging letters from around the country at their shared midday meal. Despite

---

[64]C. S. Lewis, "Learning in War Time," in *The Weight of Glory and Other Addresses* (New York: HarperOne, 2001), 47-63.
[65]Jordan, "Ordeal by Bullets."

the encouragement from around the country, they were weary, especially Clarence. Dorothy Day observed, "The strain was telling on Clarence—his eyes were sad and tired and his face showed the terrible strain he was under."[66] Clarence was a key target, Dorothy reflected, because "he is the minister, he is the founder of Koinonia, and it is his planning and vision which has kept things going since 1942. He has consistently tried to follow the teachings of Jesus, living the Gospel message of love of brother." Though they were tired, the community reported feeling renewed by God's love. As Clarence translated from 2 Corinthians,

> Just look! We catch it from every direction but we don't let them squeeze the life out of us. We don't know which end is up, but they don't upend us. We are persecuted, but never wiped out. We are banged all over, but they don't get rid of us. On every hand we bear the *slaying* of Jesus in the body so that the *life* of Jesus in our group might be clearly evident. We who live for Jesus always flirt with death, in order that Jesus' life may be all the more evident in our fragile flesh. . . . We are sure that He who made the Lord Jesus to live again will also make us alive with Him and stand us all up together. . . . And that's why we don't poop out. Even if we do look worn out on the outside, we are constantly refreshed on the inside. After all, it will turn out that our little old troubles will be more than outweighed by our eternal glory. We just don't put any stock in outward things, but in inner things. For outward things are perishable, while inner things are eternal.[67]

- Who in your congregation might be carrying a greater burden in following Jesus? Dorothy Day observed Clarence's burden. Clarence observed the heavier burden of Black community members.
- How can you help someone as an individual?
- How can you shift patterns in your church and community that would make level the paths of righteousness for all people?

Clarence believed that if Christians were not being persecuted, they were losing their saltiness. In 1994, long after Clarence's death, members of Koinonia Farm believed that their commitment to racial equality had waned. They wrote a letter to Jimmy Carter, inviting him to visit the farm, and

---

[66]Dorothy Day, "On Pilgrimage," *Catholic Worker*, May 1, 1957.
[67]Jordan, *Cotton Patch Version*, 2 Corinthians 4:8-11, 14, 16-18.

mentioned their reckoning. They said, "folks in Sumter County no longer shoot at Koinonia, as they did in our early years, but that's not because Sumter County has freed itself of racist power structures. Instead Koinonia has quit struggling. 'The intensity of persecution (of Christians) is geared not to the moral level of the non-Christians or persecutors but to the intensity of the witness of the Christian community,' . . . Jordan wrote. When we lose our salt, 'people will no longer bother to persecute Christians.'"[68] They were quoting one of Clarence's sermons on Jesus' Sermon on the Mount. Clarence said: "Whenever tension ceases to exist between the church and the world, one of two things has happened: Either the world has been completely converted to Christ and his Way, or the church has watered down and compromised its original heritage."[69]

- Are there areas of your life, or your church's life, where you have lost your saltiness?
- Do you think Clarence was right, that if Christians are walking faithfully they will be persecuted?

---

[68]Unnamed to Jimmy Carter, July 29, 1994, 17, Carter, Koinonia Farm Archive. For Koinonia's self-reevaluation in the late twentieth century, see Tracy E. K'Meyer, "What Koinonia Was All About: The Role of Memory in a Changing Community," *The Oral History Review*, 24, no. 1 (1997): 1-22.
[69]Clarence Jordan, "Sermon on the Mount," in *Clarence Jordan: Essential Writings*, ed. Joyce Hollyday (Maryknoll: Orbis Books, 2003), 120.

13

IT'S NOT SO SIMPLE

> How Clarence's unexpected approach to the civil rights movement in Americus, Georgia, reveals the complexity of the past and why we must not settle for binaries.

ALBANY MOVEMENT

As a kid, Hamilton Jordan liked his Uncle Clarence, even though Clarence was known as the black sheep of the family. Hamilton remembered family members whispering "among themselves about 'what Clarence was doing' and shaking their heads with disgust."[1] But Hamilton rarely saw Clarence, usually only at funerals and hardly at family weddings. When Hamilton asked why Clarence and Florence rarely came to the weddings, Clarence "smiled and hugged [him], then pulled back . . . 'you only see me at family funerals because you have to be invited to weddings.'" But in the summer of 1962, Clarence, Florence, and their children regularly stopped by Hamilton's house in Albany, about thirty-five miles south of Koinonia Farm. They piled out of a beat-up car, laden with pecans or peaches from the farm in a brown paper bag.[2] Hamilton learned later that Uncle Clarence stopped by so often because they were involved in the civil rights movement in Albany, Georgia, and collaborating with Black leaders there.

---

[1] Hamilton Jordan, *No Such Thing as a Bad Day* (New York: Pocket Books, 2000), 119.
[2] Jordan, *No Such Thing*, 120. One of the Jordan children logged a chronology of the Albany movement. See Chronology in Civil Rights, Koinonia Farm Archive.

CLARENCE AND CIVIL RIGHTS

The Americus movement: Marching, voting, boycotting. When I first learned about Koinonia Farm, I fully expected Clarence and other members to be actively involved in the civil rights movement. In some ways, I was falling into the old binary trap—you're either with us or against us. But as with Jimmy Carter, a puzzle emerged that left me questioning my assumptions. I watched a documentary about Koinonia and heard Clarence's daughter Jan describe her father's approach to civil rights. Her description puzzled me. Jan said that when she told her dad she wanted to participate in a march, he responded, "Jannie, I can go out and kill sheriff Chappell. I would be 'doing' something but what I'd be doing wouldn't be right. You can join in the march. That's your decision. But if you get arrested, I won't get you out. Call someone else or stay in jail. Because what you're doing isn't right."[3] So what were Clarence's views on civil rights? Clearly, he did not hold the same perspective as John Perkins, who was organizing people in marches in the same era. But more research showed me that Clarence was not against the movement—his position was more complicated.

Clarence's complicated relationship to the Americus movement broke down the dichotomy I already knew was false because history is complex, but so easily returned to: that people were either in favor of the movement or against it. Clarence's position can be characterized by a sense of individual responsibility and choice, and the commitment to do what he thought was the right thing. As his daughter Jan observed, "He was often in the center of conflict and yet he didn't instigate the controversy."[4] If John Perkins represents the first option, movement activism that opposed a second option, massive White resistance (which we know was complicated), Clarence offers a third path in the civil rights era.

In late 1962 and early 1963, Student Nonviolent Coordinating Committee workers Ralph Allen, Don Harris, and John Perdew came to Americus from Albany to join local Black leaders to work for civil rights. Voter registration was their first project. Since 1908, when Georgia put severe limits on who could vote, it had been nearly impossible for African Americans to vote in Sumter

---

[3] Jan Jordan in Kay Weiner, ed., *Koinonia Remembered* (Americus, GA: Koinonia, 1992), 77-78. The documentary is *Briars in the Cotton Patch: The Story of the Koinonia Farm* (Vision Video, 2012).
[4] Jan Jordan in Weiner, *Koinonia Remembered*, 77.

County. According to one history, "a person would have to be a Confederate veteran or descendent, a person of good character, had to be able to read and write any part of the Georgia or U.S. Constitution, or was the owner of 40 acres of land or property worth 500 with all the poll taxes paid back to 1877."[5]

Clarence used his influence in everyday life to encourage voter registration, which upset Georgia's racial hierarchy. A Black friend who also worked at the pecan factory at Koinonia recalled, "I will always appreciate Clarence for letting us know we should register to vote. He gave us the opportunity to become registered voters."[6]

Koinonia Farm also opened their property to movement organizers, perhaps because of the connections they already had through their involvement with the Albany movement. Student Nonviolent Coordinating Committee workers stayed at Koinonia Farm for several months, with at least one, Zev Aloney, living there long term. One organizer remembered that being at Koinonia meant "leaving a crazy world and coming to people who were rational."[7] The farm was a retreat and a place for organizing meetings. In 1963, Koinonia Farm hosted a workshop for about twenty project workers, and when the workers wanted to organize the local maids so they could earn more than the pittance they were paid, Koinonia again opened its doors to an initial barbecue. As with Black churches in Mississippi, this was a decision that could have deadly consequences.

While the Student Nonviolent Coordinating Committee's initial goal was voter registration, it began a mass-action campaign that involved marches to desegregate local businesses—similar to what John led in Mendenhall. Black citizens of Americus benefited from a separate Black business structure. As with other places of civil rights activity, Black-led institutions were central places for organizing and galvanizing people. John and Mabel Barnum's local Black funeral home was a headquarters for the movement, and many (though by no means all) Black churches opened their doors to the movement.[8]

---

[5]Quoted in Mills Lane, *People of Georgia: An Illustrated History* (New York: Beehive, 1975).
[6]Weiner, *Koinonia Remembered*, 53.
[7]"Civil Rights Activists Recall the Americus Four," n.d., John Perdew Material, Koinonia Farm Archive.
[8]This narrative relies on Stephen G. N. Tuck, *Beyond Atlanta: The Struggle for Racial Equality in Georgia, 1940–1980* (Athens: University of Georgia Press, 2003); Ansley Lillian Quiros, *God with Us: Lived Theology and the Freedom Struggle in Americus, Georgia, 1942–1976* (Chapel Hill: University of North Carolina Press, 2018).

Black movement leaders pointed to Koinonia as laying the groundwork for what became one of the most successful rural Georgia organizing campaigns. Charles Sherrod, a pastor and Student Nonviolent Coordinating Committee worker based in Albany, observed, "Much of the spade work has already been done by the Koinonia farm people. . . . This is a good start even if it is emblazoned with bullet fringes."[9] Local leader Mabel Barnum observed that Koinonia's endurance in the face of those bullets—not to mention the boycotts, social isolation, and dynamite—helped Black people muster courage in the face of a system that demeaned them. She said, "When the people saw that little group wasn't going to let the Klan run them off, they knew from that time on that you don't have to be scared of the Klan."[10]

Black leaders held mass meetings regularly in churches. The meetings strengthened people's resolve as they listened to speakers and sang freedom songs together. Jan Jordan recalled, "We Koinonia kids went to mass meetings on Mondays and Thursday evenings. We sang and registered voters."[11] In significant ways, the young people at Koinonia were part of the movement, which was deeply Christian. Freedom songs merged Negro spirituals with the immanent goals of people, calling on God and the people to bring what was right and good. They sang, "I woke up this morning with my mind set on freedom." They called each other to "come go to me with that land, where I'm bound. No segregation in that land . . . nothing but freedom in that land." They declared, "I ain't gone to let nobody turn me around. . . . I'm gonna keep on walking, keep on talking, walking to the freedom land."[12]

Bolstered by their worship, those in the movement went out to protest, strengthened to resist not just individuals who oppressed them but an entire system whose logic was bent on keeping them in their place.[13] And systems like these do not die easily—marchers knew that the power of love must confront the power of hate. Movement organizers also understood that while

---

[9]Quoted in Tuck, *Beyond Atlanta*, 178.
[10]Quoted in Tuck, *Beyond Atlanta*, 178.
[11]Weiner, *Koinonia Remembered*.
[12]"Americus, Georgia, Mass Meeting, August 17, 1963," n.d., Moses Moon Collection, box 6, Archives Center, National Museum of American History, www.youtube.com/watch?v=cgHFM34-Qlk&list=PLanaFQxhTXyxS9YU-mgJt6sYN37cb7vUe&index=5. Historian Evan Kutzler posted these songs on YouTube.
[13]For faith in the movement, see David L. Chappell, *A Stone of Hope: Prophetic Religion and the Death of Jim Crow* (Chapel Hill: University of North Carolina Press, 2004); Quiros, *God with Us*.

their activism might prompt violent retaliation, they were not the ones causing the violence, contrary to what local White authorities claimed. Rather, they were creating a moment in which the violence of the system was brought to light for all to see. For them, change would happen when people were confronted with the violence, and it would be embodied in new laws as well as people who were confident in their self-worth.

Clarence's views of change. But despite these noble goals, Clarence refused to march, demonstrate, or join boycotts. When movement activists encouraged people to boycott a store over its hiring practices, Clarence continued to buy from the store. When Jan asked him why, Clarence replied, "Jannie, we've been on the other end of a boycott. I know first-hand how much a boycott hurts. I can't participate in the boycott and be doing unto others as I would have them do unto me. I've had it done unto me and I didn't like it one bit."[14] Clarence did not see the means of change—a boycott—as consistent with the ends.

Clarence also did not put much faith in political systems' ability to bring change, although he did support Black voters' registration. As early as the 1940s, when writing for a high school Sunday school audience and their teachers, he noted that some people were convinced that Jesus would be a political savior, but they were mistaken.[15] For Clarence, the kingdom of God would come on earth as it is in heaven, not through political rebellion but through spiritual transformation. His sensibility does not seem to have changed much as Americus's Black residents worked for civil rights.

Clarence understood God's kingdom as encompassing—and surpassing—the movement's goals. As the phrase "civil rights movement" became common, Clarence began to speak of the "God movement," which he saw as a means *and* an end. The God movement was the kingdom of God, breaking into the world as people followed Jesus no matter the consequences. Those in the God movement would care for the land, value people over money, share in interracial fellowship, and practice the way of love because their relationship with Jesus had transformed them. They would live together as though the kingdom of God had come.

---

[14]Jan Jordan in Weiner, *Koinonia Remembered*, 78.
[15]Clarence Jordan, *Lord and Master: Part I*, Judson Keystone Graded Course XI, Part 1-Pupil (Philadelphia: Judson, 1949), 8.

Clarence's interpretation of the political imprisonments and executions during Jesus' passion reveals how he expected the kingdom of God to come. In 1949, Clarence told the story of the two thieves, or "rebels," as he translated the term, crucified with Jesus. Clarence suggested that three rebels, Barabbas (whom Pontius Pilate released instead of Jesus), Dismas, and Gesmas (the two other rebels, according to tradition), knew one another because of the familiar way one of the crucified thieves refers to Jesus. Other places in the text, people call Jesus "Teacher, and Rabbi, and Lord, and Master, and Jesus, thou Son of God." But this rebel just calls him Jesus. "This familiar, intimate name did not now fall from a stranger's lips. It went back to the shop, the schoolroom, the street corners, the playground. It revived memories of heated discussions—about a kingdom and how it should be set up." Had they grown up together? Clarence wondered. Had they debated how the Messiah would come, as many Jews did? Like other Jews, they wanted change, but the rebels wanted to bring the kingdom in through force. But Clarence saw that for Jesus, the kingdom did not come by force but was "a kingdom of the spirit, of love, of kindness and meekness, of universal brotherhood, of sharing."[16]

Clarence refused to force anyone to embrace the kingdom of God, although he urged them to repent, turning toward it and away from the false gods of the world. As the community noted in an open letter to the citizens of Americus during the attacks and boycotts of the 1950s, they had not made public statements before because they did not want to force their ideas on others but to live their own lives under God.[17] But when their lives were in tension with others—and they fully expected them to be in tension—they refused to back down. Their dominant sensibility, however, was to not force others to change. Clarence was fundamentally concerned with people's hearts; in this he was resoundingly individualistic. He noted, in response to the civil rights movement, "I'm more concerned about persuasion—about changing people from the inside."[18]

The kingdom of God would come quietly, Clarence thought. Clarence contrasted John the Baptist—along with other prophets, including civil rights

---

[16] Jordan, *Lord and Master: Part I*, 34.
[17] "An Open Letter from Koinonia Farm," n.d., in Koinonia Farm 1949–1957, Koinonia Farm Archive.
[18] "Analogy Between Prejudices, Pastor Puts Jesus in Cotton Field," n.d., in Koinonia Farm, 1958–1965 (white binder), Koinonia Farm Archive.

activists—with Jesus. Those like John attempted "to force people into the kingdom—or to mistake the way the kingdom is manifested. John was certainly aware that the Spirit of God descended on Jesus, but he overlooked the significance of its coming as a dove—quietly," Clarence said.[19] Clarence saw civil rights activists who *intentionally* revealed the extent to which the kingdom of this world gripped Christians as forcing the issue.

To be clear, Clarence was in no way arguing for a gradual change, as many White racial moderates did. His interpretation of the apostle Paul's racial position reveals his understanding. For Clarence, Paul was clearly an integrationist, living in a time with even more racial tension than his own. Clarence said Paul had three options: first, he could have rejected God's call for racial unity, saying, "'Well, after all, human beings are human beings. We've got our sacred Southern way of life and we've got to keep it.' He could have identified himself with the culture and wound up with a pretty big place of influence." Second, Paul could have tried to take a "middle-of-the-road position" saying, "Sure, God has included the Gentile, but you know it's going to take time and I'm pushing on this thing in my way, and we'll all kind of push along together, and in time things will be solved." This middle position would have been being like a White racial moderate, which was an "untenable" position and led to misery, because "when you straddle the fence you are respected by neither side and you are capable of leading neither side." Last, Paul could have taken the path he did, which Clarence thought he too was taking: living out his belief and enduring the subsequent persecution. For Paul, that meant going to jail. In Clarence's telling, when the good church people of Ephesus saw Paul "in one of the local cafes eating with" a Black man, "they thought that because he was eating with him he was going to church with him. Now it's one thing to have a sit-in in the cafeteria. It's *another* thing to have a sit-in in the church." When Paul spoke to the people to defend himself and explain that his call was "to preach the Word to the Gentiles, 'the Negroes,'" then "somebody hollered for the tar and feathers, and Paul had to be taken into the prison to be protected."[20]

---

[19]Clarence Jordan, "The Sound of a Dove," *Town and Country Church*, October 1961, in Koinonia Farm, 1958–1965 (white binder), Koinonia Farm Archive.

[20]Clarence Jordan, "The Distinct Identity," in *The Substance of Faith and Other Cotton Patch Sermons*, ed. Dallas Lee (Cascade Books, 2005), 119-121.

Clarence wanted all Christians to be like Paul, betting their lives on the unseen realities—living as though the kingdom of God *actually* had come on earth. He thought that true Christians should embody the kingdom of God today together and become pockets in the broader society where people lived out the kingdom of God. He wrote in 1949,

> How can Christ "save" the world without saving individuals who will band themselves together into small spiritual families? These will become the heart of the redeemed society, or kingdom of God, very much like the human family is the unit of the kingdoms of this world. . . . As these redemptive fellowships multiply, they become the "leaven" which leavens the whole lump of sour dough. Through them the kingdoms of this world are transformed into the kingdom of our Lord. It is by this process that he is made known to others as the Saviour of the world.

But, Clarence continued, "the church as we know it today is not such a fellowship," and "too often it has offered to the world a Saviour whom it has itself rejected."[21]

Clarence did not want to provoke controversy unnecessarily, but living in the God movement inevitably would, and one must not shy away from that. As Clarence explained to Jan when he said he would not bail her out if she marched, "Now, if you and Lena (a Black friend) are in town and in the course of your time together it would be natural to go into Walgreen's for a coke [and sit at the counter together], I not only will come to get you out of jail but I will go all the way to the Supreme Court because what you're doing is right."[22] In other words, if Jan and Lena broke segregation's rules by eating together at a public lunch counter because they were thirsty—not because they wanted to make a point—Clarence would support them.

QUESTIONS AND IMPLICATIONS

Clarence understood racism in the South to be systemic and individual. As systemic sin, it was embedded in the very culture of White Christianity and bled out into the broader society. Individuals, he thought, perpetuated it. His primary concern was not society, however, but whether Christians were

---

[21]Clarence Jordan, *Lord and Master, Part 2*, Course XI, Part 2, in the New Judson (Keystone) Graded Course for High School Young People (Philadelphia: Judson, 1949), 111.
[22]Jan Jordan in Weiner, *Koinonia Remembered*, 78.

living faithfully. He thought that society would change as Christians lived together in community, faithfully adhering to what was good, right, and true no matter the consequences, because they would interact with the larger society. But for Clarence, the key was that those in the God movement would embody an alternative way of living, a glimpse of heaven on earth, that was seen in how they cared for one another. Clarence welcomed civil rights activists to the farm, and embodied this vision by providing both a haven and a foundation for their organizing. But he did not agree with their methods.

Activists wanted to change society, to change the political, economic, and religious systems that socialized White southerners into thinking African Americans must stay in their place and dehumanized Black citizens. They cared about an alternative community, which they called the beloved community, that grew as people worshiped, marched, and ate together. But a key goal for most activists was to reveal the violence undergirding the southern way of life, so as to dismantle it. As Martin Luther King Jr. argued in his "Letter from a Birmingham Jail" in 1963, "Nonviolent direct action seeks to create such a crisis and foster such a tension that a community which has constantly refused to negotiate is forced to confront the issue. It seeks to so dramatize the issue that it can no longer be ignored."[23] Change required not going about one's life in scorn of the consequences quietly, but outright demands. As King observed, "We know through painful experience that freedom is never voluntarily given by the oppressor; it must be demanded by the oppressed."[24] For King, a key priority was changing laws and practices—changes to the system such as laws that would prevent White citizens from exploiting Black citizens.

- What do you think of Clarence's view of change compared to civil rights activists' perspective? What are the strengths and weaknesses of both positions? Can they be reconciled?

My own sense about how change happens may be more expansive than Clarence's. I think that some people need to be working as outside agitators,

---

[23]Martin Luther King, "Letter from a Birmingham Jail," *The Christian Century: An Ecumenical Weekly*, June 12, 1963, 767-773, https://teachingamericanhistory.org/document/letter-from-birmingham-city-jail-excerpts/.
[24]King, "Letter from a Birmingham Jail."

IT'S NOT SO SIMPLE

others need to work within systems, and all of us need to live into what is good, beautiful, and true in our everyday lives.

- Consider the following: Where do you live? How do you live? Do you care for the soil? Do you care for your neighbors? Do you consume more than you ought? Do you love those who persecute you?
- How is your cultural context broken and beautiful? To what extent do you refuse to embody the broken parts when they conflict with the gospel, and how much does it cost you?

People today often bifurcate various cultural issues: Are you for or against? Our minds want to make things simple. Our brains are magnificent, but they are also are cognitive misers, and we tend to identify simple categories and create stereotypes. Historical conclusions, however, usually suggest that we resist bifurcation. The study of history nearly always demands that we see things as complicated—because they are. Remembering that the world is complicated can also drive us to humility because we realize that so often we only see part of the situation. We also serve a God who is complicated and beyond our understanding. God is the one who loved Job deeply and also allowed Satan to hurt him tremendously, and the one who allowed Joseph to suffer and brought great good from it.

- Describe a situation in which things were more complicated than you originally thought, kind of like Clarence's engagement with the civil rights movement. What does allowing things to be complicated demand of us?
- On what issues do you act in a third way? On what issues should you act in a third way or, like Clarence welcomed civil rights activists, welcome those who are approaching a subject with a similar end goal but with different means?

14

COTTON PATCH GOSPEL

> How Clarence's Cotton Patch translations of the New Testament were a gift of love to White southern Christians and why we should let the translations be a mirror for us today.

AUDIENCE AND CONTEXT

"Georgia is in the Bible Belt, where the ideas of Jesus are preached with great fervor and denied with equal vigor," Clarence quipped often.[1] He thought the hypocrisy stemmed from White Christians' lack of understanding of the actual gospel message. They imagined God was remote, the kind of being you might inscribe into a stained-glass window, rather than the God who became flesh and dwelled among God's people. He wanted to preach and translate Scripture in such a way that people who thought they were Christians saw the good news—and themselves—as though for the first time.

In his "cotton patch" approach, Clarence aimed to strip "away the fancy language, the artificial piety, and the barriers of time and distance," and "put Jesus and his people in the midst of our modern world, living where we live, talking as we talk, working, hurting, praying, bleeding, dying, conquering, alongside the rest of us."[2] If people really knew Jesus as incarnate, living, breathing, stubbing his toe, and wearing diapers as a baby, they might change. When Clarence

---

[1] Gene Hunter, "Dixie Advocate of Race Equality to Speak Here," April 1963, in Koinonia Farm, 1958–1965 (white binder), Koinonia Farm Archive.
[2] Clarence Jordan, "Introduction," in *The Cotton Patch Version of Luke and Acts: Jesus' Doings and the Happenings* (Clinton, NJ: New Win, 1969), 7.

preached, he tried to make biblical stories come alive using not only modern but colloquial—everyday—speech. He wanted to bring Scripture into the world of everyday folk whose shoes were stained with red dirt and who enjoyed muscadine wine.

Early versions of the Cotton Patch translations were oral, like the Hebrew Scriptures and the New Testament letters that the Jews and the early church read out loud. When he preached, Clarence would read his text and refer back to it. He would read from his Greek New Testament, translating Scripture out loud as he went. His translation accounted for the context of the early church, and it accounted for his read on his contemporary White American church. Drawing from his expertise in New Testament from his PhD and continued studies, Clarence set the stories of Jesus and the early church in his contemporary South. To hear recordings of his preaching and translations is to hear his humor, his love of the Scripture, and his expertise both in the New Testament world and in the trouble that came for those who resisted the southern way of life.

Clarence preached nationally, and people began asking him to write down his translations. Koinonia Farm began producing Clarence's translations in pamphlet form. In the late 1960s, Clarence began working on his translations more systematically, writing them in his careful handwriting. Others, including Linda Fuller (married to Millard Fuller, who founded Habitat for Humanity), typed them. Publications from the 1960s and 1970s look like slim books. My first copy was a more recent one, published in 2004, for which Jimmy Carter wrote the foreword.

Some people have said he transposed Scripture as a musician might transpose a piece of music, taking it from one key to another. I think his work was more of a new arrangement. He took the songs—the Gospels and the letters in the New Testament—and made them sound fresh to his listeners by comparing the contexts of the early church and his contemporary society. Clarence understood the New Testament's meanings in its original contexts and put his interpretive stamp on it by imagining what it would look like if the story unfolded in his own context.

To fully understand Clarence's translations of the New Testament, we must remember his context and audience. Despite how obvious this conclusion is, I really understood it only after months of reading other sources—FBI files, newspaper clippings, letters, sermons, and interviews from the majestic Hargrett Rare Book and Manuscript Library at Clarence's alma mater, the University of Georgia, and the room known as "the closet" that houses Koinonia Farm's archival material. Books by other historians, walks around Koinonia Farm, and touring the town of Americus filled in my sense of the place and the time Clarence inhabited. As I wove an intertextual context—puzzling over Clarence and southwest Georgia's history, reading the Cotton Patch translations, looking again at other sources—I increasingly saw the Cotton Patch translations as Clarence's guidebook for living.

Clarence believed that Christians were to continue Jesus' incarnation, putting flesh on the Word of God in their particular times and places. This meant showing people what it looked like together to be children of God, people who would look like their daddy. The Cotton Patch translations reveal how Clarence understood God's call on all Christians in the South at mid-century. They are arguably his most enduring and influential legacy and, despite the distance in time and perhaps place, are relevant for us today.

But Clarence's main audience was White southerners. To get the full benefit of the Cotton Patch translations, you have to situate his translations in a thick understanding of that world.

Why White southerners as the audience? While I cannot say for certain, I can make an argument from context. Despite some integration at the farm and going to a Black church while in Louisville, Clarence's circles were mostly White. Clarence saw White southerners as the ones who needed to change, who were resisting the kingdom of God. When Clarence set the world of the New Testament in his contemporary time and place, he made the "chosen people," those who thought they knew God but really did not, the so-called good White church people. They were the ones who needed to repent.

Clarence wrote to a generation of White southerners who understood Scripture differently from him. Many White southerners saw their faith as under attack. They read Scripture to say that God ordained segregation and that civil rights activists' and the federal government's efforts to enforce integration violated their faith. The Cold War was at hand, and many understood their faith, which they tied closely with the United States's virtue, as under attack from "godless communists." At the same time, they emphasized preaching spiritual salvation and assumed that Jesus was White, pure and divine. Jesus' spiritual and racial purity extended to them, as their primary concern was for their spiritual purity.[3]

The Cotton Patch translations were meant to lead White southerners to repentance by confronting them with what living faithfully meant in their context. They were essentially a gift to those who had persecuted Clarence or stood by silently. Clarence told a reporter,

> I grew up in Georgia in the midst of fervent profession of faith in Christianity on the one hand and just as fervent refusal to practice it on the other. It occurred to me that much of this was not so much willful rebellion as failure to understand the ideas of the Gospel. The words of the scripture were coming through, but they were void of content. Thus the message was packing no punch. I felt that the words of Jesus and others were simply not hitting us with the same impact they had on hearers of the N.T. times.[4]

Before they could repent, White southerners needed to see, because they were blinded by sin. "Sin's first work," Clarence wrote in 1949, "is to blind you to its real nature. Before the wrong thing is ever done, sin puts its hands over your spiritual eyes. Sometimes we hear young people say, 'I don't see any harm in this or that.' The tragedy of it is that they don't. Too frequently it is evidence of the blindness which precedes depravity."[5]

Like other preachers and teachers, Clarence had long worked to make the Bible relevant to audiences. For him, imagining biblical stories set in contemporary times did that work, as his Sunday school materials from the 1940s—long before he began writing the Cotton Patch translations—show. Clarence suggested that while Jesus was crucified on Golgotha, it could have just as easily been a knoll outside Chicago, Boston, Atlanta, Smithville, or Croxton.[6] He offered extensive context for the New Testament, invited students and

---

[3] See Charles Marsh, *God's Long Summer: Stories of Faith and Civil Rights* (Princeton, NJ: Princeton University Press, 1997); Ansley Lillian Quiros, *God with Us: Lived Theology and the Freedom Struggle in Americus, Georgia, 1942–1976* (Chapel Hill: University of North Carolina Press, 2018); Carolyn Renée Dupont, *Mississippi Praying: Southern White Evangelicals and the Civil Rights Movement, 1945–1975* (New York: New York University Press, 2013); J. Russell Hawkins, *Because the Bible Told Them So: How Southern Evangelicals Fought to Preserve White Supremacy* (New York: Oxford University Press, 2021).

[4] "The Bible Collector, The Cotton Patch Translation," n.d., Koinonia Farm, in 1958–1965 (white binder), Koinonia Farm Archive.

[5] Clarence Jordan, *Lord and Master: Part I*, Judson Keystone Graded Course XI, Part 1-Pupil (Philadelphia: Judson, 1949), 106.

[6] Jordan, *Lord and Master: Part I*.

teachers to imagine themselves as part of key events in the Scriptures, and suggested they write newspaper articles or plays to convey what they had seen and heard. Clarence also thought more contemporary language could help bridge the gap between the past and the present. He encouraged people to read Scripture not in the archaic language of the King James Version but in the Revised Standard Version. He said that it "will amaze you how much more life the Scriptures take on. It is in modern speech, and written in story form, but is an actual translation from the Greek."[7]

Clarence's translations were different from the KJV or the RSV, however. He translated the New Testament's ideas. As one reviewer observed, "Paul's thoughts sometimes seem far above us: transpose them as this book does, however, by moving the situation from first-century Asia Minor to the present day American South, and they come alive and move helpfully closer to our thoughts and to where we live."[8]

READING SCRIPTURE

Clarence's practice and approach to Scripture. Clarence's patterns of scriptural engagement also shaped his Cotton Patch translations.[9] Clarence loved the Bible and used his imagination as he read. After Clarence died, a friend asked Florence which Scripture Clarence wanted read at his funeral. She responded, "You can read any scripture you like. He loved it all."[10] Clarence's son, Jim, remembered that on cold, gray days, Clarence would come indoors "for study and reading the gospels in Greek where in his imagination I'm sure he walked, talked—and probably swapped jokes—with Jesus and the disciples who were his heroes."[11] Though he loved the Bible deeply, Clarence

---

[7]Jordan, *Lord and Master: Part I*, 25. Note that the RSV was a controversial text among White evangelicals, who were troubled by the translation's saying not that a virgin would give birth but that "a young woman" would give birth. Peter J. Thuesen, *In Discordance with the Scriptures: American Protestant Battles over Translating the Bible* (New York: Oxford, 1999).

[8]Mary Morrison, "Two for the Road," n.d., Clarence Jordan Papers, in box 3, folder 13, Hargrett Rare Book and Manuscript Library, University of Georgia.

[9]Understanding people's practices for reading Scripture can be difficult, but we can consider the frameworks people brought to the text and how their practices shaped their frameworks. For one example, Beth Barton Schweiger, "Reading the Bible in a Romantic Era," in *The Bible in American Life*, ed. Philip Goff, Arthur E. Farnsley, and Peter J. Thuesen (New York: Oxford University Press, 2017), 69-80.

[10]Millard Fuller in Kay Weiner, ed., *Koinonia Remembered* (Americus, GA: Koinonia, 1992), 107.

[11]Jim Jordan in Weiner, *Koinonia Remembered*, 96.

would not elevate the Bible, the written Word of God, above Jesus, the living Word of God.

Deeply influenced by the Gospel of John and 1, 2, and 3 John, Clarence emphasized that Jesus was the Word of God. But Jesus, Clarence noted, was a man—flesh and blood—not ink. And the Word of God was not incarnate only in Jesus or the Bible. "In a sense," Clarence said, "the Word of God is that transmission of God's will and purposes to his people. It is the communication of Himself to those who allow themselves to be part of the extension of the Incarnation."[12] Christians, when they were living according to the Word, became the Word—became the way God communicated his love to others. The church must "mak[e] anew that communication to every generation," as each generation put flesh and blood on God's good news in its own times and places.[13]

Reading the Bible alone did not guarantee understanding its truth. One's posture toward Scripture enabled one to hear what God said. Hearing God's Word required loving Scripture and expecting to receive from it. Clarence said,

> It's only those who go to it yearning, hungering, and open and receptive and friendly—then the old Book comes out of the pages, its words glow as if they were lit with Neon, and the truth comes out to you,—at times it makes your heart wonder if you can hold it all. It makes you gust—O, I can understand how you could get pretty happy with religion sometimes. When you really want to know—when the truth of God really comes flooding in on you—it's a great experience; if you've never had it, you ought to seek it.[14]

Second, Clarence said that people must let the Holy Spirit guide them, not a preacher or theology professor. "Every time I read" the Bible, Clarence said, "if it's going to mean anything to me, I must read it with the consciousness that it's the Spirit that is the teacher, and it is He who takes these written words and brings them out and lays them upon my mind, upon my heart—makes them come alive."[15]

---

[12]Clarence Jordan, "The Church and the Bible" (Baptist Church, Brookings SC, December 3, 1952), in 2Aiii)a)I Clarence's Manuscripts and Other Writings, Koinonia Farm Archive.
[13]Jordan, "Church and the Bible."
[14]Jordan, "Church and the Bible."
[15]Jordan, "Church and the Bible."

Last, people must read and respond with action, or God will not reveal more to them. "I don't think God would make known his truth to people who have no intention of living it," Clarence observed. Instead, the Word "must always be becoming flesh. The process of translation must always be taking place. You must take it from the printed page, and make it flesh—your flesh, that the Word might dwell among you, and that they might see it, see it in you as it glows among you, and that they might give glory to the Father, who is in heaven."[16]

Corporate Scripture reading. The Koinonia community also valued Scripture deeply. Clarence spent hours with the text alone *and* read it daily with other Koinonia members. Days at the farm opened with corporate Scripture reading and study. When Dorothy Day—a Catholic who also lived in intentional community—visited, she commented that Koinonia members prayed less than her New Jersey Catholic Worker farming community but read the Bible more.

Clarence contributed immensely to those study sessions and helped others see the gospel's radical call, to be lived out in the mundane habits of eating, working, and praying. Ladon Sheets, who would give up a corporate job at IBM to join Koinonia Farm, remembered,

> I was spell-bound by Clarence's careful unfolding of major themes in the teachings of Jesus: hanging on every word and intrigued with each new understanding, yet deeply confronted by the truth I was hearing. I grew up in the church but never had I heard the gospel as Clarence presented it. The same scriptures I knew well when passed through Clarence's mind and spirit came out sounding totally different. At one point, I remember saying with at least a hint of exasperation, "But Clarence! What you are teaching is totally revolutionary!!" Through a little smile came his response, "Well, Ladon, I think you are catching on."[17]

Their discussions broke down false divisions between the sacred and the mundane. As one Koinonia member observed, listening to Clarence's sermons and talks gave him "insights into the way this man joined the spiritual and the down-to-earth parts of life, closing the gap between them that I'd always taken for granted."[18]

---

[16]Jordan, "Church and the Bible."
[17]Ladon Sheets in Weiner, *Koinonia Remembered*, 99.
[18]Don Mosely in Weiner, *Koinonia Remembered*, 109.

Clarence's shack in the pecan orchard. Clarence began to systematically translate the New Testament in the late 1960s at what seemed like a low point in Koinonia Farm's history. Koinonia had seemed to many to be the cutting edge of civil rights in the 1940s and 1950s. By the 1960s times had changed, and Koinonia, with its commitment to rural Georgia and intentional community and its complicated relationship with the civil rights movement, seemed outdated and stuck in place. Visitors still flocked to the farm, and Clarence's southern church-speaking schedule expanded, but few people wanted to join the community.[19] Only the Jordans, the Wittkampers, and the Brownes remained. They funded their lives mostly through the pecan mail-order business, but the income was not enough to fully support the three families. In 1963, Conrad and Ora Brown decided to leave after fourteen years for the good of the community. Conrad took a position at Highlander Folk School, which had allowed Koinonia to run an interracial summer camp during the boycott. He would go on to teach famed civil rights leader Fannie Lou Hamer, serving at Highlander until 1972 and then going into pastoral ministry. Now there were two families at Koinonia.

Clarence wrote in his writing shack, a short walk from the main community buildings. His writing shack itself reflects Clarence's penchant for seeing the holy in the mundane. Based on a picture I found of Clarence's shack from the 1970s showing pecan trees that were six to ten feet tall, I think he looked out at a pecan orchard (today those trees are seventy to one hundred feet tall). His study shack had boxes filled with exegetical studies of Scripture alongside instructions on curing hams; half-finished sermons lived next to beekeeping resources from the agricultural extension agent.[20] Clarence wrote the final drafts on the backs of order forms from the Delicious Pecan Company.[21] His translations of Scripture were embedded in the everyday life of the farm.

---

[19]Clarence Jordan, "Peace and Brotherhood" (Detroit, May 19, 1965), in 2Aiii)a)I Clarence's Manuscripts and Other Writings, Koinonia Farm Archive.
[20]Don Mosely described how he loved poking around in Clarence's shack and found these treasures in Weiner, *Koinonia Remembered*, 109.
[21]See, for instance, "Luke and Acts" (n.d.), in box 12, Hargrett Rare Book and Manuscript Library, University of Georgia.

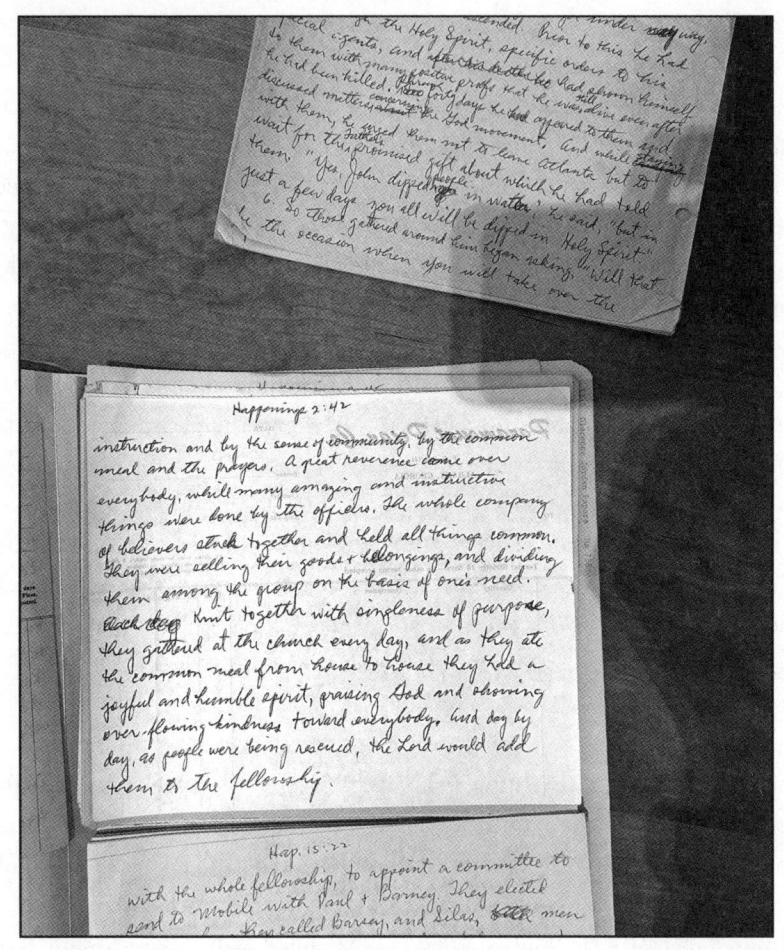

Figure 14.1. Clarence's translation of Happenings 2:42. Clarence's precise handwriting translates Acts 2:42, which he understood as not just a description of how the early church shared their resources but as a call for Christians across the ages. His scholarship and pastoral work were never far from his roots as a farmer. Photo by Karen J. Johnson, at Hargrett Rare Book and Manuscript Library / University of Georgia Libraries, Clarence Jordan Papers, 12:8

Friends observed that Clarence met God in that shack. A local friend, Mr. Ludrell, thought "the Lord had Clarence fit so He could work with him like He wanted to, because at times, He didn't want no one around him, He wanted him off to Himself, so He could deal with him the way He wanted to. I thought about that time after time, that the Lord had him to build a place off like [the shack] so He could communicate with him in that way."[22]

---

[22] Weiner, *Koinonia Remembered*, 69.

Figure 14.2. Clarence Jordan's writing shack, July 2, 2022. Today Koinonia Farm has preserved the writing shack and provided paper within for people to write their reflections about Clarence, God's work, or whatever else comes to mind. For me, it was a place of solemnity because of Clarence's good work there and death, but also frivolity as my children ran around. Honestly, I was also a little scared of the snakes, especially the venomous ones, that live in the tall grasses, and wondered how the families at the farm felt about snakes over the years. Courtesy of Karen J. Johnson

While Clarence spent most of his time in the late 1960s in the shack writing the translations and sermons, he often took breaks that reconnected him to the land and community. As Linda Fuller, who typed many of his translations, remembered, Clarence rode his little scooter to "check on the pecan trees, the peanut crop, or check on some operation in the pecan plant. He had developed so many close friendships with the employees in the pecan plant over the years and they were always happy to see him coming to give that friendly handshake, smile, and ask about their families . . . picking up nibbles of pecans as he went."[23]

SCRIPTURE AS A MIRROR

How did African Americans influence Clarence's transposition of Scripture?
I first encountered Clarence long after his death through a musical based on

---

[23] Weiner, *Koinonia Remembered*, 105.

Clarence's Cotton Patch translations while working on my doctorate. Tom Key and Russell Treyz used the translations as the basis for a musical, *The Cotton Patch Gospel*. In the theater, the Gospel stories came alive to me in a way I had never experienced. It *was* fresh, as Clarence had hoped. Jesus, the disciples, Herod, the mothers crying for their children, the people healed—all these seemed alive. They were not the stuff of stained-glass windows but real people whose stories demanded a response, which I was trying to work out in my own time and place, through where we lived, where we went to church, how I spent my free time, and what I studied. That is what Clarence wanted, but I did not yet know that.

I wondered, though, why Clarence did not portray Jesus as Black. By then, I was familiar with the history of African American artists, poets, and writers who portrayed Jesus as a lynched Black man.[24] I returned to that question years later, asking, If Clarence really wanted to call good White Christians to account, why did he not make Jesus Black? Did this show the limits of Clarence's racial understanding?

Then I asked another question: Were these questions fair? I wondered whether a White southerner could be expected to imagine Jesus as Black, even if he knew Black Christians.

After all, most of Clarence's contemporary White Christians (and many African Americans, Christian or not) imagined Jesus as White. The most popular image of Jesus in that period was Warner Sallman's *Head of Christ*, which portrays Jesus as a White man with flowing, wavy hair. While the image itself is not insidious, and people often, though not always, imagine Jesus as a member of their own cultural context, people looked on Sallman's *Head of Christ* in a context in which White southern Christians conflated Jesus' spiritual Whiteness—his spiritual purity, which was White as snow—with Jesus' imagined racial Whiteness. They used his Whiteness to convey Jesus' righteousness and vice versa. Some readers today may find this odd—how did they imagine a brown, Middle Eastern man as White? Theologically,

---

[24] For depictions of Jesus in US history related to race, see Paul Harvey and Edward Blum, *The Color of Christ: The Son of God and the Saga of Race in America* (Chapel Hill: University of North Carolina Press, 2012). For how Americans have depicted Jesus more generally, see Stephen R. Prothero, *American Jesus: How the Son of God Became a National Icon* (New York: Farrar, Straus & Giroux, 2003); Richard Wightman Fox, *Jesus in America: Personal Savior, Cultural Hero, National Obsession* (San Francisco: HarperSanFrancisco, 2004).

they used supersessionism, which divorced Jesus from his Jewish context and took him out of his physical body.[25] Clarence was raised in this context.

The more I read the sources, I saw parallels in Clarence's interpretations of Scripture to themes in African American Christianity. Clarence adopted a framework common among African American Christians—a profound sense of God's presence in the here-and-now that led to a sense of living the biblical narrative. This sense of God's immanence and the animation of the Scriptures in a community's life revealed themselves in African Americans' hope that the North would be a Promised Land, and in their freedom songs that proclaimed God's presence with them as they believed that "God's gonna trouble the water" as they let "this little light of mine . . . shine."

Clarence also gestured toward imagining Jesus as Black if he were to live in the midcentury South. Most consistently, he described Jesus' death as a lynching, a crime most commonly committed against Black men. In his 1949 Sunday school text, Clarence, in what seemed to be a direct counter to Warner Sallman's *Head of Christ*, argues that Jesus was not pale White, did not have red hair, and lacked womanly hands and features. Clarence writes, "Jesus probably had a deep brown skin, Black hair and dark brown eyes—eyes which were wonderful to behold."[26] At least once, Clarence referred to Jesus as Black. He was describing the disruptive results of the incarnation and said that in the New Testament period, "People were wandering nomads and . . . lived in tents. And so they said, 'God became one of us and lived among us, pitched his tent in our midst.' Now today we might translate it . . . 'The word became flesh and bought a home in our neighborhood— yeah, the Black bastard, and made the price of our property go down.'"[27]

Nonetheless, the images that populated that 1949 Sunday school book were of White Jesus. I do not know who chose the images in the 1949 book, Clarence or the series editor, but their power overwhelms Clarence's few words that describe how Jesus looked. Paintings and drawings of Jesus as White were common among White Christians. While similar types of sources portraying Jesus as Black were accessible to Clarence between the 1940s and

---

[25] Quiros, *God with Us*, 54. For more on how people have portrayed Christ in the US, see Harvey and Blum, *Color of Christ*.
[26] Jordan, *Lord and Master: Part I*, 18. A gendered analysis of Clarence's interpretation is important but beyond the scope of my work here.
[27] Quoted in Elaine Allen Lechtreck, *Southern White Ministers and the Civil Rights Movement* (Jackson: University Press of Mississippi, 2018), 172.

1960s, it would be expecting a lot for Clarence to go outside White Christian circles in 1949. Clarence would overwhelmingly continue to describe Jesus as White in his later Cotton Patch translations.

So why was Clarence's Jesus White? A good answer must consider Clarence's audience and context, and the parallel racial worlds he saw between the New Testament era and the mid-twentieth-century South.

Parallel racial contexts. In the Cotton Patch translations, Clarence made God's chosen people not the Jewish people but White Protestants. This meant Jesus was a White Protestant, coming to renew his people. Gentiles, the Jews' hated enemies, were usually African Americans (Clarence only translated *Gentiles* as "non-Christians" rather than "African Americans" when he understood the New Testament to be speaking religiously, not racially). The apostle Paul became a man spreading the good news to African Americans about a Savior who had been lynched by a mob of his own White Protestant kin after being persecuted by the White Christian church structure. I think Clarence translated the New Testament world this way because he thought it was the racial context in which a modern Paul would preach.

As I immersed myself in White Sumter County's boycott and violence against Koinonia Farm, Clarence's translation decisions made more sense. White southern Protestants saw themselves as God's people, faithful in a culture they perceived to be increasingly against them—from the modernist controversy and debates over teaching evolution in schools in the 1920s, to the civil rights movement's and federal government's attacks on the southern way of life, to the 1960s court cases restricting prayer in schools. In many ways they were like the Jews, a chosen people persecuted by external forces (the Romans) and despising Gentiles. By making White Christians the Jews, Clarence was also drawing on an implicit (and sometimes explicit) supersessionism, which holds that the church has replaced the Jews as God's chosen people.

Most of the chosen people, while dearly loved by God, could not see Jesus as their Messiah. Clarence held up a mirror to the White Christian church, saying, "This is who you are." It was the "good White Christians," those who thought they were saved and thought they were doing the right thing, who actually rejected Jesus.

What did this look like in the text?

In Clarence's translations of the Gospels, Jesus' parents take him to Atlanta's First Church for his dedication, where Annas and Caiaphas are co-presidents of the Southern Baptist Convention. When a Sunday school teacher, "trying to save face," asks Jesus just who his neighbor is, Jesus tells of a "Good Samaritan" traveling on the road from Albany up to Atlanta. Gangsters held a man up, and a White preacher and a White gospel worship leader both passed the injured man on the highway's shoulder. A Black man saw the fellow, "and what he saw moved him to tears. He stopped and bound up his wounds as best he could, drew some water from his water-jug to wipe away the blood and then laid him on the back seat." All the while, Clarence observed in a footnote, "His thoughts may have been along this line: 'Somebody's robbed you; yeah, I know about that, I been robbed, too. And they done beat you up bad; I know, I been beat up, too. And everybody just go right on by and leave you laying here hurting. Yeah, I know. They pass me by, too.'"[28] When Jesus asks the Sunday school teacher just who the neighbor was, the teacher refuses to acknowledge the neighbor was the Black man.

The seminary professors and denominational executives persecute Jesus. As he preaches against them, "they were afraid of their constituency. . . . So they played it cool by hiring some detectives to pose as Christians and collect evidence from his preaching, so he could be arrested and turned over to the House Subversive Activities Committee."[29] Clarence is implicitly suggesting that Jesus, like those at the farm, has been accused of communism. White Christian leaders were trying to bring Jesus before the House Un-American Activities Committee, which investigated citizens' subversive activities during the Cold War.

Clarence made the apostle Paul, who wrote most of the New Testament's epistles, a White missionary to African Americans. Many of Paul's letters were written to Black churches. Making the early church include Black Christians upset the racial order that made African Americans subservient because the unity Paul describes is not something that would happen after death. Black and White Christians, in Clarence's translations, are truly equals in Christ, and some of White readers' most beloved verses in Scripture are written to African Americans.

---

[28] Clarence Jordan, "Happenings," in *Cotton Patch Version of Luke and Acts*, Luke 10:33-34.
[29] Jordan, "Happenings," Luke 20:19-20.

As an apostle to African Americans, Paul preaches against White Christians' belief that the southern way of life will save them. In Clarence's translation of Galatians, "The Letter to the Georgia Convention," Paul reminds his beloved brothers and sisters of his "previous life as a white Southerner, how fanatically I harassed the movement and violently attacked it, and how I went far beyond most white Southerners of my age in zealously defending and promoting the traditions of our noble ancestors."[30] Paul went north for several years, then visited the other leaders in Atlanta, who "clearly grasped that I had been made responsible for getting the word to Negroes, just as Rock [Peter] had been to whites. For obviously the same one who had empowered Rock to work among whites had also empowered me among Negroes."[31] But when Rock came to Albany, Paul had to rebuke him because Rock "shrank back and segregated himself" and no longer ate with "Negroes" after the other White brothers arrived. Paul observes that the southern way of life is "not necessarily" contrary to God's principles, "for if the South's traditions can lift a man to a more noble life, then surely something good and right has come from it. . . . In a way, the Southern customs disciplined us for the Christian life, that we might be put right by faithfulness." But now they live by faith and no longer are ruled "by the deeply entrenched patterns of the culture."[32] They must therefore stop segregating, not giving up the good fight, because "THEY WHO FORCE SEGREGATION ON YOU ARE SEEKING THE APPROVAL OF SOCIETY SO THEY WON'T GET PERSECUTED FOR ACCEPTING CHRIST'S LYNCHING."[33]

QUESTIONS AND IMPLICATIONS

Clarence's idea that spiritual blindness is a tragedy because it leads to depravity, or sin, is powerful. Complicating the situation is that those who are blind do not realize they cannot see—and think they can. If we let them, our

---

[30]Clarence Jordan, "The Letter to the Churches of the Georgia Convention [Galatians]," in *The Cotton Patch Version of Paul's Epistles* (Piscataway, NJ: New Century, 1968), Galatians 1:13-14.
[31]Jordan, "Letter to the Churches of the Georgia Convention [Galatians]," Galatians 2:7-8.
[32]Jordan, "Letter to the Churches of the Georgia Convention [Galatians]," Galatians 2:12; 3:21, 23, 25.
[33]Jordan, "Letter to the Churches of the Georgia Convention [Galatians]," Galatians 6:11 (capitalization original).

encounters with Scripture, with others, and with the Holy Spirit can help us to see ourselves rightly.

- In what ways may you and/or your church community be blind? Listen to the quiet voice and confirm it with others—including those who are different from you and will have different blind spots.

While Clarence was writing for White southerners in the mid-twentieth century, the Cotton Patch translations can still be a mirror for us today, especially if we approach Scripture loving the Word, willing to listen to the Holy Spirit, and ready to take action, as Clarence said. Do not dismiss the translation as irrelevant for your context, as one White northern reporter did when interviewing Clarence about the boycott. She asked how those in the North could help and was thinking of how they could help the farm by buying their products, writing to government officials, and so on. Clarence responded that those in the North could get into just as much trouble as those at Koinonia had in the South. Clarence observed that the north had some "serious problems," especially in housing, and that it was no racial utopia. That the reporter did not expect Clarence's answer is apparent in how quickly she glossed over it. She responded that they appreciated his idea and turned back to the story of the violence in the South.[34] Wherever we live, we ought not be like that reporter. It is usually easier to see the evil "over there" than closer to home.

- How can you and your fellow Christians get into just as much trouble as Clarence wherever you are?
- What does the Cotton Patch translation say to you? How does reading the radical gospel story in the context of the mid-twentieth-century South help you see how you could better put flesh on the Word of God in your own time and place?

Clarence was most disappointed with the White church. It was this disappointment with the church that drove him to Scripture, to learn how to live in a way consistent with what he was taught. But, according to his nephew Hamilton Jordan, Clarence's disappointment with the church continued to the end of his life.

---

[34]Dorothy Dunbar Bromley and Clarence Jordan, *Report to the People* (New York, n.d.), Koinonia Farm Archive.

- What do you do with disappointment when things do not change as you would hope?

While Clarence was writing prophetically to White Christians, it would be easy to miss that Scripture also speaks to those who, as African American pastor and theologian Howard Thurman puts it, have their backs up against the wall.[35] Thurman emphasized that Jesus was a Jew, and in his culture, Jews were despised by the Romans. Drawing on the Black theological tradition, Thurman considered the gospel not from within the White power structure but from the perspective of those who are marginalized. As a New Testament scholar, Clarence knew a lot about the racial context of first-century Judaism. We should respect that knowledge. But, as Thurman did, there are other ways to transpose Scripture. My own take is that we need the diversity of voices in the church to help us see the things we miss.

- What are the strengths and weaknesses of these different perspectives?
- What do they each help you see?

Clarence wanted his translation of Scripture to help people resist the lull of imagining God as somewhere out there and instead remember that God is with us always. No matter how far we run, we cannot escape his presence. And when Christians are putting flesh on the Word, being the body of Christ, we testify to who God is.

- In what ways are you and your church putting flesh on the Word? In what ways could you improve? Whom can you look to for wisdom?

---

[35]Howard Thurman, *Jesus and the Disinherited* (Boston: Beacon, 1949).

15

THE SOIL NEVER LOSES ITS CLAIM ON US

> How Clarence's application of his vision changed over time and how meditating on Clarence's attachment to one place and his death can give us a heart of wisdom.

STAYING

Koinonia was at a crossroads as Clarence worked on his Cotton Patch translations. Not only were people not joining the community on a permanent basis, but their farming-education ministry was becoming less relevant. When Clarence returned to Georgia in 1942, farming was many people's livelihood. By the 1960s, mechanization meant that a machine could do the labor of eighty men. People were still leaving, going to southern and northern cities, and improving their crop yield would not keep them in the South. Farming was becoming a big business.[1]

Clarence wanted to sell the farm and move on, thinking perhaps its work was done. The Wittkampers did not agree, which drove the community to pray. As Florence remembered, "We began to believe that the Lord considered our work here expendable. The koinonia had witnessed and could step out of the picture. What did the Lord want us to do now? Where did He want us to go? For over a year we asked these questions."[2]

---

[1] Mills Lane, *People of Georgia: An Illustrated History* (New York: Beehive, 1975).
[2] Florence Jordan, "Koinonia," n.d., in 2A iii) b) [i] Florence's Writings, Koinonia Farm Archive.

As they asked, visitors continued to come. One White couple, Millard and Linda Fuller, would breathe new life into the community. In 1965, they stopped by Koinonia Farm for lunch with an old friend. They stayed for three months after they met Clarence. The Fullers had been wealthy but had given away most of their money after a spiritual and marriage crisis. In 1965, Millard took a job fundraising for Tougaloo College in Mississippi (whose students would support John Perkins and the Mendenhall boycott in coming years). In 1968, Millard quit and jotted a note to Clarence, asking what Clarence had up his sleeve. Clarence replied that he had nothing up his sleeve, but perhaps God had something for them together.

FUND FOR HUMANITY

Millard and Clarence met with a group of men to brainstorm about Koinonia's future. What emerged from their conversations was the concept of the partnership. They took the idea of holding all things in common and extended it outward from the farm. Their frame was explicitly Christian but did not work through institutional churches or denominations. They did not expect others to live in intentional community but invited them to join into financial and spiritual partnership with other people to do God's work. They renamed the farm Koinonia Partners and developed a threefold mission, which they understood as continuing the farm's original mission to proclaim and apply the gospel.

First, they would communicate the gospel, calling people to repent. As Millard wrote,

> Reshape your life, for God's new order of the Spirit is impinging upon you. Change your way of living. Start living out God's way in your life. Live in a spirit of partnership with God and your fellow man. Live on a reasonable standard and donate the excess to the poor. Be a peacemaker. Love. Love your neighbor as yourself . . . in deed. Reach out to all mankind in a warm and compassionate spirit of brotherhood.[3]

Second, for those who wanted to change, they developed small discipleship schools, retreats of three to four days throughout the nation.

---

[3]Millard Fuller, "Koinonia Partners," n.d., in Correspondence, Koinonia Farm Archive.

Third, they offered people an opportunity to apply their faith through the "Fund for Humanity." The fund was a form of what we today would call microfinance. It could funnel financial resources that could act as seed grants for different projects poor people wanted to undertake. Clarence saw it as being modeled on the early church, which "took the assets *which God had already given them* and cared for those in need."[4] By contributing to the Fund for Humanity, people could help create that alternate world in which people would not need to worry about what they would wear or how they would obtain food (Matthew 6:25). Millard wrote that the fund meant to "(a) provide an inheritance for the disinherited, and (b) to provide a means through which the possessed may share with and invest in the dispossessed. What the poor need is not charity but *capital*, not case-workers but *co-workers*. And what the rich need is a wise, honorable and just way of divesting themselves of their over-abundance."[5]

People contributed to the Fund for Humanity through no-interest loans and outright gifts. The fund enabled what Koinonia Partners called partnership farming, industries, and housing. The fund would provide capital to start a business, and then people who worked in the business took a reasonable living allowance and donated the rest back to the fund. In housing, Koinonia Partners facilitated building decent houses for people living in poverty and sold them using no-interest loans. As the homeowners paid back the loans, they freed the initial capital to build houses for others and were encouraged to donate some of what they would have spent on interest back to the fund to help others.

The Fund for Humanity extended the idea of Christian community outward from the farm. People did not need to live together in community and make decisions in common, as Koinonia Farm had. But they could join in the vision of the God movement Clarence translated in Acts 4, in which all the believers had what they needed:

> Not one of them considered his property to be private, but all things were shared by them. With mighty power the apostles were giving the evidence of Jesus' aliveness, and upon them all was a spirit of abounding goodwill. You

---

[4]Clarence Jordan, "Sermon on the Mount," in *Clarence Jordan: Essential Writings*, ed. Joyce Hollyday (New York: Orbis Books, 2003), 129.
[5]Fuller, "Koinonia Partners."

know, there wasn't a person in the group in need. For owners of land or houses were selling them and bringing the proceeds and placing them at the disposal of the apostles. Distribution was made to everyone on the basis of his need.[6]

As the Fund for Humanity grew, Florence took up the reins. She wrote to every person who donated to the fund for humanity. She reflected, "We knew when we wrote that first letter that there were a lot of people who had money—and who really had a conscience about it. . . . When they began to see the rest of the world . . . there wasn't this easiness: I have money, so I'm doing okay. Why should I care whether anyone else has it or not?"[7]

The fund benefited local people and eventually those around the world. Bo and Emma Johnson, a Black couple who stood by Koinonia during the boycott and violence, were the first ones to buy a Koinonia house. In 1976, Millard and Linda Fuller founded Habitat for Humanity and then the Fuller Center for Housing, which worked across the globe and in the United States to eliminate poverty housing.[8]

RETURNING TO THE SOIL

"Somehow God made us out of his old soil and we go back to it and we never lose its claim on us," Clarence knew.[9] On October 29, 1969, Clarence died in his writing shack at only fifty-seven years old. Lena Hofer found him ill when she popped by to say hello after school. She ran from the writing shack back to the community houses, calling for help. When Millard entered the shack, he saw Clarence at his desk with both feet on the ground, both hands clasped to his chair's arms, and his head leaning against the wall. Millard noted that even in death Clarence was dignified, and thought, "You've made it!"[10]

Sumter County's White citizens failed to honor Clarence. The coroner refused to come to the farm to issue a death certificate, so Koinonia members

---

[6]Jordan, "The Happenings," in *The Cotton Patch Version of Luke and Acts: Jesus' Doings and the Happenings* (Clinton, NJ: New Win, 1969), Acts 4:32-35.
[7]Florence Jordan, "Spring 1982," in 2A. Iii)b) Florence Jordan, Koinonia Farm Archive.
[8]Much is written on Habitat for Humanity. For one of Millard's narratives, see Millard Fuller, *A Simple, Decent Place to Live: The Building Realization of Habitat for Humanity* (Dallas: Word, 1995).
[9]Quoted in Bren Dubay, "Setting the Table at Koinonia Farm," *Plough Quarterly* (Winter 2015), https://www.plough.com/en/topics/community/communal-living/setting-the-table-at-koinonia-farm.
[10]Millard Fuller, "Jim and Lucine Joseph," November 19, 1969, Millard and Linda Fuller, Koinonia Farm Archive.

loaded Clarence's body into a station wagon and brought it to Americus, where the coroner wanted to do an autopsy. Florence agreed. Clarence did not think highly of expensive funerals, so they buried him in a shipping carton the next morning, dressed in his blue jeans and a plaid shirt. Koinonia men and several African American neighbors dug the grave.[11]

In the coming years, Koinonia grew. During the 1970s, among Christians and outside Christian circles communal living became a popular choice. Koinonia became a key place to live in community. Through the Fund for Humanity and offering their land, Koinonia Partners helped build more housing for local people and started several other partnership ministries. Clarence's Cotton Patch translations of the Scriptures continued to sell, and Jimmy Carter became more connected to Koinonia after his presidency through his work with Habitat for Humanity.

Race continued to play a complicated role at Koinonia, as members sought unity in a difficult context. One historian who interviewed those associated with Koinonia over the years found a racial divide over how they narrated key elements of the farm's history: the White people tended to emphasize the life in common, while the Black people emphasized the community's activism.[12]

While it is small today, the community continues. They offered my family and me a warm welcome for my research. They have returned to the common purse, are grounded by regular prayer and worship, and have committed themselves to biological farming, which goes beyond organic farming in caring for and restoring the soil. Clarence's ideas continue to shape the community as they regularly read his writing.

A few years before he died, Clarence was speaking about peace and brotherhood at the annual meeting of the Baptist Peace Fellowship. A northerner from an integrated church asked how their church could help in the South without causing trouble as outsiders. Clarence responded, first, by breaking down the boundaries of North and South (and, he jokingly added, Texas). He said that in the international Cold War context, state lines did not matter. People thought of the United States as one nation. But his second suggestion was directive—resonating with Catherine de Hueck's and John Perkins's

---

[11] Fuller, "Jim and Lucine Joseph."
[12] Tracy E. K'Meyer, "What Koinonia Was All About: The Role of Memory in a Changing Community," *The Oral History Review* 24, no. 1 (1997): 1-22.

relocation, and the work of Raleigh and Paulette Washington and Glen and Lonni Kehrein, whom we will consider next. He said, "I would like to see you approach it more from the standpoint of the incarnation, to come and live with us, rather than making a quick survey trip from which you can rapidly escape."[13]

He could have also suggested, as he did to that reporter who had asked how northerners could help the farm, that they stay where they were, addressing the problems that came from the North's racialized geographies. Despite Koinonia's best efforts to address housing and economics in southwest Georgia, people still moved north, looking for better opportunities. It is to people who worked in those northern contexts from the late 1960s through the 1990s that we now turn.

QUESTIONS AND IMPLICATIONS

While Clarence had a significant impact in his lifetime, Koinonia Farm remained small, and few people joined the shared life there until after he died. Was he successful? That question, often asked with a subtext in an American context that assumes bigger is better, requires defining success. When asked how she would define success, Florence Jordan responded, "Clarence used to say, 'I don't know what success would look like for Koinonia. There's only question I'll ever have to answer, and that is: have I been faithful?' If a person is a maturing Christian at Koinonia, that's all we can ask. We all have to keep on growing."[14] Clarence did not place ultimate value in the size of the farm or the number who joined him. He said, "It is our desire to discover and to know the will of Christ. If it leads to utter failure, I had rather it would lead there and be one with Him, than to be successful and lose him."[15]

- How do you measure success? What would replacing success with faithfulness mean for you and your church, even if it led to "utter failure"?
- Have you been faithful to what God calls you to do? Do you trust him with the results?

---

[13]Clarence Jordan, "Peace and Brotherhood" (Detroit, May 19, 1965), in 2Aiii)a)I Clarence's Manuscripts and Other Writings, Koinonia Farm Archive.
[14]Florence Jordan, "Spring 1982."
[15]Quoted in Clarence Jordan, "AT 100-4223" (n.d.), Federal Bureau of Investigation, Koinonia Farm Archive.

Clarence is buried in an unmarked grave at Koinonia Farm on Picnic Hill, along with several others, including Florence Jordan and Millard Fuller. He knew that he was made from dirt and would return to dirt. Few today live in a rural context, so close to the soil as Clarence did. But none of us can lose the soil's claim on us. The Anglican prayer for Ash Wednesday reminds us, "Almighty God, thou hast created us out of the dust of the earth: Grant that these ashes may be unto us a sign of our mortality and penitence, that we may remember that it is only by thy gracious gift that we are given everlasting life; through Jesus Christ our Savior. Amen." Living in light of our mortality can help us to number our days, that we may gain hearts of wisdom (Psalm 90:12).

Living wisely requires rightly ordering our loves, making the soil of our hearts good soil so it can produce an abundant harvest. To produce the harvest, we must act. As Clarence translated Jesus' parable of the soils,

> A farmer went out to plant his seed. As he planted, some fell on the path where they were walked on, and the birds came and ate them. Some seed fell on the rock, and though they sprouted, they dried up from lack of moisture. Still others landed in the middle of a briar patch, and the briars that came up with them choked them out. And others fell on the rich dirt and grew and yielded a hundred times over. He finished by saying, "Give this *careful* consideration." When the "students" asked what the parable meant, he said: "the seed are God's ideas. The 'path' seed represent ideas that are heard by people who let the Confuser [Satan] come and snatch the ideas from their hearts, without their ever acting on them and being helped. The 'rock' seed are the ideas which, when heard, are gladly received—but by people who have no deep roots. They live by them for a while, and when the time of real testing comes, they chicken out. The 'briar patch' seed are the ideas which are heard by busy people and are choked out by the distractions and money-making and pleasure-seeking of life, so the ideas just never mature. The 'rich dirt' seed are the ones which lie in the hearts of brave and good people who, when they hear the ideas, hold on to them and patiently spread them."

Jesus continues, "Be careful, then, how you respond. For whoever gets on the ball will be encouraged all the more, and whoever sits on his hands will have even what little he seems to have taken away from him."[16] Clarence's

---

[16] Clarence Jordan, *The Cotton Patch Version of Luke and Acts: Jesus' Doings and the Happenings* (Clinton, NJ: New Win, 1969), Luke 10:5-15, 18.

invitation into fellowship at Koinonia, and later, into partnership with God and others, was an invitation to act, to "radically restructure their lives so as to be God's partners across the land."[17]

- What radical restructuring might you and other members of your church need to do? It may not mean joining an intentional community, but we can be sure that the devil, whom Clarence called "the confuser," wants to confuse us so we run after temporal rather than eternal things. How can you restructure your life so you can give more for kingdom purposes? Would it mean living in a smaller house? Reducing your consumption in other ways? Removing activities from your life so you have more margin for others?

- Both with Koinonia Farm and Koinonia Partners, the restructuring involved people's money. They were not calling for voluntary poverty, as Catherine de Hueck sometimes did. But they were calling people to simplicity, taking enough for themselves and to share with others so everyone had what they needed. What could a community of Christians living like that do for the world?

- Clarence made this call to communal simplicity at the start of the massive expansion of consumerism and advertising in the post–World War II era, whose assumptions are often hidden from us because they seem so normal. Desire for more is rarely satisfied. Without the accountability of a community, it can be easy to deceive ourselves. What accountability are you willing to have around your money?

- Where do you see people living out the kingdom of God? How can you join them?

Koinonia Farm today has a wonderful library, which includes several books by agrarian writer Wendell Berry. Berry would call Clarence a "sticker," one who did not buy into the promise of "'mobility': our forlorn modern progress toward something indefinitely, and often unrealizably better."[18] When White neighbors had tried to force him to leave, Clarence refused. He

---

[17]Millard Fuller and Norman Dewire, "Salvation Today" (1970s[?]), in Correspondence, Koinonia Farm Archive.
[18]Wendell Berry, *It All Turns on Affection: The Jefferson Lecture and Other Essays* (Berkeley, CA: Counterpoint, 2012), 17.

loved the place and wanted to continue to live out the good news where God had planted him. He stayed in a poor place that was difficult. Some seasons and work call for movement. Before his death Clarence was making plans to relocate to Atlanta so he could travel and speak more easily, but he was not moving to improve his own comfort.

- To what extent do you fall for the promise of mobility versus staying in one place and caring for that place?
- What does it mean to live out the gospel where you are? How might Christianity disrupt the individualism, materialism, racism, or militarism of your place?

You may not agree with Clarence's positions. If you have come to this point, I hope it was only after taking his position seriously. Loving God and loving others, the two greatest commandments, will cause trouble. Millard noted that Christians will get in trouble not because they seek out trouble but because their way of life is so contrary to the world.[19]

- How is your life and the life of your church askance to the world?

---

[19]Millard Fuller to Rollin Rheinheimer, August 27, 1971, in Correspondence, Koinonia Farm Archive.

PART IV

SEEK FIRST TO UNDERSTAND

Rock of Our Salvation Evangelical Free Church and Circle Urban Ministries

> *The ministry of reconciliation can never be mere passive acceptance of a theological truth, but must include active participation. Unfortunately, the Christian church at large—to state it in the most favorable way—is guilty of benign neglect.*
>
> RALEIGH WASHINGTON AND GLEN KEHREIN,
> *BREAKING DOWN WALLS*

16

AN UNLIKELY PAIR

> How a Black career Army officer turned pastor, Raleigh Washington, and his wife, Paulette, partnered with a White couple, Glen and Lonni Kehrein, who lived in Chicago's inner city, how empathy strengthened their partnership, and the limits of most White evangelicals' thinking about race.

A MATCH MADE IN AUSTIN

Raleigh Washington never expected to move back into a poor Black neighborhood. As an African American man, he had worked hard to move up and out. But in 1983, Raleigh and his wife, Paulette, heard about Circle Urban Ministries. Circle was a community development organization led by a White man, Glen Kehrein, located in Chicago's mostly African American Austin neighborhood. Circle would grow to provide health care, legal services, family counseling, housing for the homeless, a food pantry, a school, and real estate development, but in 1983 it needed a church partner. Raleigh was finishing a master of divinity degree at Trinity Evangelical Divinity School, north of Chicago in the wealthy, White suburb of Bannockburn. He wanted to plant a church and had always assumed it would be in a middle- or upper-class context. But he was starting to think maybe he wouldn't stay in the suburbs after all.

Professional ministry was a second career for Raleigh. He had served as a lieutenant colonel in the Army, having been promoted faster than his White counterparts. But Raleigh's success and confident attitude angered some

White colleagues, and they looked for ways to remove him from active duty. After eleven failed investigations, Raleigh received notice that he had been charged with "conduct unbecoming an officer" but had no specific details. On the day before he was eligible for full retirement benefits, Raleigh was given the choice of pleading guilty and being able to retain his benefits or being dishonorably discharged. Raleigh had served nearly thirty years and had a family to feed. But, convinced he had done nothing wrong, Raleigh refused to admit any guilt. Raleigh was convinced White people's racism had driven him out. He accepted the dishonorable discharge, without the benefits.

One of Raleigh's professors told him about Circle Urban Ministries. Glen had founded it in 1974, a few years after graduating from Moody Bible Institute, which was also in Chicago. Chicago's Austin neighborhood had only recently transitioned from being a White to a Black community. Austin had experienced White flight, a phrase that did not capture the complicated nature of urban neighborhoods' changing racial geographies. But like other neighborhoods, racial change seemed to happen overnight in Austin. Children in middle- and upper-class families who had moved to the neighborhood for a better life remembered seeing their White neighbors one day, and the next, without warning, they were gone.[1] In 1960, Austin was nearly 100 percent White.[2] By 1970, it was one-third African American, and within the decade it was nearly three-quarters African American. The transition happened block by block, from east to west. Glen and his wife, Lonni, had moved into the Austin neighborhood when other White folks were leaving.

Glen was wary of meeting with Raleigh. He and Lonni also bore racial wounds.

Circle Church, located a few miles east of Austin by the University of Illinois at Chicago, had planted Circle Urban Ministries. Circle Church called itself an "open church" because, unlike most evangelical churches' implicit racial dynamics, it explicitly welcomed people from all racial backgrounds. Glen and Lonni had moved to Austin with other members of Circle Church and formed an intentional community called the Austin Community

---

[1]Shunelle Hollis, interview by author, September 30, 2021; Sheila Anderson, interview by author, April 5, 2021.
[2]Judith A. Martin, "Austin," in Encyclopedia of Chicago, accessed October 20, 2021, www.encyclopedia.chicagohistory.org/pages/93.html.

Fellowship. Like at Koinonia, fellowship members held their possessions in common. Those who worked in paying jobs funded Circle Community Center, which they later renamed Circle Urban Ministries.

But Circle Church had split along racial lines, which left the members of the Austin Community Fellowship feeling like their parents had divorced. Since Glen had been an elder at Circle Church, he and Lonni had been in the thick of the painful split. It seemed like Black and White people could not worship together or be part of the same church body. Glen felt like Circle Urban Ministries no longer had a strong church partner to which to send their clients, and they had not built strong relationships with local Black churches because of their involvement at Circle Church. They were trusting God would provide and in the meantime had, like at Koinonia, turned inward and developed a home church within the fellowship.

Glen had wanted to work with African American partners. He and Lonni knew they needed to learn from their Black brothers and sisters. Their posture of humility, of being learners and not saviors, is a lesson Lonni still emphasizes.[3] Glen and Lonni had become close with one Black family, and the husband worked with Glen at Circle. However, when this man committed adultery and Glen called him to account, the man had become angry and accused Glen of racism. This painful situation was the first in a repeated pattern. Glen would reach out to Black men for leadership, and eventually they would rebuff him. Glen's pain hurt Lonni deeply. When she learned that Raleigh and Paulette were visiting to explore planting a church, she was hesitant.

Raleigh and Paulette would offer Circle a church partner, but *how* they went about it made all the difference.

Meeting the Washingtons brought healing to the Kehreins. As Lonni recalled, "It was like homecoming." Raleigh talked with love to Lonni and Glen about what Circle Church had endured, apologizing for what had happened even though he had not been involved. The racial dynamics at the church had been painful and had seemed to require Lonni and Glen to adhere to an always-guilty way of being because they were White. Lonni remembered "bawling" because Raleigh and Paulette gave her grace, and she no longer had to perform. This dynamic of honesty, understanding, confession, forgiveness,

---

[3]Lonni Kehrein, interview by author, April 19, 2021.

and healing would come to characterize the church Raleigh planted, Rock of Our Salvation Evangelical Free Church (or simply Rock Church).

Empathy was a key aspect of how people navigated race at Rock Church, seeking to understand the perspective of another. At Rock, neither empathy nor any of the other practices required people to agree fully with one another. They did require them to stand on the level ground at the foot of the cross and look to Jesus' sacrifice.[4] Empathy is a habit of mind we can adopt in our own racially shaped contexts, given its effectiveness in building genuine and enduring community at Rock Church. We too can seek first to understand rather than to be understood—which of course requires humility.

Empathy is also necessary for doing history well. Historical empathy is not feeling what others in the past have felt; we do not have to manufacture emotions. Instead, historical empathy, similarly to how Rock Church members described it, is seeking to understand why people in the past did what they did. Humility reminds us that we will not be able to understand one another fully. But empathy demands that we try. We do not have to condone what people did, but to understand the logics and contexts that led to their actions does require withholding judgment. It requires what one historian has called a "pastoral imagination," to seek to understand others "not in terms of oneself, but in terms of themselves" by trying to see and experience the world as they did.[5] After we do this hard work of empathy, we can step back and ponder the moral significance of historical actors' actions. We will focus on empathy as we uncover what racial reconciliation looked like at Rock Church.

Raleigh and Paulette had practiced empathy for Glen and Lonni, seeking to understand their perspective. In the coming years, Pastor Raleigh and Glen would teach thousands to do the same.

I remember that it was a gray day when I first went to the Austin neighborhood in 2007. Eric, my husband-to-be, wanted to do his master of divinity internship with students. Inspired by John Perkins, we wanted to live crossculturally. We drove from Trinity Evangelical Divinity School, Raleigh's alma mater and the school where we were working on our master's degrees, south

---

[4]Lonni Kehrein, interview by author, April 12, 2021.
[5]Beth Barton Schweiger, "Seeing Things: Knowledge and Love in History," in *Confessing History: Explorations in Christian Faith and the Historian's Vocation*, ed. John Fea (Notre Dame, IN: University of Notre Dame Press, 2012), 66.

to meet John Hochevar of InterVarsity, which partnered with Circle Urban Ministries and Rock Church. John ran InterVarsity's Chicago Urban Program, which allowed college students to live, serve, and learn in the inner city.

I remember the trip there, safe inside the car, windows up and heat on to keep out the damp air, passing the run-down housing on Central Avenue, brick and clapboard buildings that had experienced years of disrepair. When you drive you are a spectator to a neighborhood, passing by quickly and removed from the heat, the rain, the sounds, and the smells. There are advantages. Speed, perceived safety, comfort. When you walk the streets of a neighborhood and take public transportation, as I would do in the coming years, you become a part of it. You can see details of those houses, potted plants on a windowsill, people sitting on the porches and visiting. You can smell food cooking and the person on the bus sitting by you who has not bathed. You can say hello and stop to chat, what Catherine de Hueck would refer to as her "chit chat apostolate." You can get a sense of the neighborhood and lay the foundation for empathy. But that first day we drove. We pulled into a parking lot with a high wrought-iron fence around it, and I walked somewhat nervously into the building that Circle Urban Ministries and Rock Church co-owned.

It was a huge, old brick building—some portions over one hundred years old. The building had housed a convent and the Catholic Siena High School. The nuns sold their building to Chicago Public Schools when the neighborhood changed from White to Black. Chicago Public Schools had used the school initially, but then it had stood vacant until 1984, when Circle Urban Ministries moved in. During its vacancy, the building had declined. "Neighborhood entrepreneurs," as our mentor John called them, stole the copper pipes and other valuable materials, leaving it a decaying shell. Slowly, Circle and Rock restored the building to provide for the community, relying on volunteer labor and fundraising. Like the Israelite leader Nehemiah, they were rebuilders of broken walls. The building's newest branch, which had been built right before Austin's White flight, was being remodeled to house a charter school, replacing the private school Circle had run. The school, Catalyst Circle Rock, was a partnership among the Lasallian Brothers, Circle and Rock, and Chicago Public Schools.

If I was nervous as we stepped out of the car onto the streets, I was excited to be in a place where my ordinary heroes lived and worked. Eric and I had read *Breaking Down Walls: A Model of Reconciliation in an Age of Racial Strife*, which Glen and Raleigh had published in 1993. By then, Raleigh and Paulette had moved on from Rock Church, but Glen and Lonni were still serving at Circle. Eric and I decided to serve with InterVarsity, stepping into the institutional partnership John had forged with Circle and Rock the summer after we married in 2007.

Then we stayed for six more years, learning from the saints at Rock Church and Circle Urban Ministries about what it meant to be a disciple of Jesus. The place where God worked was the Austin neighborhood of Chicago. It was holy ground.

Fifteen years later, I would complete a series of oral history interviews with longtime members of Rock Church and Circle Urban Ministries to learn about their experiences in the ministries. Those interviews form a portion of the source base for the writing that follows.

TOOLKIT

I brought to Rock Church an important metacognitive understanding about how my church background in a White, evangelical, suburban church had conditioned me to see the world in a fundamentally different way from my Black brothers and sisters. One of my professors in seminary, Dr. Peter Cha, had assigned a book called *Divided by Faith*, written by two Christian sociologists, Michael Emerson and Christian Smith, that had helped me see some of my own assumptions.

We all have frameworks we use to navigate our lives. These frameworks could also be understood as toolkits, full of tools we use to understand the world. Emerson and Smith studied White and Black evangelicals and found that both groups use three foundational theological tools to filter their experiences.[6] Those tools are freewill individualism, relationalism, and antistructuralism. A story can help unpack these terms.

When I was six, I accepted Jesus as my personal savior in a McDonald's parking lot as I rode in the minivan of my mom's dear friend, who still loves Jesus and who had witnessed to me. Since then, I have grown in my personal relationship with Jesus.

---

[6]Michael Emerson and Christian Smith, *Divided by Faith: Evangelical Religion and the Problem of Race in America* (New York: Oxford University Press, 2000).

That story is true. How I told it also reveals my reliance on the evangelical toolkit. "I accepted Jesus" reflects freewill individualism. I am an individual who made a choice, and my choice affected my life. Freewill individualism means that we evangelicals emphasize free choice and responsibility. When it comes to race-related issues, we can emphasize how a person's individual choices were the primary mover in their life situation.

Relationalism, the second tool, is also part of my story. I said that I made a choice to enter into a relationship with Jesus. Evangelicals emphasize relationships, not only with God but with other people. While, on the positive side, we are good at building into our relationship with Jesus and with others, and healthy relationships require empathy, this also means that it is easy to think about racial discrimination only in terms of relationships between individuals. The relationship in my conversion story is primarily about me and Jesus, but I was also influenced by my mom's friend. Relationalism is a great strength but cannot in itself account for how race has worked in America.

My story was inherently antistructural. I did not think of my relationship with Jesus as influenced by other structures, such as my church, or contexts, such as where I live, and unless I am intentional, it is easy to dismiss other people's experiences (and not be empathetic) if they do not fit with my sense of the world as based on an individual's decisions. Antistructuralism means that evangelicals tend to operate without overarching structures (compare most evangelical churches to, say, Roman Catholic churches with their hierarchies).

While we could debate the strengths of these three subtexts theologically, they have a profound impact on the extent to which White evangelicals like me can see how race might function in American society. *Divided by Faith* shows how, despite sharing a theological toolkit as well as other common theological commitments such as Jesus' divinity and Scripture's inerrancy, Black and White evangelicals conceptualize race in the United States in vastly different ways. White evangelicals used the toolkit to understand race in America, seeing racial problems as the result of individual racism that a person might hold in their heart toward another person. They consistently claimed that they did not experience any racial effects and did not account for race's systemic pervasiveness. Their contexts, influenced by race's positive effects, made it difficult to see race's adverse consequences, and they had few people in their inner circles who could help them see race's negative effects.

By contrast, Black evangelicals said they experienced the effects of race daily. These Black evangelicals had the same toolkit as the White evangelicals but did not always use the toolkit to understand their racial experiences because of how pervasively race affected their lives. They could not explain race in America as simply a problem between individual people. Their experiences demanded different tools.

One group of White evangelicals was an exception in the study. Those who lived in in non-White contexts sounded more like their Black peers, and they were able to articulate the personal *and* systemic ways race operated in America. In my mind, these White evangelicals had another tool in their toolkits: they had developed empathy by living in a minority-majority context, and they could not ignore the experiences of their Black peers even if they did not have the same experiences. For most White evangelicals, however, the theological toolkit containing individualism, relationalism, and antistructuralism only exacerbated their inability to see race.

Michael Emerson, one of the book's coauthors, remembered that he conducted the research for *Divided by Faith* as he and his wife (both White) moved into a neighborhood in Minnesota where they were the minority. He had felt that he heard from God at a Promise Keepers conference to listen to what grieved God and to be part of the solution. Promise Keepers is an evangelical parachurch organization for men. Emerson had returned home and read all he could about race and religion in America. But "without the transformation that we were encountering in our personal lives, I would not have grasped the divergences that I was hearing as Black and white Christians described their lives to me. I would have dismissed them, pushed them aside, explained them away. But here it was, so clearly different in ways that I now had to wrestle with to understand fully." Emerson's conclusions were difficult because they implicated those he loved who were White. He remembered, "Writing *Divided by Faith* made me physically ill. It felt like the final nail that was breaking us from the world that I had known and trusted. The world of my friends and family and heroes. I didn't want to write the book; but I had to."[7]

---

[7] Michael O. Emerson, "Foreword," in *Christians and the Color Line: Race and Religion After Divided by Faith*, ed. J. Russell Hawkins and Phillip Luke Sinitiere (New York: Oxford University Press, 2014), ix-xii.

Emerson and Smith's book was published in 2001. In 2013, before Ferguson and Black Lives Matter changed the national conversation about race, Ryon Cobb, another evangelical Christian sociologist, conducted follow-up research to see whether evangelicalism's toolkit still blinded White evangelicals to how racialized American society is. He found that it did.[8]

Reading *Divided by Faith* changed my life because I began to see that American society is shaped by race and that the practices and subtexts of my faith, paired with my racial context, limited my ability to see how that was working. Rock Church helped me understand race—and forgiveness and justice—even more.

My journey was similar in some ways to that of Glen, who came of age in Chicago in one of the most pivotal years in US history: 1968. The tools he had to understand the massive and intense racial conflict wracking the city were not up to the task of understanding the depths of what was happening. But he made the crucial choice to listen to Black people and try to understand their experiences and would later live in a Black neighborhood. From that vantage point, he would begin to see the deep systemic forces—from religious assumptions to housing practices—shaping race in the North.

QUESTIONS AND IMPLICATIONS

The toolkit idea was transformational for me, but like most social sciences, it is a model that accounts for the majority of people, and there can be exceptions.

- Does your understanding of race tend more toward a structural or a personal framework? What are the benefits of both?
- How might your own theological toolkit help or hinder your ability to see the effects of race in the United States?

Despite their best efforts, Glen and Lonni were wounded racially. Pastor Raleigh and Paulette brought the healing balm to them, in part by practicing empathy by seeing and acknowledging their pain.

- What healing do you need along racial lines? Name it and ask God to work in your life.

---

[8]Ryan Cobb, "Still Divided by Faith? Evangelical Religion and the Problem of Race in America," in Hawkins and Sinitiere, *Christians and the Color Line*, 128-40.

- Some of your need may not be from a wound inflicted by others. It may be from a callousness or refusal to learn from someone from a racial group different from you. What steps can you take to put yourself in positions of learning from others, or, if you are White, to put yourself under the leadership of someone who is from a different racial background?

I argued that empathy is essential to do history well and that, as Rock Church's history will show, also necessary to develop strong relationships.

- To what extent do you practice empathy? Are there people toward whom or situations in which you find it hard to extend empathy?
- Remember that to empathize or understand does not mean to condone what someone has done. Nonetheless, are there some people to whom or situations in which we ought not to practice empathy? My sense is that we always must because empathy is a form of love, but I may be wrong.

17

GOING BACK TO THE FUNDAMENTALS

How White evangelicals became so individualistic in the twentieth century and how Circle Church helped (and hurt) Glen and Lonni as they ministered to Black children living in a public housing project.

RACE IN THE NORTH

Glen Kehrein looked west from Moody Bible Institute and saw Black neighborhoods ablaze. It was April 1968, and Martin Luther King Jr. had just been assassinated. Glen's relationships with a handful of Black students at Moody had begun to sensitize him to how African Americans and White people experienced the world differently. Chicago's African Americans were angry and felt hopeless after such a beloved leader had been killed. Even more terrifying for White folks at Moody, some of the violence was close to campus. As Glen recalled, "I felt like I was being torn in two: part of me intensely opposed the violence; the other part was caught up and angered by the injustice that ignited it."[1]

Although Glen did not know her at the time, a young African American girl who lived close to Moody had a similar experience of fear, but for different reasons. Sheila Anderson would later join Rock Church and work for Circle. Sheila's parents were involved in a Black church but sent their children

---

[1] Raleigh Washington and Glen Kehrein, *Breaking Down Walls: A Model for Reconciliation in an Age of Racial Strife* (Chicago: Moody Press, 1994), 40.

to the Moody Church, which has close ties to Moody Bible Institute, for Sunday school. Sheila often joined other children at Sonshine Gospel Ministry for Bible study, where Glen and Lonni volunteered. Unlike Glen, Sheila was not scared of those rioting but of the White National Guard men who had been called out to create peace and who patrolled her neighborhood. Sheila's mother sent Sheila and her sister out to buy milk and bread, forgetting the curfew order. More than fifty years later, Sheila remembered seeing a tank roll up to them, and a man in a uniform with what seemed to be a huge gun jumped out and started swearing at them to get home. The girls ran home, terrified and crying. Sheila then refused to go outside, afraid she would be shot.[2]

Black Chicagoans loved King, and his murder sparked anger and amplified hopelessness that racial and economic conditions would change.[3] They were tired of living in overcrowded apartments, with little access to swimming pools during the hot summers. They were tired of rats biting their children in the night and of overcrowded schools in Black neighborhoods while schools in White neighborhoods had empty seats. They were tired of the slums. In 1966, King had joined Chicago civil rights organizers in the Chicago Freedom Summer, which became a campaign to end slums and allow African Americans to live wherever they chose in the city, a process known as open housing. King had chosen Chicago because of the support of the local people and because, given his leadership style, he thought that Chicago would provide a victory for the movement.

But Chicago's racial dynamics were less obvious than the ones that King (and Clarence Jordan and John Perkins) were navigating in the South. Chicago's mayor, Richard Daley, had supported the civil rights movement in the South. Black aldermen served on the city council and, beholden to Daley,

---

[2]Sheila Anderson, interview by author, April 5, 2021.

[3]Black Chicagoans were by no means unified. There had been conflict between King and some of Chicago's Black leaders, who did not appreciate King's bringing attention to the inequality because they were trying to make change through the complicated political system of patronage that Mayor Daley controlled. See, for instance, Darlene Gordon, "Resisting the Struggle: Why Blacks Opposed Dr. Martin Luther King, Jr. in Chicago, 1966–1967" (PhD diss., DePaul University, 2005); James Ralph, *Northern Protest: Martin Luther King, Jr., Chicago, and the Civil Rights Movement* (Cambridge, MA: Harvard University Press, 1993); Mary Lou Finley, Bernard LaFayette Jr., James R. Ralph Jr., and Pam Smith, eds., *The Chicago Freedom Movement: Martin Luther King Jr. and Civil Rights Activism in the North* (Lexington: University Press of Kentucky, 2015).

opposed King's work in Chicago. Chicago also had an open housing law on the books, which was some of the fruit of its mayor-appointed commissioner on human relations, Ed Marciniak. Marciniak was a Catholic interracialist who knew Catherine de Hueck and had been close with members of Chicago's Friendship House, which Catherine planted there in 1942. He had accepted the position as commissioner of human relations to try to make change through the governmental process. Throughout the summer of 1966, then, Marciniak had been in the position of supporting open housing but being protested against by fellow White Catholics who had joined the Black marchers. Race in Chicago was complicated, to say the least.

SHEEP GONE ASTRAY: NORTHERN EVANGELICALS AND INDIVIDUALISM

Glen had come to a point of disillusionment with White Christians and even Christianity. He concluded that White Christians were "either oblivious or unsympathetic to the legitimate needs of the Black community around us."[4] He likely did not know that this experience was common among African Americans, who left Christianity disillusioned by White Christians' inability and unwillingness to live out Jesus' teachings. This dynamic was the one Clarence and John had wrestled with and that Catherine had seen among working-class Canadians and African Americans. When the body of Christ failed to be the church, sheep fell away. As Glen recalled,

> Either my faith made sense and would help me live out a faith-driven ethic that dealt with things like injustice and poverty and racism, or it was . . . just a joke. I cried out, "Oh God, what do I do?" but there was no burning bush to guide me; I didn't know what to do. I began a journey, searching for a way to become part of the solution rather than resigning myself to being part of the problem.[5]

Glen's cousin, who was a year behind him at Moody, concluded that Christianity was a sham and left the faith because, he thought, "when it comes to really living out the teachings of Jesus, it's a joke."[6] Glen somehow held on.

Glen's experience of White evangelicalism was not an exception. While White, more-liberal Catholics worked with Jews and mainline Protestants to

---
[4] Washington and Kehrein, *Breaking Down Walls*, 38.
[5] Washington and Kehrein, *Breaking Down Walls*, 41.
[6] Washington and Kehrein, *Breaking Down Walls*, 41.

support open housing across the state of Illinois, White evangelicals were largely silent or opposed open housing. In the north, White evangelicals rarely supported segregation with the violence that Perkins experienced from White evangelicals in the South, but they did argue that open housing was not a Christian necessity. Many White evangelicals were leaving the city as part of a larger exodus to the suburbs in the post–World War II era. They left for many complicated reasons, but race played a key factor. Those with stronger church polities left more slowly, while others replanted their churches in the suburbs more quickly, sometimes leaving behind a "mission" to serve African Americans who moved into the neighborhood.[7]

Part of the lack of work for open housing, and for civil rights more generally in the North among White evangelicals, was due to just not knowing about racial disparities because of the physical distance between Black and White people. As the saying goes, "In the South they don't care how close you are, as long as you don't get too big; in the North, they don't care how big you are, as long as you don't get too close."[8] Northern White evangelicals were not concerned that Black people—Christians and otherwise—were advancing and desiring to live in nicer neighborhoods. They just did not want Black people to live in their neighborhoods. They thus missed a key element of what God has done for his children through Jesus—united people who were once far apart together in Christ as an example of God's manifold wisdom to all the principalities and powers in the unseen realm of his power (Ephesians 3:1).[9]

---

[7] Mark Mulder, *Shades of White Flight: Evangelical Congregations and Urban Departure* (New Brunswick, NJ: Rutgers University Press, 2015); Amanda Seligman, *Block by Block: Neighborhoods and Public Policy on Chicago's West Side* (Chicago: University of Chicago Press, 2005); Darren Dochuk, *From Bible Belt to Sun Belt: Folk Religion, Grassroots Politics, and the Rise of Evangelical Conservatism* (New York: Norton, 2010).

[8] Quoted in Susan Neiman, *Learning from the Germans: Race and the Memory of Evil* (New York: Farrar, Straus & Giroux, 2019), 189.

[9] These dynamics continue. More recently, sociologists have found that White people say they want to live in more diverse neighborhoods, but when a neighborhood's demographics become more than 20 percent minority, White people move away at faster rates. See Jeannine Bell, *Hate Thy Neighbor: Move-In Violence and the Persistence of Racial Segregation in American Housing* (New York: New York University Press, 2013). In 2010, the typical White American lived in a neighborhood that was 75 percent White, while the typical Black American lived in a community that was only 35 percent White. One study found that White evangelicals are mostly suburban residents, with 51.8 percent living in suburbs or exurbs, 18.4 percent living in urban areas, and 29.8 percent living in rural areas. By contrast, about 70 percent of Black evangelicals and Hispanic evangelicals live in urban areas, compared to 18.5 percent of Black evangelicals and 14 percent of Hispanic

Many White evangelicals also assumed that their ability to move to the suburbs was due to their own hard work alone. Individualism was shaping their perspective. While hard work and industry certainly contributed to their ability to move, White evangelicals' efforts happened in a context shaped by governmental and banking policies that favored them and suburbanization, which was largely off limits to African Americans.[10] Often unaware of how much the government had influenced their ability to own their own homes (see chapter three), White evangelicals insisted they had a right to choose to whom they could sell their property. What they did not see was that they were limiting other people's freedom to choose where they wanted to live.

UNDERSTANDING THE FUNDAMENTALS

White evangelicalism had not always looked that way, and Glen's school had been part of the changes. In the nineteenth century, evangelicals were often on the edge of reform, working for abolition, promoting women's education, trying to make earth as it is in heaven for all people. But in the early twentieth century, White evangelicals had shifted from emphasizing love of God and love of neighbor to focusing more on an individual's relationship with God.

The shift developed in response to contextual changes. As the factories fueling the Industrial Revolution drew Catholic immigrants and rural Americans to cities, middle-class American Protestants faced a dilemma. How should they address the pressing needs of poverty and the growing number of what they perceived to be unchurched people in the United States? These dynamics developed as scientific ways of thinking increasingly shaped American intellectual and theological life, along with the rise of German higher criticism, which tried to make Christianity "relevant" to contemporary needs.[11] American Christians wanted certainty. Some Protestants

---

evangelicals living in urban or exurban neighborhoods. See John Green and Ann Greenberg, "America's Evangelicals," referenced in Mark T. Mulder and James K. A. Smith, "Subdivided by Faith? An Historical Account of Evangelicals and the City," *Christian Scholar's Review* 38, no. 4 (Summer 2009): 430-31.

[10]This history is complicated. For African Americans in suburbs, see James Dorsey, *Up South: Blacks in Chicago's Suburbs (1719–1983)* (Bristol, IN: Wyndham Hall, 1986); Andrew Wiese, *Places of Their Own: African American Suburbanization in the Twentieth Century* (Chicago: University of Chicago Press, 2004).

[11]Mark A. Noll, *The Scandal of the Evangelical Mind* (Grand Rapids, MI: Eerdmans, 2022).

emphasized what they called Christianity's social gospel, how God would meet the physical needs of people on earth and transform society. Others, troubled that their fellow Christians were abandoning an emphasis on a person's vertical relationship with God, emphasized what they called the fundamentals of the faith. Between 1910 and 1915, Quaker Oats director Henry Parsons Cromwell and other corporate executives underwrote a series of tracts known as "The Fundamentals" to defend the faith.

These so-called fundamentalists increasingly adopted an eschatology—a view of the end times—that was premillennial, differing from nineteenth-century evangelicals. Most American evangelicals in the nineteenth century were postmillennialists, thinking that Jesus would return *after* the thousand-year reign and that their efforts to reform American society would hasten Jesus' return. The premillennial theology of a growing group of late nineteenth- and early twentieth-century evangelicals meant they believed Jesus would return *before* the thousand-year reign of God.[12] This theology meant that evangelicals had less reason to work for reform or really devote themselves to the common good beyond the personal saving of souls.

Moreover, many evangelical leaders would embrace dispensational premillennialism. They read C. I. Scofield's *Scofield Reference Bible*, which included extensive notes and instruction on how to read the Bible scientifically to understand how it showed that humanity's history was divided into separate dispensations in which God engaged the world differently. This meant, for instance, that Jesus' Sermon on the Mount teaching that the poor are blessed was not relevant for the contemporary moment. It was a great reversal, as evangelicals no longer led in social reform.[13] The gospel was being fractured, separating love for neighbor from love of God and tearing apart personal righteousness from seeking justice.

These changes in eschatology and how people read the Bible coincided with the growth of individualism, which shaped how Christians approached spiritual formation. Nineteenth-century evangelicals assumed that Christians were formed in community, but twentieth-century evangelicals,

---

[12]Mark Noll, *A History of Christianity in the United States and Canada* (Grand Rapids, MI: Eerdmans, 1992), chap. 14.

[13]David Moberg, *The Great Reversal: Reconciling Evangelism and Social Concern* (Eugene, OR: Wipf & Stock, 2007).

influenced by the logics of business, began seeing Christian formation as individualistic. When Quaker Oats director Cromwell became Moody's president, he made the school a center of these ways of thinking. Cromwell his colleagues marketed evangelicalism to middle-class consumers, downplaying its potentially radical and subversive nature. They assumed upward mobility and understood people as individuals making rational decisions. This slow, almost imperceivable shift from radical reform and concern for the least of these to a comfortable, consumer-oriented individualism became a nearly imperceptible framework through which evangelicals filtered their experiences.[14]

These were the fundamentals Glen inherited. And they were not robust enough to help him really understand the pain in his Black friends' lives while at Moody. Glen observed, "The weak response of white evangelicals exposed the fact that my kind of Christians either did not care or that we had insulated ourselves for so long that we did not know how to care. Either option was intolerable to me." Pushing against the individualism characterizing his faith tradition, Glen thought, "But I couldn't very well point a finger at the church without pointing at myself: I, too, was part of the problem."[15]

What is the problem with the world? I am. But that is not the only problem, and the solution is not only my own heart change. Glen did not yet know that.

Glen was dating a young woman also from rural Wisconsin named Lonni Bulkley, whom he met in high school. When she was nineteen, Lonni moved to Chicago to be by Glen. He invited Lonni to serve at Sonshine Gospel Mission's Awana Club. One of Sonshine's ministries was working with local youth, many of them African American and living in the Cabrini Green housing project. Despite many parents' best efforts, life for Black children at Cabrini Green was racially segregated and full of gang violence and poverty, an unintended consequence of twenty thousand people living in twenty-three high rises on just seventy acres of land.[16]

---

[14]Timothy Gloege, *Guaranteed Pure: The Moody Bible Institute, Business, and the Making of Modern Evangelicalism* (Chapel Hill: University of North Carolina Press, 2015).
[15]Washington and Kehrein, *Breaking Down Walls*.
[16]Cabrini Green was a low-income housing project. Like other public housing in Chicago, it was intended to help people, but the concentrated poverty was detrimental to its inhabitants. See Ben Austen, *High-Risers: Cabrini-Green and the Fate of American Public Housing* (New York: HarperOne, 2018).

The children Glen and Lonni worked with were smart. But Lonni could not understand a word they said. Many African Americans learn how to code switch, speaking one way when around White people and another when with fellow Black people. Like most White people crossing cultural barriers, Lonni needed to learn how to understand the girls she was trying to serve, beginning with their speech. She remembered, "I thought they were speaking a foreign language."[17] Nor could she tell them apart (a common experience when seeing someone from a different racial background).

Lonni refused to dismiss the girls. Instead, she built relationships, which led her to wonder at their resilience. When one of the girls was absent from the club, Lonni asked the others why. The girl's two closest friends responded that a brick had dropped from a Cabrini Green tower and hit her as the three had been walking. They had carried her home, and she had died. The child died through no fault of her own but because of the effects of concentrated poverty that had been largely created by generations of policies and sensibilities. Lonni's experience with these young girls changed her life. Later she would reflect that she had no idea that people might not want her help.[18] She just wanted to help them, just wanted to fix things.

Lonni and Glen married and together tried to address individual and systemic needs with the tools in their evangelical toolkit: save one person at a time through reaching them with the gospel. The toolkit worked on one level, making a difference in the lives of individuals as they entered into personal relationships with Jesus. But problems of race and poverty in America cannot merely be addressed at the individual level. They need organizational and policy solutions as well—which John Perkins, working for civil rights in Mississippi, knew well. Glen and Lonni also needed support in their work, as well as people who could teach them to see more clearly.

CIRCLE CHURCH: CHRIST'S BROKEN BODY

Their first church community supported the young couple's work but could not lead them in it. Glen and Lonni married at Salem Evangelical Free Church and began serving several times a week in the church's Awana Club, which used Scripture memory, games, and fellowship to bring children to faith in

---

[17] Lonni Kehrein, interview by author, April 7, 2021.
[18] Kehrein, interview.

Jesus. Since Glen believed that the children needed to become part of a church, and he and Lonni brought about thirty African American children to church on Sundays. But Glen's questions about social inequality were still unanswered. He and Lonni began dreaming about founding an organization that would be fully evangelical—emphasizing salvation and living a holy life— and would meet a neighborhood's social needs. Though they loved Salem, the church was not asking or answering their questions, questions with which John and Vera Mae Perkins had grappled. What did the gospel have to say to poverty and racism?

Circle Church would help them begin to answer their questions. One Sunday, they decided to visit the church. Circle Church's leaders, David Mains, Clarence Hilliard, and Ka Tong Gaw, wanted their congregation to be intentionally crosscultural and to welcome people from all racial and ethnic backgrounds. The three men modeled the diversity in their leadership. Head pastor Maines was White, and associate pastors Hilliard and Gaw were Black and Chinese American, respectively. The members were highly educated, with many young families and students in bachelor's, master's, and doctoral programs. About 80 percent were White, 5 percent were Asian, and 15 percent were African American.[19] By sociological standards, because no more than 80 percent of the population was one race, the church was multiracial. That morning, the church was signing its "Declaration of an Open Church." Glen remembered the declaration as "Circle's vision of different races and classes coming together, not to assimilate into the culture of the majority, but to appreciate and celebrate in Christian harmony their differences in culture, class, and race."[20]

Circle Church was part of a movement within evangelicalism that was hopeful that it could merge personal piety with social action. They wanted to reverse evangelicalism's early twentieth century fracturing of the gospel, when evangelicals turned away from social concern. In 1973, Ron Sider organized a meeting at Chicago's downtown YMCA, close to both Moody Church and Grant Park, where five years earlier Mayor Daley's police had violently clashed with leftist protestors outside the Democratic National Convention. John Perkins came up to Chicago for the meeting, and Pastor

---

[19]Washington and Kehrein, *Breaking Down Walls*, 74.
[20]Washington and Kehrein, *Breaking Down Walls*, 74.

Hilliard was there too. The group confessed, "We have not acknowledged the complete claim of God on our lives" and had "not demonstrated the love of God to those suffering social abuses." They also deplored "the historic involvement of the church in America with racism and the conspicuous responsibility of the evangelical community for perpetuating the personal attitudes and institutional structures that have divided the Body of Christ along color lines." They declared, "We proclaim no new gospel, but the Gospel of our Lord Jesus Christ who, through the power of the Holy Spirit, frees people from sin so that they might praise God through works of righteousness."[21]

Although the Chicago meeting's final product, the Chicago Declaration of Evangelical Social Concern, suggested unity, the coalition was fragile. Black participants had worked hard to convince all the White members to address racism in the statement. Black evangelicals also disagreed over what constituted Christian responses to racism. Many in the 1960s had seen Martin Luther King Jr.'s model of beloved community as a goal. But other young Black evangelicals became disillusioned with their treatment at White evangelical colleges and were intrigued by Black Power's budding analyses that questioned whether it was possible for White and Black people to live together in unity without White people dominating culturally.[22] Some Black Power advocates, such as the Illinois Black Panther Party leader, Fred Hampton, worked interracially, but it seemed like the White establishment would not accept their leadership or critique. Chicago

---

[21] Chicago Declaration of Evangelical Social Concern, in *Jerry Falwell and the Rise of the Religious Right: A Brief History with Documents*, ed. Matthew Avery Sutton (Boston: Bedford/St. Martins, 2013), 45-47. See also David R. Swartz, *Moral Minority: The Evangelical Left in an Age of Conservatism* (repr., Philadelphia: University of Pennsylvania Press, 2014); Peter Goodwin Heltzel, *Jesus and Justice: Evangelicals, Race, and American Politics* (New Haven, CT: Yale University Press, 2009).

[22] David R. Swartz, "Identity Politics and the Fragmenting of the 1970s Evangelical Left," *Religion and American Culture* 21, no. 1 (2011): 81-120. Black Power was a complex movement that emerged most prominently in the 1960s with the Black Panther Party and the Student Non-violent Coordinating Committee's shift in the late 1960s. It is also part of a larger tradition of Black nationalism with deep roots. Some groups, such as the Nation of Islam, of which Malcolm X was a member before he left the sect in 1964, were separatist, while others cooperated with other racial groups and prioritized Black leadership in communities, businesses, and the arts, also emphasizing Black people's beauty. While many narratives about Black Power assume that it was secular, many Black Christians embraced aspects of it. See Kerry Pimblott, *Faith in Black Power: Religion, Race, and Resistance in Cairo, Illinois* (Lexington: University of Kentucky Press, 2017); Matthew J. Cressler, *Authentically Black and Truly Catholic: The Rise of Black Catholicism in the Great Migration* (New York: New York University Press, 2017).

police officers assassinated Hampton in December 1969, supported by the FBI's Counter Intelligence Program, which sought to dismantle the Black Panther Party.

Glen had watched his Black friends at Moody navigate this painful dynamic. His friend and Air Force veteran Rev. Mel Warren had destroyed his diploma from Moody when he graduated in 1969. Warren called Moody racist, saying it segregated dormitories, prohibited interracial dating, and did not allow local Black children to use their gymnasium. Moody leadership disagreed, saying the institution did not segregate dormitories, had lifted its ban on interracial dating, and could not open the gym because of insurance issues.[23] No matter official policies, life as a Black student at a White Christian institution was difficult. While Moody may not have had an official ban on interracial dating, testimony from students who attended after Warren's graduation suggest that when Black men dated White women, many people frowned on the relationships. Further, many White students, knowing little about Black culture or physical features, would wonder about Black students' hair and other aspects of their physical and cultural lives in invasive ways.[24] Some Black students endured this dynamic without letting it bother them. Others were tired of White people's questions and ignorance, tired of explaining themselves repeatedly, tired of what they saw as a White-washed theology that did not account for their experiences and questions. Glen observed that Warren and other Black students felt Moody "gave little thought to the needs of its minorities, assuming that they would merely assimilate into the white culture."[25]

Within this fraught context, Circle Church became Glen's and Lonni's spiritual home. They asked the leadership whether they could join Circle Church with the caveat that they would be bringing about thirty Black children with them into the church's fold. The leaders said yes, and other church members helped Glen and Lonni transport the children to church. The couple soon joined the "Black Module," a ministry group that Pastor Hilliard led with the aim of making the church more attractive to African Americans. Circle Church was not perfect, but it was Christ's body, broken.

---

[23]"Bible Institute Grads Rip Diplomas; Protest Racism," *JET*, March 1970.
[24]DuRhonda Palmore, interview by author, September 22, 2021.
[25]Washington and Kehrein, *Breaking Down Walls*, 36.

Lonni would remember that the Black Module changed her life. When she was growing up in rural Wisconsin, she had no interaction with African Americans. Living in Chicago meant she talked with Black people, but most were children. Lonni had no Black adults in leadership over her. Not so at Circle Church. In the Black Module under Pastor Hilliard's leadership, Lonni submitted to African American leadership for the first time. In our conversation over four decades later, she emphasized repeatedly how important it is for White people to be under the leadership of those racially or ethnically different from them. She and Glen knew they needed to learn if they were to fulfill what they saw as a growing call to minister among African Americans.

White people felt uncomfortable in the Black Module. Pastor Hilliard's confrontational style toward White members of the Black Module let them feel the pain of interracial relationships that Black people often experienced. A key part of White members' experience in the Black Module was instruction, learning simple things like greeting a Black man on the street rather than crossing over to the other side. Lonni remembered crying often and thinking that perhaps she was learning some of what it was like to be someone without privilege in America. She would tell herself that while she might be uncomfortable, she was not like Black women in the nineteenth century's internal slave trade who said goodbye to their young children that were sold west. These confrontations made Lonni look inward, made her realize that while she did not think she was prejudiced, she did think more highly of herself sometimes in subtle ways when she compared herself to those with different skin colors.[26]

More detrimentally, White people also developed self-hate in the Black Module. Their hatred mirrored the self-hate many African Americans subtly imbibed living in a world that assumed White people, White culture, and White beauty standards—thin hips, smooth hair, light skin—were normative. Black Power advocates pushed against these standards, telling African Americans to stop putting chemicals on their skin and hair to make them lighter and straighter and instead to embrace how God had made them because "Black is beautiful." But within the Black Module, there was little room for celebrating both Black and White cultures. Glen remembered that the Black

---

[26]Lonni Kehrein, interview by author, April 12, 2021.

Module made him "hate the fact that I was white. No matter how educated I became, I could never escape the blight of my whiteness."[27]

Nor could Glen enjoy full fellowship with his African American brothers and sisters. As he recalled, his Black friends "made it a requirement to exclude whites from the brotherhood; to admit that a white person really understood was to surrender power."[28] This dynamic was painful for Glen, and he would later critique it as not Christian. But he could understand how even Christians would resist fellowship with other Christians they perceived as unwilling to fairly share power. In the coming years, most of the Black members of Circle Church would perceive their fears realized: that Circle Church favored White people who refused to share authority and value minority members' input.

Gratitude and trepidation characterized Glen's memories of Circle Church and the Black Module. Discomfort was good; self-hate and isolation were not. Twenty years later he would frame the Black Module's problem as being focused on racial education alone rather than education and relationship. Glen realized when he was older that education and relationship could lead to racial reconciliation, the power of God bringing people together in Christ through the hard work of forgiveness.

Nonetheless, Circle Church provided Glen and Lonni an institutional context where they grew spiritually in part because they had learned to wonder about others' experiences. This wondering was another tool in their toolkit, and was giving them the ability to practice empathy. Circle Church also represented an important stream of evangelicalism in America that diverged from most contemporary evangelicalism—a group of people reuniting evangelism and social reform with an eye toward the least, the last, and the lost. With the fellowship at Circle Church—despite its brokenness—Glen and Lonni were going back to the actual fundamentals of the faith.

QUESTIONS AND IMPLICATIONS

Glen did not let himself off the hook when he saw White evangelicals' indifference to African Americans' suffering, even though he had been trying to serve African Americans and learn more about their experiences. With humility, he allowed himself to be implicated in a larger structure.

---

[27]Washington and Kehrein, *Breaking Down Walls*, 75.
[28]Washington and Kehrein, *Breaking Down Walls*, 75.

- What parts of Glen's story can you relate to and why?
- How does corporate responsibility play into the life of the local and broader church experience today?
- Do you defend yourself when accused, or do you have a sense of corporate responsibility?

Lonni's experience in the Black Module made her build grit. She was uncomfortable but chose to stay and reflect on her life based on what she was learning.

- How might you need God to search you and point out any anxious ways in you?

Circle Church celebrated differences and did not expect that people assimilate to another culture.

- If your church is diverse, do you implicitly require assimilation, or do you celebrate different cultures? If so, how?

Being a part of the Black Module and submitting to African American leadership helped Glen and Lonni to see how subconsciously they expected to be comfortable and catered to culturally. Research on interracial/multiracial/multiethnic congregations suggests that often White people expect people of color to assimilate to their preferences. In our interviews, Lonni said that submitting to leadership from someone of a different race made a huge difference in her life.

- What are the costs and benefits of being led by someone from a different cultural or racial background?
- Who is in leadership in your church? How do you share power?
- Your ability to influence that dynamic is likely complicated, possibly limited, but where is a place you could start?

I argued that the fundamentalist/modernist divide limited evangelicals' understanding of the gospel by bifurcating personal salvation and righteousness from seeking justice (two things that are inseparable in Scripture).

- How does knowing this history change your understanding of social concern?
- Does a framework of individualism guide your approach to your faith? What are the strengths and weaknesses of that approach?

18

THE FUNKY GOSPEL

Why the Kehreins relocated to Chicago's Austin neighborhood as other White people left, how Circle Church split, and why empathy is necessary for good history and good relationships.

A STRATEGIC LOCATION

Glen was hooking up a stove for Eric and me in our new apartment on Erie Street in the Austin neighborhood in 2007. He was our landlord. As we chatted in the sunny yellow kitchen with a gray linoleum floor, I could not believe I was talking to one of my heroes. Our conversations after that often turned to race in America, and one day he gave me a book by a sociologist to read. The binding was bent open to a page on which the author said Christians must stop wondering why American churches remained bastions of segregation and instead act because segregation in churches was "a sinful denial of everything Christianity stands for."[1] Glen was still part of a multiracial church, but he knew well how difficult they could be to hold together.

It was no surprise Glen gave me a book by a sociologist. In 1971, he began studying sociology at Wheaton College, where Circle Church's Pastor Gaw taught. Glen wanted to understand why Chicago was so segregated and why White evangelicals were overwhelmingly opposed to racial change or indifferent to African Americans' position in American society. Above all, he wondered how Christians could best address these issues. Sociology had

---

[1]Orlando Patterson, *The Ordeal of Integration* (Washington, DC: Civitas Counterpoint, 1998), 199.

given Glen more tools for his toolkit because it looked at social systems *and* the individuals within them.

Glen and Lonni worked out their answers to questions about the causes of segregation as they worked out their salvation with fear and trembling where segregation caused the most widespread pain: in a poor Black community. There, Glen helped create a church community that lived into the reality of the unity of God's people.

When Glen graduated, he worked for Circle Church under Pastor Hilliard to develop neighborhood programs. Because members commuted to church from across the city, the leaders wanted to establish a presence in different neighborhoods. Members of the Black Module wanted to work on two main initiatives: neighborhood outreach and intentional Christian community.

John Perkins's Voice of Calvary inspired the White members of Circle Church's Black Module. They had learned about John Perkins's Voice of Calvary, which by then in Mendenhall had a Bible institute, health center, a gym, Genesis One Christian School, a farm, a summer camp, and a neighborhood outreach, all with the intention of strengthening the community holistically, physically, socially, and spiritually. When John moved to Jackson, Voice of Calvary had become more interracial, as White people from outside Mississippi had joined the staff. Glen remembered, "To have an effective ministry in the city, most of us believed we needed to intentionally live in the neighborhood in order to serve it. This required some sacrifice of people's lifestyles. . . . That's where we felt the vision of Christian community intersected with the vision for outreach."[2]

Glen thought they should establish an intentional community that also conducted outreach through social services because it would "have a stabilizing effect before the neighborhood deteriorated badly." Chicago's neighborhood change was block by block, with White residents resisting Black neighbors before leaving quickly. The population change was coupled with the movement of industry and businesses away from the city, depleting the tax base.[3] At first, housing costs would rise as Black middle- and upper-class homebuyers paid a premium to move into a "nicer" neighborhood. But then,

---

[2]Raleigh Washington and Glen Kehrein, *Breaking Down Walls: A Model for Reconciliation in an Age of Racial Strife* (Chicago: Moody Press, 1994), 76.

[3]Thomas J. Sugrue, *The Origins of the Urban Crisis: Race and Inequality in Postwar Detroit* (Princeton, NJ: Princeton University Press, 2005); Amanda Seligman, *Block by Block: Neighborhoods and Public Policy on Chicago's West Side* (Chicago: University of Chicago Press, 2005).

because of blockbusters' fearmongering and the hidden structures of the mortgage system, prices would drop (see chapter three). Because of the overcrowding in Chicago's Black neighborhoods, Black Chicagoans wanted to "move up and move out."[4] But Glen wanted to move in. To him, the Austin neighborhood on the western edge of Chicago looked like the place to be.

Glen and Lonni were adding two more tools to their toolkit: analyzing their context at the levels of groups and systems and doing so from a marginalized community. They were beginning to see more clearly.

A WHITE GROUP IN A CHANGING NEIGHBORHOOD

Few Black members of the Black Module were interested in relocating to Austin and living in intentional community.[5] At the time, Austin had the second-highest crime rate in Chicago. Nonetheless, the Kehreins and other White members of the Black Module bought property they could share in common and named themselves the Austin Community Fellowship. Intentional communities were increasingly common in the 1970s—down in Georgia, Koinonia had thirty-six members of the community, with more who had bought low-cost housing nearby and with many more people living there for shorter terms.[6] Like others, Austin Community Fellowship members shared cars, housing, and money. But families remained intact, and spouses were faithful. Lonni remembered their Black neighbors calling them the "good Christians."[7]

Other White people would join. They sought authentic relationships, an Acts 2 community, and crosscultural ministry.[8] Those who worked in paying jobs funded those who would work in various ministries of the Circle Community Center (which would become Circle Urban Ministries when they relocated a few years later). Glen wanted Circle Community Center to put flesh on the gospel. The Circle Community Center tried to fill the holes left by White flight by providing professional services and caring for kids. But

---

[4]Arthur Jackson used this phrase to describe Kansas City growing up, as people wanted to migrate toward a middle-class perspective. Arthur Jackson, interview by author, October 5, 2021.
[5]Washington and Kehrein, *Breaking Down Walls*, 76.
[6]Andrew S. Chancey, "Koinonia Farm," in *New Georgia Encyclopedia*, 2005, www.georgiaencyclopedia.org/articles/arts-culture/koinonia-farm/.
[7]Lonni Kehrein, interview by author, April 12, 2021.
[8]Murray Sitte, interview by author, September 27, 2021.

before two years were up, Glen and Lonni would feel like they had been orphaned.

LISTENING TO THE FUNKY GOSPEL

A leadership debate over "the funky gospel" split Circle Church along racial lines. Pastor Hilliard wanted to preach a sermon with that title and shared the content with Pastors Mains and Gaw. The three worked together on their sermons. But Mains, the head pastor, said Hilliard could not preach this sermon because it was not doctrinally sound. Hilliard disagreed. Hilliard thought the sermon was orthodox and understood Mains's response to be limited by Mains's White racial perspective.

The elder board, which Glen served on, decided to remove both men from the pulpit until the conflict was resolved. Hilliard and the Black parishioners interpreted this decision as "silencing the pastor." Mains thought he had done nothing wrong and should not be removed. Reflecting years later, Glen noted that the elders never dealt with the content of the sermon. They never grappled with the truths or heresies it might contain. They did not listen to their friend.

They missed an important opportunity to practice empathy. "Wounds from a friend can be trusted, but an enemy multiplies kisses" (Proverbs 27:6).

While drafts of the sermon are unavailable, we can begin to reconstruct its themes using other sources. Lonni recalled in the oral history interview she and I did that Hilliard was drawing from liberation theology. Liberation theology emphasizes Jesus' presence among the poor and oppressed and was then prominent among Catholics in Latin America.[9] We can also use the *Christianity Today* article Hilliard wrote about the funky gospel to explore his understanding of the subject, albeit a few years later.

What did Hilliard mean by "funky"? In the *Christianity Today* article, Hilliard wrote that "funky stands opposite to honky—liberated, authentic, creative." He contrasted funky to honky's commitment to the status quo, which he saw as fundamentally oppressive. He argued, "We and our leaders have been preaching a honky Christ to a world hungry for the funky Jesus of the Bible. The honky Christ stands with the status quo, the funky Jesus moves

---

[9] For an important example, see Leonardo Boff and Clodovis Boff, *Introducing Liberation Theology* (Maryknoll, NY: Orbis Books, 1987).

apart from the ruling religious system. Jesus stood with the poor and oppressed and disinherited. He came for the sick and needy."[10]

Drawing from theologian James Cone, Hilliard argued that the best symbol for Jesus in America was a Black person because Jesus "came into the world as the ultimate 'nigger' of the universe. He moved to the bottom of the social order.... In a deeper sense, however, Christ Jesus became Blacker than Black since 'he was made sin for us.' And he died on the cross, a death reserved for the niggers of his day. The system sought to lock him eternally into that despised, Black status—damned forever."[11] Hilliard argued that Jesus' followers must move to the bottom of the social order, as Jesus had done, "to become niggers with him," to become Black in a theological sense, which meant willing to be an outcast at the bottom of society.[12]

This framework might be jarring. Yet Hilliard's language is precise and draws on accurate interpretations of the United States's racial history. There are certainly stories of interracial friendship and mutual submission—some of which I am highlighting in this book—along with resistance among Black folks to their racial subjugation. But time and again, other racial groups have not wanted associate with those who are "Black" because to be Black is to be lowly, to be despised and rejected by others, to be oppressed and afflicted, to be ugly. To be Black in the overarching experience of American history perhaps is to be described as Scripture describes Jesus. Hilliard was using one of the key tenets of the tradition of formal Black theology, which began in the 1960s—that Jesus was Black, that Jesus was a "nigger"—to make clean the bride of Christ.

But there is a longer tradition within Christianity that imagines Jesus as Black and reflects aspects of Black Americans' historical place in US society.

---

[10]Clarence Hilliard, "Down with the Honky Christ—up with the Funky Jesus," *Christianity Today*, January 30, 1976. Hilliard was drawing from Christian theologian James Cone, who has a robust oeuvre. His first book was a response to Malcolm X's repeated assertions as a member of the Nation of Islam that Christianity was a White man's religion and that Black people needed a religion that emerged from their own cultural heritage. See Cone, *Black Theology and Black Power* (Maryknoll, NY: Orbis Books, 1969).
[11]Hilliard, "Down with the Honky Christ."
[12]For an overview of Black theology from an evangelical perspective, see Bruce Fields, *Introducing Black Theology: Three Crucial Questions for the Evangelical Church* (Grand Rapids, MI: Baker Academic, 2001). In my mind, one key problem of liberation theology is its reliance on Marxist analysis to understand the world, which assumes a group of oppressors and oppressed and promotes revolution. This framework does not allow for nuance, which I see in human history and in Scripture.

This tradition influenced Catherine de Hueck when she lived in Black Harlem. Black artists in the 1920s drew and sang about Jesus in their context, one full of the "strange fruit" of lynched Black bodies hanging from trees that jazz singer Billie Holiday later sang about.[13] To them, it made sense that Jesus would have been a Black man, lynched, were he in the United States. As Roman society downgraded Jews, so did White society hinder African Americans' flourishing. As the Romans crucified criminals, so did White people lynch Black "criminals," with other Whites in the nation turning a blind eye and refusing to pass legislation outlawing lynching.[14] This framework is a tradition within American Christianity (not just Black American Christianity), and White people like me must not cast it aside because it seems strange.

I remember the first time I read Black theology in seminary. I puzzled over Cone's description of Jesus' Blackness. My first hurdle was grappling with Cone's use of *Blackness* not to refer to a skin color but to a category of people. When he called Jesus a "nigger," he was referring to Jesus' position in the larger society. It seemed strange to compare Jesus, the man from Nazareth, so directly to racial categories in the United States. I wondered whether it was right to start theology with one's experiences.

But within my puzzling was an assumption that my own theology was not influenced by my experiences; Black people's theology might be influenced by their experiences, but my theology was somehow untainted by experiences. My professor, Dr. Bruce Fields, a wise Black scholar doing the difficult work of teaching in a White context, helped me realize that we all come to Scripture with lenses influenced by our experiences.[15] Our lenses do not detract from the truth of Scripture, but they limit our ability to comprehend Scripture's truth fully. My inability to see means that I need my brothers and sisters in Christ who wear different blinders (I think Black theology has flaws) to help me understand scriptural truths. My desire to know Jesus, to be conformed to the image of Christ rather than to the image

---

[13]For depictions of Jesus in US history, see Paul Harvey and Edward Blum, *The Color of Christ: The Son of God and the Saga of Race in America* (Chapel Hill: University of North Carolina Press, 2012).

[14]For another articulation of Jesus and Jews as oppressed people, and an argument for what that means for those with their backs against the wall, see Howard Thurman, *Jesus and the Disinherited* (Boston: Beacon, 1949).

[15]Fields, *Introducing Black Theology*.

of the world, means I need to listen when a brother or sister from a different background speaks.

I hear in Hilliard's honky Christ/funky Jesus message a call to stand apart from the status quo and to follow Jesus downward, toward those at the bottom of society. His message speaks to American Christians' shared past, even if that past is sometimes hidden to White eyes.

Nonetheless, Hilliard's language was difficult for many listeners—and can still be difficult today. Calling Jesus a "lynched nigger" *could* startle people enough to make them listen and consider the idea. At the same time, the phrase *could* close off communication. I have tried to help us listen to Hilliard, to practice empathy and understand his perspective—because Christian love demands it but also because good history requires it.

But I also wonder why the elders did not discuss and debate the sermon's content. Did they really listen to Hilliard? Remember, Glen recalled that the elders did not want to debate the content. He reported that their main goal was to hold the church together. Did they think that dealing with the sermon's assumptions and arguments would break the church up? Did they implicitly assume that if they ignored the sermon's ideas, they would go away? If so, were they operating out of a set of theological assumptions that assumed Jesus could not be "Black," as Hilliard defined it?

DIFFERING INTERPRETATIONS OF THE SPLIT

Those interpreting the events focused on different threads in the tangle of church conflict at Circle, as is often the case in telling histories. Looking at the different interpretations of what happened may help us understand the complicated racial dynamics we see among ourselves.

In a 1980 article, David Mains, the head White pastor, interpreted the division as based on the leaders' pride in their ability to solve social issues, precipitated by the "minority element" within the church seeking to prioritize race above other issues. First, hubris. Mains remembered, "We wanted to draw from all those people [living in Skid Row, Black ghettos, the University of Illinois Chicago Circle Campus, and the medical community] and show that the church of Christ could break down the walls, and all of us could live together in peace before the world." But, he recalled, "we consistently underestimated the stranglehold of the enemy," and the problems "hundreds of years in the making" did not "softly melt away" as they had anticipated.[16] Mains thought that they did not understand the depth, complexity, and strength of race in America. Mains's words after the division are haunting: before the split, they assumed they were successful. But if he could do it again, he would have thought less about the church's success and instead have said, "I will do what can be done, and maybe others will join me. Someday my son or my son's son will finally see significant change in one small corner of a major metropolitan area." Mains's chastened humility is wise.

If Mains saw pride as the context, too much concern about race among the "minority element" was the immediate cause for the split in his mind. Mains's article reads as an us-versus-them, with "us" as White and in control, and "them" as minorities who have to receive power: "We gradually gave the minority element more and more power within the church." He remembered that the "minority element" wanted to "express in absolute terms that the number one priority of the church should be to address social issues, with the minority pastor answerable to no staff leadership."[17] Mains did not want to describe the conflict in detail, but his brief description raises questions. It reads as though he blames African Americans in the church for prioritizing race above other issues and for not being able to let go of racial concerns. The subtext of this argument is common among White evangelicals—who are not racial minorities and therefore are able often to avoid thinking in racial terms unless they choose to. The argument, more simply, is that minorities overemphasize race.

Evangelism professor Dr. Soong-Chan Rah and pastor Gary Vanderpol emphasize in their book *Return to Justice* that race shaped the conflict. They argue that Mains wanted to exercise his authority. But when differences of opinion arose, Mains could accept only minorities who agreed with his way of thinking. As pastors, Rah and Vanderpol argue that members of a majority group in a church must embrace not only those who accept their way of thinking.[18] In their interpretation, Hilliard was a victim

---

[16]David Mains and Philip Yancey, "My Greatest Ministry Mistakes," CT Pastors, 1980, www.christianitytoday.com/pastors/1980/spring/80l2015.html.
[17]Mains and Yancey, "My Greatest Ministry Mistakes."
[18]Soong-Chan Rah and Gary Vanderpol, "Circle Church and the Test for Integration," in *Return to Justice: Six Movements That Reignited Our Contemporary Evangelical Conscience* (Grand Rapids, MI: Brazos, 2016).

of pastoral authority paired with racialized cultural assumptions about right and wrong.

My analysis of Mains's 1980 reflection could support Rah's and Vanderpol's view. Mains remembered that he had emphasized that they were a team but had not emphasized that he was the leader of the team. So when "a staff member [Hilliard] submitted a sermon to the team" and Mains saw what he thought were "doctrinal problems, [he] could not allow the sermon to be preached. [Hilliard] responded by going over my head to the board of elders."[19] What Mains failed to account for in his article is that pastoral authority, when stacked with race, becomes complicated.

Glen pulled out a different thread in the tangle in *Breaking Down Walls*. He emphasized that Mains and Hilliard did not have a strong relationship binding them together when the inevitable conflict arose because of their differences, racial and otherwise. Interracial relationships must weather storms—perhaps more than intraracial relationships—and theirs could not handle the tempest because Circle Church was built on racial understanding rather than racial reconciliation. For Glen, racial understanding meant White people learning about minorities' experiences without anyone holding an unwavering commitment to remain in relationship. Racial reconciliation demanded empathy from both Black and White people, with a conviction—bordering on a covenant—from all people that they would work through conflicts and refuse to give up on the relationship.

Glen knew that Pastor Clarence Hilliard did not agree with his interpretation. Glen notes in *Breaking Down Walls*,

> As I showed Clarence a draft of this chapter, it became apparent that we have some significant differences in our perspectives. I want to emphasize that this chapter represents my conclusions, as drawn from my reflections of eighteen years. This account should not be taken as the definitive word. . . . My intent is that we learn from the past, from both our successes and mistakes. . . . To [Circle Church and its leaders] I owe a deep debt of gratitude for much of my early spiritual growth and ministry guidance.[20]

In the end, the church split along racial lines. Pastor Hilliard left, along with all the Black members. Soon after, Pastor Mains left as well. Glen grieved

---
[19] Mains and Yancey, "My Greatest Ministry Mistakes."
[20] Washington and Kehrein, *Breaking Down Walls*, 84n1.

that "not even one personal relationship with a fellow Black believer survived the holocaust."[21]

QUESTIONS AND IMPLICATIONS

Many people then—and now—think of the Austin neighborhood as a throwaway neighborhood. Glen and Lonni thought otherwise. Glen saw the Austin neighborhood as strategic for his ministry goals, and living in Austin enabled him to see needs more clearly. Living in Austin had great benefits.

- How does your location strengthen or limit your ability to fulfill ministry goals?
- How can your location be a tool in your toolkit to understand race and live faithfully?
- While the Kehreins found Austin appealing, no Black members of Circle's Black Module wanted to live in community in the Austin neighborhood. What aspects of how you do church life and community welcome or push away certain groups of people?

I called us to listen to Hilliard's sermon and to practice empathy.

- What did you learn from listening to the funky gospel?
- Think about a conflict you have had with another person. Can you understand their perspective, even articulate it back to them in a way they would say accurately depicts their view, even if you don't agree with what they're saying? How might this be an act of love?

As we know, it is the nature of historical accounts to differ, and the split at Circle Church was complicated. All accounts agreed that race had a hand in the split.

- Which interpretation of Circle Church initially resonates with you more? Why? What could you learn from other interpretations?
- In what ways do you see racial and other types of authority stacked in your context, as they were with Pastor Hilliard as a Black man submitting to Pastor Mains as a White man? What are the consequences?

---

[21] Washington and Kehrein, *Breaking Down Walls*, 81.

19

LIFE IN THE AUSTIN NEIGHBORHOOD

How the Washingtons decided to relocate to the Austin neighborhood, different reasons Austin was so poor, and why the benefits of living there outweighed the costs.

GOD OF THE NATURAL AND SUPERNATURAL

Glen and Lonni developed relationships with other African Americans in the neighborhood, but their ministry partnerships with Black Christians continued to fail. So when they met Raleigh and Paulette Washington and heard they were considering planting a church in the Austin neighborhood, they wondered whether Raleigh and Paulette could be an answer to prayer. Could they be covenant partners in ministry? Glen decided to take a chance. He offered space at Circle Community Center for Raleigh's church plant, should Raleigh want it. Raleigh rejoiced at the open door. But he and Paulette had one hesitation.

Ministering in the Austin community meant moving to a poor community. For Raleigh—and for many of the Black professionals who would later move into the Austin neighborhood as part of Circle and Rock—moving to Austin contrasted his assumptions about the good life. This may have been why no Black people from the Black Module had joined the Austin Community Fellowship. A common narrative among African Americans held that success was leaving the 'hood, getting out to a better life.

Raleigh knew about downward mobility. In seminary he had heard John Perkins speak. Raleigh appreciated John's emphasis on relocation, moving to communities most people tried to leave, preaching the gospel, and partnering with them to develop their community. But while Raleigh understood John's call for relocation intellectually, the idea did not capture his imagination until he met Glen and Lonni. Raleigh marveled that Lonni and Glen not only moved downward economically but also crossed racial lines. When he and Paulette looked at how Glen and Lonni had chosen to live, they wondered how they could not make the same choice.

We do not always know how our decisions will affect others.

From an outside perspective, the cost for Raleigh and Paulette would be great. He and Paulette were concerned about poverty and oppression, but Raleigh had been on an upward trajectory most of his life. Raleigh had been born in the projects in Florida, was raised by a single mother, and had gotten out. He had graduated from college and served as a high-ranking officer in the military. His was a success story, and he had never thought he would move back into a poor neighborhood. Ministering in the suburbs would have been a natural fit.

But God is God not only of the natural. Sometimes, perhaps more than we think, God calls his people to supernatural decisions.

God seemed to be calling Raleigh and Paulette to one such decision. Paulette thought God was orchestrating their steps. She had prayed that if God wanted them to minister in Chicago, God would provide a home. Paulette had drawn a floor plan of her ideal home, including a claw-foot bathtub. The money for her dream home was scarce. Raleigh had just graduated from Trinity Evangelical Divinity School, and the couple had little money, especially without the retirement benefit they had planned on from the Army. At the end of their first visit with Glen, Glen asked whether there was anything else they needed before they left. Despite Raleigh's efforts to quiet her, Paulette responded that they needed a house. Glen responded that the house across the street from him was for sale. He brought them by and asked whether they could go inside. When they did, Paulette saw that the house matched her dreams, right down to the claw-foot bathtub. Then, through what seemed like a series of miracles, they were able to purchase the house.

WHY WAS AUSTIN POOR AND BLACK?

Pastor Raleigh and I think differently about systemic racism. This became obvious to me when conducting our oral history interview. To put it another way, we would prioritize different causes when answering the question, "Why was/is Austin poor and Black?" While I am aware of the effects of individuals' personal choices, I tend to emphasize how racialized assumptions became embedded in America's systems and led to unequal economic and social outcomes for African Americans and other racial minority groups. I appreciate the theological toolkit of individualism, relationalism, and antistructuralism, but when it comes to race I want to pay attention to the structures.

Pastor Raleigh, by contrast, highlights personal responsibility, sounding more like a typical White evangelical regarding race. He believes that fundamentally the United States's system of laws is fair, but that individuals who are personally racist can corrupt those laws and bend the system to benefit themselves or their race. Empathy—because I am a sister in Christ and I am a historian—requires me to understand Pastor Raleigh's perspective.

Like all of us, Raleigh's views of race were shaped by his personal history. Born in 1938 in the Jim Crow South in a similar context to John Perkins, Raleigh faced the degradation separate water fountains symbolized: White people's demands that Black people stay "in their place." But somehow, Raleigh did not experience some of the worst results of this discrimination—a lowered self-worth and a hatred of White people. As a child, he always wanted to prove his self-worth by beating the White kids at whatever sport they played. As an adult, he was grateful for a handful of individual White people who were kind in his life because they prevented him from thinking all White people were evil.

Although born into segregation, Raleigh grew up in a nation that was making progress toward equality. CIO labor unions integrated in the 1930s, and during World War II Black Americans called the nation to a double victory—abroad against fascism and at home against racism. In the 1950s, the military where John Perkins and Raleigh Washington would serve was finally integrated, and Black Americans began advocating for laws requiring segregation to change, for equal pay, and for the enforcement of their constitutional right to vote. By the 1960s, the legislative branch passed legislation that improved racial inequality, especially in the South. The 1964 Civil Rights Act prohibited segregation in public places, the 1965 Voting Rights Act gave the federal government the power to enforce equal access to the polls, and the 1968 Fair Housing Act prohibited discrimination in home sales. Raleigh thinks that the civil rights movement worked because so much of the law is no longer explicitly racist.[1] I agree that key aspects of the law have become less racist, although scholars still debate this argument.[2]

Raleigh's experience of justice with the Army is a testimony to the changes making it more difficult for individuals use the law in a prejudicial way. Remember that Raleigh had been discharged from the military without honor a day before he would have received full retirement benefits after being found guilty of conduct unbecoming of an officer. Though given the option of admitting his guilt and still receiving the benefits, Raleigh insisted he had done nothing wrong. A White attorney friend had been working on reversing the ruling and suggested Raleigh reach out to a military law specialist. Supported financially by a "concerned couple," Raleigh did, and the specialist applied to have the Army Board of Correction of Military Records hear his case. The chances were one thousand to one that his case would be heard, but the court accepted the case and granted a reversal several years into Raleigh's work at Rock Church. Raleigh was reinstated in the Army for one day and enjoyed a full retirement parade.[3] He also received his retirement benefits.

Raleigh understood his trial as the way God moved him to Rock Church. He remembered, "With my loyalty and drive, I would not have retired early from the military and entered the ministry. . . . The Scripture kept running through my mind, they 'meant it for evil . . . but God meant it for good'" (Genesis 50:20).[4] In his case, justice was blind, and although racially motivated people had tried to hurt him, right had prevailed.

A FLY IN MILK

Partnering with Circle not only meant moving back into a poor neighborhood; it also meant planting a multiracial church. Raleigh had not gone to seminary intending to lead an interracial church, but he was well-equipped to sit in the messiness of interracial dynamics and to lead the

---

[1]Raleigh Washington, interview by author, September 14, 2021.
[2]See, for instance, Richard Rothstein, *The Color of Law: A Forgotten History of How Our Government Segregated America* (New York: Liveright, 2017) and Michelle Alexander, *The New Jim Crow: Mass Incarceration in the Age of Colorblindness* (New York: New Press, 2010).
[3]Raleigh Washington and Glen Kehrein, *Breaking Down Walls: A Model for Reconciliation in an Age of Racial Strife* (Chicago: Moody Press, 1994), 97-98.
[4]Washington and Kehrein, *Breaking Down Walls*, 98.

congregation in growing humility, love of neighbor, and strong relationships across racial lines.

Raleigh's career in an integrated military and the personal relationships he developed there gave him skills to connect across racial lines. The military was a great racial leveler, but White people and a form of White culture also dominated. When Raleigh went to officer training school, he was the only Black officer candidate there, a fly in milk, as he would recall. Nonetheless, as Paulette reflected, because the Army drew recruits from across the country and from a variety of racial backgrounds, Raleigh developed racial sensitivity.[5] He learned to see people as individuals and not let stereotypes define a person.[6]

In the Army, Raleigh developed close relationships with White people, which strengthened his belief that a person's character mattered more than their race. Those friends proved themselves true when they stood up for him, taking the hard road, against racism. For example, in 1960, Raleigh and three White friends tried to eat out off base in Indiana. Three restaurants refused to serve the integrated group. Raleigh suggested that his friends drop him off at the base and go out to eat without him. But they refused. At the fourth restaurant, Louis Taglia secured seats for the whole party, ordered the most expensive meal on the menu for Raleigh, and paid for it. As Raleigh remembered, "The damage to my dignity by being rejected by three restaurants was completely destroyed by the love of one man who would not let that evening go without us eating together because he cared for me."[7]

Raleigh's training at Trinity Evangelical Divinity School also equipped him for his ministry in the Austin neighborhood. Raleigh attended the seminary in part because of its location. Trinity Evangelical Divinity School is in the wealthy Chicago suburb of Bannockburn, just four miles west of Fort Sheridan, where Raleigh had been stationed.[8] It is the seminary for the Evangelical Free Church of America but draws students from across the globe. It offered connections to White churches and the National Association of Evangelicals. There Raleigh learned to preach exegetically. Like John Perkins,

---

[5]Paulette Washington, interview by author, September 16, 2021.
[6]Washington, interview, September 14, 2021.
[7]Washington and Kehrein, *Breaking Down Walls*.
[8]Bannockburn and neighboring Deerfield have their own hidden histories of racial exclusion. See Johnson, *One in Christ*, chap. 7.

Raleigh expounded on a biblical text, eschewing much of the emotionalism that characterized traditional Black preaching, which he critiqued.

Raleigh trained for ministry during an era of increasing emphasis on the individual. Among evangelicals, psychology had become prominent starting in the 1970s with radio shows such as *Focus on the Family* and *Psychology for Living*, which led to a greater focus on individuals' well-being and a therapeutic culture, even among more leftward-leaning evangelicals.[9]

Raleigh's experiences in the military and seminary made him different from Black evangelicals such as Clarence Hilliard who were more influenced by the Black Power movement and Black theology. If someone were to mock Raleigh, they might call him an Oreo, Black on the outside and White on the inside. (Raleigh would later embrace this stereotype at Rock Church, using humor to disarm people and help them draw closer together.) Calling someone an Oreo assumes that some ways of being are more authentically Black. I wonder whether that is true. Both Raleigh and Hilliard sought to live faithfully, although their approaches to racial division and justice differed. But one was not Blacker than the other. Hilliard was more focused on systemic issues—policies and practices that led to White people's views being prioritized over others'—while Raleigh would prioritize relational concerns, addressing those dynamics interpersonally. Their differences remind us of the obvious: not all Christians will agree about how to approach race, and all will fall short in some ways. But this work of racial healing is God's work, and we join him in it, however imperfectly. As we practice empathy, we need not agree with others completely to walk forward with them.

THE COSTS AND BENEFITS OF DOWNWARD MOBILITY

Even though Raleigh's experiences in White institutions had prepared him to minister to White people, most of his congregation at Rock Church would be Black and living in the Austin neighborhood. Raleigh and Paulette, Glen and Lonni, and others who relocated or chose to stay paid a price for living there.

Those outside the neighborhood can look at statistics and analyze the situation from a distance, but Black and White members of Rock Church living

---

[9]David R. Swartz, "Identity Politics and the Fragmenting of the 1970s Evangelical Left," *Religion and American Culture* 21, no. 1 (2011): 104. Hilde Løvdal Stephens, *Family Matters: James Dobson and Focus on the Family's Crusade for the Christian Home* (Tuscaloosa, AL: University of Alabama Press, 2019).

in the 'hood listed the many reasons people would want to leave.[10] Why would you want to live in a place with higher crime, with trash on the streets, where you should not walk after dark, with obvious drug trafficking, and with loud music at all hours of the night? Beyond the experiences of day-to-day life, why would you choose to live where your home's value would not appreciate at the same rate (if at all) as other neighborhoods?

Many family members of Rock Church folks asked these questions and disliked the Rock members' decisions to live in the Austin neighborhood.[11] Rock Church members often validated their family members' concerns. Some suggested their families were right to be concerned for their safety. But they also observed that most of their neighbors also disliked the less savory aspects of their neighborhood, and while they might be able to move, their neighbors were trapped.

Many Rock members also described the many benefits of living in the Austin neighborhood. Proximity meant church members were available to meet needs, which not only benefited the neighborhood but was gratifying to those who shared their gifts. Because they were on the ground daily, they were able to see the needs of the community and use their gifts to advance God's kingdom. For instance, one White engineer recalled walking by Circle's unfinished building and grieving the loss to the community because the space was not being used. She thought to herself, "Someone ought to do something about this." Then she recalled feeling the Holy Spirit say, "Why not you?" For over twenty years, she helped rehabilitate the building. Now the community has a school and state-of-the-art auditorium.[12]

Church members also offered the community stability because they would not move, which created evangelism opportunities. Living in the neighborhood meant that there was a natural opportunity to invite neighbors to church. Proximity gave authenticity to their evangelism, enabling them to connect with their neighbors. The same White engineer brought many neighborhood kids with her to Rock Church. A desire for a more effective evangelistic ministry led her to move from suburban Oak

---

[10] Arthur Jackson, interview by author, October 5, 2021.
[11] Bob Stannard and Carole Stannard, interview by author, July 4, 2021; Jackson, personal communication.
[12] Rock Church member, interview by author, September 27, 2021.

Park to Austin so she could have a Chicago area code. She wanted the children she served to see her as a neighbor, sharing their lives, rather than an outsider coming to help.[13] Like Clarence Jordan said, the incarnation was God moving into the neighborhood.

White people living in the neighborhood spoke with gratitude about the richness of their crosscultural experience. Because they were intentional (see chapter twenty-one), they developed crosscultural relationships that benefited them deeply. Bob and Carole Stannard, both White, moved into the neighborhood because Bob was working for one of Circle's ministry offshoots as a family practice doctor. Bob grew up in the neighboring suburb of Oak Park. Though he lived right next door to Austin, his parents warned him to never cross Austin Boulevard, the street dividing the two communities. In college, Bob developed a deep relationship with God and a desire to serve the underserved as a medical doctor. He and Carole were attracted to the opportunity to serve with like-minded people. Carole also worked at Circle, teaching in various capacities. Initially, it would seem the Stannards brought all the social capital—values and relationships enabling people to thrive—to the neighborhood. Bob is an amazing doctor who sacrificially gives to his patients, and Carole has nurtured hundreds of children.

But Bob and Carole say that they gained more than they have given. To offer just one example, living in the Austin neighborhood gave them another mother through their across-the-street neighbor, Mama Council. Mama Council was an African American woman who found faith at Rock Church, where she also learned to read. Many days, Bob would go across the street to share an RC Cola with Mama Council, and she would care for his family and their children. There is great social capital even in poor neighborhoods. Rock Church members found their neighbors to be committed to helping one another and welcoming others as family.[14] They experienced a more communal way of life that subtly resisted the individualism characterizing much of American evangelicalism. Like John Perkins, even as they acknowledged the problems, Carole and Bob looked for strengths rather than weaknesses in their community.

---

[13]Rock Church member, interview by author, September 27, 2021.
[14]Carol B. Stack, *All Our Kin: Strategies for Survival in a Black Community* (New York: Basic Books, 1983).

We must ask what difference proximity makes. Or, if trying to reach and serve "the least, the last and the lost," can one do this from a distance? Those who came to join Rock Church and Circle Urban Ministries argued that proximity was essential for effective evangelism. Sociological research suggests that economic segregation is harmful to those on the bottom rungs of society, to those trapped in poverty. Downward mobility was costly to those who moved or stayed when they could have left. But it also led to surprising benefits in the mundane aspects that give life its richest meanings: a hug from a child, a drink shared with a neighbor, seeing God's beauty anew. In the Austin neighborhood, a group of people came together as the body of Christ.

A LIGHT IN THE NEIGHBORHOOD

Raleigh and Glen made Rock Church and Circle Urban Ministries ministry partners. Circle was in a sense the hands and feet of Rock Church, offering the tangible help that neighbors needed. Raleigh and Glen described Circle as the outreach arm of Rock Church. Through their intentionally overlapping work, Rock Church and Circle Urban Ministries were able to be a light in the neighborhood because people lived in the community. Many of Rock's key ministry focuses were outward facing to the immediate neighborhood, influenced by the relationship with Circle. Through physical structures, events, and people, Rock Church and Circle Urban Ministries brought light to the Austin neighborhood.

Rock Church's first location was in Circle's eight-thousand-square-foot building. But as Rock Church and Circle Community Center grew, Glen and Raleigh felt like they needed more space for both ministries. Glen learned that the Chicago School Board was selling a 150,000-square-foot building at the corner of Central and Washington. The building had originally been Siena High School, a Catholic high school and convent, but as the Austin neighborhood changed racially, the sisters had sold the building to the Chicago School Board. Chicago Public Schools used the building as an annex to the Austin High School, just a few blocks away, when the school was bursting with three thousand students.[15] But by 1984, there were fewer

---

[15] Washington and Kehrein, *Breaking Down Walls*, 92.

students, and the building was shuttered. Vandals had removed copper and other items of value from the building, leaving it largely unusable.

Glen and Raleigh went to see the building. The men were excited. Glen recalled, "As we came to a room the nuns had used as a chapel, Raleigh's eyes lit up. 'This would be the perfect size to develop an emerging church. God wants us here! We could put 50 in this room and it wouldn't feel empty—but we could squeeze 150 in here, too.'" The building would take millions to restore, even with volunteer help. Glen remembered "groaning inside just thinking about shoveling out all the debris, getting electricity to the different rooms, and replacing the heating plant." But Raleigh observed, "Think what it would say to the people of the community to see this building restored! Just occupying this location would take it out of the hands of the drug dealers and gang bangers, and that itself would bring hope to the neighborhood."[16]

Glen and Raleigh were able to purchase the building for $80,000. A donor and friend who had been supporting Circle Community Center felt led to give $100,000 for the purchase of the property, leaving some money to board up the windows and clear out the debris. With the move, Circle Community Center changed its name to Circle Urban Ministries. Hours of sweat equity from church members, ministry leaders, and outside volunteers, alongside generous donations, transformed the building.[17]

How a place looks matters to the feel of a community, and what happens in that place can either build up or tear down a community. As Rock Church members observed, the building would become known in the community as a place where people could get help and not be judged. One member noted that for Circle to survive for so long in a rough neighborhood meant that neighbors respected the ministry.[18]

Neighbors got to know Rock and Circle through Rock's evangelism. One key strategy was Rock's yearly Harvest ministry. Harvest was born when Paulette Washington had what she saw as a vision from God, who told her to host a banquet and invite people who could not repay her. They started with a small luncheon for neighborhood women. Shunelle Hollis, who would eventually serve as the coordinator for Harvest, came to Rock Church through the Harvest

---

[16] Washington and Kehrein, *Breaking Down Walls*, 92-93.
[17] Charles Butler, interview by author, October 4, 2021.
[18] Sandra Jackson, interview by author, October 5, 2021.

ministry, attending in the second year. She remembered the intentionally intimate setting and appreciated how people related to one another personally.

Harvest grew from a small luncheon to being a multiday event held under a tent, with giveaways for the neighborhood. Rock leaders wanted Harvest to be a demonstration of Jesus' love, to show neighborhood people that Rock Church loved them, and to share the gospel. The door prizes, the warm welcome, and the insistence that people come as they are were meant to tell people that they did not need to dress up or pay up to be worthy of God's love.[19] Raleigh observed that Harvest was only possible because of the partnerships he and Glen developed with other Christian organizations.[20] Groups outside the community, including an Evangelical Free church in Minnesota, Wheaton College students and others, served at the event and donated door prizes. Raleigh and Glen were bringing the resources of the more wealthy members of the body of Christ into the neighborhood.

People also make a place flourish. Pastor Raleigh hired Arthur Jackson in 1987 as assistant pastor. Like Raleigh, Arthur held a degree from a White-dominated institution, Dallas Theological Seminary, and like Raleigh, Pastor Jackson did not go to seminary sensing a call to minister in a poor urban community. He grew up in an integrated school and observed that racially mixed schools had more resources than all-Black ones. Racially, he had been conscious of his inferior status as a Black person and had adopted the mindset, like many other Black folks, that if he could move up and move out, he should. The Army drafted Arthur to serve in Vietnam, and he recalled no discrimination. After seminary, he had no desire to move back into a low-income Black neighborhood. But when Pastor Jackson and his wife, Shirley, visited Rock and heard Raleigh's vision, they believed God was calling them to relocate, even though the salary was less than they needed to support their family of seven. Jackson thought he could learn from Raleigh as a leader. The couple moved from their Texas three-bedroom home to a second-floor apartment on West Erie Street, where the Washingtons and Kehreins lived.

Pastor Jackson worked within the ministry and out in the neighborhood.[21] He walked the streets of Austin and went into people's homes, ministering to

---

[19]Shunelle Hollis, interview by author, September 30, 2021.
[20]Paulette Washington, interview by author, September 14, 2021.
[21]Jackson, interview.

those who were, as he said, below a GED and with PhDs. He served both African Americans in the church and the community and White folks, and preached occasionally. While Pastor Jackson is an example of someone who was hired to work for the church, Raleigh commissioned all members of the church body for ministry.

Their ministry was not perfect. One person I interviewed reflected that sometimes Circle and Rock presented poor Black community members in too negative a light at times to attract donor support, emphasizing the pain and need in the neighborhood and not the goodness, strength, and beauty.[22]

Catherine de Hueck had done that, too. This frame can be common for White, especially college-educated people doing crosscultural ministry in a poor context—although it may be a temptation for Black folk too. People like me who are White, middle class, and educated can assume we are "White saviors," as I implicitly believed when we first moved to the community years after Pastor Raleigh had moved to another calling. Why wouldn't I? Everything in my training and education led me to be a problem solver. Eric and I were leading InterVarsity's Chicago Urban Project, a program for college students to learn about justice and live in an urban environment under the leadership of a church and community-development ministry. We began right after the director of the summer enrichment program we were supposed to help resigned, without fully preparing the summer staff, who were community members, for their work. Eric and I wanted to jump in and fix it, but a wise mentor held us back, showing us how to follow the lead of those in the community.

By letting others exercise leadership rather than taking over, we joined Rock's and Circle's more dominant legacy of community empowerment. They were living out John Perkins's admonition to live among "the people" and learn from them, and to help them become leaders who make great changes in their community. Several people from the community who received help and experienced transformation through Rock and Circle went on to become agents of change in the neighborhood. Rock and Circle empowered local people to lead and to serve.

---

[22]Louise Bonner, interview by author, September 24, 2021.

Brother Andre Hinton's story puts flesh on this vision. Andre grew up with some familiarity with Christianity, but his Catholic faith had not given him a close relationship with Jesus. He was homeless for a season and heard Circle could provide him clothing, so he went there for help. A month later, he decided to attend Rock Church. He was surprised at the mixture of Black and White attendees but felt relatively comfortable because it reminded him of his mixed Catholic congregation growing up. Pastor Raleigh shared the message of salvation with Brother Andre, and Andre immediately began sharing the good news with his friends. Andre volunteered as a chaplain at Circle and eventually moved into a paid position, evangelizing on the streets and meeting people's needs. Today Andre is well-known on Austin's streets, helping meet people's needs and sharing the gospel.

QUESTIONS AND IMPLICATIONS

Many of Rock Church's leadership and members' decisions to live in or stay in the Austin neighborhood should startle us because it is so contrary to contemporary expectations as well as the vast swath of more recent evangelical history in the North. We do not serve a God of comfort but one who calls us to sacrifice in obedience. Each of us must consider *where* God is calling us to live. Part of that consideration should include reckoning with the racial geographies and their histories, which shape where we live.

- What does it mean, given this history, to love your neighbor as yourself, to want what you want for your neighbor? And who is your neighbor? This could be the fulfillment of John Perkins's vision of pairing your life with others, perhaps for a season or perhaps for your life.
- What are your assumptions about upward mobility? What would you give up if you moved to a poorer neighborhood? What would be the costs? What might be the gains?
- What neighborhoods around you need beacons of light? Look closely, because if you're an outsider it's easy to miss the lights that are already shining. How could you join those lights shining? How could you invest your resources in places that need it most?
- Do you have a deficit mindset when it comes to poor places, or a strengths mindset? How can you acknowledge problems while also

celebrating the strengths? To see a person's strengths is to see their dignity as people made in God's image.

As with Raleigh and me, there are clearly differences among how people, even brothers and sisters in Christ, approach and understand race in America.

- How do you deal with those who approach race differently than you do? How might there be synergy between you even if your understanding of race is different? How could accounting for other analyses make you more effective?

Raleigh's life experiences had prepared him to lead an interracial church.

- What in your past has equipped you for interracial relationships? What blind spots do you have?
- In what ways is your church intertwined with other ministries that address social needs? Could a partnership be more effective than creating your own ministry?

20

THE CHALLENGES OF "COLORBLINDNESS"

How Pastor Raleigh led Rock Church in approaching racial (and other) differences, why they were not colorblind, and what reconciliation required of church members then—and what it might require of us now.

SEEING COLOR AND MOVING BEYOND IT

How did Rock Church operate? Its members were from different racial, economic, and class backgrounds. People who were just learning to read worshiped alongside those with medical degrees and doctorates.

In nearly all my interviews, when I asked what make Rock Church work, church members started by emphasizing that Jesus had united them. They built their relationships on the work of reconciliation they believed God had already done through Jesus. They accepted one another because they knew that God was a God of love who did not look at people's outward appearances but at their hearts. People at Rock held the truth at the front of their minds that God did not love a person less or more whether poor or rich, whether addicted to alcohol or to spending. For Rock Church, God's love was the starting point and the thing that held them together.[1]

---

[1] Sandra Jackson, interview by author, October 5, 2021.

How did this unity function at the day-to-day level? Long-term church members developed a way of interacting with one another that saw the other person's race—their color, Rock members would call it—but then moved beyond color to see the person. Their perspective was not colorblind, a term often used to describe what is often a well-meaning desire to ignore or downplay racial difference. Frankly, people will almost always notice the phenotypical traits of a person. The challenge is putting the right emphasis on color, which could look differently in different contexts. Rock Church members saw others as individuals, which included paying attention to how a person's racial experiences shaped them in painful and funny ways. They casually joked that White people liked hummus or that if you wanted to make a Black person feel welcome in your home, just pick up a bucket of fried chicken.

I like hummus. I also like fried chicken. People at Rock also knew that those stereotypes did not always match reality.

Nonetheless, this ability to joke—and to see race and put race in its proper place—was hard won. It was not a form of cheap reconciliation. Instead, it was the fruit of intentionality in the hard work of interracial relationships. People adopted postures of curiosity, asking, "Help me understand." They engaged rather than avoided difficult questions and the differences between them. Their conversations did more than acknowledge differences but brought those differences to the surface, interrogating them. They discussed personal relationships, racial differences, how race had worked in US history, and how it was operating in the present. In these conversations they tried not to criticize or judge. Instead, they wanted to understand and accept one another because they knew that God accepted each of them as members of his body.[2] They were practicing empathy.

Their dangerous work—dangerous because it could hurt, offend, rebuke, and open wounds—made Rock Church a haven. Because they intentionally worked hard to understand one another and love one another despite differences and disagreements, people felt free at Rock. They did not wonder whether someone was treating them differently because of their race, education, or job.

---

[2]Jackson, interview.

Their experiences reveal that we may be able to see beyond race, by which I mean seeing people as individuals rather than assuming racial stereotypes about them. But we cannot start there or we will miss key components of who one another are. And we must use more tools than the typical evangelical toolkit offers.

Raleigh and Glen offered their congregation eight principles to follow that would help them build relationships across racial lines in their book *Breaking Down Walls*. These tools were hard won but effective. They said that first people must be *committed to a relationship* with a particular person from another race, fighting for the relationship as one might fight for a marriage to remain intact. Next, people must be *intentional*, working hard to get to know the other person. Third, people must have *sincerity*, being open and honest, investing time in the relationship, and taking the initiative to share their own lives. Fourth, people must develop *sensitivity*, "the intentional acquisition of knowledge in order to relate empathetically to a person of a different race and culture."[3] Fifth, they must embrace their *interdependence*, recognizing that people from different backgrounds need one another. The goal of the church, they said, should be "to reflect the unity of the body of Christ in the midst of its diversity; to experience how God has gifted different parts of the body in building up the whole to draw alienated, hurting people to the good news of Jesus Christ."[4] Sixth, they must embody *sacrifice*, embracing discomfort for the sake of the relationship and relinquishing "an established status or position to genuinely adopt a lesser position . . . to facilitate a cross-cultural relationship."[5] Seventh, they must practice *empowerment*, forgiving past sins, repenting on behalf of others. Black people, they said, needed to blame less, and White people needed to stop denying their past. They wanted people to take responsibility. Last, they said people should embrace the *call* to be reconcilers—all people were called to be reconciled to one another, whether across racial lines or not. Rock Church used these tools to make reconciliation work.

---

[3]Raleigh Washington and Glen Kehrein, *Breaking Down Walls: A Model for Reconciliation in an Age of Racial Strife* (Chicago: Moody Press, 1994), 141.
[4]Washington and Kehrein, *Breaking Down Walls*, 181.
[5]Washington and Kehrein, *Breaking Down Walls*, 185.

Figure 20.1. Raleigh Washington and Glen Kehrein celebrate the publication of their book *Breaking Down Walls*. The cakes, made by the mother of a Rock leader, and their suits show their playfulness around race. Raleigh wore a white suit and had a white cake, while Glen donned a black suit and stood by a cake with chocolate frosting. Courtesy of DuRhonda Palmore

BEING UNCOMFORTABLE AT CHURCH

While Rock Church members used these principles in their personal relationships with one another, Pastor Raleigh, Glen, and the elders made sure they were also embedded into the liturgies of the church throughout the year and in weekly worship. Worship at church is more than singing. It includes preaching, giving, praying, Communion, and passing the peace. But the singing part of worship is central for most American churches, and it is often the part of the worship service we label "worship." Singing draws people together—emotionally, spiritually, and physiologically. Neuroscientists have discovered that when we sing together, our hearts actually beat at the same time, slowing down together, offering a calming, unifying effect.[6] Singing can also lead to racial unity and

---

[6]Claire Groden, "Many Hearts, One Beat: Singing Syncs Up Heart Rates," *Time*, July 10, 2013; Anna Haensch, "When Choirs Sing, Many Hearts Beat as One," NPR, July 10, 2013, www.npr.org/sections/health-shots/2013/07/09/200390454/when-choirs-sing-many-hearts-beat-as-one.

empathy, helping us see God anew if we inhabit the songs from a culture different from our own.

But singing songs that are not familiar can be uncomfortable. When I started attending Rock Church, I did not like it. Among other things, I wanted songs that were familiar. One of my mentors, Carole Stannard, told me that if I was comfortable at church there was something wrong, so I should embrace the discomfort. I did, and as I participated in the singing part of worship, I came to love gospel music, music that our then-worship leader Reggie Harris referred to as down-home music. That music—with its repetition and clapping—made me feel like I was part of Rock Church, made Rock Church feel like home. As I sang, I dwelled in a different worship culture. I realized that growing up, I had sung about *my* relationship with God. But with these brothers and sisters, we sang about *our* relationship with God.

Rock's music and structure of service demand attention. Nationally, Rock Church became known for its worship services. Rock's leaders intentionally crafted worship services to reach those in need and build unity. Significantly, they did not assume that more mature Christians should feel comfortable, which was why Carole told me church was not about me being comfortable.

In 1983, Raleigh hired Paul Grant as Rock Church's music minister. Paul grew up in Ohio in a Black Pentecostal context and moved to Chicago to attend Moody Bible Institute, Glen's alma mater. Paul found Moody through the Moody radio program *Songs of the Night*. There were more Black students at Moody than when Glen was a student a decade and a half before.

DuRhonda Baskett was one of them. She grew up on Chicago's South Side and attended Moody after three years at the University of Illinois's Circle Campus. DuRhonda decided to transfer after rededicating her life to God. DuRhonda and Paul married and moved to a house on Austin Boulevard, colloquially called the "Mason-Dixon line" because it separated the interracial but mostly White suburb of Oak Park from the Austin neighborhood. In addition to serving as Rock's music minister, Paul worked nights at Republic Airlines to pay the bills. He served this way until 1985, when Circle was able to hire him as a chaplain, until his death in 1991 in a boating accident. DuRhonda also worked in both ministries, serving as an administrative assistant to both Raleigh and Glen.

As music minister, Paul chose songs that would appeal to both the Black and White members but emphasized culturally Black songs. Raleigh thought that when non- or lapsed Christians came to church, they needed to encounter something familiar. As Pastor Jackson put it, while Paul wanted to make the music accessible to everyone, it definitely had a "gospel vibe."[7]

DuRhonda's sister and brother-in-law, Charles Butler and his wife, Donna, joined the church in 1984. The Butlers were also Moody graduates. Charles served as the director of Christian education and volunteered in the music ministry. He also served in Circle Urban Ministries as program director overseeing the food and clothing pantries, the transitional homeless shelter for families that helped them secure stable incomes and housing, the job placement ministry, the chaplaincy, youth leadership development, an after-school ministry, and an adult literacy program.[8] When Paul Grant died tragically in a boating accident, Charles stepped in as music director.

Charles continued leading Rock Church in worship with a "gospel vibe." He observed that while Black and White folks might sing the same hymns, they sang them differently. Black gospel church leadership requires a set of skills that includes "melodic and verbal improvisation techniques, modifications of vocal timbre, patterns of congregation/choir/soloist interaction, repertoire, common verbal couplets, and shared worship expectations among others."[9] In one small example in layperson's terms, DuRhonda told me that gospel music requires clapping on beats two and four, while most White people typically clapped on beats one and three.[10]

Although the music was more culturally Black, Pastor Raleigh did not preach in a traditional Black church type of way. The music gave people emotional release, and Pastor Raleigh's teaching reached people's minds. He drew from his exegetical training at Trinity Evangelical Divinity School, carefully unpacking scriptural texts' meaning.

Everyone was a little uncomfortable at Rock Church until it became home. Some African Americans remembered how unusual the services felt to them.

---

[7] Jackson, interview.
[8] Charles Butler, interview by author, October 4, 2021.
[9] Brian Schrag, "Motivations and Methods for Encouraging Artists in Longer Traditions," in *The Oxford Handbook of Applied Ethnomusicology*, ed. Svanibor Pettan and Jeff Todd Titon (Oxford: Oxford University Press, 2015), 324.
[10] Butler, interview.

Rock Church seemed quiet. While people responded to the pastor occasionally with an "Amen," it was not as dialectical as most Black churches.[11] Many were surprised at the presence of White people in the congregation, and they had to adjust their expectations.

Other Black attendees appreciated the church's relatively egalitarian nature. As Sheila Anderson remembered, Paulette was different from the other pastors' wives (or first ladies, as they are called in many Black churches) whom she had known.[12] Pastor Raleigh and Paulette were open and welcoming. They broke down barriers and invited people into fellowship. Yet, Raleigh was clearly in charge; once people were part of the church, he expected them to participate in ministry, especially outreach ministry, when asked. For instance, he always wanted a proportionate mix of Black and White choir members when he and other leaders traveled to minister at other churches, and he would call choir members who had already declined a trip and ask them to come.

White folks adjusted their expectations as well. Unlike in many racially mixed congregations, they were a minority and submitting to Black leadership. But worshiping God in a crosscultural context allowed them to experience God in different ways from what they were familiar with. As one White member observed, living in our own bubbles cuts God's grace short and limits our opportunities to receive what God has for us.[13] Many White people mentioned feeling a new freedom to worship God at Rock, expressing themselves in ways they had not before. Attending the church meant letting go of some of their expectations. But in laying those down at the foot of the cross, people found God.

Everyone had to give up something to worship together, and they practiced grace when people worshiped differently—hands up or hands down, responding "Amen!" or staying silent. Throughout, Pastor Raleigh and the other leaders emphasized bringing people together. Worship was not just about an individual and God but also *us* and God.[14]

---

[11]Sheila Anderson, interview by author, April 5, 2021.
[12]Anderson, interview.
[13]Murray Sitte, interview by author, September 27, 2021.
[14]Shunelle Hollis, interview by author, September 30, 2021.

FUDGE RIPPLE

Pastor Raleigh and Glen helped the people grow their commitments to reconciliation and discipleship not only through the warp and woof of their services but also through fudge ripple meetings, the central component of the church's yearly liturgies related to reconciliation. But while there was certainly laughter at these meetings, they were no laughing matter.

When Eric and I joined Rock Church, fudge ripple meetings were no longer regular parts of the church calendar. But the people who welcomed us had been formed by these meetings. And when I asked people in our interviews years later what reconciliation looked like at Rock Church, nearly everyone responded with a discussion of fudge ripple meetings.

The meetings emerged from Raleigh's and Glen's commitment to working out the conflicts that arose between them. But they knew they needed to build the conditions for those relationships to happen for the church as a whole. They reflected, "Conflicts are inevitable, but one of the things Glen learned from his Circle Church experience was that cross-cultural relationships could not survive if differences were left unresolved. . . . I [Raleigh] rarely let issues lie around unresolved, mostly because of my personality: I've never been afraid of conflict." They wanted to extend these dynamics to the whole church because they knew "as a whole church we had to be intentional about resolving differences and diffusing tensions."[15] The linchpin for reconciliation at Rock Church was intentionality, both for individuals and as a part of the regular liturgy of church life.

They held the meetings every quarter, intending to create a regular space for the congregation to check in with one another. Raleigh and Glen wanted "to create an atmosphere that encouraged Black people and white people to be open with their inner thoughts. In our society that usually happens only in guarded, racial seclusion."[16] All churches have conflict. Interracial churches may have more. Raleigh and Glen wanted people to discuss issues simmering beneath the surface regularly, so the issues would not boil over and destroy the church. Instead, fudge ripple meetings moved people toward reconciliation. As Raleigh and Glen reflected, "our goal is to be preventive rather than

---
[15] Washington and Kehrein, *Breaking Down Walls*, 94.
[16] Washington and Kehrein, *Breaking Down Walls*, 145.

prescriptive.... Contrary to popular assumptions, we don't outgrow the need for these meetings, any more than a married couple gets to the point where they never have to do problem solving any more." They trusted that "whatever is brought into the light can be dealt with through the body. One reason church or individual conflicts get so brutal is that so much has been kept in the dark.[17]

On fudge ripple Sundays—as on other days—racial humor abounded. People at Rock referred to one another as those of the darker and lighter hues, or the chocolates and vanillas. They ate fudge ripple ice cream and Oreo cookies. A container in the shape of a giant Oreo cookie served as a receptacle for questions to discuss as a group. Because people talked openly about race, the humor did not deprecate people or racial groups; it brought them together.

Fudge ripple Sundays were structured to give people time to process things in their own racial group but ultimately brought them together to try to understand one another and to recommit to loving one another. Before church, the chocolates met together with Pastor Raleigh to discuss issues and concerns. Then the entire congregation gathered for worship. After church, the vanillas met together with Pastor Raleigh. Last, everyone met to discuss issues that arose in the separate meetings and other subjects Pastor Raleigh and the elders thought needed discussion.

Pastor Raleigh told the congregation that it was not sinful to raise questions and disagree when they met together. But if they left the meeting and talked about these issues in the parking lot—especially if Black people talked with other Black people about White people, or if White people talked with other White people about Black people—that was sin. They wanted to deal with the issues together, rather than going somewhere else and griping about them. While people could ask questions during the combined meeting, Raleigh knew anonymity might help people raise difficult issues. Those present could write questions on three-by-five-inch cards and deposit them in the giant Oreo for Raleigh to read. Raleigh never wanted to shame people or make them feel embarrassed with their questions. Even in the questioning, there was an attitude of love and acceptance.

---

[17]Washington and Kehrein, *Breaking Down Walls*, 132.

Any subject was fair game. They discussed why White evangelicals thought the more Christian vote was for a Republican, while Black evangelicals leaned toward Democrats.[18] They discussed the history of race in America, which helped people understand where others were coming from.[19] They deliberated over interracial marriage, particularly as Black men in the congregation married White women. Black people wondered why White people were always so nosy, asking questions about their past. White people responded that these questions were gestures of friendship, of trying to get to know someone better. Pastor Raleigh encouraged the Black people to reframe White people's questions and volunteer some information. White people learned to let Black people "unpack their own luggage" (as one longtime Rock Church member told me when I was asking lots of questions). Some subjects were lighter—like why African Americans pluralize the name of grocery stores such as Jewel(s) and Aldi(s). These discussions of racial hurt, past and present, led to healing.[20]

The chocolates and the vanillas did not always see eye to eye. But because Pastor Raleigh coached them to ask, "Help me understand," they did grow in their understanding.[21] Participants learned to avoid judging or dismissing people. Pastor Raleigh encouraged them to recognize and name their own perspectives, which could help them see their bias, and seek to understand how others thought about an issue. Participants learned to enter hard discussions regularly, a practice few people would do on their own. Church leadership providing these opportunities mattered.

Fudge ripple discussions revealed the diversity within racial groups. Pastor Jackson recalled that the meetings helped people within the racial groups see their own diversity and prevented them from making their experiences normative.[22] For instance, Pastor Raleigh might joke that if a White person wanted

---

[18] When I first came to Rock Church, voting patterns surprised me. In the mostly White enclave where I grew up, White Christians voted Republican. In the mostly Black Austin neighborhood, Black Christians voted for Democrats. Both would say they were voting to protect life. Then, the Republicans emphasized life in the womb and at the end of life, while the Democrats seemed more concerned about poverty-related issues. For a history of the rise of White evangelicals' commitment to the Republican party, see Daniel K. Williams, *God's Own Party: The Making of the Christian Right* (New York: Oxford University Press, 2010).
[19] Jackson, interview.
[20] Hollis, interview.
[21] Doug Hansen, interview by author, September 25, 2020.
[22] Jackson, interview.

to make her Black friend feel comfortable sharing a meal, that White person should pick up a bucket of fried chicken (a stereotypical Black food). But not all Black people like fried chicken. Nor do all Black people pluralize the names of grocery stories.[23] As they discussed these issues, stereotypes crumbled. People came to know that this White brother was an introvert and would not ask questions, while that Black sister never called the grocery store Aldi "Aldis."

Fudge ripple meetings may not be essential to build strong cross-racial relationships and to have authentic interracial worship, but some sort of regular, structured check-in seems important. As Pastor Jackson told me, many of the people—like him—at Rock Church had many years of experience in interracial relationships, but nonetheless the public forum reminded even those people that their experience was not like everyone else's. When Pastor Jackson left Rock Church to serve as head pastor at an interracial church in Oak Park, he did not implement fudge ripple meetings.[24] When I asked why, Pastor Jackson said that he did not want his new church to be "Rock Church west" and that congregations needed to determine what would work best for them. However, the church he went to did not, in one sociologist's opinion, achieve the "elusive dream" of mutual embrace of people from different racial backgrounds. Nonetheless, at Rock, the fudge ripple meetings did foster deep, committed interracial relationships, community, and the ability to talk about race in thoughtful, humble ways. Those I interviewed who were no longer members at Rock Church reflected that they had never found such deep community in another setting, even though they knew how to build it.

RACIAL RECONCILIATION REQUIRES INTENTIONALITY, HUMILITY, AND FORGIVENESS

Raleigh expected that the congregation would be intentional in developing crosscultural relationships but kept the vision of reconciliation front and center to prevent the congregation from drifting. One church member recalled that at least once a month, Raleigh would ask how they were doing

---

[23]Merdise Lee, interview by author, April 17, 2013.
[24]Jackson, interview; Korie Edwards, *The Elusive Dream: The Power of Race in Interracial Churches* (New York: Oxford University Press, 2008).

with their intentionality in crosscultural relationships. Who were they inviting over for dinner, who were they spending time with? The congregation listened and responded, although it was difficult.

Crosscultural relationships take effort, and being around others who are making the effort makes intentionality easier. Steve and Trina McIlrath, both White, remembered being each weekend, after a week of living crossculturally. Steve taught math at the local high school, and Trina worked at Circle before staying home to raise their children. On the weekends, they often felt tugged between wanting to rest and Raleigh's prompting to pour into crosscultural relationships. Raleigh's voice won out—because that's what other Rock Church members were doing too.

Intentionality made a difference. Sometimes it is okay to just want to be with someone of your own race, to take a break from interpreting. But working through the difficulty can help form a "new we."[25] Reggie Harris, an African American man who would become a worship leader, recalled how Judd Wood, a White man, remembered his name when he came to visit Rock Church and then invited him to play racquetball and get together. The pair became fast friends.

Building interracial relationships also required humility. Members of Rock Church adopted a posture of genuine learning, asking, "Help me understand" often, not just at fudge ripple meetings. As learners, they would not assume their assumptions were right or that they understood another person's position. Trying to understand builds connections, not walls.

Members of Rock Church believed that *anyone* could hold prejudiced attitudes or, they would say, be racist. By this they meant that anyone could hold assumptions about other people based on racial categories. Their framework did not understand racism through the lens of power. A power-based racism framework would say that those who exercise more power in a society are the only ones technically capable of racism. Rock Church members were talking about personal views. Some scholars—and many activists on the left—disagree with Rock Church's racism framework.[26] But

---

[25]Chris Rice, who cofounded the Duke Divinity School Center for Reconciliation, shared this term with me.

[26]Several of the African Americans I interviewed noted that Rock Church's perspective contradicts contemporary notions of racism.

Rock Church's admission that anyone can be racist and that everyone is racist in some ways levels the playing field. Members described their perspective as bringing them together at the foot of the cross, where the ground is level for all sinners.[27]

In their humility, Rock Church members knew they needed forgiveness. They needed to forgive and to be forgiven. People on both sides of the racial divide forgave one another and did so often. White people confessed their own sin and apologized to Black people for what had happened in the past, particularly in America's racial history. Black people, too, forgave their White brothers and sisters for what had happened and confessed their own prejudice.

In the end, these postures moved people beyond racial reconciliation toward simple reconciliation. Reconciliation was not just chocolates and vanillas coming together but individual people seeing one another as individuals, taking responsibility and bringing healing to one another. Seeing one another as individuals demanded they account for the experiences of color but did not end there. They could appreciate reconciliation because they had worked through the racial issues, the racial contexts, and the racial assumptions that people who live in America cannot escape. As one White member observed, "It's about doing life together, being in proximate relationships. You see color, appreciate the nuance of color because people's experiences are shaped by their color, and to ignore that color, those experiences is to ignore a key part of who they are. But you don't want to classify people based on how they look."[28]

For many, reconciliation continues to be work—although they value people as people, they also know that America's racial dynamics mean they will have to work hard to connect with others, especially those who are not already close friends. People came to Rock Church for many reasons, and some were drawn particularly by the work of racial reconciliation there. But as they stayed at Rock and in the neighborhood, their lives became less about the ideals of reconciliation and more about simple actions. When you live by others, you do life together. You can help with the community garden, sit on

---

[27]Reggie Harris and Sareta Harris, interview by Sarah Lambert and Lauren Whitfield, March 25, 2018.
[28]Steve McIlrath and Trina McIlrath, interview by Alexis McIlrath, March 18, 2018.

the front porch, be a part of what's happening on the block.[29] These simple actions were characterized by a willingness to ask questions and to be changed. They were becoming more and more like their teacher, Jesus.

RACIAL RECONCILIATION IS PART OF DISCIPLESHIP

As important as fudge ripple meetings were, racial reconciliation was *not* Rock Church's ultimate vision. Fudge ripple meetings were a tool Pastor Raleigh and the elders used to form disciples of Jesus who were in right relationship with God and others. Pastor Raleigh's wanted to help people become whole and healthy believers who took responsibility for their relationship with God, who repented from their sin, and who lived into the possibilities that God had in store for them. But given their racial context as Americans, being reconciled across racial lines was essential to being a disciple of Jesus. Reconciliation and dealing with racial sin were aspects of discipleship. Members knew that Jesus was the foundation for racial healing, but they cared deeply about their own discipleship.[30] Many joined the fellowship because of the authentic leadership, strong teaching, and commitment to discipleship they saw in Rock's leaders.[31]

As they became whole and healthy, they were better able to do the difficult work of building interracial relationships. The habits of mind and character traits people developed as they matured in Christ were also required for good interracial relationships—and vice versa. As people worked through the difficulties inherent in interracial relationships, they developed the virtues necessary to be more like Jesus.

Rock Church members and leaders talked about sin and helped members address sin in their own lives, whether racial sin or otherwise. People at Rock confessed their sin and turned from it. Talking about racial sin helped people from the community find relationship with Jesus. As Andre Hinton observed, at Rock Church he found White people taking responsibility for their ancestors' past actions and apologizing. This small, genuine act brought tremendous healing. In his ministry of evangelism and discipleship, Andre has found that the church's racial witness and acts of confession have helped

---

[29]McIlrath and McIlrath, interview.
[30]Harris and Harris, interview.
[31]Jackson, interview; Sitte, interview; Jackson, personal communication.

THE CHALLENGES OF "COLORBLINDNESS"

draw others into relationship with Jesus. Seeing the repentance, the forgiveness, and the mutual accountability enabled those far from God to begin to believe that if God could deal with racism, God could also help them with their own sin.[32]

QUESTIONS AND IMPLICATIONS

Rock Church members argued anyone could be prejudiced. This perspective enabled them to come together.

- What do you think of their argument and experience? What is the cost of admitting your own prejudice? What might be the weaknesses of this perspective?
- What do you think about how Rock Church members accounted for race in their relationships with each other? What makes it difficult to have conversations about race?

When I worshiped at Rock Church, it took about two years before I began to really love going to church. I had to commit to Rock Church, despite the discomfort—which meant services that were longer than I wanted, preaching that was different from what I was used to, and new songs to learn.

- What cultural norms dominate at your church? What would be the cost of representing other cultures in the service? What would be the benefits? Would you be willing to stick it out through discomfort?

While fudge ripple meetings may not be essential to build strong crossracial relationships and to have authentic interracial worship, they enabled a generation of Rock Church members to develop empathy and strong interracial relationships.

- What do you think of fudge ripple meetings? How could you modify the practice to fit your church or situation?
- What regular practices do you have that help you prevent issues—racial or otherwise—from blowing up? What practices could you implement?
- How could you help your church discuss racial issues, no matter your position within the church? To what extent might conversations foster reconciliation?

---

[32]Andre Hinton, interview by author, October 13, 2021.

- What opportunities do you have in your church to discuss conflict regularly? If you have something like fudge ripple, how could you apply some of its principles?
- When Rock ministry leaders traveled to other churches, they invited them into relationships of reconciliation and asked them to apply what they learned in intentionally cross-racial relationships. How many cross-racial relationships do you have? What would it take to develop those?

Racial reconciliation was not an idol, something people prioritized more than God, at Rock Church. But Rock Church members believed that dealing with racial sin and hurt was necessary to be in right relationship with God and others.

- Could *not* talking about race be a form of idolatry, because we don't want to step into discomfort or confess sin?

Fudge ripple meetings involved confessing sin to one another. In the book of James, James says we are to confess our sins to one another to receive healing (James 5:16).

- How might confession of racial sins and lamenting past racial hurt bring healing in your local church?

21

PROPHETIC HOPE

How Rock Church's witness can complicate binaries of the left and right, why relocation might be a good option, and how Rock Church and Circle lived into an eschatological reality.

CARRY YOUR OWN LOAD AND CARRY ONE ANOTHER'S BURDENS

Combined, Rock Church's and Circle Urban Ministries' partnership and approach do not fit nicely into simple categories about how to approach race. Their histories also complicate how race and class intersect to form poor, racialized communities like the Austin neighborhood. Broadly speaking, those on the political right today tend to emphasize individual initiative as determining a person's life outcomes, downplaying the contexts that shape them. Those on the political left, by contrast, emphasize oppressive systems, thinking less about personal responsibility. What wisdom do Rock's and Circle's histories offer both groups?

Pastor Raleigh preached that the fullness of life in Christ meant a person could overcome their past. While they might be wounded by a history not of their own making, they were not bound to that past. They needed to take ownership of their part in the suffering and change. Raleigh preached a basic gospel message: all have sinned and fallen short of God's glory; all can repent and accept the forgiveness Jesus offered on the cross; all can live into a new life. People were empowered to carry their own loads.

A key part of discipleship, Pastor Raleigh preached, was taking responsibility and acting. He preached that God could heal a person, but that person must also make changes. Congregants remember Raleigh preaching against a victim mentality that would accept handouts.[1] Pastor Raleigh knew what it was like growing up poor with a single mom. But he believed that with God's strength people could overcome.

Significantly, he never implied that people must overcome on their own, or with only God's help. Instead, Christians must help one another. Raleigh encouraged those who had found healing to help others. Reflecting his belief that absent fathers were a foundational cause of the Austin neighborhood's problems, Raleigh encouraged Rock members to help single moms and devoted much of his fundraising to the youth ministry to provide mentoring and relationships for the young people. Circle's ministries provided a homeless shelter, a school, health care, law services, and food. Rock Church's members' decision to live in the neighborhood offered friendship, volunteers in the church's vast children's program, and opportunities to bring resources to their neighbors. Those who wanted to turn their lives around could join a community that supported their efforts. While they were called to carry their own loads, they joined a community in which people carried one another's burdens.

This community was full of people who took responsibility for their own sin and acknowledged the pain caused by their racial ancestors. White people and Black people both needed to confess prejudice, hatred, and fear of one another. They did not want power dynamics to simply invert, so Black people could exercise power over White people. Instead, they worked toward mutual submission, where all members of a church were looking out for the good of others. In short, they wanted Christians to love one another. Love requires intention. It does not come automatically.

Several Rock Church members I interviewed were troubled by how contemporary racial dynamics are sometimes characterized by Black people exercising power over White people. They observed that some approaches to race in America have a "victim mentality," a tendency to blame others for one's problems.[2] They suggested that some people of color's emphasis on their

---

[1] Sandra Jackson, interview by author, October 5, 2021.
[2] Charles Butler, interview by author, October 4, 2021; Doug Hansen, interview by author, September 25, 2020.

identity as victims of racial harm gave them undue power over White people. Insisting this was a form of racism, they said it could not lead to reconciliation. No one, they argued, was perfect and should hold the upper hand. Love among God's children required forgiveness, which could lead to unity.

POLICY IS PART OF THE MULTILAYERED SOLUTION THAT MUST INCLUDE RELATIONSHIPS

By some standards, Rock Church and Circle Urban Ministries fell short. Racial hierarchies, those on the left argue, are embedded in national, state, and municipal laws. Policy therefore is the solution.[3] Others understand these policies to be perpetuating Whiteness—which means that culturally White ideas of beauty, culture, and ways of being are seen as a standard that people should strive for.

Rock Church and Circle Urban Ministries did not prioritize changing policies in their work. They were more concerned with evangelizing, meeting immediate needs, stabilizing the neighborhood, and then developing the community economically. If we applied John Perkins's four tasks of the church to their combined work, they would thrive in the tasks of evangelism, social action, and community and economic development but fall short in seeking justice. Nonetheless, Rock's and Circle's work in evangelism, social action, and community development made a difference and should not be dismissed. They made change at the local level in meaningful ways.

The people whose lives were transformed through Rock and Circle may be the most significant fruit, but change also manifested in the buildings in the neighborhood. I saw the change on Parkside Avenue, the street directly west of Circle's and Rock's building. When Circle and Rock moved into the abandoned high school, neighbors called that block "murder row." Empty buildings stood open, housing drug deals and prostitution. For the task of evangelism, the buildings' lack of locked doors made it easy to enter them to invite people to church and share information about Circle's services.[4] The easy access also meant police regularly removed bodies from the buildings. Circle worked on John Perkins's third task, community development, and secured funding to tear down the derelict buildings and replace them with

---

[3]See, for instance, Ibram X. Kendi, *How to Be an Antiracist* (New York: One World, 2019).
[4]Andre Hinton, interview by author, October 13, 2021.

affordable housing. Now, newer, well-kept houses line Parkside, and it is no longer called murder row. But the peace that Circle and Rock brought with this restoration has required vigilance to maintain. Current Rock Church members pray on the street corners by the buildings drug dealers use for transactions, providing a presence for good on those corners.

Issues of justice and reconciliation have many layers. Circle addressed social needs and community development. Rock Church called people to relationships, which may be an essential component of justice. Most of the Rock Church members I interviewed insisted that relationships across racial lines—racial reconciliation—were essential for true justice because they were the glue that held justice together.

CONSIDER LIVING IN AN IMPOVERISHED PLACE

Uncommon is the person who will practice downward mobility, even if they are committed to justice. Some professors and colleagues in my PhD graduate program who cared deeply about social justice were amazed at my husband's and my decision to live in the Austin neighborhood. It seemed so strange. Why not work for justice from a distance? Others from my hometown's more conservative community appreciated our decision but did not relocate. They were generous givers, supporting missionaries from a distance but some also volunteered in Austin because we were there. Many people at Rock Church could have lived somewhere else. But love demanded proximity, and proximity produced empathy.

Understanding the histories behind race and class segregation shows that we cannot engage racial issues in America today without paying attention to racial—and by extension class—geographies. Put simply, Americans tend to live in communities that are segregated racially and economically. While personal preference contributes to that segregation, we inherit these racial and economic geographies and those who are in more comfortable places have little incentive—perhaps apart from the gospel's call—to disrupt them.

Living in a community makes a person better able to understand the perspective of their neighbors. It builds empathy, the additional tool that White evangelicals who live in places where they are minorities can use to understand race.

Living in a poor neighborhood does not require working there to make a difference. While this may seem obvious, it took me years to realize it. At first,

I thought that those who moved to the neighborhood or stayed needed to also be doing full-time ministry like Glen and Lonni and Pastor Raleigh and Paulette. After that first summer working with InterVarsity, my husband, Eric, began teaching at the charter school that partnered with Circle and Rock. In my mind, we were living out the model, despite my being in graduate school and not working in the community. Our living in the neighborhood *did* make a difference for Eric's students. They could not easily dismiss their White teacher because he shared their burdens. When Eric began working at a school in a different community, I struggled with our changing callings, though we served at Rock and volunteered at Circle. But I soon realized that many Rock Church members lived in the neighborhood and worked outside it.

Living in the neighborhood still made a difference. Our presence helped the block and helped bring stability to the community. We walked the streets of Austin, greeting our neighbors. We enjoyed the beauty of the community garden next to our house that Ms. Mary, who lived on the block, had founded years ago. We thanked Carl from across the street for tilling the soil. We joined in the work, sharing raw green beans with kids who learned that a green bean grows on a plant. In faltering and stumbling ways, we built relationships. We joined God in his kingdom work.

NO ONE IS COLORBLIND, SO DON'T TRY TO BE

Rock Church members joked about CPT (colored people's time, which is slower than White people's time) and how White people smell when it rains. The humor took the edge off the pain when they sat in discomfort about racial differences. They asked for help understanding and helped one another. They assumed that if there was a conflict in a cross-racial relationship, race had something to do with it.[5] In essence, they refused to be colorblind or ignore race.

Rock Church's leadership enabled this focus. Pastor Raleigh and Glen's decision to institutionalize racial discussions in fudge ripple meetings helped people practice having difficult discussions, uncovering racial assumptions and dismantling stereotypes. They learned to bring peace, if not always agreement. They did this by paying attention to race.

But the strange thing is, by talking about race so much, members began to move beyond race. They saw one another primarily as brothers and sisters

---

[5]Glen Kehrein, interview by author, April 19, 2021.

in Christ rather than chocolates or vanillas, while still remaining aware of how racial histories and contemporary dynamics shaped the lives of their brothers and sisters of lighter and darker hues.

This work is hard. In my teaching experience, White students hesitate to name race for reasons ranging from discomfort with talking about race to a genuine desire to see people as individuals because they believe that God has made each of us beautifully and wonderfully. But Rock members were able to embrace all of who other members were, including the varied ways others related to race in America.

Seeing and naming difference has other advantages too. To use metaphors, Rock Church was not a melting pot, in which everyone became the same. Nor was it a salad, in which the parts do not really mix. Instead, as one Rock leader put it, the church became a sort of stew, racially and culturally, with distinct ingredients flavoring one another.[6] When you're a part of the stew, you can see yourself more clearly and adopt habits and wisdom from other cultures. For instance, in my own time at Rock, I learned to identify some of my cultural strengths and assumptions. I realized that my focus on timeliness is useful for productivity. I also began to see the limits of my individual approach to God and began thinking more about *we* approach God, not just how *I* approach God.

THE PARADOX OF GROWING INFLUENCE

Vision leaks and people drift if they do not intentionally focus on their goals. Pastor Raleigh and Glen kept Circle and Rock focused on making disciples through reconciliation, outreach, and community development in the Austin neighborhood. The church was growing. At its height it had up to 450 people on a Sunday morning.[7]

Their impact increased beyond the Austin neighborhood as the church received national denominational and media attention. Rock Church became known as the "Jackie Robinson" of the Evangelical Free Church of America, a White denomination, for integrating it. When the EFCA women's ministries chose Rock Church and Circle Urban Ministries as their annual ministry focus to support through funding and prayer, Pastor Raleigh and Glen's influence grew as they and fellow church members traveled to showcase

---

[6]Butler, interview.
[7]Butler, interview.

racial reconciliation in action. Even after the year was complete, Rock Church kept receiving invitations to send delegations to other churches. Raleigh's compelling speaking ability coupled with the vision of Black and White people standing together in one of the most segregated cities in the North appealed to the denomination's White Christians. Raleigh and Glen's talks on the road formed the foundation for their book, *Breaking Down Walls*.[8]

Raleigh and Glen would bring other ministry staff members and laypeople with them. Rock corporately modeled reconciliation, whether it was the mixed-race gospel choir, the dance ministry led by Sandra Jackson, a Black math teacher, or conversations in the homes of those who hosted them.[9] In turn, when (mostly White) volunteers came to work at Circle, Rock Church members hosted them, building bridges.

Pastor Raleigh's vision for reconciliation grew beyond the neighborhood. It dovetailed with that of Bill McCartney, a White college football coach who founded Promise Keepers, a parachurch ministry aiming to help men live faithful Christian lives. McCartney wanted to embed racial reconciliation into the ministry. Promise Keepers diversified the staff, and by 1996 nearly 40 percent of the 487 employees were African American. McCartney used the tools of individualism and relationalism in his approach to reconciliation, saying, "This is a heart issue and things are only going to improve when we can establish individual relationships across color lines. We need to get involved in each others [sic] lives."[10] Pastor Raleigh served on Promise Keepers's board, and McCartney asked Raleigh to develop a racial reconciliation department. Pastor Raleigh did, and then McCartney said he sensed God calling Raleigh to work at Promise Keepers. Pastor Raleigh and Paulette prayed and felt like they should move to Colorado, where Promise Keepers was headquartered, but Rock Church had a policy that no one who was a deacon or pastor could leave without the elder board's blessing.

The elders prayed and affirmed Raleigh's call to Promise Keepers but said they did not think he was released from Rock.[11] So Raleigh began traveling

---

[8]Butler, interview.
[9]Jackson, interview.
[10]Jeff Coen, "Promise Keepers Out to End Racial Friction," *Chicago Tribune*, October 26, 1996. See also the various discussions of Promise Keepers in Michael Emerson and Christian Smith, *Divided by Faith: Evangelical Religion and the Problem of Race in America* (New York: Oxford University Press, 2000).
[11]Raleigh Washington, interview by author, September 14, 2021.

between Chicago and Colorado, serving in both ministries, for two years. Rock's elders and the church struggled. Raleigh wanted Glen to join him, but Glen felt called to the Austin neighborhood. He knew that effective ministry there required a presence in the community and did not feel called to leave. The elders and the church watched the men struggle through the consequences of Raleigh following what he saw as a call on his life. Although there was less acrimony, many felt like their parents were separating, as Glen and Lonni had when Circle Church split. In 1998, the elder board unanimously gave their blessing for Raleigh to leave Rock Church and work full time at Promise Keepers. They did not want to see him go but felt he had made his decision.[12] In the end, the growth of Rock Church's influence weakened Glen and Pastor Raleigh's relationship because it was rooted in the Austin neighborhood.

The church appointed Pastor Raleigh's brother, Abraham Lincoln Washington, as senior pastor. If Pastor Raleigh bled reconciliation, Pastor Linc bled transformation.[13] Pastor Linc inherited the legacy of fudge ripple meetings, but his primary concern was deliverance, seeing people trapped in sin made free.[14] Eric and I joined Rock Church during Pastor Linc's tenure. We had read Pastor Raleigh and Glen's *Breaking Down Walls* and were excited for fudge ripple meetings. But though Pastor Linc and Glen worked closely together, Pastor Linc rarely led fudge ripple meetings. We learned about reconciliation from church members who continued the habits of reconciliation they had learned from Pastor Raleigh and Glen, but the work was no longer as prominent at the institutional level.

Glen and Pastor Raleigh's relationship struggled after Pastor Raleigh moved. Reflecting years later, Raleigh told me that their difficulty came from their relationship being built on their ministry partnership. They cared about one another deeply and personally, but their relationship was bound by their shared ministry rather than by a simple personal relationship. "If I had it to do again," Pastor Raleigh said, "I would be equally committed to the partnership, but I would be more committed to the relationship."[15]

---

[12]Murray Sitte, interview by author, September 27, 2021.
[13]Steve McIlrath and Trina McIlrath, interview by Alexis McIlrath, March 18, 2018.
[14]Hinton, interview.
[15]Washington, interview.

Glen and Pastor Raleigh reconciled before Glen died in 2011. Glen had battled colon cancer for a year. I was working on my dissertation during his battle, and we had Glen and Lonni over for dinner. We had prepared a special meal that fit within Glen's regulated diet. After dinner, we sat in our family room talking about ministry and calling, and Glen told Eric and me that we should expect to begin to build credibility in the neighborhood only after a decade of living there. We were about three years in. When Glen died the following year, Rock Church was packed for Glen's funeral, as Black and White people came from the neighborhood, the city, and across the country. Former Austin Community Fellowship members sang, and Rock Church choir members rose out of the audience and went to the front of the gym where the funeral was held, singing songs from their days at Rock together to celebrate Glen's life.

Figure 21.1. Raleigh Washington and Glen Kehrein embrace outside Circle Urban Ministries and Rock Church as they celebrate a portion of Washington Boulevard in Chicago being named "Reverand Raleigh B. Washington Drive," in honor of Pastor Raleigh's work. Courtesy of DuRhonda Palmore

Glen, together with Raleigh, had cast a vision for what reconciliation and restoration could look like, and many had lived that out in a poor neighborhood. Karen Mains, wife of Circle Church's David Mains, reflected when Glen died,

> Glen and those like him have such a clear and demanding understanding of what can be that it is as though they have visited ahead and have come back, in some way, to tell us what it is they have seen. There can be a world where justice rules. We can mend broken cities and dysfunctional communities. The redemption Jesus offers can save souls and through His people even rehabilitate city blocks. Families can lift themselves out of poverty. Single moms can raise children who go to college. Prisoners can be set free. We do not have to settle for the ruinous, debilitating, humanity-destroying *status quo*.[16]

Karen Mains observed that Glen did not settle. He had an eschatological vision; he lived as though the kingdom of God was already among us, which it is. He could see it perhaps better than many of us. I wonder, did he strengthen his vision by taking baby steps of faith? With each step he took into the darkness, did he see more light in front? Or could he see it all at once?

A GLIMPSE OF WHAT COULD BE

A wise student of mine learning about Rock Church and Circle Urban Ministries wondered whether their model was replicable. Like other foreign students, he had to learn about the United States's racial dynamics. He thought Rock and Circle did good things. He saw how, for those willing to submit to the disciplines that lead to reconciliation, their experience was a glimpse of heaven. But he puzzled over how contrary these experiences were to the trajectories of race and class in United States. Could Rock and Circle do any more than be pockets of hope? The reconciliation Rock Church offered and the proximity in the neighborhood Circle facilitated are uncommon. After all, most Americans want to move out of poor neighborhoods. If they care about justice, they care from a distance. Americans want to be comfortable in their churches and by default avoid the messiness of conversations about race.

After Glen's death, Circle Urban Ministries navigated the travails of changing leadership. Currently, it serves 10 percent of Austin's population a

---

[16]Karen Mains, "Remembering the Future: Honoring the Life of Glen Kehrein," Hungry Souls, accessed April 19, 2022, www.hungrysouls.org/newsletter/issue-11-01.html.

year, and it hopes to increase its influence to 15 percent of the neighborhood.[17]

Rock Church has also stabilized under the leadership of Pastor Rob Stevenson. The church is still interracial, but it is much, much smaller. Yet it is a crucial witness and resource for Christians of all colors. In 1988, Glen argued that while monoracial churches might grow faster, they actually hindered "the power of the gospel, because at its core, the gospel is the message of reconciliation: us being reconciled to God and to each other. We don't have vehicles within our society to act on that reconciliation." Segregated churches mean "that we have Bible-believing evangelicals who at their core are very racist, yet they experience very little contradiction with that because they're never challenged."[18]

Rock Church and Circle Urban Ministries are not alone. Glen, along with John Perkins, was a founding member of the Christian Community Development Association in 1989. It started with three organizations, and when Glen died there were over three hundred. The Christian Community Development Association is a network of Christians

> committed to seeing people and communities wholistically restored. We believe that God wants to restore us not only to right relationships with Himself but also with our own true selves, our families and our communities. Not just spiritually, but emotionally, physically, economically and socially. Not by offering mercy alone, but by undergirding mercy with justice. To this end, we follow Jesus' example of reconciliation. We go where the brokenness is. We live among the people in some of America's neediest neighborhoods. We become one with our neighbors until there is no longer an "us" and "them," but only a "we." And, in the words of the Prophet Jeremiah, "we work and pray for the well-being of our city [or neighborhood]," trusting that if the entire community does well and prospers, then we will prosper also.[19]

---

[17]"Our Impact," Circle Urban Ministries, accessed April 19, 2022, https://circleurban.org/our-impact/.

[18]Quoted in Robert Kachur, "Fudge Ripple at the Rock," *Christianity Today*, March 4, 1988.

[19]"About Christian Community Development Association," *Christian Community Development Association* (blog), accessed April 19, 2022, https://ccda.org/about/. For the history of the About Christian Community Development Association, see Peter Goodwin Heltzel, "The Christian Community Development Association: A Quiet Revolution," in *Jesus and Justice: Evangelicals, Race, and American Politics* (New Haven, CT: Yale University Press, 2009), 160-77. See also John M. Perkins, *Beyond Charity: The Call to Christian Community Development* (Grand Rapids, MI:

Nonetheless, Christian Community Development Association–type ministry is not the common framework for American Christianity, and churches like Rock remain rare. Those I interviewed who had left the church said they had never encountered such deep community anywhere else. One would think that they would be able to create community, replicating it because they had been trained at Rock.

While I, like most Americans, hope Rock's and Circle's vision will expand and many people will want to follow it, I wonder whether their smallness is not the problem that I, with my limited vision, imagine it to be. Maybe the key to their strength was not their impact on changing the neighborhood or solving racial problems in America. Maybe their greatest impact is in a small group of people embodying an eschatological reality—living as though the kingdom of God has actually come on earth. God's economy, after all, is different from our own. Perhaps Rock was and is just a small glimpse of heaven. But I do think that by the power of the Holy Spirit, Christians can study the past, understand the present, and restore the ruins visible in America that point to the deep divisions and lack of neighbor love in American Christianity. All things are possible.

QUESTIONS AND IMPLICATIONS

Rock's and Circle's ministries and histories do not fit nicely into either perspective on the right or the left.

- What other correctives to the right and left do Rock Church and Circle Urban Ministries offer? How has your thinking changed? How might your actions change?

I argued that Rock and Circle's testimony demonstrates the importance of proximity when doing ministry among people who are poor. One obvious way to do this would be to relocate and live in a poor community. When we made the decision to purchase a house in the neighborhood, Glen and others suggested that we move close to another Rock Church member because of the support they would offer as we lived in the neighborhood.

- What it look like for you to relocate?

Baker Books, 1993); Wayne Gordon and John M. Perkins, *Making Neighborhoods Whole: A Handbook for Christian Community Development* (Downers Grove, IL: InterVarsity Press, 2010).

- Who do you know who is living in a neighborhood where you might want to move?

Perhaps moving is too much of a step for you. In my interviews with Lonni Kehrein, she emphasized putting yourself under the leadership of someone from a racial group different from your own. That might be one option. I would hesitate to let fears that you will cause gentrification hinder relocating or investing in a poor community. Many think "urban pioneers" cause gentrification, but studies show that state-private partnerships drive it more. Market-driven solutions enabling poor people to remain coupled with policies that advocate for fair housing can help people from many income levels remain in a place. My main caution would be that you remember God is at work through his church already in poor communities and you are joining his work, not leading it.[20]

- What other steps could you take to put yourself among those who are in economic need or to begin exploring whether a move might be in your future? Where could you go to church? Whom could you visit? Where could you volunteer to learn from others?

Rock Church and Circle Urban Ministries offer a glimpse of what could be. Like Clarence Jordan and those at Koinonia Farm, they lived as though God's Word was true—and contrary to American notions of individualism, self-justification, and upward mobility.

- What aspects of the possibilities seem closest to heaven?
- Who have you seen who lives as though heaven really were on earth? What characterizes their life? What can you learn from them?
- How might you move toward that vision?

---

[20]Claire Bolton, "Enacting Critical Community Development through Anti-Gentrification Policy Advocacy," *Community Development Journal* 57, no. 2 (2022): 213-33; Claire Bolton, Katherine Hankins and Andy Walter, "'Gentrification with Justice': An Urban Ministry Collective and the Practice of Place-Making in Atlanta's Inner-City Neighbourhoods," *Urban Studies* 49, no. 7 (2012): 1507-26; Soong-Chan Rah, "Rethinking Incarnational Ministry," in *CCDA Theological Journal*, ed. Chris Jehle, Soong-Chan Rah, and Brandon Wrencher, 2013; Robert Lupton, *Theirs Is the Kingdom: Celebrating the Gospel in Urban Life* (New York: HarperCollins, 2010).

CONCLUSION

Tears streamed down my face as I left our house in the Austin neighborhood for the last time in 2013. I remembered worshiping with my Rock Church family, sharing meals with neighbors, chatting with others over their fences as I walked to the train, walking around the neighborhood, and working in the community garden next door. I had sought to work toward what Catherine de Hueck called the "chit chat apostolate" during her time in Harlem, stopping on her walks to talk with people and be Christ to them. Knowing Catherine, I imagine she did it better than me, but I aspired to it anyway.

Eric and I had invested deeply in the house emotionally, physically, and financially. Before we bought it, our 1911 Queen Anne bungalow had been a drug house, abandoned by previous owners. After renting from Glen and Lonni for two years, we had found the house in 2009 after the housing market crash. It was next door to two Wheaton College alumni from our church who led the weekly Bible study we joined. When we walked into the house and saw the original woodwork intact, we saw the possibility of redemption. Although it was on the city's demolition list, we could restore it. We wanted to invest in the neighborhood, putting down roots as John Perkins had in Mississippi and as Glen and Lonni had in Chicago. As I left, I remembered how Glen had said we should stay for at least ten years. We were leaving after six.

Our neighbors on the block always asked when we were going to have children. They all thought we rattled around in that big house, and it needed to be full. Now I was pregnant with our first child and was facing my limitations. Months earlier I had accepted a position at Wheaton College, which is in a suburb west of Chicago. Eric and I had agonized over the decision, nearly moving to Mississippi for a job there instead because we knew that my working at Wheaton and commuting from the Austin neighborhood would dismantle the smallness that characterized our lives. Our social life and church were both in the neighborhood, and as a graduate student I had ambled around the city for my work but had done most of my writing and reading at home. Living, working, and worshiping in the same neighborhood meant there were many layers of overlap and opportunities to build community. Working at Wheaton would mean an hour commute for me each way by train. The town in Mississippi where I had received a job offer was small, and there we could have continued living and working in a context where I was a minority, following John's relocation principle.

I accepted Wheaton College's offer because I felt more peace about it. It would allow us to stay in the Chicago area near family and would allow me to teach evangelical students, to whom I felt a calling. I had originally planned to commute like the handful of faculty members who lived in Oak Park and River Forest, the suburbs just west of the Austin neighborhood.

But now I was pregnant, and those ten hours of weekly commuting looked costly, both in terms of paying for childcare and in time away from my baby. Our values were crashing into Chicagoland's racial geographies and systemic sin. If we moved to Wheaton, we wanted to be close to the college because we had one car, which Eric would need for his commute. But Wheaton was majority White and pretty wealthy, with its own complicated racial history, as I would later learn, shaped by the housing dynamics that had made the Austin neighborhood predominantly African American. Would I actually live there?

We answered yes, but with great fear. In Wheaton, we would raise our child in a context of relative comfort. Worshiping at Rock Church and studying Catherine de Hueck had taught me the dangers of comfort and the benefits of discomfort. Comfort could make me not trust God. Discomfort, leaning into the tensions in life—as studying history requires of us—opened me to see God in new ways. Although initially I had not liked Rock Church's long church services, which ended when the Holy Spirit said they were over, had resisted the ten minutes of passing the peace, and had longed for familiar worship songs, now I knew that God was in the waiting, the hugs and greetings, and the Black church songs. When we first moved to the neighborhood, I had been afraid—afraid because I did not know whether the fireworks I heard cracking were gunshots, afraid because I stood out with my White skin, afraid because I had heard so many negative things about the community. Now I was aware of potential dangers in the Austin neighborhood, but I could see beauty in neighboring families inviting me to a lavish birthday celebration, the wonder of new life every year in the garden, the goodness of people watching out for me on the block. God was working in all of these.

I worried about the dangers of the suburbs.

I knew my tendency toward materialism, envy, and greed—tendencies that had been dampened living in a place where there was such material need. How would I hold up? What patterns would my son fall into, living in such a wealthy place? I had learned from John Perkins, Catherine de Hueck, and Glen and Lonni to resist narratives of upward mobility—a lesson that would only be reinforced when, in the coming years, I studied Clarence Jordan and researched John, Catherine, and the Rock Church family with the eyes of a scholar. Living in the Austin neighborhood had taught me that it is more effective to serve those in material need when you live by them and can learn from them. I had named the upward mobility narrative as an idol, though, and knew I was not trying to live into it. I would have to continue to see it for the idol it was, balancing the needs of my growing family with the wants that masquerade as needs.

Sin, I knew, resided not only in my heart but also in the social systems all around me. I worried about my participation in systemic sin, which is sin that is embedded in social systems. I had navigated the sin of the Austin neighborhood. Could I resist the social sin of Wheaton? Living there would certainly mean contributing to a sinful system, even if my intent was not in line with its purposes. Median household income in the town of Wheaton is more than three times that of the Austin neighborhood. Wheaton had a history, shaped by zoning, federal investment in suburbanization, and other policies that had determined its demographics. Some of those dynamics have led to sin—excluding particular people who seem undesirable, though some were brothers and sisters in Christ. We make our decisions within larger contexts we cannot control.

We moved reluctantly. Over the ensuing years, I have thought deeply about our decision. I continue to think that Christians should assume downward mobility as our first option, and upward mobility should be the exception. But Christians also have freedom—and perhaps this was what Glen and Raleigh were saying when they said not all were called to relocate. As Pastor Raleigh and Glen discussed of the calling to reconciliation in their book,

Breaking Down Walls, they said that all are called to be reconcilers, like Christians are called to evangelism. But some people have a special call, and God places "certain people in pioneering efforts to apply those principles of racial reconciliation in service to the poor, the oppressed, and the needy."[1]

Life is complex. Clarence's complicated engagement with the civil rights movement has reminded me that in many things, there's not a right and a wrong approach. As Clarence did, I keep the question, "Am I being faithful?" on my mind. There are seasons to our lives, and living close to my work has allowed me to raise four young children while working full time. This season has helped me realize my limits as a human. Pregnancy and nursing have taxed my body, and the past decade or so in the suburbs has felt like a blur in which I am hanging on. Rather than living in the Austin neighborhood, my teaching and writing here in the suburb of Wheaton have been my practice, my discipleship related to racial justice and reconciliation.

I may be called to move again to a poor community where I am a minority, relocating following John's wisdom. I may also serve where I am planted, being a "sticker" like Clarence and Glen were, and stay here in this suburb. People here are teaching me to ask what opportunities there are to serve individuals and to shape policies. Race and class touch many aspects of our lives, even when they are not obvious. No matter where we live, we can pay attention to who is elected as prosecutors and judges, and influence zoning, voting, and school redistricting for good. We can wonder what policies in our towns, at our schools, in our churches, and at our workplaces we could be asking about and praying about.[2] As Pastor Raleigh and Glen observed,

> Institutional racism occurs in the Christian church when believers operate out of ignorance, tradition, and the status quo, accepting the disparity between racist without questioning why. Institutional racism is often motivated by fear. Fear of the unknown, fear of people different from ourselves, fear of being inconvenienced, fear of losing our budget if we support this black program, fear that the "quality of life" is going to go downhill—all kinds of fears motivate whites to respond in a self-preserving way.[3]

---

[1] Raleigh Washington and Glen Kehrein, *Breaking Down Walls: A Model for Reconciliation in an Age of Racial Strife* (Chicago: Moody Press, 1994), 214.
[2] Vincent Bacote, *Reckoning with Race and Performing the Good News: In Search of a Better Evangelical Theology* (Boston: Brill, 2020).
[3] Washington and Kehrein, *Breaking Down Walls*, 203.

CONCLUSION

We can often have the most impact at a local level in small ways. No matter where we live, we can seek out relationships with those who are different from us. As Catherine's life reminds us, God works through us in the little things.

I remember ultimately that I am joining God in his work. I do not have to solve the church's and the nation's problems, but as Pastor Raleigh preached, I am responsible for my response to God's call. I am responsible for what I do with the gifts I have been given. For me, taking responsibility has meant caring for my family and students, creating spaces for them—as I have tried to do for you in this book—to learn about, pray about, discern, and ultimately act in ways that bring justice and righteousness. That space is not the only type of space in which to engage racial issues—we need spaces to address real trauma, for instance—but we also need a gentle space where we can be humble, admit that we do not know it all, and ask, as I learned at Rock, "Help me understand." Learning matters. Investing in the life of the mind, although a great privilege, is a joy that can make a difference as we expand our sense of who is in the communion of saints, seeing a "new we" that includes people from all tribes, tongues, and nations.

I teach my students that racial and economic issues, and how our faith intersects with them, are not just topics those on "the left" or particular ethnic or racial groups should care about. They are problems so knotty and complicated that no one group of people and no particular discipline can untangle them. I can teach them to understand America's and Christianity's racial past using the discipline of history—as I have done here—teaching students to discern the truth in stories, to see how context influences people's thoughts and actions, to humbly recognize the limits of their knowledge, and to practice empathy rather than judgment.

They—and we—can study history with courage, rather than imbibing narratives about our heritage that make us feel good. Since we serve a God who has forgiven our sins, we need not fear the sins of the past, nor try to distance ourselves from those sins. We can be implicated in the present. We do not have to defend ourselves because God knows our failings. We can learn to love the dead as we would love the living, trying to understand that person in their context, while still recognizing sin.

Doing history can inspire us to act in the present. Since we do not have to hide from the pain of the past and can learn from the wisdom of those who came before us, we can be free to respond to pain in the present. We can learn about ordinary heroes and also walk in the hard-won wisdom those heroes' lives offered.

TIMELINE

Year (Month)	Catherine de Hueck and Friendship House	John and Vera Mae Perkins	Clarence Jordan and Koinonia Farm	Rock Church and Circle Urban Ministries	National and Global Events
1891					Pope Leo XIII publishes encyclical *Rerum Novarum*, laying groundwork for Catholic social teaching Immigrants to US from "White" countries seen in US as members of different White races
1896	August: Catherine born in Russia				May: *Plessy v. Ferguson* establishes segregation as constitutional in US. The case is a part of the larger rise of Jim Crow in the American South
1903					W. E. B. DuBois publishes *The Souls of Black Folk*, providing a picture of African Americans' place in society as a cultural center
1908					Georgia passes voter-restriction laws targeted at hindering African American citizens from voting Model T invented
1910	Catherine's family returns from abroad and settles in St. Petersburg				Great Migration of African Americans out of rural South begins. It will dip in 1930s and resume until 1970. White city dwellers respond with violence (covered primarily in Black press) and restrictive covenants. Later, banks will practice redlining
1911					Survey of chain gangs in Georgia shows 180 White prisoners to 2,000 African American prisoners
1912	Catherine and Boris marry		Clarence Jordan born		
1914					World War I begins. This, along with increasing racism against (often Catholic) immigrants in US, leads Catholic bishops to emphasize Americanizing lay Catholics. They shift to geographic parish model but set aside national parishes to serve only African Americans
1915					Film *Birth of a Nation* is released. Reviving the image of Ku Klux Klan, the film heightened racial tensions throughout US, glorifying violence against African Americans and supporters of racial equality

Year (Month)	Catherine de Hueck and Friendship House	John and Vera Mae Perkins	Clarence Jordan and Koinonia Farm	Rock Church and Circle Urban Ministries	National and Global Events
1919	Bolshevik soldiers imprison Catherine and Boris in their villa, intending them to die Catherine and Boris are evacuated from Russia to England Catherine is received into the Roman Catholic Church				Germany and most Allied Powers sign the Treaty of Versailles, ending World War I Summer: Race riots occur across US. Riots help transition White races into White race January: Alabama ratifies Eighteenth Amendment, being first state to affirm prohibition, which will lead to the rise of bootlegging businesses like the one John Perkins was born into Claude McKay writes the poem "If We Must Die" in response to growing violence against Blacks perpetuated by Whites. The poem indicates the rise of The New Negro, who will resist racial violence. McKay will later become a Catholic through the influence of Catherine's Friendship House
1921	Catherine and Boris immigrate to Canada July: Catherine's son George is born. In the ensuing years, Catherine works as a speaker on the Chataqua circuit				In Harlem this year and throughout the 1920s, literature, music, and art flourish in a movement known as the Harlem Renaissance. Many artists depict Jesus as a lynched Black man
1924					Johnson Reed Immigration Act restricts immigration from countries Congress deems less desirable to protect the racial bloodlines of the United States
1927	Catherine de Hueck's friendship with Father John LaFarge, leader of Catholic interracial movement, begins				
1929	Catherine's friend, Black journalist and children's author Ellen Tarry, moves to Harlem. Tarry will help pave way for Catherine among Harlem's Black intelligentsia				American stock market crashes
1930		John Perkins born	Americus, the closest town to Koinonia Farm, builds segregated playground, showing segregation's continued strength, even amid the progressive impulses that supported building playgrounds for African American children		

Year (Month)	Catherine de Hueck and Friendship House	John and Vera Mae Perkins	Clarence Jordan and Koinonia Farm	Rock Church and Circle Urban Ministries	National and Global Events
1931	Catherine lives among the poor and infiltrates communist organizations				March: Communist Party's legal team defends nine Black teenagers in Scottsboro case, making friends among African Americans for Communist Party May: Pope Pius XI publishes *Quadragesimo Anno*, which addresses the church's role in changing social and economic issues, including socialism
1932	Catherine founds the first Friendship House in Toronto to stop spread of communism among working class and to help church live up to its social teachings				Highlander Folk School of Tennessee is founded, becoming center for civil rights study and action
1933			Clarence Jordan graduates from University of Georgia with a degree in agriculture; begins studies at Southern Baptist Seminary in Louisville, KY. Will pastor three churches during seminary		January: Hitler comes to power in Germany June: Home Owners Loan Corporation is created. Its logics will be adopted by private banks to practice redlining
1934					Federal Housing Authority is created. Its logics will also be adopted by private banks to practice redlining
1935					Congress of Industrial Organizers (CIO) is founded, which organizes workers of all races and skilled and unskilled workers Mississippi funds White schools three times more than Black schools Communist Party in Russia increases influence on workers around world, starting more open clubs, running summer camps, drawing ties between communism and Christianity
1936	Catherine is run out of Toronto, and Friendship House there closes		Clarence and Florence Jordan get married, will go on to have four children Clarence earns ThM from Southern Clarence begins to teach at the African American Simmons University, until 1941		
1937					Canadian Communist Party Membership increases to 15,000 people, from 5,000 members in 1934

Year (Month)	Catherine de Hueck and Friendship House	John and Vera Mae Perkins	Clarence Jordan and Koinonia Farm	Rock Church and Circle Urban Ministries	National and Global Events
1938	Catherine moves to New York's Harlem community and founds Friendship House			Raleigh Washington born in the segregated South	
1939			Clarence finishes doctoral program in New Testament at Southern Baptist Theological Seminary		Film *Gone with the Wind*, seen by millions of Americans, becomes highest-grossing film in America Hitler invades Poland C. S. Lewis publishes his famous essay, "Learning in Wartime"
1940					Germany begins attacks on Western Europe
1941					Japan bombs Pearl Harbor, and US joins World War II
1942	Catherine moves to Chicago		Clarence and Florence Jordan and Martin and Mabel England establish Koinonia Farm. Koinonia Farm endorses pacifism, which troubles neighbors who support World War II as a good war		
1943					Pope Pius XII writes *Mystici Corpus Christi*, reiterating how church is "mystical body of Christ"
1944			Two more families move to live at Koinonia Farm, both African American		
1945					September: World War II ends with Japanese surrender
1946		John's brother Clyde shot and killed by a Mississippi deputy sheriff	Future president Jimmy Carter receives naval commission and leaves Sumter County, where Koinonia Farm is, until 1953		
1947	Catherine publishes *Friendship House*. Catherine and her second husband, Eddie Doherty, move to Combermere, Canada, to found a Friendship House there, which becomes Madonna House. Madonna House is still active today	John moves to California			
1948				Glen Kehrein born in Wisconsin	Supreme Court Case *Shelly v. Kramer* declares restrictive covenants on homes unenforceable by state, further limiting their power US military is formally integrated. Both John Perkins and Raleigh Washington will serve in the integrated military

Year (Month)	Catherine de Hueck and Friendship House	John and Vera Mae Perkins	Clarence Jordan and Koinonia Farm	Rock Church and Circle Urban Ministries	National and Global Events
1949		John Perkins visits Mississippi and reconnects with Vera Mae Bradley, who later becomes his wife White author Lillian Smith publishes *Killers of the Dream*, a critique of southern racial hierarchy	Clarence writes Sunday school book for high schoolers White members of Koinonia who are also members at Rehobeth Church (where many Koinonia members attended) begin to leave the church because of hostility from other church members over Koinonia Farm's racial commitments		
1950			Rehobeth Church expels remaining White Koinonia members		July: First US troops arrive in Korea for Korean War
1951		John and Vera Mae marry. John is drafted to fight in Korean War shortly after their wedding			In a Cicero housing riot just outside Chicago, Whites attack the apartment of the Clarke family. The Clarkes are Black Catholics, and their White neighbors do not like that they are attempting to move into all-White Cicero. Housing violence plaguing American cities finally becomes national news
1953					July: Armistice signed ending organized combat in Korean War
1954		January: John returns to California after army obligation is over Spencer Perkins, son of Vera Mae and John, is born. Spencer's involvement in a church's children's ministry will later lead John to convert to Christianity			May: Supreme Court rules to end legally segregated schools in *Brown v. Board of Education* July: Mississippi Citizens' Council is established to resist school integration
1955			Jimmy Carter appointed to Sumter County School Board Rufus and Sue Angry, nearby sharecroppers, move to Koinonia		May: *Brown v. Board of Education* II, the Supreme Court rules that all schools must integrate August: Emmett Till is lynched September: Emmett Till's open-casket funeral is held, bringing national attention to the horrors of racially motivated violence. Seventeen days later, the trial of Till's murderers occurs. They are both found not guilty, and later boast in the press about killing him December: Montgomery Bus Boycott begins, which propels Martin Luther King Jr. to national leadership Ellen Tarry publishes her autobiography *The Third Door*, which details her life as an African American woman and her hope for interracial justice, which she had worked for through Friendship House

Year (Month)	Catherine de Hueck and Friendship House	John and Vera Mae Perkins	Clarence Jordan and Koinonia Farm	Rock Church and Circle Urban Ministries	National and Global Events
1956		Violence and a boycott against Koinonia Farm begin			Mississippi State Sovereignty Commission is established. It conducts surveillance of civil rights activity, including John's
1957			State of Georgia comes close to meeting all its agricultural needs, one of Clarence's goals		Martin Luther King Jr. visits Highlander Folk School
1958			Fewer than ten people (including children) remain at Koinonia Grand jury investigating attacks on Koinonia includes flawed final report by Georgia's attorney general suggesting Koinonia as instigator of violence against farm April: Clarence gives lecture at Martin Luther King Jr.'s Church in Montgomery, Alabama		
1959					Ross Barnett elected governor of Mississippi; he provides state funding for Citizens' Councils to promote their message in Mississippi and nationally
1960		John, Vera Mae, and their family return to rural Mississippi	Boycott of Koinonia ends Sumter County schools integrate	Raleigh joins military as an officer in the Adjutant Generals Core after graduating from Florida A&M with BA in psychology, where he had a baseball scholarship and did Reserve Officers Training Corps (ROTC)	John F. Kennedy becomes first US Catholic president
1962		John and Vera Mae established the Voice of Calvary in Mississippi Student Non-violent Coordinating Committee workers come to Americus, Georgia from Albany to work for civil rights/ voter's registration rights			May: The Catholic Church makes Martin de Porres, son of a freed Black slave, a saint October: James Meredith integrates Ole Miss; rioting follows his arrival for three days

Year (Month)	Catherine de Hueck and Friendship House	John and Vera Mae Perkins	Clarence Jordan and Koinonia Farm	Rock Church and Circle Urban Ministries	National and Global Events
1963			Conrad Brown leaves Koinonia due to financial limits of farm Koinonia hosts 23 people as part of a civil rights workshop, though Clarence does not agree with the civil rights movements' tactics		January: "Born of Conviction," statement by 28 ministers, reinforces Methodist denomination's support of integration, but the southern White ministers who supported it will soon leave their posts at White churches April: Martin Luther King Jr. writes "Letter from a Birmingham Jail," condemning White moderates June: Byron de la Beckwith murders NAACP leader Medgar Evers in the driveway of Evers's Jackson, Mississippi house November: John F. Kennedy assassinated; Lyndon Johnson becomes president
1964					Two hung juries leave Beckwith free Summer: Student Non-violent Coordinating Committee organizes Mississippi Freedom Summer, bringing White college students south to register Black voters June: KKK members kill three civil rights volunteers investigating a church burning in Philadelphia, Mississippi, which brings national attention to the violent resistance to civil rights in Mississippi July: Congress passes the Civil Rights Act August: At the Democratic National Convention, Black and White leaders from the Mississippi Freedom Democratic Party try to take the seats of the delegates from Mississippi's regular Democratic party (which has an all-White primary, unlike the MFDP). They refuse to compromise and take the at-large seats November: Lyndon Johnson elected president
1965		John Longstreet partners with John and Vera Mae to help African Americans register to vote in Mississippi	Millard and Linda Fuller meet Clarence at Koinonia Farm. They will go on to live at the farm and later found Habitat for Humanity		Freedom of school choice plan is established in Mississippi Jimmy Carter dissents against his church when it upholds segregation August: Voting Rights Act prohibits discrimination by race in voting

Year (Month)	Catherine de Hueck and Friendship House	John and Vera Mae Perkins	Clarence Jordan and Koinonia Farm	Rock Church and Circle Urban Ministries	National and Global Events
1966		Reverend Odenwald, pastor at White First Baptist Church in Mendenhall and friend of John, commits suicide John promotes cooperatives, partnering with Father A. J. McKnight, a Black Catholic Priest John helps form the Simpson County Development Corporation Simpson County Civic League (which helps Black voters register) elects Nathaniel Rubin as chair Violence against Perkins family increases Johnson administration gives War on Poverty funding to Perkinses			Jimmy Carter loses governor race. He will run again in 1970 and win
1968			Koinonia Farm reincorporates as Koinonia Partners, reflecting Clarence's sense that his role, though not his calling, was changing	Raleigh returns from voluntarily serving in Vietnam, where he was promoted to major, and receives bronze star for meritorious service Raleigh and Paulette meet Glen experiences racial awakening while a student at Moody Bible Institute in Chicago in wake of riots following Martin Luther King Jr.'s assassination	April: Martin Luther King Jr. is assassinated Fair Housing Act is passed, making redlining illegal
1969		December: John arrested. From jail, he and other community leaders start a boycott against shops in Mendenhall. They have several demands, including ending segregation in downtown Mendenhall	October 29: Clarence dies while translating the New Testament in his writing shack at 57 years old		Responding to litigation by Black families, the Supreme Court rules that Mississippi's "freedom of choice" delaying tactic to integrate schools, which relied on brave Black families like the Perkinses to carry the burden of integration, was not effective. Mississippi schools had to end segregation, which they did in 1970 Fannie Lou Hammer establishes Freedom Farm Cooperative, joining in nationwide trend

Year (Month)	Catherine de Hueck and Friendship House	John and Vera Mae Perkins	Clarence Jordan and Koinonia Farm	Rock Church and Circle Urban Ministries	National and Global Events
1970		In response to the Supreme Court's ruling that Mississippi must immediately integrate schools, White Christians in Mendenhall help establish a segregated private school. While complicated, White Christians across the South followed a similar pattern		March 21: Glen and Lonni marry	
1971		John and Vera Mae move their family to Jackson for John's safety and commute to Mendenhall for ministry		Glen and Lonni visit Circle Church on Easter Sunday and decide Circle is where they need to be Fall: Glen Kehrein enrolls at Wheaton College, where Circle Church's Pastor Gaw also works	
1973				June: Glen and Lonni move into Chicago's Austin neighborhood, inspired by John's Voice of Calvary model in Mendenhall. Circle Church supports their efforts to start community center there, but no Black members of Black module want to join the intentional community	Mississippi's Sovereignty Commission is decommissioned
1975					Home Mortgage Disclosure Act passed, making accessible information on financial institutions' lending practices
1976		John publishes *Let Justice Roll Down* and *A Quiet Revolution*. The first book is his autobiography and the second articulates his vision for the church. He will go on to develop the three *R*'s of relocation, reconciliation, and redistribution	Reporters contact Koinonia Farm to determine Carter's relationship with it during 1950s and 1960s, and members at Koinonia say they have no recollection or evidence of his help, despite his claims to the contrary Millard and Linda Fuller found Habitat for Humanity	Circle Church splits amid controversy over Pastor Clarence Hilliard's "Funky Gospel" sermon. Members of Austin Community Fellowship and Circle Community Center feel alone without guidance of Black leadership and Black friends	Jimmy Carter runs for president
1977					Community Reinvestment Act passed, meaning there is legal responsibility for financial institutions to invest in underprivileged communities by helping to finance home loans
1978		John splits Voice of Calvary, now in Jackson, off from the ministry still operating in Mendenhall, which becomes The Mendenhall Ministries			

Year (Month)	Catherine de Hueck and Friendship House	John and Vera Mae Perkins	Clarence Jordan and Koinonia Farm	Rock Church and Circle Urban Ministries	National and Global Events
1979				Paulette Washington accepts Jesus as her personal Savior; two weeks later, Raleigh does same	
1980				May: Raleigh is discharged from the military without honors after refusing to retire (and keep his benefits) because retiring would mean admitting he had been guilty of conduct unbecoming of an officer September: Raleigh enters Trinity Evangelical Divinity School to study for an MDiv	Jimmy Carter keeps copy of *The Cotton Patch Gospel* in his desk at the Carter Center
1981		Voice of Calvary ministry name changed to Mendenhall Ministries in Mendenhall to distinguish it from John's ministry in Jackson. Dolphus Weary leads the organization and partners with Artis Fletcher, who pastors the Mendenhall Bible Church. John and Vera Mae mentored both men and their wives, Rosie Weary and Carolyn Fletcher			October: musical *Cotton Patch Gospel* makes its debut
1983				Raleigh graduates from Trinity and founds Rock Church, which holds services at Glen's Circle Urban Ministries Paul Grant is hired as Rock Church's music director, becoming fully on staff in 1985 DuRhonda Baskett joins Rock Church. She becomes an integral part of many ministry opportunities at Rock Church Charles and Donna Butler, sister and brother-in-law of DuRhonda Baskett, join church. Charles will go on to serve as program director of Circle Urban Ministries	

Year (Month)	Catherine de Hueck and Friendship House	John and Vera Mae Perkins	Clarence Jordan and Koinonia Farm	Rock Church and Circle Urban Ministries	National and Global Events
				Austin High School closes one of its buildings in the wake of White flight. The building will later become the location of Rock Church	
1984				July: Circle Urban Ministries purchases old Austin public high school in what seems to be miracle December: Glen and Lonni leave Austin Community Fellowship, which had functioned as church, and officially join Rock Church	
1985	December 14: Catherine dies in Canada at 89 years old			June 2: Rock Church holds its first service in new chapel, with 75 people	
1987			Florence Jordan dies at 74 years old		
1988				*Christianity Today* publishes extensive article about Rock Church, focusing on its interracial ministry	
1989		Christian Community Development Association founded (CCDA). Founding members include Glen and John		Army Board of Military Corrections reverses Raleigh's case; he is reinstated for one day and retires with honor and full benefits	
1993				*Breaking Down Walls*, which Raleigh and Glen cowrote, is published. They gives eight principles for racial reconciliation and leading congregations in how to engage all neighbors	
1994				Raleigh joins Promise Keepers's board of directors and will begins to work as vice president for reconciliation in 1996, commuting between Chicago and Denver	Byron de la Beckwith, who murdered Medgar Evers, is finally convicted and sentenced to life in prison
1998			Dolphus and Rosie Weary, mentees of John and Vera Mae, found the Rural Education and Leadership Development Fund to aid underprivileged rural communities by grassroots activity	Rock Church elder board gives its blessing for Raleigh to leave Rock Church	

Year (Month)	Catherine de Hueck and Friendship House	John and Vera Mae Perkins	Clarence Jordan and Koinonia Farm	Rock Church and Circle Urban Ministries	National and Global Events
2007				Karen and Eric Johnson move to Austin neighborhood and join Rock Church	
2010			President Jimmy Carter speaks at Koinonia Farm celebration		
2011				November: Glen dies of colon cancer, after Glen and Raleigh reconcile	
2013				Karen and Eric Johnson move to Wheaton, IL	

SUGGESTED READING

The footnotes contain significant sources for civil rights, Christianity, and the Great Migration. I have highlighted below a handful of helpful books for further study of these ordinary heroes.

CATHERINE DE HUECK

Doherty, Catherine de Hueck. *Fragments of My Life*. Notre Dame, IN: Ave Maria, 1979.
———. *Friendship House*. New York: Sheed and Ward, 1947.
Duquinn, Lorene Hanley. *They Called Her the Baroness: The Life of Catherine De Hueck Doherty*. Staten Island, NY: Alba House, 2000.
Johnson, Karen J. *One in Christ: Chicago Catholics and the Quest for Interracial Justice*. New York: Oxford University Press, 2018.
Tarry, Ellen. *The Third Door: The Autobiography of an American Negro Woman*. 2nd ed. London: Staples, 1965.
Wild, Robert A., ed. *Comrades Stumbling Along: The Friendship of Catherine de Hueck Doherty and Dorothy Day as Revealed Through Their Letters*. New York: Alba House, 2009.

JOHN PERKINS

Berk, Stephen E. *A Time to Heal: John Perkins, Community Development, and Racial Reconciliation*. Grand Rapids, MI: Baker Books, 1997.
Marsh, Charles. *The Beloved Community: How Faith Shapes Social Justice from the Civil Rights Movement to Today*. New York: Basic Books, 2007. (Marsh also discusses Clarence Jordan.)
Perkins, John M. *Dream with Me: Race, Love, and the Struggle We Must Win*. Grand Rapids, MI: Baker Books, 2017.
———. *Let Justice Roll Down: John Perkins Tells His Own Story*. Ventura, CA: G/L, 1976.
———. *A Quiet Revolution: Meeting Human Needs Today; A Biblical Challenge to Christians* (Waco, TX: Word Books, 1976).
———, ed. *Restoring At-Risk Communities: Doing It Together and Doing It Right*. Grand Rapids, MI: Baker Books, 1995.

Slade, Peter, Charles Marsh, and Peter Heltzel. *Mobilizing for the Common Good: The Lived Theology of John M. Perkins*. Jackson: University Press of Mississippi, 2013.

CLARENCE JORDAN

Jordan, Clarence. *The Cotton Patch Gospel*. Macon, GA: Smyth & Helwys, 2004.

———. *The Substance of Faith, and Other Cotton Patch Sermons*. A Koinonia Publication. New York: Association Press, 1972.

K'Meyer, Tracy Elaine. *Interracialism and Christian Community in the Postwar South: The Story of Koinonia Farm*. Charlottesville: University Press of Virginia, 1997.

Lee, Dallas. *The Cotton Patch Evidence: The Story of Clarence Jordan and the Koinonia Farm Experiment (1942–1970)*. Eugene, OR: Wipf & Stock, 2011.

ROCK CHURCH

Washington, Raleigh, and Glen Kehrein. *Breaking Down Walls: A Model for Reconciliation in an Age of Racial Strife*. Chicago: Moody Press, 1994.

INDEX

Adams, Dennis, 137
Albritton, Caryoln. *See* Fletcher, Carolyn
Americus, 144, 147-48, 172-83, 197-203
   See also Georgia
Anderson, Sheila, 245-46, 289
Angry, Rufus, 164, 177-78
Angry, Sue, 164, 177-78
Atkinson, Harry and Allene, 173
Austin neighborhood, 236-37, 259-62, 268, 269-82, 300, 313
   See also Chicago
Barnett, Ross, 102, 111
Barnum, John and Mabel, 198-99
Beckwith, Byron de la, 103, 129
Birdsey, Herbert, 182
Black church, 40, 79, 95-96, 98, 118, 121-22, 127, 216-17, 262-65
Black pride, 60-61, 135, 254-56, 262-65
Black theology, 50-51, 262-65
Bolshevik Revolution, 22-23
Bowers, Sam, 128
brotherhood of man, 163-64
   See also mystical body of Christ
Brown, Currie, 76
Browne, Conrad, 161, 213
Buckley, Joe, 76
Burgamy, Charles, 175-76, 178-79
Butler, Charles, 288
Butler, Donna, 288
Camper, Rosie. *See* Weary, Rosie
Canada. *See* Toronto
Carter, Earl, 186-87
Carter, Jimmy, 147-8, 183-92, 194-95, 227
Carter, Rosalynn, 184, 186, 189
Catholicism
   African American conversions, 46
   Catholic Action, 64-66
   interracialism (see *Friendship House*)
   segregation, 45-48
   social teaching, 12, 29-31
   See also Hueck, Catherine de; mystical body of Christ

Catholic Worker, 60
Chicago, 245-47
Christian Community Development Association (CCDA), 309
Chicago Declaration of Evangelical Social Concern, 253-54
Christianity
   Black church (*see* Black church)
   California, 98-99
   Catholicism (*see* Catholicism)
   holistic gospel, 105-6, 117-39
   housing segregation, 45-48, 248-49
   race, 96, 106-12, 146-48
   segregationist theology, 106-12
   southern, 95, 106-12, 149-50, 208-10
   See also fundamentalist/modernist divide
churches, multiracial, 272
   See also Circle Church; Rock of Our Salvation Evangelical Free Church
Circle Church, 236-37, 252-57, 262-68
Circle Community Center. *See* Circle Urban Ministries
Circle Urban Ministries, 235-40, 261, 277-82, 308-9
Citizens' Councils, 102
civil rights movement, 12-13, 71-78, 100-104, 127-40
   Albany movement, 196
   Americus movement, 197-200
   desegregation, 71, 198-200
   education, 130-4, 175-7
   faith, 127-136, 199-200
   legislation, 71, 271-2
   nonviolence, 76, 129-130, 143, 161, 204
   northern, 246-7
   voter registration, 82, 127-9, 197-8
   white moderates, 102, 145, 176, 202
   white resistance, 100-104, 128, 132-4, 144-5, 175-83
closed society, 85-92
Cogely, John, 60

INDEX

colorblindness, 61, 283-98, 303-4
   assimilation, 65-66
communism, 18, 22-23, 25, 27-28
   accusations, 160-61, 171, 179, 219
   African Americans, 34-37
   anti-communism, 24-29, 72
Congress of Industrial Organizations (CIO), 42, 94, 271
cooperative movement, 122-24, 135
Cotton Patch translation, 168, 184, 190, 194, 202-3, 206-22
Cromwell, Henry Parsons, 250-51
Day, Dorothy, 33, 60, 143-45, 194, 212
Depression, Great, 27-8, 32, 34, 36, 42, 44
Doherty, Catherine. *See* Hueck, Catherine de
Du Bois, W. E. B., 42, 50-51
ecclesiology, 117-40, 155-64, 166-71
   See also mystical body of Christ
economic development, 120-24
economics, 12, 19, 25-38, 85
   corporate sharing, 144, 153, 157-62, 224-26, 230
   downward mobility, 99-100, 114, 117-18, 159-60, 269-70, 274-77, 279, 281, 302-3, 310-11 (*see also* poverty, voluntary)
   empowerment, 122-123
   idolatry (*see* mammon)
   race, 85
   race and Christianity, 38, 43-44, 54-64
Eisenhower, Dwight, 178
Emerson, Michael, 240-42
England, Mabel, 144, 157
England, Martin, 144, 155-57, 166
eschatology, 200, 250-51, 308, 310
Evangelical Free Church of America, 304-5
evangelicalism
   Black, 254-55, 262-65
   toolkit, 240-43, 252, 259-61, 285
   White, 78-79, 172-76, 180-81, 208-10, 218-20, 240-43, 247-51
Evers, Charles, 129
Evers, Medgar, 76, 90, 103
Falls, Arthur, 36, 48-49, 60
Fellowship Center, 152
Fields, Bruce, 264
Fletcher, Carolyn, 73, 77, 124, 137-38
Fletcher, Artis, 77, 87, 124, 137-38
Friendship House, 17-67
Friendship House (book), 25-26, 27, 51-53, 78
forgiveness, 23, 134-6, 296-97, 300-301
Fortson, Warren, 186, 190-91
Fuller, Linda, 207, 215, 224, 226
Fuller, Millard, 224-26

fundamentalist/modernist divide, 249-52
Gaw, Ka Tong, 253, 259, 262
Georgia, 146-49
   See also Americus
God movement, 167-70, 200-204
Grant, DuRhonda (née Baskett), 287-88
Grant, Paul, 287-88
Great Depression, 27-8, 32, 34, 36, 42, 44
Great Migration, 39-48, 72, 94-95, 99, 153
Griggins, Suzanne (née Keys), 137
Habitat for Humanity, 184, 224-26
Harlem, 13, 17-18, 33-37, 39-44, 49-51, 54-64
Harlem Renaissance, 34, 50-51
Harrigan, Ann, 15, 39-40, 54, 58
Harris, Reggie, 287, 288
Hamer, Fannie Lou, 82, 124, 161, 213
Hayes, Mitchell, 129
Highlander Folk School, 161, 171, 213
Hill, Alfoncia, 134
Hilliard, Clarence, 253-57, 260, 262-68, 274
Hinton, André, 280-81, 296-97
historical thinking, 3, 5, 7-9
   agency, 50-51, 53
   complexity, 32-33, 48, 49-51, 58-64, 103, 110-11, 174-75, 196-205, 315-16
   context, 3, 9, 26-27, 32, 60-61, 66-67, 78-81, 105-12, 115, 148, 151-53, 207-10
   contingency, 34-35, 53
   continuity and change, 138-39
   empathy, 238, 257, 262-65, 267, 270-72, 284, 291-93, 302
   historical consciousness, 3-4, 53
   historical narratives, 19-21, 24, 28-29, 32, 45, 49-51, 62-64, 76, 92-93
   humility, 25, 64, 93, 112-14, 145-46, 151-52, 154, 164-66, 183-93, 237
   sourcing, 20, 26, 52-53, 106, 148
   strangeness of the past, 8
   racial pioneers, 48
Hollis, Shunelle, 27
Holloway, Scottye, 131-33, 138
housing
   segregation, 13, 42-49, 302-3
   proximity to poor people, 29-30, 37-38, 65-66
Hueck, Boris de, 22-23, 34
Hueck, Catherine de, 11-13, 17-67, 72, 78, 80, 85, 92, 100, 104, 148, 152, 160, 227, 239, 247, 264, 313
Hueck, George de, 23
Huemmer, Doug, 72
incarnation, 153, 190, 208, 211-12, 222
individualism, 99, 105-6, 126, 250-51

INDEX

interracial cooperation
  communists, 35-36
  friendship, 51
  Koinonia Farm, 163-66
  labor, 42
interracial justice, 18
Jackson, Arthur, 279
Jackson, Sandra, 305
Jesus
  and race, 50-51, 216-19, 222
  See also incarnation
Jordan, Clarence, 143-231, 246-47, 276, 311, 315, 316
Jordan, Hamilton, 189-90, 221
Jordan, Florence (née Kroeger), 144, 151, 157-58, 163, 173-74, 185-86, 191, 196, 223, 226
Jordan, Jan, 188, 197, 199, 203
Jordan, Jim, 145, 180, 210
Jordan, Robert, 181-82
Kehrein, Glen, 235-37, 245-311
Kehrein, Lonni (née Bulkley), 251-57, 262
Keys, Suzanne, 137
King, Ed, 110
King, Martin Luther, Jr., 74, 130, 165-66, 171, 204, 246-47
Koinonia Farm, 143-231
Korean War, 97
Kroeger, Florence, *see* Jordan, Florence
Ku Klux Klan (KKK), 112, 128, 132, 137, 165-66, 175-76, 179, 181
LaFarge, John, 34
Lewis, C. S., 4, 80, 193
Longstreet, John, 127
Mains, David, 253, 262, 265-8
mammon, 25-26, 145, 159-60, 172
Marciniak, Ed, 247
McCartney, Bill, 305
McIlrath, Steve, 294
McIlrath, Trina, 294
McKay, Claude, 35, 41, 50, 56
McKnight, Father A. J., 122
McNeil, Neil (archbishop of Toronto), 25, 27-29, 32
Mendenhall, 71-78, 103-12, 117-34, 136-39
Mendenhall Ministries, 131, 136-39, 260
  See also Voice of Calvary
Meredith, James, 95
Mississippi, 6, 71-73, 85-93 100-104
Mississippi State Sovereignty Commission, 75-6, 102-3, 112, 129
Moody Bible Institute, 245-46, 251, 255, 287, 288
Mosely, Don, 184-85

Mulvoy, Father Michael, 34, 37, 57
mystical body of Christ, 55-64
National Association for the Advancement of Colored People (NAACP), 35, 42, 90, 129
Nelson, Claud, 158
New York. *See* Harlem
Newsome, Jesse, 128
Odenwald, Robert, 106-7, 111
Palmore, DuRhonda. *See* Grant, DuRhonda
Payne, Deborah, 132-33
Perkins, Clyde, 91
Perkins, John, 71-140, 143, 145, 147-48, 153, 197, 198, 224, 227-28, 238, 246, 247, 253, 260, 269-70
Perkins, Spencer, 97, 112, 132
Perkins, Vera Mae (née Bradley), 72, 74, 77, 96-97, 99-100, 103, 121, 132, 134, 136
Porres, Blessed Martin de, 15, 52
poverty, voluntary, 30, 66, 230
Promise Keepers, 242, 305-6
Quadragesimo Anno, 32
race
  ethnic identity, 45-46
  north, 95, 177-78, 246-67
  ownership, 89, 122-24, 134
  southern, 72, 85-95, 146-48
  stereotypes, 55
  white saviors, 58-64, 280
  See also Christianity; economics; housing; racism
race riots, 35, 40-41, 92, 245-46
racism
  prejudice, 270-72, 294-95
  systemic, 5, 48, 270-72, 316
  See also sin
reconciliation, racial, 140, 267, 283-298, 302, 304-6
  See also forgiveness
Red Squad, 28, 32
remembering, 10-11, 92-93, 112-114, 167, 192-93, 285
repentance, 3, 7, 23, 26, 32-33, 38, 112-114, 154, 293-97
Rerum Novarum, 12, 31
research process, 19-20, 39, 60-61, 81-83, 105, 107, 138-39, 178, 183-192, 197, 214, 216, 240-43
Rock of Our Salvation Evangelical Free Church, 237-38, 277-82, 283-98, 309
Rubin, Nathaniel, 128, 134
Russian revolution. *See* Bolshevik Revolution
Scottsboro Boys, 35
segregation, 48-49
  See also Christianity; housing; race
Sheets, Ladon, 212

Sherrod, Charles, 199
Sider, Ron, 253
Silver, James, 91-92
sin, 291
    corporate, 10, 22, 26, 29-32, 51, 81-82, 203-4, 315
    individual, 23, 25-26, 62, 203-4, 209-10, 315
    prejudice, 47-48, 107
    segregation, 259
Singletary, John Leonard (Jack), 187, 189
Smith, Lillian, 107-8, 114
social action, 119-20
social gospel, 2, 148, 249-50
Southern Way of Life, 73, 106-12, 163-64, 166, 202, 220
spiritual formation, 8-10 21, 30-31, 47, 159-60, 229-30, 250-51, 286-89
Stannard, Bob, 276
Stannard, Carole, 276, 287
Stevenson, Rob, 309
Student Nonviolent Coordinating Committee (SNCC), 82, 127, 197-99
Sunshine Center. *See* Fellowship Center

supercessionism, 218
Taglia, Louis, 273
Tarry, Ellen, 34, 36-37, 50-51, 56, 58-64
Till, Emmett, 87
Toronto, 26-33
Trinity Evangelical Divinity School, 235-36, 238, 264-65, 270, 273-74
Voice of Calvary, 72, 118, 260
Warren, Mel, 255
Washington, Abraham Lincoln, 306
Washington, Paulette, 270, 273, 278-79, 289
Washington, Raleigh, 235-38, 269-311
Weary, Dolphus, 77, 96, 105, 118, 124, 135, 137-39
Weary, Rosie (née Camper), 77, 124, 135, 137-38
Wheaton College, 259, 313-14, 317
White flight, 236, 248, 260-61
Williams, John Bell, 101
Wittkamper, Will, 167, 213, 223
Wood, Judd, 294
World War I, 22, 41
World War II, 90-91, 144, 166-67, 271
Wright, Richard, 37
Young, Andy, 165-66